THE CLASSICAL EPIC

THE
MAGILL
BIBLIOGRAPHIES

Other Magill Bibliographies:

Black American Women Novelists—Craig Werner
Classical Greek and Roman Drama—Robert J. Forman
Contemporary Latin American Fiction—Keith H. Brower
English Romantic Poetry—Bryan Aubrey
Masters of Mystery and Detective Fiction—J. Randolph Cox
The Modern American Novel—Steven G. Kellman
Restoration Drama—Thomas J. Taylor
Twentieth Century European Short Story—Charles E. May
The Victorian Novel—Laurence W. Mazzeno

THE CLASSICAL EPIC

An Annotated Bibliography

Thomas J. Sienkewicz
Capron Professor of Classics
Monmouth College

SALEM PRESS

Pasadena, California   Englewood Cliffs, New Jersey

Library of Congress Cataloging-in-Publication Data

Sienkewicz, Thomas J., 1950
    The classical epic / Thomas J. Sienkewicz
            p. cm—(Magill bibliographies)
    Includes index.
    ISBN 0-89356-663-2 (alk. paper)
    1. Epic poetry. Classical—History and criticism—
Bibliography. 2. Epic poetry, Classical—Bibliography.
3. Homer—Bibliography. 4. Virgil—Bibliography.
I. Title. II. Series.
Z7018.E63S55   1991
[PA3022.E6]   90-48884
016.883'0109—dc20   CIP

To Bernice, a great lover of the Classics

CONTENTS

EDITORIAL STAFF

Publisher
FRANK N. MAGILL

Advisory Board
KENNETH T. BURLES
DAWN P. DAWSON

Series Editor
JOHN WILSON

Production Manager
KATHY HIX

Copy Editor
JO-ELLEN LIPMAN BOON

ACKNOWLEDGMENTS

A bibliography such as this could not have been completed without the help of many dedicated librarians and their staffs, especially those at Monmouth College in Monmouth, Illinois, at Knox College in Galesburg, Illinois, and at Bowdoin College in Brunswick, Maine. Particular thanks to Harris Hauge, Eleanor Gustafson, and Skip Burhans for their help and technical assistance and to Bernice Fox for reading various portions of this work. To my aunt, Frances Liguori, and to my sisters, Doris Sienkewicz and Toni Gallo, who helped me beat the library system in New Jersey. And, last but not least, to my wife, Anne, and my children, who had to endure the painful birthing of this bibliography. In the end, of course, responsibility for any errors and inaccuracies is mine alone.

THE CLASSICAL EPIC

INTRODUCTION

When you start on your journey to Ithaca,
then pray that the road is long,
full of adventure, full of knowledge.

from "Ithaca" by C. P. Cavafy
translated from modern Greek by Rae Dalven

This bibliography serves as a guide for an epic journey. Its itinerary is indeed long; it begins in Bronze Age Greece at least four thousand years ago and continues into twentieth century America. On this trip, you are invited to become better acquainted with three Classical epics, Homer's *Iliad* and *Odyssey* and Vergil's *Aeneid*, poems which together not only make up the core of ancient Greek and Roman literature but also serve as the centerpiece of the Classical tradition upon which Western culture is based.

One hundred years ago, a college student in America or Europe would generally have read Vergil's *Aeneid* in the original Latin, if not the Homeric poems in the original Greek. Even fifty years ago, most college-bound high school students in the United States would have read at least part of the *Aeneid* in Latin. As we approach the end of the twentieth century, however, that is no longer the case. Most people who read these epics today do so in translation and require a basic introduction to the Greco-Roman culture in which they were created. This bibliography provides such an introduction and suggests sources of information about essential features of these ancient epics.

This is a selective bibliography. It does not include references to everything written about Homer and Vergil. The production of such a comprehensive bibliography would indeed be a Herculean task, one beyond the scope or intent of this series. Nor is this bibliography intended for specialists and general Classical scholars, for whom there are many other bibliographic sources which better suit their needs. Rather, this bibliography is directed toward the first-time reader of the Classical epics in English translation. In particular, the annotations in this bibliography are designed to help the more advanced high school student and the general college student find a path through the wealth of material which has been written about Homer and Vergil and to discover sources for course papers and projects on the *Iliad*, the *Odyssey*, and the *Aeneid*.

For the most part, citations refer to easily accessible references. Articles in periodicals or scholarly journals are usually cited only when they have been reprinted in volumes more available to the general reader, and the books mentioned are those likely to be found in the public library of a small-sized American city or in the library of a small college without a Classics major. The library you use will probably not have all the books listed in this bibliography, but it should have at least some of them.

Any steps you take on this journey with Homer and Vergil and any efforts you make to become better acquainted with their three epics will be rewarded in several ways. For one, the student of Homer and Vergil gains knowledge about another world, about the civilization of the ancient Greeks and Romans. Homer's world, in fact, is a prism which illuminates, simultaneously, the Mycenaean civilization of the Greek Bronze Age and the society of archaic Greece in the eighth century B.C. The world of Homer's heroes also anticipates the society of fifth century Athens, the plays of Aeschylus, Sophocles, and Euripides, and the philosophy of Socrates, Plato, and Aristotle, all of which were profoundly influenced by the Homeric poems. So, too, the world of the *Aeneid* reflects the civilization of Rome. Indeed, to read Vergil's poem is to learn something of that imperial consciousness which made Rome the dominating power in the Mediterranean world from about 200 B.C. until about A.D. 400.

As you become more familiar with Homer's and Vergil's epics, you will also come to appreciate better our own Western heritage. These three works are so much a part of our cultural inheritance that, in a real sense, all that was written in the Greco-Roman period, as well as most of the literary products of the Renaissance and Neoclassical periods and much subsequent literature, has felt the presence of these two Classical poets in some way. They have inspired such direct literary imitations as Dante Alighieri's *Divine Comedy* and John Milton's *Paradise Lost*, and their influence can also be seen in such well-known English poems as John Keats's "On First Looking into Chapman's Homer" and Alfred, Lord Tennyson's "Ulysses." Even in the late twentieth century, references to Homer and Vergil appear in the most unexpected places, such as the autobiography of Joe Paterno, the successful Pennsylvania State University football coach, whose enthusiasm for Vergil cannot be understood without reading Vergil and without becoming more familiar with the long history of Homeric and Vergilian influence in the Western world.

For this reason, this bibliography includes a representative sample of literary works, especially from Great Britain and the United States, which have been directly influenced by the Classical epics of antiquity. It is not a complete list. For example, despite the strong links between the Homeric poems and such ancient Greek plays as Sophocles' *Ajax* and *Philoctetes* and Euripides' *Trojan Women* and *Cyclops*, no dramatic works are included in this bibliography. Also, since epic writers after Vergil are, as a rule, influenced by both Vergil and Homer, I have cited these works, such as Milton's *Paradise Lost* and Torquato Tasso's *Jerusalem*, only under Vergil. The student working on the influence of Homer on later epics should look not only at the section in Homer but also at the section in Vergil. I hope that this part of the bibliography will provide the new reader of Homer and of Vergil with exposure at first hand to the way that these poets have become part of the fiber of Western literature.

In addition to these examples of direct imitation of the ancient epics, there are many scholarly studies of the influence of these poems upon later literature and upon

Western culture in general. Such works (including Aristotle's *Poetics* and T. S. Eliot's major essay "What Is a Classic?") illustrate how these epics have become the starting point of both ancient and modern literary criticism. In this way, when we read Homer and Vergil, we learn as much about ourselves as we do about the ancient Greeks and Romans.

There is, however, a third reward for your efforts. As you learn more about Homer and Vergil, you will also come to enjoy all three of these poems and to appreciate them for their intrinsic literary value. The plots of these epics and the characters portrayed in them provided entertainment and education to readers and audiences for thousands of years before the invention of motion pictures, television, and videotape players. The *Iliad*, the *Odyssey*, and the *Aeneid* lead us to a timeless and universal form of entertainment, the good story told well.

These works are very much alike in some ways and in other ways are very different. First, all three are epics, long narrative poems written in a serious way about heroes. All include a divine apparatus; that is, the gods participate in the action. All begin *in medias res*, that is, not at the beginning of the story but in the middle. Invocations, similes, assembly scenes, catalogues, and other features considered characteristics of the epic can also be found in each poem. References to many of these poetic features appear in the bibliographic sections entitled "Literary Studies."

Later epics, such as Dante's *Divine Comedy* and Milton's *Paradise Lost*, have followed these poems as models. The epic genre, as known in Western culture, has been defined, to a great extent, by these Classical examples. Another section of the bibliography, entitled "General Studies of the Epic Form," deals with the epic as a genre and with the basic differences between oral and literary epics or between primary and secondary epics. Citations referring to the form of an epic also appear in other sections, such as those dealing with literary studies of the *Iliad*, the *Odyssey*, and the *Aeneid* and with the influence of these three epics on later literature.

All three poems were also composed in meter but not in rhyme. This meter, called dactylic hexameter, is a rhythm not easily translatable into English. In fact, many of the better translations use prose or meters more natural to English, such as iambic pentameter or the heroic couplet. Users of this bibliography will find that citations indicate whether a particular translation is written in prose or verse. While some may feel that prose translations are more "readable," any reader using a prose translation should refer at least periodically to a translation in verse as a reminder of the poetic nature of the original epic.

Translating Homer and Vergil is inevitably a difficult task. The poems of Homer were composed in a Greek very different from that spoken in the fifth century of the Athenian dramatists, or from the biblical (or Koine) Greek spoken in the time of Christ, or from the language used in modern Greece. So, too, the Latin of Vergil is the sophisticated Latin of the Augustan poets of Rome, imbued with a love of things Greek and of indirectness which even some of Vergil's contemporaries would find occasionally difficult to follow. Neither Homer's Greek nor Vergil's Latin translates very well into English. Since the Renaissance, each generation has produced its own translators, many of whom are represented in this bibliography. Some translations, such as Alexander Pope's Homer and John Dryden's Vergil, have met the test of time and have been published in countless new editions. Other translations, such as the version of the *Odyssey* published in 1895 by S. H. Butcher and Andrew Lang, served the special needs of a particular time and place and will probably not continue to be used as the translations of Pope and Dryden have. Over the years, critics, poets, and translators themselves have expressed a variety of theories about the best way to translate Homer and Vergil into English. Some of these opinions are collected in those sections of the bibliography entitled "On Translating Homer" and "On Translating Vergil."

While the twentieth century translations of Homer by Richmond Lattimore and of both Homer and Vergil by Robert Fitzgerald have been hailed by contemporary critics, it is difficult to say how well these translations will satisfy the needs of the next generation. The translations of Lattimore and Fitzgerald are certainly the place where English readers at the end of the twentieth century should begin their journey with Homer and Vergil, but, short of learning ancient Greek and Latin and reading the epics in their original languages, every reader should approach these epics not just from one but from several translations. Only with the help of two of more translations can the English reader begin to appreciate the complexity and beauty of the epics in their original languages. For this reason, I have made a special point in this bibliography of listing a variety of translations, some written for American, others for British readers; some using twentieth century language, others the English of the nineteenth or even the eighteenth centuries. Each of these translations is very different from the next. Take particular care to choose the ones which best suit your needs.

Even proper names may present a problem for new readers of these poems. The Greeks and Romans often had different names for the same character. Thus, the Greek god known as Zeus in the Homeric poems is the same deity whom Vergil calls Jupiter; similarly, the Homeric hero Odysseus is known as Ulysses in the *Aeneid*. For this reason, many translations and studies of the epics contain glossaries which explain these various names. I have included references to such glossaries in the citations.

The spelling of Greek personal and place names also creates obstacles for English readers. Some writers and translators prefer to use traditional, Latinized spellings of Greek names, such as Aeolus, Circe, Ithaca, and Nausicaa. Others simply transcribe Greek names into English and write Aiolos, Kirke, Ithake, Knossos, and Nausikaa. With place names, one occasionally finds modern Greek spellings—Ithaki rather than Ithaca, for example. Another option is to use the more familiar Latin spellings for the main characters, such as Achilles, Athena, and Eurycleia, and to use more literal Greek spellings for the less common names, such as Alkinoös, Antikleia, and Phoinix. For the sake of consistency, I have chosen to use traditional forms such as Athena, Circe, Ithaca, and Cnossus in this bibliography. In titles,

. retain the spelling preferred by the author.

.ame of the author of the *Aeneid* is not spared orthographic confusion either. .t's full Latin name was almost certainly Publius Vergilius Maro. Even in .y, however, the variant "Virgilius" appeared, perhaps because the poet's nickname, Parthenias, was translated into the Latin word *virgo* ("virgin," .len") and also by association with the Latin word *virga* ("rod" or "magic "), which fit the poet's image as a magus, or magician. Although "Virgil" is .bly more common in English, I employ the form "Vergil" in this bibliography .cause it is closer to the poet's real name, except in titles, where I follow the spelling of the author.

It is helpful for the new reader of Homer and of Vergil to be aware of the way in which the ancient epics are organized. All three epics were divided into books, twenty-four for each of the Homeric poems and twelve for the *Aeneid*. The length of each book is generally thought to correspond approximately to the number of lines which would fit on a roll of papyrus. Regular reference to these books and lines (for example, 8.278) in English translations makes it much easier for the reader to compare translations and to follow references in more scholarly studies of the epics. Thus, I have generally indicated in the bibliography whenever a particular translation includes regular reference to such books and lines.

The plots of all three epics were well known to the ancient general public, and neither Homer nor Vergil had to explain the identity of main characters or the general plot outlines. Modern readers, however, do not usually come to the epics with the same prior knowledge. Therefore, I have included sections in the bibliography in which a reader may find references to plot summaries and background of these epics. It may be helpful to read one or two of these before reading anything else.

The *Iliad* is the story about the Trojan War, not about the whole war, but about an incident which takes place in the tenth year of the war between the Greeks and the Trojans. The plot centers on a quarrel between two Greeks, Agamemnon, the leader of the Greek forces, and Achilles, the best warrior on the Greek side. Just as the war is being fought over a woman, Helen of Troy, who had been stolen by the Trojan prince Paris from Menelaus, her Greek husband and brother of Agamemnon, so in the *Iliad* Agamemnon and Achilles quarrel over a woman, Briseis, Achilles' war prize, whom Agamemnon takes away. In anger, Achilles refuses to fight until the girl is returned to him and does not return to the conflict until his best friend, Patroclus, is slain by Hector, champion of the Trojans and Paris' brother. The grief-stricken Achilles in turn kills Hector, and the poem ends with the ransom of Hector's body by his father, Priam, King of Troy.

The plot of the *Odyssey* follows that of the *Iliad* chronologically. This epic is about the homecoming of Odysseus, one of the companions of Agamemnon and Achilles at Troy. Like the *Iliad*, the *Odyssey* begins toward the end of the story, in the tenth year of the hero's wanderings following the war and just before Odysseus returns to Ithaca, his island home. In a flashback, Odysseus himself narrates the ten years of adventures which precede the beginning of the *Odyssey*. Then, the epic describes the hero's return to his island home of Ithaca, the slaughter of the haughty suitors of his wife, Penelope, and his reunion with his family.

To a great extent, the plot of the *Aeneid* is a blending of both the Homeric poems. It describes the flight of Aeneas, a Trojan prince, from burning Troy after the city's capture by the Greeks and the journey of Aeneas to Italy, where he fights a war with some Italian tribes for the hand of a Latin princess, Lavinia. Like Odysseus, Aeneas is a much-traveled hero; like Achilles, he is a war hero. He is also the national hero of Rome and reflects a conscious effort on the part of Vergil to transform the traditional story of Aeneas into a poem about the greatness of Rome and about Augustus Caesar, the ruler of Rome at the end of the first century B.C.

Within the mythological and thematic unity which binds these three epics together there are several features which set Vergil's poem apart from its Homeric anteced-ents. First of all, there is the very fact of Vergil's conscious imitation of the Homeric tradition. It is not by chance that the greatest Roman poet based his masterpiece on the *Iliad* and the *Odyssey*. While the Romans had conquered Greece politically more than one hundred years before the birth of Vergil, culturally the conqueror had been conquered by the conquered. As Vergil's friend and fellow poet Horace observed in his *Epistles* (II, 2.156-157):

> Captive Greece took captive her fierce conqueror
> And introduced her arts into rude Latium.

Educated Romans long before Vergil had begun to look to Greece for literary and intellectual inspiration. Vergil's great hero, Aeneas, is a figure from Greek myth-ology, and Vergil's epic is a splendid attempt by a Roman to meet the Greeks on their own poetic grounds, to produce an epic in Latin which could compete success-fully with Homer's poems.

Vergil's *Aeneid*, then, is very much a literary epic, a bookish poem produced in writing for a reading public immersed in Greek culture and filled with a fondness for subtlety and sophisticated language. On the other hand, the Homeric poems are intrinsically oral; they are products of a long tradition of spoken, performed poetry which dates back hundreds of years before the poems were put into written form. Only with the work of Milman Parry, Eric Havelock, and others in the twentieth century have the full implications of this distinction between oral and literary epic been appreciated. The poetic language of Vergil is, in many ways, closer to the rhetorical interests of a modern poet who strives for originality and the unusual turn of phrase, while the language of Homer is more traditional, based more on an elaborate system of recurring words and phrases upon which the poetic line, as well as the poem itself, is built. Thus, Homer's repetition of the formulaic expression "when early-born, rosy-fingered Dawn appeared" to describe daybreak may initially appear monotonous and even unimaginative to the modern reader. So, too, Homer's description of Odysseus as "many-turned" instead of "wily," can even appear fixed and automatic, at least on the surface, when one realizes that these epithets occur regularly at the same point in the poetic line. On the other hand, Vergil's repeated use of the epithet "pious" in reference to his hero Aeneas is not so much the result of oral tradition but of intentional, literary imitation of Homer's style.

Homeric formulas and epithets are features which make the *Iliad* and the *Odyssey* in many ways more like oral, traditional epics performed in such parts of the world as Yugoslavia, Turkey, and Africa than literary productions such as the *Aeneid*. The special nature of Homeric language is reflected in the bibliographical section on oral composition, with its special attention to epithets, formulas, and themes. There is no equivalent in the Vergilian section of the bibliography.

Another striking difference between Homer and Vergil is in the area of biography. We know quite a lot about Vergil's life, including the dates of his birth (October 15, 70 B.C.) and death (September 21, 19 B.C.). While some of the biographical details which survive in the ancient lives of the poet—incidents such as Vergil's deathbed request that the unfinished *Aeneid* be destroyed rather than published—read like exaggerations and cannot be accepted as historical fact, many other details, such as the poet's friendship with Horace and his ties with the emperor Augustus, are probably accurate. Several sources for such information about Vergil can be found in the bibliographical section entitled "Biography."

For Homer, on the other hand, the picture is quite different. While there is an ancient biographical tradition for Homer, including the story that the poet came from the island of Chios and was blind, the picture is blurred by the oral nature of the Homeric poems and by the implication that "Homer" may not have existed at all, that the *Iliad* and the *Odyssey* are actually the result of a long oral tradition, of contributions by many individual singers over the course of several centuries. Some of this information is collected in the citations listed under the subheading of Homeric biography. However, Homeric biography and the circumstances surrounding the composition of these poems have, over the years, become the subject of an intense scholarly debate known as the "Homeric Question." On one side stand the "analysts," who argue on the basis of textual inconsistencies within the poems and on the basis of the formulaic nature of Homeric language that the Homeric poems could not have been the composition of a single individual, that the poems evolved over several centuries and with the contributions of generations of singers. On the other hand, there are the "unitarians," who resolutely affirm the unity of the Homeric poems, who claim either that both poems are the product of a single poet known as Homer or that each poem was composed by a single poet, the *Iliad* by "Homer" and the *Odyssey* by someone else who lived about a generation later than "Homer." Of special note in the history of the Homeric question is the theory of Samuel Butler, the nineteenth century British man of letters, who argued forcefully that the *Odyssey* was actually composed by a woman. In the twentieth century, Robert Graves developed Butler's theory into a novel entitled *Homer's Daughter*.

Mixed into this controversy about authorship are questions about literacy—Was Homer literate or not?—and dating—When did "Homer" live and when were his poems put into final written form? Even in ancient Greece, these questions could not be answered with any authority, and the poet was said to have lived as early as c. 1000 B.C. or as late as c. 750 B.C. His literacy and the writing down of his poems are tied to the introduction of the Greek alphabet, c. 850 B.C. If he lived before that date, "Homer" simply could not have been literate, nor could the poems have been written down, by "Homer" or any other Greek. Even after that date, however, the literacy of the author of the Homeric poems is not certain and the poems may not have existed in writing, at least in the form we know today, until the Pisistratid era in Athens, c. 540 B.C. The work of Eric Havelock, cited frequently throughout this bibliography, has, in particular, questioned the ties between the Homeric poems and literacy as it is understood today.

At times the debate about the Homeric question has taken on the vehemence of religious polemic, and it is unlikely that any real resolution of the controversy will ever be found. There is no indisputable evidence, no "smoking gun" which proves that Homer really did or did not live and did or did not write the *Iliad* or the *Odyssey*. All these questions on the authorship of the Homeric poems are discussed in the bibliographic section entitled "The Authorship of the Homeric Poems."

While orality is a distinctive feature of the Homeric poems, the political nature of Vergil's poem sets it apart from the *Iliad* and the *Odyssey*. In a very real sense, the *Aeneid* can be read as a propaganda tract celebrating the accomplishments of Augustus Caesar, who ruled Rome at the time Vergil was composing the *Aeneid* and who, as a member of the Julian family, could claim descent from Vergil's hero Aeneas, through his son Julus. Vergil's choice of a patriotic theme is, in fact, supported by Horace, who suggested in the *Art of Poetry* that literature should be both useful and sweet (*utile et dulce*). The Romans relished such a blend of the practical and the aesthetic and felt that an inspiring element of patriotism could only improve a poetic theme.

The often-intense nationalism of the *Aeneid* may, however, present a problem for many twentieth century readers, who are not always prepared for Vergil's mix of literature and politics. On this score, readers of Vergil in nineteenth century England or America could appreciate Vergil's aesthetic goals much more readily than we can. Twentieth century equivalents of such patriotic poems as Walt Whitman's "O Captain, My Captain," John Greenleaf Whittier's "Barbara Fritchie," or Tennyson's "The Charge of the Light Brigade" simply do not exist. Perhaps Vergil's nationalism is one reason that the Roman poet has become less popular at the end of the twentieth century than he was at the beginning—a phenomenon frequently lamented by authors cited in this bibliography. Readers interested in the historical and political background to Vergil's poem should pay particular attention to the citations listed in the subsection of the bibliography entitled "The Social and Political World of Vergil."

Modern readers of the *Aeneid* are usually more interested in the first half of the poem, especially the love affair between Aeneas and Dido, than in the second half of the poem, which describes the war between Aeneas and Turnus, between the

Trojans and the Latins. In fact, Vergil's Aeneas does not always please modern eyes. Not only does he abandon Dido for his "duty," but the epic also ends with the savage and merciless slaying of Turnus by Aeneas. Indeed, much of the discussion about Aeneas in the section on character studies is devoted either to the troubling relationship between Aeneas and Dido or to the question of Aeneas' cruel behavior toward Turnus.

Vergil shares this war theme and the savagery of his main character with Homer, whose portrayal of Achilles is no less difficult for a modern reader to accept. The section on character studies in the *Iliad* is dominated by Achilles, his anger toward Agamemnon, his stubborn refusal to change his mind in the embassy scene in *Iliad* 9, his ruthless slaughter of Hector, and his memorable pity for Hector's father, Priam, at the end of the epic.

It is no surprise that the Classical epic which has been most popular and the most discussed in the twentieth century is the *Odyssey*. This epic combines a domestic theme with elements of the fantastic, a blend which is much more to the taste of twentieth century Americans. The *Odyssey* includes the themes of both science fiction, with its quest and journeys to where no man has gone before, and soap operas, with their everyday squabbles and experiences such as adultery, marriage, and coming-of-age. New readers of the *Odyssey* will be particularly interested in interpretations of Odysseus' varied adventures, references to which can be found not only in the subsection on the *Odyssey* entitled "Studies of Individual Books, Episodes, and Passages," but also in the subsection on Homeric poetry entitled "Homer's Sources."

Many of the difficulties faced by the new reader of Homer and Vergil are problems of scholarship. Much of the best which has been written about these epics was not originally written in English, and it is not always easy to find translations. Thus, the work on Homer by the great German scholar Ulrich Wilamowitz von Möllendorf, *Die Ilias und Homer* (1916; the *Iliad* and Homer) remains essentially inaccessible to the English reader, despite its intrinsic value and the influence it has had on twentieth century scholars on both sides of the Atlantic. English translations of important works of foreign scholarship, such as Viktor Pöschl's work on Vergil, remain all too rare.

Other important works, even when written in English, have been published in scholarly journals which are not readily available in public libraries or even small college libraries in the United States. Sometimes, this need has been partially filled by critical anthologies, including several volumes in the Modern Critical Views and Modern Critical Interpretations series edited by Harold Bloom. Many other studies, heralded by scholars, are not included in this bibliography simply because the new reader would be able to obtain a copy only with difficulty.

At other times, scholars themselves have been at fault and have addressed their works about Homer and Vergil exclusively to other scholars. All too often, quotations from the epics are given only in the original languages, and footnotes are filled with obscure references in foreign languages. This tendency is, to a certain extent, excusable, since the English-speaking Classical scholar has long been expected to understand not only ancient Greek and Latin but also at least French and German, if not Italian. I have tried as much as possible to warn the reader when a particular citation contains foreign quotations without translation, and I commend, in particular, those scholars and publishers who include translations, especially from Homer and Vergil, in their studies. Only in this way can the reader without Greek or Latin become more acquainted with much of the very exciting scholarship which has been written about both Homer and Vergil, especially in the twentieth century. Classical scholars may lament the need to quote their beloved authors in translation, but perhaps these translations will be the vehicle for a Classical revival in the years to come.

Scholarly commentaries of the Classical epics, in particular, illustrate the rift between scholarship and the general reader. Many of these commentaries contain a wealth of information and valuable interpretation, but all too often they are useful only to those readers who have at least some understanding of Latin or Greek. All too rare are those commentaries, such as James Hogan's on the *Iliad*, which are written specifically for the general reader. Several such commentaries exist for both the *Iliad* and the *Aeneid*; curiously, the *Odyssey* lacks such a commentary, despite the popularity of this epic in the twentieth century. Scholars will miss in this bibliography citations for many valuable Homeric and Vergilian commentaries, especially the series on individual books of the *Aeneid* published by Oxford's Clarendon Press, which are not included in this bibliography because of their more technical and scholarly nature.

Sometimes, the number of citations is a good guide to the importance of a reference. Erich Auerbach's essay "Odysseus' Scar," first published in 1953 as a chapter in *Mimesis: The Representation of Reality in Western Literature*, has appeared in a number of reprints and anthologies. This essay is not only one of the most influential twentieth century studies of Homer's *Odyssey* but also a major work of general literary criticism. Similarly, Adam Parry's essay "The Two Voices of Virgil's *The Aeneid*," frequently reprinted since it first appeared in 1963, has greatly influenced subsequent discussions of Aeneas' character. Studies such as these are the ones which every student of Homer and of Vergil should read.

Classicists are a conservative lot. This characteristic is particularly evident in this bibliography from the large number of citations of early twentieth century and even nineteenth century studies of Homer and Vergil. Despite their age, works such as R. C. Jebb's *Homer: An Introduction to the "Iliad" and the "Odyssey,"* published in its fifth edition in 1894, and J. W. Mackail's *Virgil and His Meaning to the World of To-day*, published in 1922, remain good general introductions to the Classical epics of Greece and Rome. Sometimes, however, one must beware of antiquity even when dealing with ancient authors. This warning holds especially true for studies of the Homeric world and its ties with the Mycenaean world. The decipherment of Linear B tablets by Michael Ventris in 1952 and subsequent study of this archaeological evidence by later scholars have so revolutionized knowledge of Mycenaean society that much of the scholarship written before 1952 must be read with caution and must be qualified by later citations. Readers interested in the decipherment story and in the society which it reveals should refer, in particular, to the citations listed in the section entitled "The Homeric World."

With these few guidelines to the use of this bibliography, you should now take your copies of Homer and Vergil in hand and begin your epic journey. Along with the twentieth century Greek poet C. P. Cavafy, who is quoted at the beginning of this introduction, I hope that your journey is a long one, filled with knowledge and adventure.

General Studies of the Epic Form

Beye, Charles Rowan. "Epic Technique." In *The "Iliad," the "Odyssey," and the Epic Tradition*. Garden City, N.Y.: Doubleday, 1966.
References by Homer and Hesiod to the craft of the singer are followed by an explanation of several special aspects of the Homeric epics and of epics in general, both oral and literary. These features are character delineation, catalogues, battle narratives, repetitions, and similes.

Bowra, C. M. *Heroic Poetry*. New York: St. Martin's Press, 1961.
A comparative study of the characteristics of heroic epics especially in ancient Greece, the Near East, and northern Europe. Considers similarities among traditional oral epics such as the *Iliad*, the *Odyssey*, the *Epic of Gilgamesh*, *Beowulf*, the *Elder Edda*, and the *Song of Roland*. Contains chapters on such topics as the hero, narrative, language, compositional techniques, oral tradition, and the bard. Also discusses different types of heroic outlook in these poems, examines the relationship between poetic narrative and historical events, and surveys the evolution and decline of heroic epic traditions. Contains a few untranslated Greek words and an index.

_____. "Some Characteristics of Literary Epic." In *From Virgil to Milton*. New York: St. Martin's Press, 1961. Reprinted in *Virgil: A Collection of Critical Essays*, edited by Steele Commager. Englewood Cliffs, N.J.: Prentice-Hall, 1966.
Discusses some of the differences between the oral Homeric epics and literary epics such as Vergil's *Aeneid* and John Milton's *Paradise Lost*. The oral epic is based more on phrases and formulas than on individual words and portrays a more traditional hero concerned with personal honor and fame.

Clark, John. "The Development and Nature of Epic Poetry." In *A History of Epic Poetry*. Edinburgh, Scotland: Oliver & Boyd, 1900.
An introduction to a historical survey of the epic in medieval and modern

Europe. Traces the genre from its preliterate origins to the poems of ancient Greece and India and develops a general definition of the genre based especially upon characteristics of the Homeric epics and Vergil's *Aeneid*. Discusses such topics as epic action, the language of epic poetry, and the use of the gods and national themes in epic.

Conway, Robert Seymour. "The Architecture of the Epic." In *Harvard Lectures on the Vergilian Age*. Cambridge, Mass.: Harvard University Press, 1928. Reprint. New York: Biblo and Tannen, 1967.
Considers several basic principles of classical epic and applies them to Vergil's *Aeneid*. Focuses on two features of epic narrative: *in medias res*, the principle of beginning in the middle rather than at the beginning of the story; and the expectation that an epic plot be varied but unbroken.

Cook, Albert. *The Classic Line: A Study in Epic Poetry*. Bloomington: Indiana University Press, 1966.
Considers the poetic features of epic by examining several examples of the genre. Shows how an epic poem differs from lyric and has its own rules about diction, syntax, and rhythm which can be molded to suit the goals of individual poets. Suggests that epic poems tend to lack the ornamentation and poetic figures which are a basic feature of lyric. Includes separate studies of each of the Homeric poems, of Vergil's *Aeneid*, of medieval epic, of Dante Alighieri's *Divine Comedy*, and of John Milton's *Paradise Lost*. Also includes an index.

Foerster, Donald M. *The Fortunes of Epic Poetry: A Study in English and American Criticism, 1750-1950*. Washington, D.C.: Catholic University of America Press, 1962.
This survey of critical attitudes toward the epic form begins with the rigid Neoclassical models based upon Homer and Vergil and moves to the eighteenth century discovery of the "primitive" epic and the nineteenth century English Romantic redefinition of the genre as lyric, spontaneous, and natural. Considers the rivalry among epic, lyric, and novel forms in the nineteenth and twentieth centuries. Includes notes and an index.

Greene, Thomas. *The Descent from Heaven: A Study in Epic Continuity*. New Haven, Conn.: Yale University Press, 1963.
This study of the European epic form includes a chapter on epic norms concerning imagery, the hero, structure, and language as well as individual studies of both Homeric epics, Vergil's *Aeneid*, the English epics of Edmund Spenser and John Milton, and the Italian Renaissance epics of Ludovico Ariosto and Jacopo Sannazzaro. Finishes with an index and a short appendix on the Hittite epic *Kumarbi*.

Hayley, William. *An Essay on Epic Poetry*. London: J. Dodsley, 1782. Reprinted with introduction by M. Celeste Williamson. Gainesville, Fla.: Scholars' Facsimiles & Reprints, 1968.

An influential eighteenth century verse essay tracing the history of the epic genre from antiquity to the author's own day and providing an overview and definition of the epic genre. Shows affection for classical authors such as Homer and Vergil and enthusiasm for more recent epic poets such as Dante Alighieri and Edmund Spenser. Argues for the liberation of the genre from the artificial rules of Neo-classicism and expands the scope of epic to include satire, history, and romance. Suggests that the genre could be improved, especially with the introduction of more female principal figures and with a stronger emphasis upon nationalism. Williamson's introductory essay explains the historical significance of Hayley's essay.

Johnson, John W. "The Characteristics of Mande Epic." In *The Epic of Son-Jara*. Bloomington: Indiana University Press, 1986.

Expands the traditional definition of an oral epic to include the characteristics of West African epic. There are sections on poetic, narrative heroic, and legendary traits of this epic. This essay accompanies a translation of and commentary on the performance of the West African epic *Sunjata* by the singer Fa-Digi Sisòkò.

Lewis, C. S. *A Preface to "Paradise Lost."* New York: Oxford University Press, 1942.

In the first half of this appreciative study of John Milton's *Paradise Lost*, Lewis, the author of the *Chronicles of Narnia*, studies the characteristics of the epic form. Considers differences between the "primary" epic of Homer and the epics of Vergil and John Milton, which he calls "secondary" not because they are inferior but because they are outgrowths of primary epic. Primary epics are oral, aristocratic, and public, while secondary epics are more literate and personal. Contains an appendix and index.

Lord, Albert B. "Homer and Other Epic Poetry." In *A Companion to Homer*, edited by Alan J. B. Wace and Frank H. Stubbings. New York: Macmillan, 1963.

An examination of the Homeric epics in the context of other oral epic poetry. There are sections on the nature of oral epic, oral technique concerning form and subject, the problem of writing oral compositions, the ritual and magical origins of epic, and the purposes of epic. Examples are especially drawn from South Slavic epics. Not all foreign-language quotations are translated.

Mason, H. A. "Being Serious." In *To Homer Through Pope: An Introduction to Homer's "Iliad" and Pope's Translation*. New York: Harper & Row, 1972.

In order to consider the seventeenth century idea of an epic as a serious poem, several translations of the speech of Sarpedon in *Iliad* 12 and the speech of Clarissa in Alexander Pope's *The Rape of the Lock* are compared. Homeric epic is seen to be a mixture of both the serious and the comic.

Merchant, Paul. *The Epic*. New York: Methuen, 1971.
Part of the Critical Idiom series of books dealing with various literary genres, forms, and movements, this book examines several types of epic, including the classical epics of Homer and Vergil, the medieval poems of Dante Alighieri and Geoffrey Chaucer, the works of the Renaissance writers Edmund Spenser and John Milton, and the modern novel. There are extensive quotations in English from various epics. Includes a select bibliography and index.

Newman, John Kevin. *The Classical Epic Tradition*. Madison: University of Wisconsin Press, 1986.
Studies the significant contributions of Callimachus, a third century B.C. Hellenistic poet, to the epic genre and suggests that Callimachus' definition of epic as a mixture of dramatic, lyric, and comic became a model used by later epic poets such as Vergil and Dante Alighieri, novelists such as Leo Tolstoy and Thomas Mann, and twentieth century Russian film directors such as Sergei Eisenstein and Vsevolod Pudovkin. Includes two illustrations, a valuable glossary of critical terms, a select bibliography, and an index.

Nilsson, Martin P. "The Origin and Transmission of Epic Poetry." In *Homer and Mycenae*. London: Methuen, 1933. Reprint. New York: Cooper Square, 1968.
Examines several oral epic traditions, including those of France, Scandinavia, Yugoslavia, the Kirghiz of Central Asia, and the Atchinese of Sumatra. Notes that these traditions share with the Homeric epics such features as stock expressions, typical descriptions, archaic language, and a background in the olden days. Concludes with a brief description of the genesis of the Greek epics in the Mycenaean period and their further development during the following centuries.

Okpewho, Isidore. *The Epic in Africa*. New York: Columbia University Press, 1979.
Shows how the principles of oral epic, observed especially in the Homeric epics and in the Yugoslavian epic tradition, can be applied to African oral epics such as the *Sunjata* of West Africa and the *Mwindo Epic* of Zaire. Compares the oral language, the narrative style, and the portrayal of heroes in the European and African epic traditions. Contains a selected bibliography and index.

Otis, Brooks. "From Homer to Virgil: The Obsolescence of Epic." In *Virgil: A Study in Civilized Poetry*. Oxford, England: Clarendon Press, 1963.
Considers the epic form and literary theory about epic in the ancient world from Homer to Vergil. Surveys the mythological, historical, and imitative epics of

Classical and Hellenistic Greece and Republican Rome. The *Aeneid* is seen to be a new kind of epic based upon a subjective style. There is an appendix on historical epic in the Hellenistic Greek period. Not all quotations are translated.

Ridley, M. R. *Studies in Three Literatures*. London: J. M. Dent & Sons, 1962. Considers the poetic possibilities of the Greek, Latin, and English languages in several literary genres, including epic. Characteristics of primitive and literary epics are discussed with particular reference to the Homeric epics, Vergil's *Aeneid*, and John Milton's *Paradise Lost*. Includes an index.

Van Doren, Mark. *The Noble Voice*. New York: Henry Holt, 1946. Ten long poems in the Western poetic tradition are the focus of this book by an important twentieth century American poet and novelist. Discusses the works of Homer, Lucretius, Vergil, John Milton, Dante Alighieri, Edmund Spenser, William Shakespeare, William Wordsworth, and George Gordon, Lord Byron.

HOMER

General Studies

Atchity, Kenneth. Introduction to *Critical Essays on Homer*, edited by Kenneth Atchity, Ron Hogart, and Doug Price. Boston: G. K. Hall, 1987.
This introductory essay, providing useful summaries of the twenty-two items in a critical anthology on Homer, begins with observations on the oral and literary features of the Homeric epics and offers some perspective on the contribution each item has made to Homeric studies.

Atchity, Kenneth, Ron Hogart, and Doug Price, eds. *Critical Essays on Homer*. Boston: G. K. Hall, 1987.
This book contains more than its title suggests. In addition to a collection of seventeen essays representing the diversity of twentieth century Homeric scholarship, there are Homer-inspired poems (such as W. H. Auden's "The Shield of Achilles," John Donne's "A Valediction: Forbidding Mourning," Wallace Steven's "The World as Meditation," and C. P. Cavafy's "Ithaca"), as well as Jorge Luis Borges' reflections on blindness. An introductory essay by Atchity, a selected bibliography, and an index are included.

Auslander, Joseph, and Frank Ernest Hill. "Blind Homer." In *The Winged Horse: The Story of the Poets and Their Poetry*. Garden City, N.Y.: Doubleday, 1927.
Part of an introduction to poetry and its appreciation written for children, this chapter includes comment upon the Homeric question, summaries of both Homeric poems, a discussion of some of their literary characteristics, and observations on Homer's influence in both ancient Greece and the modern world.

Austin, Norman. *Archery at the Dark of the Moon: Poetic Problems in Homer's "Odyssey."* Berkeley: University of California Press, 1975.
This book is a reaction to twentieth century studies of the Homeric poems as traditional oral compositions lacking more elaborate literate structures. The author examines the Homeric formulaic language, poetic symbolism, and ways of thinking in order to suggest that in literary matters the author of the *Odyssey* was not a primitive. Includes endnotes, a bibliography, and an index.

Bassett, Samuel Eliot. *The Poetry of Homer*. Berkeley: University of California Press, 1938.
This appreciation of the poetic quality of the Homeric poems is part of the Sather Classical Lectures series. Presents in the first chapter the strongly unitarian view that a single poet composed both poems. The remaining chapters consider various ways in which Homer creates an illusion of reality in his poems and examines

special poetic features of the poems, including Homer's use of description and dialogue. Some untranslated Greek words. Contains notes and an index.

Bérard, Victor. *Did Homer Live?* Translated by Brian Rhys. New York: E. P. Dutton, 1931.
Seeks links between the Homeric poems and the eastern Mediterranean cultures of Egypt, Phoenicia, and ancient Israel. Offers a textual history of the Homeric poems, a history of Bronze Age Greece and its ties with the East, and a theory of composition for the Homeric poems which assumes the development of writing in the thirteenth century B.C. and a written Phoenician model for the *Odyssey*. Later scholarship, especially studies of the oral language of the Homeric epics and the decipherment of Linear B, have made obsolete much of this unitarian argument, but Bérard's theories have had great influence on writers such as James Joyce.

Beye, Charles Rowan. *The "Iliad," the "Odyssey," and the Epic Tradition*. Garden City, N.Y.: Doubleday, 1966.
In addition to individual interpretative essays on the Homeric epics and on Vergil's *Aeneid*, there are chapters on the nature of Homeric poetry, the Homeric world, and special features of epic technique.

Bloom, Harold, ed. *Homer*. New York: Chelsea House, 1986.
A volume in the Modern Critical Views series, this book contains twenty-four studies on Homer published between 1933 and 1986. Topics include Homeric oral language, similes, epic structure, the Homeric hero, and interpretative discussions of both Homeric poems. Features include an introduction, chronological chart, list of contributors, bibliography, and index.

_____. *Homer's "The Iliad."* New York: Chelsea House, 1987.
A volume in the Modern Critical Interpretations series, this book contains selections from eight studies of the *Iliad* published between 1951 and 1985. Discusses features of Homer's oral language, Homeric psychology, the role of the gods in human life, and the Homeric hero, especially in the *Iliad*. Contains an introduction, chronology, bibliography, and index.

_____. Introduction to *Homer*, edited by Harold Bloom. New York: Chelsea House, 1986. Reprinted in *Homer's "The Iliad,"* edited by Harold Bloom. New York: Chelsea House, 1987.
Compares and contrasts the Homeric representation of the self, deity, the hero, and war with that found in the earliest part of the Bible, known as the Yahwist strand.

Bowra, C. M. *Homer*. New York: Charles Scribner's Sons, 1972.
In addition to studies of both Homeric poems, this book considers features of oral composition, obstacles faced by the modern reader of the Homeric poems, historical background to the Greek Heroic Age, the role of action in the Homeric poems, and Homer's creative blending of the heroic ideal with the everyday activities of human life. Includes an introduction, thirty-nine plates, a bibliographical note, and an index.

_____. "Homer and Hesiod." In *Ancient Greek Literature*. London: Thornton Butterworth, 1933.
An overview of Homeric poetry in the context of other poetry of the period, including the *Homeric Hymns* and the works of Hesiod. Bowra argues that the *Iliad* and the *Odyssey* were heroic epics composed by a single poet for recitation in the ninth or eighth century B.C. Includes plot summaries and brief studies of Homeric language and characters. The plot of the *Iliad* is derived from traditional lays about heroic strength and that of the *Odyssey* from folktales of adventure and popular tales celebrating heroic wit and cunning. Contains a bibliography and index.

Butler, Samuel. *The Authoress of the "Odyssey."* 2d ed. London: Jonathan Cape, 1922. Reprint. Chicago: University of Chicago Press, 1967.
Written by the author of *The Way of All Flesh*. While Butler's expressed intent is to prove not only that the *Iliad* and the *Odyssey* were written by different authors but also that the *Odyssey* was written by a woman in Greek-speaking Sicily, the book is actually a poetic interpretation of the epic. In addition to a paraphrase of the plot and the argument about authorship, there are chapters on the character of Penelope, on the geographic background of the poem, and on the date of composition. There are some untranslated Greek passages. Includes illustrations, maps, and an index.

Camps, W. A. *An Introduction to Homer*. New York: Oxford University Press, 1980.
A brief study of the character of Homeric poetry. Topics of individual sections include plot outlines of the two Homeric poems; similarities and differences between the *Iliad* and the *Odyssey*; Homeric society; the supernatural; character portrayal; and poetic characteristics of the epics. There are detailed endnotes and two appendices, one on the structure of the poems and another on their topography.

Carpenter, Rhys. *Folktale, Fiction, and Saga in the Homeric Epics*. Berkeley: University of California Press, 1946.
Volume 20 in the Sather Classical Lectures series. In this study, the author examines elements of folktale and hero legend in the Homeric epics and empha-

sizes the differences between the world of Homer and the Mycenaean world. Carpenter concludes that the poems were composed by two different individuals c. 700 B.C. Contains a map and index.

Clark, Frank Lowry. Introduction to *A Study of the "Iliad" in Translation*. Chicago: University of Chicago Press, 1927.
Discusses some typical, universal features of Greek literature which explain its influence on later cultures and especially on British literature. Outlines the history of Greek literature and summarizes outstanding characteristics of the Greek language in general and of Homeric verse in particular. Homer's verse is compared to that of Vergil and of Henry Wadsworth Longfellow.

Durant, Will. "The Heroic Age." In *The Story of Civilization*. Vol. 2, *The Life of Greece*. New York: Simon & Schuster, 1939.
Although published before the decipherment of Linear B, this essay remains a good introduction to Homer and his world. In addition to summaries of the *Iliad* and the *Odyssey*, there are sections on the Greek invasion of the Aegean world c. 2000 B.C., on the heroic myths of Greece, on the Dorian conquest of Greece, and on Homeric civilization, including its art and its social, economic, and political structures. Features include a chronological table, illustrations, glossary, bibliography, endnotes, and indexes.

Edwards, Mark W. *Homer: Poet of the "Iliad."* Baltimore: The Johns Hopkins University Press, 1987.
This book is divided into two parts. Part 1 is especially concerned with poetic aspects of the Homeric poems but also includes essays on religious and social features of the Homeric epics. Part 2 is a commentary on ten books of the *Iliad*. Contains an introduction, afterword, general bibliography, and index.

Finley, M. I. "Bibliographical Essay." In *The World of Odysseus*. Rev. ed. New York: Viking Press, 1965.
This short discussion of literature written about Homer focuses on general works in English. Includes sections entitled "Homer and History," "Homer, Mycenae, and Archaeology," "Institutions," and "A Note on Translations of Homer."
_____. *The World of Odysseus*. Rev. ed. New York: Viking Press, 1965.
A sketch of the society in which Homer conceived his heroes to live. There are chapters on Homer's place in Greek history, the Homeric question, and economics, social structure, and values in the Homeric world. Includes a bibliographical essay, notes, indexes, and a foreword by Mark Van Doren.

Fitzgerald, Robert. "[On Translating Homer]." In *Critical Essays on Homer*, edited by Kenneth Atchity, Ron Hogart, and Doug Price. Boston: G. K. Hall, 1987.
This abridgment of the postscript appended to Fitzgerald's translation of the

Odyssey includes approximately half the original essay. Discusses the Greek singer, the Homeric formula, Fitzgerald's travels to Ithaca, and the problems of translating Homer.

_____. "Some General Considerations." In *The Odyssey*, by Homer, translated by Robert Fitzgerald. Garden City, N.Y.: Doubleday, 1961.
The second half of a postscript to his translation of the *Odyssey*. Considers such topics as the Homeric question, the Greek singer, the Homeric formula, Homer's humor, the structure of the *Odyssey*, and the relationship between the *Iliad* and the *Odyssey*.

Flacelière, Robert. "The Trojan War: Homer." In *A Literary History of Greece*, translated by Douglas Garman. Chicago: Aldine, 1964.
Historical background on the Trojan War and on Greece in the Bronze and Iron ages, with sections on Minoan and Mycenaean art. An overview of the Homeric question concludes with the author's assertion that a single author wrote both Homeric poems. Plot summaries and discussions of both epics, with sections on Homer's art, personality, and portrayal of character. In the last section, the history of the poems from the time of Homer until the Roman era is summarized. Contains a foreword, seventeen plates, a chronological table, bibliographies, and an index.

Grant, Michael. "Homer." In *Greek and Latin Authors: 800 B.C.-A.D. 1000*. New York: H. W. Wilson, 1980.
This essay considers the Homeric question, oral performances of Homer, and the relationship between Homer and history. Includes a summary of the plots of both Homeric epics, a discussion of characterization in Homer, interpretations of the epics, comments on Homer's later influence, and a note on works falsely attributed to Homer, including other poems in the epic cycle and the *Homeric Hymns*. Appendices include a list of works of doubtful attribution and a chronological list of authors arranged by century. Also includes a preface, "List of Authors Included," twenty-five illustrations, a pronunciation key, and bibliographies.

_____. "The Wrath of Achilles." In *Myths of the Greeks and Romans*. New York: New American Library, 1962.
Following a summary of the plot of the *Iliad*, the author offers historical background to the Mycenaean age, an analysis of several Homeric characters, including Achilles and Helen, a study in the qualities of a Homeric hero and his gods, and the influence of Homer upon later art and literature.

Graves, Robert. Introduction to *The Anger of Achilles*, by Homer, translated by Robert Graves. Garden City, N.Y.: Doubleday, 1959.

In this introductory essay to his translation of Homer's *Iliad*, Graves discusses such topics as professional storytellers in ancient Greece, the content of the Homeric epic cycle, Homer's humor, his attitude toward the gods, the character of Achilles, the popularity of the *Iliad* in antiquity, and some problems in translating Homer.

Griffin, Jasper. *Homer*. New York: Hill & Wang, 1980.
This short work contains a chapter on the general features of the Homeric epics as well as studies of each epic, with special attention to the meaning and influence of the poems. Contains a preface, bibliographies, and an index.

_____. "The Homeric Epic." In *Homer*. New York: Hill & Wang, 1980.
Includes plot summaries of both epics and some background to the Homeric age. Argues that the two Homeric poems were composed by different poets. Discusses features of Greek heroes and poetic characteristics of the epics.

Havelock, Eric A. *The Greek Concept of Justice: From Its Shadow in Homer to Its Substance in Plato*. Cambridge, Mass.: Harvard University Press, 1978.
Studies the transformations in Greek attitudes toward justice and morality between Homer and Plato, that is, between the ninth century and the fourth century B.C. Includes observations on the function of epic in preliterate society, on the didactic nature of Homer's formulaic language, and on the moral and legal issues of both the *Iliad* and the *Odyssey*. The Homeric poems are considered to portray not the values of the Mycenaean world in which the stories take place but the ideas of maritime Greece in the ninth through seventh centuries B.C., in which the Homeric poems were composed. Contains endnotes, a bibliography, and an index.

Heubeck, Alfred. "General Introduction." In *A Commentary on Homer's "Odyssey."* Vol. 1, *Introduction and Books I-VIII*, edited by Alfred Heubeck, Stephanie West, and J. B. Hainsworth. Oxford, England: Clarendon Press, 1988.
This introduction to a scholarly commentary on the *Odyssey* provides a broad overview suitable for the general reader. Focuses on the Homeric question and the "redactor hypothesis" that a single poet united several independent poetic strands into the poem known as the *Odyssey*. Considers the epic to be the product of both the traditional oral language described by Milman Parry and the hand of a single literate poet. Suggests that writing encouraged the compressed plot of the *Odyssey*. Compares the two Homeric poems and emphasizes transformation of the Homeric gods from irrational and impulsive powers in the *Iliad* into representatives of wisdom and fate in the *Odyssey*. Also discusses Homer's characterization of Odysseus. There are a few untranslated Greek words.

Hogan, James C. Introduction to *A Guide to the "Iliad."* Garden City, N.Y.: Anchor Books, 1979.

This introduction to a commentary accompanying Robert Fitzgerald's translation of the *Iliad* includes sections containing plot summaries of both Homeric epics, background from the Trojan saga, and discussion about topics such as Homer and history, the composition of the epics, Homeric language and syntax, typical scenes, and the poetry and themes of the *Iliad*.

Holoka, James P. "Homer Studies: 1971-1977." *Classical World* 73 (1979): 65-150.

This sweeping overview of Homeric scholarship includes references to work in several languages besides English. Arranged thematically, with sections on Homer's language, style, and worldview, on studies of both the *Iliad* and the *Odyssey*, on ancient scholarship, history, archaeology, and Homeric influence. Under each heading, there is a list of bibliographical references followed by brief editorial comments on selected entries.

Jebb, R. C. *Homer: An Introduction to the "Iliad" and the "Odyssey."* 5th ed. Boston: Ginn, 1894. Reprint. Port Washington, N.Y.: Kennikat Press, 1969.

Despite its date of publication, this book, written by an important nineteenth century classical scholar, remains a good general introduction to Homeric studies. The four chapters deal with the following topics: the general literary characteristics of the poems; social and religious aspects of the Homeric world; Homeric influence and criticism in antiquity; and the Homeric question. Greek references in parentheses or notes. Includes five appendices on more technical aspects of Homeric language and on the house at Tiryns (with plan), a bibliography, and footnotes.

Kirk, Geoffrey S. "Homer." In *The Cambridge History of Classical Literature*. Vol. 1, *Greek Literature*, edited by P. E. Easterling and B. M. W. Knox. New York: Cambridge University Press, 1985.

The first part of this essay deals with the Homeric question and the place of the Homeric poems in the ancient Greek tradition of oral poetry. The second part contains a detailed summary and an interpretation of the *Iliad*. The last part is a close comparison of the two Homeric poems with particular attention to the special use of folktale themes in the *Odyssey*. Extensive passages of both epics are quoted in translation; there are some untranslated Greek words. Contains a preface, fourteen plates, footnotes, a metrical appendix, an appendix of authors and works with bibliography, a general bibliography, and an index.

_____. Introduction to *The Language and Background of Homer: Some Recent Studies and Controversies*, edited by Geoffrey S. Kirk. Cambridge, England: W. Heffer & Sons, 1964.

In this essay, the author offers some background to the twelve scholarly essays collected in this volume and suggests the contribution each has made to Homeric studies. Kirk also lists six important directions for Homeric research to pursue in the future: language studies about Linear B and Homer's formulaic system; oral poetry; the archaeology of Bronze Age Greece; the study of Mycenaean society; the structure of the Homeric poems; and the history of the poems.

_____. Introduction to *The Odyssey*, by Homer, translated by Walter Shewring. New York: Oxford University Press, 1980.
Introduces various aspects of the *Odyssey* to readers of a prose translation of the poem. Provides background to the story and a summary of the plot. Offers some observations on the Homeric question, the date and possible method of composition of the poem, some differences between the *Iliad* and the *Odyssey*, and the character of Odysseus.

_____, ed. *The Language and Background of Homer: Some Recent Studies and Controversies*. Cambridge, England: W. Heffer & Sons, 1964.
This book is a collection of twelve essays originally published in scholarly contexts between 1947 and 1961. Topics include oral poetry, the language of Homer, and Mycenaean features of the Homeric poems. Not all Greek is translated. Some essays are written for the Homeric scholar rather than the beginning student. Contains an introduction and notes.

_____. *The Songs of Homer*. Cambridge, England: Cambridge University Press, 1962.
Examines the Homeric poems in the context of Greek oral heroic poetry from the Mycenaean period to the time of Homer and presents a comprehensive view of the nature of the poems, their relation to earlier Greek culture and poetry and the effect of oral composition upon their structure. Provides historical background, an overview of the nature of oral composition, an examination of the way that oral epic may have developed in Greece between 1600 and 600 B.C., and an explanation of the textual transmission of the Homeric poems. Studies structural and general features of both the *Iliad* and the *Odyssey*. There are maps, plates, and an index.

Kitto, H. D. F. "Homer." In *The Greeks*. Baltimore: Penguin Books, 1952.
Examines several passages from the *Iliad* in order to show how Homer embodies the essential Greek spirit, including a vividness of description, an absence of natural background, a sense of humanity, intellectual power, and moral seriousness. Emphasizes Homer's role as the educator of Greece and considers briefly the Homeric question and the relationship between the *Iliad* and the *Odyssey*. Includes a map.

Lattimore, Richmond. Introduction to *The "Iliad" of Homer*. Chicago: University of Chicago Press, 1951.
Lattimore precedes his translation of the *Iliad* with background on the story of the fall of Troy and a summary of the plot of the *Iliad*. Other topics discussed include the date of Homer, the epic cycle, the unity of Homer, Homeric formulas and similes, the role of the gods, and Homer's characterizations of Hector, Achilles, and Ajax.

Lesky, Albin. "The Homeric Epic." In *A History of Greek Literature*, translated by James Willis and Cornelis de Heer. 2d ed. New York: Thomas Y. Crowell, 1966.
This chapter of Lesky's survey of Greek literature from its origins through the sixth century A.D. is a good introduction to Homeric studies. There are sections on such topics as epic poetry before Homer, the Homeric question, methods of composition of both epics, language, and the role of the gods. Contains a select bibliography and an index.

Levi, Peter. "Homer." In *A History of Greek Literature*. New York: Viking Penguin, 1985.
Surveys the history of the Greek language, linguistic features of Homeric poetry, the Homeric question, the date of the poems, and the Greek epic tradition. Discusses the role of the gods in the *Iliad*, especially the seduction of Zeus in book 14. Emphasizes the adventure and sea themes of the *Odyssey*, which is compared to the *Iliad* and to other epics. Both Homeric poems are interpreted as studies in the breakdown and restoration of moral order. Includes charts, bibliographies, and an index.

Lorimer, H. L. *Homer and the Monuments*. London: Macmillan, 1950.
An examination of the world of Homer in regard to archaeological evidence from Bronze Age Greece. Includes a short history of Greece from the Neolithic period through the introduction of the alphabet, a survey of relations between Greece and the other nations in the late Bronze and early Iron ages, a discussion of anachronistic references by Homer to the use of cremation and of iron weapons, and information on writing, weaponry, dress, and architecture in Bronze Age Greece. Studies evidence concerning authorship of the Homeric poems and concludes that each poem was composed by a single author between c. 750 and c. 680 B.C. Contains a preface, thirty-two plates of archaeological finds from the Bronze Age, sixty-one figures, mostly of armor, and indexes.

Mason, H. A. *To Homer Through Pope: An Introduction to Homer's "Iliad" and Pope's Translation*. New York: Harper & Row, 1972.
Based upon the premise that both the Greek scholar and the Greekless reader would benefit from approaching the Homeric poems in translation, especially

those of Alexander Pope and John Dryden. Includes studies of the basic structure of *Iliad* 1, Pope's and Dryden's translations of the book, Homeric similes, the concept of the epic hero, and the serious tone of epic. Twentieth century translations of the *Iliad* and the *Odyssey* are discussed in epilogues. Not all Greek phrases are translated. Includes an index.

Michalopoulos, Andre. *Homer*. Boston: Twayne, 1966.
Part of Twayne's World Authors series, this volume offers a critical study of Homer and his works. The following subjects are covered in individual chapters: background to Mycenaean civilization and the Homeric question; general introductions to both the *Iliad* and the *Odyssey*; the tragedies of the *Iliad*; the character of Achilles; and observations on comparisons between Achilles and Odysseus and on the status of women in Homer. Contains a preface, chronological chart, epilogue, notes, selected bibliography, and index.

Miller, Walter. Introduction to *The Iliad*, by Homer, translated by William Benjamin Smith and Walter Miller. New York: Macmillan, 1944.
In this short introduction to a verse translation of the *Iliad*, Miller summarizes the traditional biography of Homer, the mythic background and general features of the poem, including Homer's character portrayal, treatment of the gods, and the links between the *Iliad* and historical events. There is also a glossary of Greek and Trojan heroes and of the gods grouped as supporters of the Greeks or the Trojans.

Mueller, Martin. Introduction to *The Iliad*. Boston: Allen & Unwin, 1984.
Discusses the historical background of the Homeric poems, oral composition and the nature of the Homeric formula. Considers various views of Homer, including acceptance of the Homeric poems as a cultural code in fifth century B.C. Greece, identification of Homer and Nature in eighteenth century Europe, and recognition that literate and oral compositions can use similar forms of rhetoric. Argues that Milman Parry's theory of an inherited and fixed oral language must be balanced by the recognition of a more poetic and flexible method of composition and interpretation for the Homeric poems.

Murray, A. T. Introduction to *The Odyssey*, by Homer, translated by A. T. Murray. Cambridge, Mass.: Harvard University Press, 1919.
In this short introduction, the translator summarizes the ancient life of Homer, the controversy concerning whether Homer was a real person, the history of the Homer texts, ancient critics of Homer, and his aims as a translator.

Murray, Gilbert. *The Rise of the Greek Epic*. 3d ed. Oxford, England: Clarendon Press, 1924.

This study of the origin of the Homeric epics, and especially the *Iliad*, is based upon the analytic theory that the poems originated in an ancient poetic tradition. Includes an overview of Greek history and society in the Bronze and Dark ages, a study of traditional elements in the *Iliad*, a general appreciation of the *Iliad*, and some comments on the Homeric question and the transmission of the Homeric texts. There are ten appendices and an index.

Nagler, Michael N. *Spontaneity and Tradition: A Study in the Oral Art of Homer*. Berkeley: University of California Press, 1974.
Using an approach to the Homeric poems based upon the theories of generative linguistics, Nagler illustrates his theory of spontaneous composition in the context of an inherited, traditional frame of thought and language. Examines traditional phrases and motifs in the *Iliad* and the *Odyssey* and offers a general interpretation of the *Iliad*. Includes a discussion of the Homeric question and comparisons of the Homeric epics with other epics, such as *Gilgamesh* and *Beowulf*. There are two plates, a bibliography, and indexes.

Nagy, Gregory. *The Best of the Achaeans: Concepts of the Hero in Archaic Greek Poetry*. Baltimore: The Johns Hopkins University Press, 1979.
Uses careful linguistic analysis of the Homeric poems, of other archaic Greek poetry, including Hesiod and Pindar, and of poetry in various Indo-European traditions in order to show how Achilles, the hero of the *Iliad*, possesses religious features of a traditional Greek cult hero. Establishes a coherent theory about the evolution of the Homeric poems and their place in Greek and Indo-European culture and considers the relationship of Homer's *Iliad* with an earlier poem about the heroic rivalry between Achilles and Odysseus. Examines the themes of heroic and poetic immortality, praise and blame, and the image of the warrior-poet in early Greek poetry. Contains an introduction, appendix, bibliography, and indexes.

Nilsson, Martin P. *Homer and Mycenae*. London: Methuen, 1933. Reprint. New York: Cooper Square, 1968.
Surveys the links between the Homeric epics and the Mycenaean world. Discusses issues related to the Homeric question, the nature of oral epic poetry, and characteristics of Homeric language and style. Includes a history of the Mycenaean age, a description of Mycenaean state organization, and a discussion of datable elements in the Homeric poems and of the origin of Greek mythology. Includes maps, plans, illustrations, and an index.

Packard, David W., and Tania Meyers. *A Bibliography of Homeric Scholarship: Preliminary Edition, 1930-1970*. Malibu, Calif.: Udena, 1974.
A computer-generated bibliography listing all works on Homer published in

several languages over a forty-year period. Works are organized alphabetically with no annotation.

Page, Denys L. *History and the Homeric "Iliad."* Berkeley: University of California Press, 1959.
Considers Hittite documents, Trojan excavations, and the catalogue of ships in *Iliad* 2 as good evidence that the Greek sack of Troy actually occurred. Argues that little from the world described in Linear B Tablets from Pylus and Cnossus survives in the Homeric poems. Examines some archaeological and linguistic relics from the Mycenaean world in the *Iliad*. Includes a preface, endnotes, maps, plans, an index, and an appendix on the multiple authorship of the *Iliad*.

Perry, Walter Copland. *The Women of Homer*. London: William Heinemann, 1898.
While the main subject of this book is the favorable position and character of women in Homer, considerable attention is also devoted to general views of Homer, both ancient and modern, and especially to the author's enthusiastic opinion of Homer as a poet. Includes chapters on marriage, female dress, and the position of women in the Homeric poems and discussion of individual characters, such as Andromache, Helen, Penelope, Athena, and Aphrodite. Contains some untranslated foreign language quotations. There are twenty-two illustrations and an appendix of ancient citations in the original languages.

Rees, Ennis. Introduction to *The Odyssey*, by Homer. Indianapolis: Bobbs-Merrill, 1977.
Topics discussed in this short essay include the Homeric question, the later influence of Homer, background to the Trojan War, and the role of the gods.

Ridley, M. R. "Primitive Epic." In *Studies in Three Literatures*. London: J. M. Dent & Sons, 1962.
The Homeric epics, English and Scottish border ballads, the Icelandic sagas, and the Germanic *Sigurd* are used to illustrate the qualities of primitive epic. Homer is shown to be a master of characterization and the simile.

Rieu, E. V. Introduction to *The Iliad*, by Homer, translated by E. V. Rieu. Baltimore: Penguin Books, 1950.
Rieu's introduction to his translation of the *Iliad* includes a comparison of the *Iliad* and the *Odyssey*, a summary of the plot of the *Iliad*, and a consideration of such topics as Homer's originality, the Homeric question, the historical accuracy of the Homeric poems, and Homer's method of character portrayal.

_____. Introduction to *The Odyssey*, by Homer, translated by E. V. Rieu. New York: Penguin Books, 1946.
In this essay, the translator summarizes the plots of both Homeric epics and

considers some aspects of Homer's poetry, including his treatment of women and
the gods. Some of the difficulties in translating Homer are also discussed.

Romilly, Jacqueline de. "Homer." In *A Short History of Greek Literature*, translated
by Lillian Doherty. Chicago: University of Chicago Press, 1984.
This essay is divided into two parts. The first part deals with the Homeric
question and the oral composition of the epics and suggests the composite
language, structure, and civilization of the poems as evidence for layers of
composition in the poems. The second part summarizes the plots of the poems
and discusses such aspects of the Homeric world as the gods, the human ideal,
love of life, and literary art. Contains a preface, a translator's note, a chronological map, tables, a bibliography, an index, and an appendix on the epic cycle and
the *Homeric Hymns*.

Rose, H. J. "Homer and the Ancient Epic." In *A Handbook of Greek Literature
from Homer to the Age of Lucian*. 4th ed. New York: E. P. Dutton, 1951.
Includes plot summaries of both Homeric epics, a detailed introduction to the
Homeric question, and discussion of other works, now lost, included in the
ancient epic cycle.

Rouse, W. H. D. *Homer*. New York: Thomas Nelson and Sons, 1939.
This short study by a popular translator of the Homeric poems includes summaries of both epics, historical and archaeological background, information about
the geographic world of Homer, a general appreciation of Homeric poetry, and
a survey of English translations of Homer. Contains illustrations, maps, and an
index.

Rubino, Carl A., and Cynthia A. Shelmerdine, eds. *Approaches to Homer*. Austin:
University of Texas Press, 1983.
A collection of nine scholarly papers which approach Homeric studies from a
variety of directions, including comparative linguistics, archaeology, historical
studies, word studies, and literary criticism. Questions raised include the nature
of the Homeric hero, problems of Homeric narrative, and the later influence of
Homer. An introduction by the editors summarizes the essays. Not all Greek is
translated. Includes endnotes and an index.

Schein, Seth L. *The Mortal Hero: An Introduction to Homer's "Iliad."* Berkeley:
University of California Press, 1984.
This book is more than a literary study of the *Iliad*. The author emphasizes
thematic, ethical, and artistic aspects of the poem in the context of the poetic
tradition in which it developed. There are chapters on the poetic tradition, the
gods, heroism, Achilles, and Hector. Includes a preface, endnotes, a bibliography, a general index, and an index of passages cited.

Scott, John A. *Homer and His Influence*. Boston: Marshall Jones, 1925.
In this study of the Homeric contribution to Western civilization, the author discusses the following topics: the Homeric question, the biographical tradition about the poet, Homer's use of the Greek poetic tradition, translations of Homer, a comparison of the two Homeric poems, and Homer's influence on later Greeks, on the Romans, and on English literature.

Silk, M. S. *Homer: The "Iliad."* London: Cambridge University Press, 1987.
This introduction to the *Iliad* begins with background on the Homeric world and oral composition, surveys the general features of the poem, including structure, style, and characterization, and ends with some comments on the influence of the *Iliad* on world literature. Includes a preface and annotated bibliography.

Smyth, Herbert Weir. "Epic Poetry." In *Greek Literature*. New York: Columbia University Press, 1912. Reprint. Freeport, N.Y.: Books for Libraries Press, 1969.
Emphasizes the dominance of the *Iliad* and the *Odyssey* among ancient Greek epics and the influence of the Homeric poems on later literature, both as an authority in the ancient world and as a model in European literature of the seventeenth to nineteenth centuries. The influence of the Homeric poems is based upon their realistic and individualized portrayals of human nature. Foreign language quotations are not translated. Index.

Steiner, George, and Robert Fagles, eds. *Homer: A Collection of Critical Essays*. Englewood Cliffs, N.J.: Prentice-Hall, 1962.
This volume is a collection of seventeen essays, one excerpt from a novel, and eight poems connected with Homer. In addition to critical studies, there are appreciative essays by such writers as Leo Tolstoy, Ezra Pound, and Franz Kafka. Represented poets include W. H. Auden, Robert Graves, and C. P. Cavafy. Includes a bibliography and notes on the editors and authors.

Taplin, Oliver. "Homer." In *The Oxford History of the Classical World: Greece and the Hellenistic World*, edited by John Boardman, Jasper Griffin, and Oswyn Murray. New York: Oxford University Press, 1988.
In this chapter of a history of Greece, profusely illustrated with 407 illustrations, nine color maps, and six other maps, the author includes short essays on both the *Iliad* and the *Odyssey*, with special attention to the heroes of each epic and to the ways in which the two epics complement each other. There are also discussions of oral tradition, oral composition, and the relationship between Homer and history. Includes bibliographies, a table of events, and an index.

Thomas, C. G., ed. *Homer's History: Mycenaean or Dark Age?* New York: Holt, Rinehart and Winston, 1970.

Part of the European Problem Studies series, this collection contains excerpts from fourteen essays dealing with the historical background of the Homeric poems. These essays, mostly published between 1955 and 1965, were written by such Homeric scholars as C. M. Bowra, D. L. Page, and T. B. L. Webster. Topics covered include archaeology, economic organization, religion, political structure, Homer's sources, and his later influence. Each article is introduced by a brief note stating the significance of the study and providing biographical information about the author. Includes introduction, illustration, chronological chart, and bibliography.

Trypanis, C. A. "Epic Poetry." In *Greek Poetry from Homer to Seferis*. Chicago: University of Chicago Press, 1981.
The first chapter of a survey of Greek poetry from its Homeric beginnings until the early twentieth century. There are sections on the origins of the Greek poetic tradition, the Homeric epics, Hesiod, the Homeric hymns, and other ancient epic poetry. The section on the Homeric epics includes discussion of the poet Homer, the composition of the poems, Homeric narrative, the worlds of men and of gods in Homer, and the poetic excellence and influence of the poems. Contains endnotes, bibliography, and index.

_____. *The Homeric Epics*. Translated by William Phelps. Warminster, England: Aris & Phillips, 1977.
This book has chapters on the Homeric question, the structure of the Homeric poems, their date of composition, epic narrative technique, men and gods in the Homeric epics, their poetic achievement, and their later influence. Contains preface, bibliography, footnotes, and index.

Vivante, Paolo. *Homer*. New Haven, Conn.: Yale University Press, 1985.
This study is intended to introduce the general reader to the poetic quality of the Homeric poems. The author discusses such topics as reading Homer, Homeric narrative, character portrayal, Homer's representations of nature, especially in similes, and historical background to the Homeric poems. Contains a select bibliography and index.

Wace, Alan J. B., and Frank H. Stubbings, eds. *A Companion to Homer*. New York: Macmillan, 1963.
While written especially for those reading Homer in Greek, this collection of twenty-three scholarly essays contains much of value to the general reader. There is extensive material on the Homeric poems, their authorship, and the Homeric world. Discusses the archaeological record at Troy, Mycenae, and other sites and considers the geography, history, and culture of Greece in the Homeric period. Includes sixty-nine maps and figures and forty black-and-white plates, as well as indexes.

West, M. L. "Homeric and Hesiodic Poetry." In *Ancient Greek Literature*, edited by K. J. Dover. New York: Oxford University Press, 1980.
This contribution to a multiauthored survey of Greek literature from the Homeric period through the sixth century A.D. is written by the author of several important scholarly editions of early Greek authors. This essay includes sections on the Homeric question and oral composition, on each of the Homeric poems, on the *Homeric Hymns*, on the poetry of Hesiod, and on the date of Homer. West shows how Homer controls the narrative and prepares for events in the *Iliad* and how the *Odyssey* was created from several narrative strands. The volume includes maps, a chronological table, a bibliography, and an index.

Whitman, Cedric H. *The Heroic Paradox*. Edited by Charles Segal. Ithaca, N.Y.: Cornell University Press, 1982.
This posthumous collection of six essays covers Greek drama, Homeric heroes, the plot of the *Iliad*, and the Homeric question. An introductory essay by the editor discusses the many contributions of Whitman to Greek studies, including the study of Homer. Contains vita of the author, bibliography, and index.

_____. *Homer and the Heroic Tradition*. Cambridge, Mass.: Harvard University Press, 1958.
In this affirmation of the unity of Homeric thought and structure, the author discusses such topics as Homer's portrayal of the Mycenaean world, the writing of the Homeric poems, Homer and Geometric art, and imagery, characterization, and the gods in the Homeric poems. Special features include a map, a chronological chart, a structural chart in flyleaf, endnotes, and an index.

Wilkie, Brian, and James Hurt. "Homer." In *Literature of the Western World*. Vol. 1, *The Ancient World Through the Renaissance*, edited by Brian Wilkie and James Hurt. New York: Macmillan, 1984.
This brief introduction to Robert Fitzgerald's translation of the *Odyssey* includes a discussion of the influence of the *Odyssey* and the Bible, comments on the Homeric question, and the role of the gods in the epic. Includes a bibliography.

Woodhouse, W. J. *The Composition of Homer's "Odyssey."* Oxford, England: Clarendon Press, 1930.
The main purpose of this book is to find signs in the *Odyssey* of the epic's sources and method of composition. In addition to close studies of many episodes in the *Odyssey*, especially those which take place on Ithaca, the book includes character studies, comparisons of the *Iliad* and the *Odyssey*, and a strong affirmation of the unitarian position that the *Odyssey* was composed by a single poet. While each chapter is introduced by several passages in Homeric Greek without translation, the main body of the chapter can be read without reference to these passages.

The Homeric World

Overviews

Beye, Charles Rowan. "The Poet's World." In *The "Iliad," the "Odyssey," and the Epic Tradition*. Garden City, N.Y.: Doubleday, 1966.

Shows how the Homeric epics are an amalgam of different historical periods, namely Mycenaean Greece and Greece of the eighth century B.C. Discussion of Mycenaean artifacts mentioned in Homer, of Homer's political and domestic structures, and of the role of the gods in the Homeric poems.

Bradford, Ernle. *Ulysses Found*. New York: Harcourt, Brace & World, 1963.

In this book, the author combines ancient evidence, modern scholarship, and his own sailor's knowledge of the Mediterranean in order to identify the places mentioned in the *Odyssey* and to retrace the route of Odysseus. Sailing days and routes mentioned in the poem are considered to reflect actual voyages. A chronology of Odysseus' voyage and a discussion of the location of Odysseus' Ithaca are contained in appendices. Features include an introduction, thirteen illustrations, six maps, a select bibliography, a genealogical chart of Odysseus, endnotes, and an index.

Camps, W. A. "The World of the Poems." In *An Introduction to Homer*. New York: Oxford University Press, 1980.

A brief discussion of the general features of Homeric society, including professions, political power, marriage, domestic life, and the law.

Edwards, Mark W. "History and Society." In *Homer: Poet of the Iliad*. Baltimore: The Johns Hopkins University Press, 1987.

The links of the Homeric poems with the society of eighth century B.C. Ionia and with the preceding Dark Age and the Mycenaean period are briefly surveyed. There are sections on archaisms in Homer and on society and weapons in the Homeric poems.

Havelock, Eric A. "The Society Reported by Homer." In *The Greek Concept of Justice: From Its Shadow in Homer to Its Substance in Plato*. Cambridge, Mass.: Harvard University Press, 1978.

Examines such features of the Homeric epics as the catalogues of ships and of Trojan forces and Homeric descriptions of domestic architecture, life on Ithaca, voyaging, fighting, farming, and civic life and concludes that the world Homer describes is the maritime world of the Greek city-states in the ninth through seventh centuries B.C. The setting in the Mycenaean age is used only to facilitate use of the stories as repositories of cultural values. Includes endnotes, a bibliography, and an index.

Jebb, R. C. "The Homeric World." In *Homer: An Introduction to the "Iliad" and the "Odyssey."* 5th ed. Boston: Ginn, 1894. Reprint. Port Washington, N.Y.: Kennikat Press, 1969.
This essay surveys various aspects of Homeric society, including the law, religion, architecture, and social customs. Greek words are in parentheses and notes.

Keller, Albert G. *Homeric Society: A Sociological Study of the "Iliad" and "Odyssey."* New York: Longmans, Green, 1913.
Works from the assumption that the Homeric poems can be used by themselves to provide an accurate picture of life in the Homeric age. There are chapters on industry, government, religion, social life, and knowledge of and contact with non-Greek peoples. Book and line references to relevant passages of the *Iliad* and the *Odyssey* are provided in footnotes. A good resource for information about the way these subjects are treated in the Homeric poems, but this work must be supplemented by archaeological evidence in order to obtain a more historical perspective on the Homeric world. Includes a bibliography and indexes.

Kirk, Geoffrey S. "The Historical Background of the Homeric Poems." In *The Songs of Homer*. Cambridge, England: Cambridge University Press, 1962.
In this first part of a work on the composition of the Homeric epics, the author describes the rise of Mycenaean culture, the Linear B tablets and life in a late Mycenaean palace-state, and Greek society from the decline in Mycenaean culture in the twelfth century B.C. until the time of Homer in the eighth century B.C.

Kitto, H. D. F. "The Country." In *The Greeks*. Baltimore: Penguin Books, 1952.
This description of the geography and climate of Greece includes a section on the economic life of Greece in the Dark Age. Passages from the *Odyssey* are used to illustrate agricultural practices, crafts, trades, commerce, and city life in the period. Includes a map.

Michalopoulos, Andre. "The Dawn of Civilization and Homer." In *Homer*. Boston: Twayne, 1966.
In this introductory essay to a general study of Homer, the author provides some historical background to the Homeric epics. Topics covered include the rise of Greek mythology and the anthropomorphic gods, a history of Greece through the Bronze Age, the legend of Troy and historical evidence for the Trojan War, the Homeric question, and the ancient biographical tradition about Homer.

Mireaux, Émile. *Daily Life in the Time of Homer*. Translated by Iris Sells. New York: Macmillan, 1960.
This description of life in the Homeric period is based primarily upon the

evidence of the Homeric poems themselves. There are chapters on such topics as family life, the manor house, economy, and government. Suggests that the Homeric poems depict a basically feudal and traditional society which shows signs of approaching social upheaval. Includes an index.

Murray, Gilbert. "The People." In *The Rise of the Greek Epic*. 3d ed. Oxford, England: Clarendon Press, 1924.
While this overview of Greek history and society in the Bronze and Dark ages is written from the scholarly perspective of the early twentieth century and must be modified by later discoveries, especially the decipherment of Linear B, Murray provides some insight into the ways in which Greek social and religious customs may have changed between the Bronze and Dark ages. Examines, in particular, modifications in the Greek tribal structure and Greek ethical attitudes, including the Greek concepts of *aidos* ("shame") and *nemesis* ("retribution"). There is some untranslated Greek.

Onians, Richard B. "The Earliest Greeks." In *The Origins of European Thought About the Body, the Mind, the Soul, the World, Time, and Fate*. Cambridge, England: Cambridge University Press, 1951.
In this brief introduction to a study of European concepts of consciousness, the immortal soul, and temporality, Onians describes some of the characteristics of Homeric heroes and Homeric society. Illustrates these heroes' nobility of soul but barbarity of action.

Seymour, Thomas D. *Life in the Homeric Age*. New York: Macmillan, 1908.
A close description of life in Greece in the ninth century B.C. based upon careful examination of the Homeric poems. Frequent reference to Homeric vocabulary, with detailed explanation. Chapters on geography, religious beliefs, and many other aspects of Homeric society, including government, the family, and agriculture. There are maps, photographs, drawings of artifacts and art from the period, plans, indexes, and a bibliography.

Silk, M. S. "Homer's World and the Making of the *Iliad*." In *Homer: The "Iliad."* London: Cambridge University Press, 1987.
Places the *Iliad* in the context of the Mycenaean world, which it recalls, and the Greek world of the eighth century B.C., in which it was composed. Includes a discussion of oral composition and the Homeric question and background on the language, society, and religion of the *Iliad*.

Vermeule, Emily. "The World of Odysseus." In *Greece and Rome: Builders of Our World*, edited by Merle Severy. Washington, D.C.: National Geographic Society, 1968.
Vermeule's contribution to a profusely illustrated volume of essays written by

outstanding classical scholars provides a historical and cultural background to the Homeric epics. The archaeological discoveries of Heinrich Schliemann at Troy and Sir Arthur Evans at Cnossus are described, as is the decipherment of Linear B by Michael Ventris. The Mycenaean world is re-created by the story of a fictional sea captain named Aktor of Troizen. The destructions of Thera and Troy are also described.

Vivante, Paolo. "Age and Place of Homer." In *Homer*. New Haven, Conn.: Yale University Press, 1985.
In this essay, the author places the Homeric poems in a general historical context and argues that a single author composed both Homeric epics. The date of Homer, his place in eighth century B.C. Ionian Greece, and his method of composition are discussed. Homer's ability to unite description and temporal reality is seen to be his essential poetic contribution.

Homer's Past: Archaeology and History

Bowra, C. M. "The Greek Heroic Age." In *Homer*. New York: Charles Scribner's Sons, 1972.
Surveys characteristics of the Heroic Age of the Greeks and of other peoples. Discusses evidence for the historical reality of events of this age, especially the story of the Trojan War. The catalogue of ships in *Iliad* 2 is analyzed as a historical document of the Mycenaean period. Argues for the Mycenaean origin of the Homeric hexameter.

_____. "Homer's Age of Heroes." *Horizon* 3 (January, 1961): 74-93. Illustrated. Reprinted without illustrations as "Problems Concerned with Homer and the Epics," in *Homer's History: Mycenaean or Dark Age?*, edited by C. G. Thomas. New York: Holt, Rinehart and Winston, 1970.
After summarizing the main problems surrounding the question of authorship of the Homeric poems, Bowra highlights the three ways that modern scholarship has learned more about the Homeric age and the historical background of the poems: archaeological discoveries, especially those of Heinrich Schliemann and Carl Blegen at Troy; information from Egyptian and Hittite records; and the decipherment by Michael Ventris of the Mycenaean script known as Linear B. A comparison of Homer's description of the Mycenaean world with the historical evidence shows that Homer, as an oral poet, merges the Mycenaean world with aspects of his own, later age.

Carpenter, Rhys. "Possibly One Mycenaean Relic in the Poems." In *Homer's History: Mycenaean or Dark Age?*, edited by C. G. Thomas. New York: Holt, Rinehart and Winston, 1970.

In this excerpt from *Folktale, Fiction, and Saga in the Homeric Epics*, Carpenter compares Homeric statements about culture and society with archaeological evidence from the Mycenaean period and concludes that only one Homeric item, a helmet of boars' teeth, is supported by historical evidence. The Homeric poems, a combination of saga and fiction, show no knowledge of the Mycenaean age.

_____. "Saga and Fiction." In *Folktale, Fiction, and Saga in the Homeric Epics*. Berkeley: University of California Press, 1946.
Challenges the view that the Homeric poems contain recollections of the distant, Mycenaean past. By comparing the epic of *Beowulf* with its historical reality, the author maintains that a feature of heroic epic is the vivid illusion of historical actuality.

Chadwick, John. *The Decipherment of Linear B*. 2d ed. Cambridge, England: Cambridge University Press, 1967.
This book describes one of the most exciting archaeological discoveries in the twentieth century, namely Michael Ventris' decipherment of the Mycenaean script known as Linear B in 1952. Much to the astonishment of many classical scholars, Ventris proved that the writing was a very early form of Greek. Chadwick, coauthor with Ventris of the first collection of deciphered Mycenaean documents, here explains how Ventris unlocked the key to the script. He considers some early objections to the theory and illustrates what the deciphered tablets reveal about life in Mycenaean Greece. Of particular note are comparisons of Homeric and Linear B words for various objects. The second edition includes a postscript outlining progress made between 1958 and 1967. Contains three plates, seventeen figures, and an index.

_____. "The Greek Dialects and Greek Pre-History." In *The Language and Background of Homer: Some Recent Studies and Controversies*, edited by Geoffrey S. Kirk. Cambridge, England: W. Heffer & Sons, 1964.
Summarizes the traditional theory that the three dialects of ancient Greece results from three waves of invasion and suggests that the dialects are better understood as regional developments of late Bronze Age forms of Greek. Includes a map and three charts.

Dow, Sterling. "The Greeks in the Bronze Age." *XIe Congrès International des sciences historiques*, Stockholm, 1960. Reprinted in *The Language and Background of Homer: Some Recent Studies and Controversies*, edited by Geoffrey S. Kirk. Cambridge, England: W. Heffer & Sons, 1964.
A summary of early Greek history, including the settlement of Greece, sites in the Neolithic and early Helladic periods, the Minoan empire and the myth of the

Minotaur, the relations between Greek states in the late Bronze Age, and the events leading up to the Trojan War.

Durant, Will. "Before Agamemnon." In *The Story of Civilization*. Vol. 2, *The Life of Greece*. New York: Simon & Schuster, 1939.
This introduction to the historical background of the Homeric world includes a summary of the excavations of Troy and Mycenae by Heinrich Schliemann and a description of both archaeological sites and of Mycenaean civilization.

Finley, M. I. "Homer and the Greeks." In *The World of Odysseus*. Rev. ed. New York: Viking Press, 1965.
In this chapter of a book on the Homeric world, the author considers Homer's place in Greek history, the birth of the Greek language and civilization, and the date of the Homeric poems. In particular, the rise of writing in Greece and the development of Greek mythology are discussed.

_____. "Lost: The Trojan War." In *Aspects of Antiquity: Discoveries and Controversies*. 2d ed. New York: Penguin Books, 1977.
An overview of historical aspects of the Trojan War, including ancient sources, a brief outline of the tale, doubts about the tale's historical basis, the archaeological discoveries of Heinrich Schliemann, and Mycenaean and Hittite evidence for the war.

Gladstone, William. Preface to *Mycenae*, by Heinrich Schliemann. 2d ed. New York: Charles Scribner's Sons, 1889. Abridged in *Homer's History: Mycenaean or Dark Age?*, edited by C. G. Thomas. New York: Holt, Rinehart and Winston, 1970.
This essay by the well-known British statesman illustrates the enthusiastic late nineteenth century response to Schliemann's archaeological discoveries at Mycenae. Gladstone offers some general reflections on the artifacts discovered by Schliemann and lists the items of evidence which connect Schliemann's discoveries with the Homeric poems.

Kirk, Geoffrey S. "The Historical Background of the Homeric Poems." In *The Songs of Homer*. Cambridge, England: Cambridge University Press, 1962.
Traces the history of Greece from c. 1600 B.C. to c. 600 B.C. with particular attention to the rise of Mycenae as a political power in Greece, historical evidence for the Trojan War, the decipherment and significance of the Linear B tablets, life in a Mycenaean palace-state, the decline of Mycenaean society, and aspects of Greece in the Dark Age.

_____. "Objective Dating Criteria in Homer." *Museum Helveticum* 17 (1960): 174-190. Reprinted in *The Language and Background of Homer: Some*

Recent Studies and Controversies, edited by Geoffrey S. Kirk. Cambridge, England: W. Heffer & Sons, 1964.

Lists objects mentioned in the Homeric poems which can be securely dated to the Mycenaean, Geometric, or later periods and suggests that archaeology and language require careful evaluation as the main criteria for dating such objects.

Levin, Saul. *The Linear B Decipherment Controversy Re-examined*. Albany: State University of New York Press, 1964.

A detailed critique of Michael Ventris' decipherment in 1952 of the Linear B tablets from Mycenaean Greece. While accepting the general correctness of Ventris' transcription of the script into Greek, Levin argues that very few of the linguistic values applied by Ventris to individual characters have been verified. Argues for the presence of another language on the tablets in addition to Greek and cautions that many interpretations of the Linear B documents and of life in the Mycenaean world remain pure guesswork.

Lorimer, H. L. "The Age of Illiteracy in Greece." In *Homer and the Monuments*. London: Macmillan, 1950.

This essay is a good example of the limited knowledge of writing in Bronze Age Greece before the decipherment of Linear B in 1952 by Michael Ventris. Lorimer refers to the Linear B tablets only as "Minoan script." Her belief that this script was never used to write in Greek was a commonly accepted scholarly position in 1950 but was soon proven incorrect by the work of Ventris. Also discusses Homeric references to writing and the development of the Greek alphabet. Includes two tables illustrating the alphabets used by the earliest Phoenicians and Greeks.

_____. "Arms and Armour." In *Homer and the Monuments*. London: Macmillan, 1950.

The archaeological evidence concerning the armor and arms of Bronze Age Greece is closely compared with Homeric references to various types of armor and arms. In general, the Homeric poems retain a vivid recollection of weaponry from the Bronze Age. Includes forty-eight figures depicting Bronze Age artifacts. There is some untranslated Greek.

_____. "Cremation and Iron." In *Homer and the Monuments*. London: Macmillan, 1950.

Deals with anachronistic references in the Homeric poems to cremation and the use of iron weapons, neither of which were common in Bronze Age Greece. Discusses archaeological evidence for the increased frequency of both cremation and iron weapons in Greece in the period following the Dorian invasion, c. 1000 B.C. Includes a list of the few iron objects found in Greek Bronze Age sites, discusses the dating and provenance of these objects, and examines specific Homeric references to the metal.

_____. "Prehistoric Greece." In *Homer and the Monuments*. London: Macmillan, 1950.

This historical survey of Greece from the neolithic period through the introduction of the Greek alphabet (c. 750 B.C.) is essentially an archaeological study of Greece in the Bronze Age and of the evolution of Helladic culture between 3000 and 1000 B.C. Examines burials, pottery, dwellings, and other material remains from various parts of Greece, especially from Mycenae, in order to piece together a picture of migrations, invasions, cultural breaks, colonization, and empire building in this period in which the Homeric poems originated. Argues that the catalogue of ships in *Iliad* 2 is essentially a relic of the Bronze Age. Although written before the decipherment of Linear B, this essay remains useful.

Murray, Gilbert. "The Historical Context of the *Iliad*." In *The Rise of the Greek Epic*. 3d ed. Oxford, England: Clarendon Press, 1924.

Presents the *Iliad* as a poetic combination of tradition and fiction in which some historical elements survive. While rejecting the theory of a historical chronicle as the basis of the epic, Murray considers the historical possibilities of the catalogue of ships in *Iliad* 2 and of such characters as Helen, Achilles, and Agamemnon.

Nilsson, Martin P. "Datable Elements of Civilization in Homer." In *Homer and Mycenae*. London: Methuen, 1933. Reprint. New York: Cooper Square, 1968.

Shows how the Homeric poems refer to objects from widely different time periods. While Nestor's cup in *Iliad* 11, Odysseus' helmet in *Iliad* 9, and Hector's body shield in *Iliad* 6 are all from the Mycenaean period, Homer's references to the commercial activities of the Phoenicians must be dated to the eighth and seventh centuries B.C., and the headdress of Andromache in *Iliad* 22, the plaited hair of Euphorbos in *Iliad* 17, the cuirass of Agamemnon in *Iliad* 11 and the brooch of Odysseus in *Odyssey* 19 are all datable to the seventh century B.C. Notes differences between Mycenaean and Homeric burial practices.

_____. "The History of the Mycenaean Age." In *Homer and Mycenae*. London: Methuen, 1933. Reprint. New York: Cooper Square, 1968.

Lists several reasons for believing that the Mycenaeans were Greeks, a position later proven by the decipherment of Linear B. Collects evidence for dating the Greek migration c. 2000 B.C. and traces the progress of this migration by studying linguistic and archaeological evidence. Considers how Greek myths, especially the story of the Trojan War, fit into this historical picture.

Page, Denys L. "Background to the Trojan War." In *History and the Homeric "Iliad."* Berkeley: University of California Press, 1959.

Thirteenth century B.C. Hittite documents from Turkey provide some external written evidence for events which were possibly related to the Trojan War, including the existence of an Asian league and the presence of Greeks on the coast of Turkey. Minor differences between the Hittite documents and the *Iliad* are noted.

_____. "Documents from Pylos and Cnossos." In *History and the Homeric "Iliad."* Berkeley: University of California Press, 1959. Abridged in *Homer's History: Mycenaean or Dark Age?*, edited by C. G. Thomas. New York: Holt, Rinehart and Winston, 1970.
Linear B Tablets from the palace archives of Mycenaean Greece are used to provide details about the elaborate political and social structures of Mycenaean civilization, about which the Homeric poems retain only the dimmest memory.

_____. "The History of Troy." In *History and the Homeric "Iliad."* Berkeley: University of California Press, 1959.
A detailed examination of the excavations at Troy reveals important evidence concerning the history of the city and its relationship with the early Greeks. Shows how Troy VIIa was destroyed by fire within fifty years of the traditional date of the fall of the city.

Palmer, Leonard R. "The Case for a Mycenaean Basis." In *Homer's History: Mycenaean or Dark Age?*, edited by C. G. Thomas. New York: Holt, Rinehart and Winston, 1970.
In this excerpt from *Mycenaeans and Minoans*, Palmer argues that the Mycenaean system of land tenure, based upon dedication of large tracts to the gods, is reflected in the Homeric poems. Includes close examination of Mycenaean terminology for economic organization.

Rouse, W. H. D. "The Excavations." In *Homer*. New York: Thomas Nelson and Sons, 1939.
A life of Heinrich Schliemann, the story of his discovery of the site of ancient Troy, and a description of the several strata of cities on the site.

_____. "The Greeks Before Homer." In *Homer*. New York: Thomas Nelson and Sons, 1939.
While this description of the civilization of Bronze Age Greece and its destruction by Greek invaders is somewhat outdated by the decipherment of Linear B, the description of Homeric Greek society, derived mostly from the Homeric epics, is more reliable. Includes information on political organization, agriculture, religion, and poetry in the Homeric world.

_____. "Mycenae and Tiryns." In *Homer*. New York: Thomas Nelson and Sons, 1939.

A brief reference to the excavation of Mycenae by Heinrich Schliemann leads to a description of general features of Mycenaean society, including armor and housing.

_____. "Where the Greeks Came From." In *Homer*. New York: Thomas Nelson and Sons, 1939.
Provides information about the Indo-European origins of the ancestors of the Greeks, including their religious and social customs, tools, agriculture, language, and poetry. Special attention is paid to their domestication of the horse. The beliefs and customs of the Icelandic Norsemen are considered parallel to those of the nomadic ancestors of the Greeks.

Seymour, Thomas D. "The Troad." In *Life in the Homeric Age*. New York: Macmillan, 1908.
A geographic description of the region around the site of Troy and a history of interest in the region from the visit of Alexander the Great in the fourth century B.C. until the nineteenth century A.D. archaeological excavations of Heinrich Schliemann. Description of the excavations at Troy by Schliemann and Wilhelm Dörpfeld.

Trypanis, C. A. "Men and Gods in the Homeric Epics." In *The Homeric Epics*, translated by William Phelps. Warminster, England: Aris & Phillips, 1977.
Includes an overview of government, social structure, domestic life, and the role of the gods and of fate in the Homeric poems as well as studies of the characters of Achilles, Hector, and Odysseus.

Wace, Alan J. B. "The Early Age of Greece." In *A Companion to Homer*, edited by Alan J. B. Wace and Frank H. Stubbings. New York: Macmillan, 1963.
Surveys what is known of Neolithic and Bronze Ages cultures in Greece (4000-1100 B.C.). Archaeological evidence of pottery and architecture is emphasized. Includes figures, illustrations, an appendix on chronology, and a chronological chart of Bronze Age Greece.

_____. "The History of Homeric Archaeology." In *A Companion to Homer*, edited by Alan J. B. Wace and Frank H. Stubbings. New York: Macmillan, 1963.
In this short essay, the author summarizes the contribution archaeology has made to Homeric studies. The excavations of Heinrich Schliemann at Troy and Mycenae are highlighted. Includes a map.

Webster, T. B. L. *From Mycenae to Homer*. 2d ed. New York: W. W. Norton, 1964.
The author combines the evidence of archaeology, especially that of early Greek

pottery, with literary knowledge of Mycenaean civilization derived from the decipherment of Linear B documents in order to describe the development of the Homeric poems in their cultural context. Includes introduction, illustrations, chronological table, map, endnotes, and index.

Whitman, Cedric H. "The Memory of the Achaeans." In *Homer and the Heroic Tradition.* Cambridge, Mass.: Harvard University Press, 1958.
Homer's poems are considered in the context of the Mycenaean world, which they accurately describe. The identity of the Trojans and Achaeans and the early history of Mycenae are discussed.

Homeric Geography

Bérard, Victor. "Homer and the East." In *Did Homer Live?*, translated by Brian Rhys. New York: E. P. Dutton, 1931.
Examines possible ties between the Homeric poems and the cultures of the eastern Mediterranean, especially Egypt and Phoenicia. Argues from archaeological finds, Egyptian history, and passages from the *Odyssey* that the world of the *Odyssey* is the mercenary and nautical world of the Bronze Age Mediterranean. Bérard's dating of the arrival of the Achaeans (Greeks) to the fifteenth and fourteenth centuries B.C. can no longer be accepted; the use of Greek on Linear B tablets has proven that the first Greeks arrived about 2000 B.C.

_____. "The Phoenicians and the *Odyssey.*" In *Did Homer Live?*, translated by Brian Rhys. New York: E. P. Dutton, 1931.
Associates the lands visited by Odysseus in the *Odyssey* with real places in the western Mediterranean, suggests a Semitic origin for many Homeric place names, and argues that the ultimate source for these adventures was a Phoenician sailors' manual.

Blegen, Carl W., Alan J. B. Wace, and Frank H. Stubbings. "The Principal Homeric Sites." In *A Companion to Homer*, edited by Alan J. B. Wace and Frank H. Stubbings. New York: Macmillan, 1963.
Summarizes what is known from archaeological evidence about four major sites in Homeric Greece. Blegen describes the various levels of Troy discovered by Heinrich Schliemann and other archaeologists and discusses the date of the Trojan War. Wace gives a history of Mycenae and its archaeological monuments and discusses its heroic tradition. Stubbings outlines the topography of both modern Ithaki and Levcas and argues that Ithaki is the site of Odysseus' home. Blegen, the excavator of ancient Pylus, gives a brief description of the site. Includes maps, figures, and photographs.

Bradford, Ernle. "Ithaca and Levkas." In *Ulysses Found*. New York: Harcourt, Brace & World, 1963.

This appendix to an analysis of the geographic and navigational accuracy of the *Odyssey* deals with the so-called "Ithaca problem." Includes summaries of the theory of Wilhelm Dörpfeld that the island of Levkas best fits the description of the Homeric Ithaca and of the difficulties involved in identifying the modern Greek island of Ithaki with the Homeric Ithaca. Chronology of the voyage in an appendix.

_____. *Ulysses Found*. New York: Harcourt, Brace & World, 1963.

A detailed attempt by a sailor to locate the places in the Mediterranean associated with Odysseus' adventures in the *Odyssey*. Discussion of Odysseus' departure from Troy includes a geographic description of Tenedos, the hero's place of embarkation, information about the type of ship Odysseus sailed, and reference to his first adventure, the pirate raid on the Cicones from *Odyssey* 9. Odysseus then travels to the Land of the Lotus-Eaters, here identified with the island of Jerba, off the coast of modern Libya. From there, Odysseus travels to the Island of the Cyclopes, identified with Sicily. The home of Aeolus, the wind god, is considered to be the Italian island of Ustica. Argues that Bonifacio on the French island of Corsica, not Leontini in eastern Sicily or Formiae in western Italy, is the home of the Laestrygonians, because only Corsica has a harbor the right distance from Ustica. Suggests that Odysseus' journey from the island of Aeolus to his home in Ithaca and back to Aeolus' island was an unrealistic poetic invention. Accepts as accurate the traditional identification of Cape Circeo, on the western coast of Italy, as the site of Circe's home, and associates Circe with the Italian goddess Feronia.

_____. "Voyage in Search of Fabled Lands." In *Greece and Rome: Builders of Our World*, edited by Merle Severy. Washington, D.C.: National Geographic Society, 1968.

A profusely illustrated summary of the author's travels described in *Ulysses Found*. The author sails in the Mediterranean along the hypothetical route of Odysseus in the *Odyssey* and paraphrases the story of Odysseus' voyage. Includes two maps.

Butler, Samuel. "That Ithaca and Scheria Are Both of Them Drawn from Trapani and Its Immediate Neighborhood." In *The Authoress of the "Odyssey,"* by Samuel Butler. 2d ed. London: Jonathan Cape, 1922. Reprint. Chicago: University of Chicago Press, 1967.

Introduces the author's argument that Homer's descriptions of both Ithaca and Scheria are based upon the ancient town of Drepanum (modern Trapani) in Sicily and that the geography of the entire poem reflects the background of the Sicilian female who wrote the poem. Includes a detailed description of features of Trapani which can be linked with events in the *Odyssey*.

Carpenter, Rhys. "The Setting of the *Odyssey*." In *Folktale, Fiction, and Saga in the Homeric Epics*. Berkeley: University of California Press, 1946.
An examination of geographical references in the epic concludes that the setting of Odysseus' adventures is the western, not the eastern, Mediterranean and that the *Odyssey* reflects Greek penetration into the West in the late seventh century B.C.

_____. "Trouble over Troy." In *Folktale, Fiction, and Saga in the Homeric Epics*. Berkeley: University of California Press, 1946.
Notes that the archaeological evidence and the epic tradition offer contradictory locations for ancient Troy and concludes that the Hellespont could not have been the location for the war in the epic tradition until the Greeks colonized Asia Minor. Also speculates that the Etruscans were the historical models for the Trojans.

Gordon, Cyrus H. "Further Observations on Homer." In *Before the Bible*. New York: Harper & Row, 1962. Reprinted in abridged form as "The Epics Drawn from a Common Eastern Mediterranean Tradition," in *Homer's History: Mycenaean or Dark Age?*, edited by C. G. Thomas. New York: Holt, Rinehart and Winston, 1970.
Discusses Mycenaean civilization in the larger context of eastern Mediterranean cultures, including those of the Egyptians, Mesopotamians, and Phoenicians. Illustrates antecedents for both the *Iliad* and the *Odyssey* in various literatures of the Near East, including the *Epic of Gilgamesh*, and discusses parallels between the Homeric epics and the Bible. Finds Near Eastern concepts about religion and government, including the idea of covenant, in the Homeric poems.

Hammond, N. G. L. "The Physical Geography of Greece and the Aegean." In *A Companion to Homer*, edited by Alan J. B. Wace and Frank H. Stubbings. New York: Macmillan, 1963.
A survey of the general geographic characteristics of various regions of Greece, including Attica, the Peloponnesus, Thrace, and the islands. Geological, climatic, and agricultural features are discussed. Includes two photographs.

Keller, Albert G. "Ethnic Environment." In *Homeric Society: A Sociological Study of the "Iliad" and "Odyssey."* New York: Longmans, Green, 1913.
Considers Homeric knowledge of and attitudes toward non-Greek societies, such as the historical Scythians, Ethiopians, and Egyptians, and the mythical Cyclopes. In particular, an overview of Phoenician culture and its influence in the Mediterranean world in the time of Homer is followed by a brief survey of references to the Phoenicians in the *Odyssey*.

Leaf, Walter. *Troy: A Study in Homeric Geography*. London: Macmillan, 1912.
Proves the accuracy of Homeric geography by comparing the text of Homer with
the natural features of the area around Troy and the Troad in Turkey. In addition
to summarizing the archaeological work of Heinrich Schliemann and Wilhelm
Dörpfeld at Troy, Leaf includes observations from his own travels in the Troad
and concludes that Homer's catalogue of Trojans in the *Iliad* is based upon an
authentic geographic document. With maps, plans, and illustrations.

Lorimer, H. L. "The Foreign Relations of Greece in the Late Bronze and the Early
Iron Age." In *Homer and the Monuments*. London: Macmillan, 1950.
Homeric references to various peoples of the Near East, especially the Phoeni-
cians and Egyptians, are compared with archaeological evidence for commercial
and other contacts between these regions and Greece between c. 1200 and c. 700
B.C. Concludes that Homer frequently blends together contemporary and Bronze
Age features.

Mireaux, Émile. "The Background and Setting." In *Daily Life in the Time of
Homer*, translated by Iris Sells. New York: Macmillan, 1960.
Describes the size and shape which Greeks in the time of Homer gave to the
world. Locates the foreign lands with which they were familiar. Contrasts the
modern concept of a universe governed by fixed natural laws with the Greek
view of the world as a smaller, more unpredictable living organism. Includes a
discussion of the place of the Greek gods in this universe.

Page, Denys L. "Achaeans in Hittite Documents." In *History and the Homeric
"Iliad."* Berkeley: University of California Press, 1959.
Examines written evidence from the fourteenth to thirteenth century B.C. Hittite
Empire in Turkey to show that Achaeans (Greeks) and Hittites were in contact
for about 150 years preceding the Trojan War.

_____. "The Homeric Description of Greece." In *History and the Homeric
"Iliad."* Berkeley: University of California Press, 1959.
Uses linguistic evidence, including noun-epithet combinations, to show how the
catalogues in *Iliad* 2 accurately describe the political geography of Mycenaean
Greece and of Troy.

Rouse, W. H. D. "Ithaca." In *Homer*. New York: Thomas Nelson and Sons, 1939.
Describes the modern Greek island of Ithaki and argues that it was probably the
island known as Ithaca by the poet of the *Odyssey* but discounts the importance
of geographic accuracy in the *Odyssey*.

_____. "The Places of the Story: The Troad." In *Homer*. New York:
Thomas Nelson and Sons, 1939.

A description of the Troad, the region in modern Turkey where the Homeric Troy was located. Specific sites are associated with Homeric places and events. A citadel on the island of Astypalaea provides some idea of what the Troy of Homer looked like.

Seymour, Thomas D. "Homeric Cosmography and Geography." In *Life in the Homeric Age*. New York: Macmillan, 1908.
In addition to a description of the geography of the Homeric world, there is a discussion of Homeric concepts concerning the sun, the year, constellations, and atmospheric phenomena. Examines the geographic accuracy of the catalogue of ships in *Iliad* 2 and questions the poet's familiarity with more than the names of these places. Considers the actual locations of such Homeric sites as Pylus and Ithaca. Includes several maps and illustrations.

Simpson, Richard Hope. "Mycenaean Greece and Homeric Reflections." In *Approaches to Homer*, edited by Carl A. Rubino and Cynthia A. Shelmerdine. Austin: University of Texas Press, 1983.
The catalogue of ships in *Iliad* 2 is seen to be an accurate reflection of the geography of Mycenaean Greece. Homer was not a historian but an oral poet. He relied not on an eyewitness account but on oral tradition. There are some untranslated Greek quotations.

Thomas, Helen, and Frank H. Stubbings. "Lands and Peoples in Homer." In *A Companion to Homer*, edited by Alan J. B. Wace and Frank H. Stubbings. New York: Macmillan, 1963.
Evidence from the Homeric poems is used to describe the political and social world of Homer. There are separate sections on the Greeks and their allies, the Trojans and their allies, and the rest of the world. There are some untranslated Greek quotations. Includes several maps.

Homeric Society

Atchity, Kenneth, and E. J. W. Barber. "Greek Princes and Aegean Princesses: The Role of Women in the Homeric Poems." In *Critical Essays on Homer*, edited by Kenneth Atchity, Ron Hogart, and Doug Price. Boston: G. K. Hall, 1987.
In this essay, the authors combine ethnographic studies of matriarchal and patriarchal systems with a close examination of the weaving metaphor in the Homeric epics in order to contrast the rights of women in the Homeric world with those of women in Classical Athens.

Beattie, A. J. "Aegean Languages of the Heroic Age." In *A Companion to Homer*, edited by Alan J. B. Wace and Frank H. Stubbings. New York: Macmillan, 1963.

This essay moves in reverse chronological order from the Aegean languages of the Classical Age, to the Dark Age, to the Aegean languages of the Heroic Age, and to the language of the Achaeans. Also includes sections on borrowed elements in Greek and the establishment of the Greek language. There are some untranslated Greek words.

Bowra, C. M. "The Creative Outlook." In *Homer*. New York: Charles Scribner's Sons, 1972.
Comparison of Homeric society to that of the Mycenaean world shows that Homer's description of the Heroic Age results as much from the poetic imagination as from historical reality. Composed for an aristocratic audience, the Homeric poems reveal an appreciation for the heroic ideal and for the everyday joys and sorrows of life.

_____. "The Meaning of a Heroic Age." In *The Language and Background of Homer: Some Recent Studies and Controversies*, edited by Geoffrey S. Kirk. Cambridge, England: W. Heffer & Sons, 1964.
Originally published in 1957 as the Earl Grey Memorial Lecture at the University of Newcastle in England, this essay compares the Homeric poems to oral epics from several cultures in order to describe the ideals of a heroic society. Bowra considers some of the situations under which a heroic age develops, under which groups of individuals emerge into power and eminence, especially in war.

Butler, Samuel. "The House of Odysseus." In *The "Odyssey" Rendered into English Prose*. London: Jonathan Cape, 1922. Reprint. New York: E. P. Dutton, 1925. In this appendix, reprinted from his *The Authoress of the "Odyssey,"* Butler describes significant architectural features of Odysseus' palace on Ithaca. Includes a drawn plan of the building.

Calhoun, George M., and T. B. L. Webster. "Polity and Society." In *A Companion to Homer*, edited by Alan J. B. Wace and Frank H. Stubbings. New York: Macmillan, 1963.
This sweeping overview of Homeric society is divided into two parts. Calhoun summarizes the political and social structures suggested in the Homeric poems with sections on government, law, family, and religion. Webster qualifies this picture with evidence from Linear B tablets. There are some untranslated Greek words.

Finley, M. I. "The Case Against a Mycenaean Basis." In *Homer's History: Mycenaean or Dark Age?*, edited by C. G. Thomas. New York: Holt, Rinehart and Winston, 1970.
In this excerpt from the scholarly article entitled "Homer and Mycenae: Property and Tenure," the author finds no references in the Homeric epics to basic

features of Mycenaean economic organization, such as communal land holding
and conditional tenures, and concludes that the Homeric world is totally post-
Mycenaean. The Homeric poems reflect features of Greek society after the fall
of Mycenaean civilization and are not reliable sources for life in the Mycenaean
world.

_____. "Homer and Mycenae: Property and Tenure." In *The Language and
Background of Homer: Some Recent Studies and Controversies*, edited by Geoffrey S. Kirk. Cambridge, England: W. Heffer & Sons, 1964.
Argues that the Mycenaean culture revealed in the Linear B tablets is different
in many ways from that described in the Homeric poems and that the Homeric
world is completely post-Mycenaean.

_____. "Household, Kin, and Community." In *The World of Odysseus*.
Rev. ed. New York: Viking Press, 1965.
The importance of class status to the standing of a Homeric hero is considered.
Questions of kinship and kingship are discussed in terms of such topics as
assemblies in the *Iliad*, Penelope's suitors, and the Greek custom of guest-
friendship.

_____. "Wealth and Labor." In *The World of Odysseus*. Rev. ed. New
York: Viking Press, 1965. Reprinted in *The "Odyssey" of Homer*, edited by
Albert Cook. New York: W. W. Norton, 1967.
This essay provides an overview of the organization of Homeric society. Topics
discussed include the local economy, trade, the organization of the household,
and the relationships between freemen and slaves, nobles and the common
people.

Keller, Albert G. "Government, Classes, Justice, Etc." In *Homeric Society: A
Sociological Study of the "Iliad" and "Odyssey."* New York: Longmans, Green,
1913.
Views the concept of kingship, relationships between the classes, and the types
and rights of the people in assembly, especially in passages from the *Iliad*.
Discusses questions of Homeric law, homicide, war customs, and, especially,
guest-friendship.

_____. "Industrial Organisation." In *Homeric Society: A Sociological Study
of the "Iliad" and "Odyssey."* New York: Longmans, Green, 1913.
Relies primarily on the Homeric poems themselves as evidence for such topics
as hunting, fishing, agriculture, food preparation, manufacturing, trade, and the
status of craftsmen in the Homeric world. Manufacturing includes woodworking
and metalworking, weaponry and armor, shipbuilding, home construction,
furniture, and textiles.

_____. "Marriage and the Family." In *Homeric Society: A Sociological Study of the "Iliad" and "Odyssey."* New York: Longmans, Green, 1913.
Examines family life as it is depicted in the Homeric poems and considers attitudes toward the status of women and children, illegitimacy, kinship, succession, concubinage, adultery, divorce, and remarriage in the Homeric world. Describes such marriage practices as the selection of spouses, the dowry, and the marriage ceremony.

_____. "Property." In *Homeric Society: A Sociological Study of the "Iliad" and "Odyssey."* New York: Longmans, Green, 1913.
A short description of the concept of private property as descried in the Homeric poems. Considers landholding, slavery, and customs of inheritance.

Lorimer, H. L. "Dress." In *Homer and the Monuments*. London: Macmillan, 1950.
Compares the archaeological evidence for dressing habits by both men and women in Bronze Age Greece with Homeric references to clothing. Includes several illustrations of clothing on Bronze Age figures. There is some untranslated Greek.

_____. "The Homeric House." In *Homer and the Monuments*. London: Macmillan, 1950.
Archaeological evidence for domestic and public architecture in Bronze Age Greece is compared with references in the Homeric poems. Similarities between the plan of Tiryns and the house of Odysseus are noted. Various parts of the Homeric house are explained. Homeric references to religious temples are shown to be late interpolations and do not reflect the religious customs of Bronze Age Greece. Includes several plans.

Mireaux, Émile. "Blood Vengeance and the Family." In *Daily Life in the Time of Homer*, translated by Iris Sells. New York: Macmillan, 1960.
Considers the private obligations of vengeance within the family and between families in the Homeric world. Derives evidence for private methods of compromise and settlement from scenes in the *Iliad*, especially Achilles' reconciliation with Agamemnon. Describes methods of prosecuting offenses such as adultery, rape, and theft and public methods of settlement, including judicial duels, the process of ordeal, and acts of suicide.

_____. "Homer's Women." In *Daily Life in the Time of Homer*, translated by Iris Sells. New York: Macmillan, 1960.
Studies the portrayal of women and their lives in the poetry of Homer and Hesiod. Describes the conduct of women in the home, their family life, marriages, betrothals, childbirth customs, and women's participation in religion and mystery cults.

_____. "The Life of a Nobleman." In *Daily Life in the Time of Homer*, translated by Iris Sells. New York: Macmillan, 1960.
A detailed description of the life, duties, and prerogatives of the lord of a Homeric manor. Includes information about his place in the clan, members of his entourage, body care, clothing, ornaments, wealth, property, hunting, travel, hospitality, banquets, and festivities.

_____. "The Lower Classes and the Cultivation of the Land." In *Daily Life in the Time of Homer*, translated by Iris Sells. New York: Macmillan, 1960.
Examines the working and living conditions of free laborers, slaves, servants, shepherds, fishermen, and poor lot holders. Describes life in the fields at various points in the year.

_____. "The Manor House." In *Daily Life in the Time of Homer*, translated by Iris Sells. New York: Macmillan, 1960.
Uses references to homes in the Homeric poems. Describes the general features of the Homeric manor, especially the plan and use of the *megaron*, as well as information on home decoration, furnishings, doors, and fastenings.

_____. "Peasants and Soldiers." In *Daily Life in the Time of Homer*, translated by Iris Sells. New York: Macmillan, 1960.
In addition to information on the training and life of a soldier, this chapter examines the life of peasants in regard to their *kleros*, or lot of land, its right of possession, conservation, and exploitation.

_____. "Public Workers and Craftsmen." In *Daily Life in the Time of Homer*, translated by Iris Sells. New York: Macmillan, 1960.
Considers the special skills, duties, rights, rank, and status of Homeric *demiourgoi*, public manual workers such as blacksmiths, carpenters, metalworkers, and potters. Discusses the connection between these crafts and the rise of civic and urban life.

_____. "Wanderers and Expatriates." In *Daily Life in the Time of Homer*, translated by Iris Sells. New York: Macmillan, 1960.
Evidence from the Homeric poems is used to describe the life of seafarers, beggars, exiles, and mercenaries. Includes information on commerce and coinage.

Nilsson, Martin P. "State Organization in Homer and in the Mycenaean Age." In *Homer and Mycenae*. London: Methuen, 1933. Reprint. New York: Cooper Square, 1968.
Suggests that the form of kingship held by Agamemnon in the *Iliad* is essentially Mycenaean. Compares Homeric kings with those in the Teutonic epic tradition. Describes the features of government in the Homeric poems, including the

powers of kings, the role of the army assembly and the duties of vassals and retainers. Suggests that the Homeric poems provide some evidence for a feudal political organization in the Mycenaean period and for its replacement by more fragmented aristocratic rule in post-Mycenaean times.

Palmer, L. R. "The Language of Homer." In *A Companion to Homer*, edited by Alan J. B. Wace and Frank H. Stubbings. New York: Macmillan, 1963.
This supplement to a grammar of Attic Greek shows the special features of the Homeric morphology and syntax. The general reader may benefit from the discussion of Greek dialects, tradition and corruption of the Homeric text, and the constitution of the Homeric dialect. Greek examples are not translated. Includes a language map of the Aegean and a synopsis of the chapter.

Perry, Walter Copland. "Dress of Women in Homer." In *The Women of Homer*. London: William Heinemann, 1898.
A detailed consideration of the types of apparel worn by women and of the Homeric vocabulary for this clothing in the *Iliad* and the *Odyssey*.

_____. "Excursus." In *The Women of Homer*. London: William Heinemann, 1898.
Depicts a deterioration in the character and status of women from the favorable portrait found in the Homeric poems to a degraded one in Classical Greece and especially in ancient tragedy and comedy. Some untranslated foreign language quotations.

_____. "Marriage." In *The Women of Homer*. London: William Heinemann, 1898.
Examines marriage customs, the relationship between a husband and wife, and the status of married women in the Homeric epics.

_____. "Position of Women in the *Iliad* and the *Odyssey*." In *The Women of Homer*. London: William Heinemann, 1898.
Considers the life of children, the relationship of parents and children, and the life of women in the Homeric epics. The status of women in the Homeric epics is seen to be superior to that of women in Classical Greece. There is an appendix of ancient citations in the original languages.

Seymour, Thomas D. "Agriculture, Plants, and Trees." In *Life in the Homeric Age*. New York: Macmillan, 1908.
A summary of agricultural practices in the Homeric poems. Describes plowing and harvesting techniques. Includes botanical lists of cultivated types of flowers and trees and food and industrial crops.

_____. "Animals, Fishes, Birds, and Insects." In *Life in the Homeric Age*. New York: Macmillan, 1908.
A Homeric bestiary describing the living creatures, both real and mythic, wild and domesticated, which are mentioned in the Homeric poems. Special attention to the types, care, and use of horses, dogs, cattle, and other domesticated animals. Lists Homeric vocabulary and knowledge of various wild creatures of sea, land, and air.

_____. "Dress and Decoration." In *Life in the Homeric Age*. New York: Macmillan, 1908.
Explains how references to clothing in the Homeric poems allude not to the Mycenaean period but to the customs of the ninth century B.C. Describes various forms of dress, their manufacture, and the wearing occasions for the dress of both Homeric men and women. Includes sections on jewelry and styles of hairdressing. Illustrations and figures.

_____. "Homeric Arms." In *Life in the Homeric Age*. New York: Macmillan, 1908.
Discusses changes in Greek arms and armor between the twelfth and seventh centuries B.C. Evidence from archaeology and the Homeric poems is combined to describe the form and purpose of such defensive armor as shields, cuirasses, greaves, and helmets, and such offensive weapons as swords, spears, knives, axes, and bows. Also considers the form and use of chariots in the Homeric poems.

_____. "Homeric Food." In *Life in the Homeric Age*. New York: Macmillan, 1908.
Describes the eating habits of Homeric Greeks, including the number of meals, banquet customs, table etiquette, types of food, and food preparation. Includes information on grape cultivation and wine drinking.

_____. "Homeric Property." In *Life in the Homeric Age*. New York: Macmillan, 1908.
This illustrated chapter describes forms of landownership, size of fields, techniques of farming, and types and care of domesticated animals on a Greek farm in the Homeric period.

_____. "The Homeric State." In *Life in the Homeric Age*. New York: Macmillan, 1908.
Examines the nature of Homeric kingship, various words for ruler, types of advisory councils and public assemblies, the duties of a herald, international relations, and indications of community and civic life in the Homeric poems.

_____. "Homeric War." In *Life in the Homeric Age*. New York: Macmillan, 1908.
Summarizes various aspects of warfare in the *Iliad*, including types of combat, size of the forces, military organization, tactics, arrangement of camps, fortifications, casualties, and field medicine. Discusses the various causes for war mentioned in both Homeric poems.

_____. "House and Furniture." In *Life in the Homeric Age*. New York: Macmillan, 1908.
Combines evidence from archaeology and the Homeric poems to describe the features of the Homeric house, including architectural form, materials of composition and use of rooms. Description of various types of Homeric furniture, including chairs, tables, and bed. Includes illustrations and a plan of the *megaron* at Tiryns.

_____. "Sea Life and Ships." In *Life in the Homeric Age*. New York: Macmillan, 1908.
Describes the methods of sea travel, ship construction, and the life of sailors in the Homeric poems. Includes the Homeric vocabulary for various parts of a ship and a description of each part.

_____. "Slavery and Servitude." In *Life in the Homeric Age*. New York: Macmillan, 1908.
Contrasts modern forms of slavery with Homeric practices. Discusses the status and responsibilities of both male and female slaves within the Greek family unit.

_____. "Trade and the Crafts." In *Life in the Homeric Age*. New York: Macmillan, 1908.
Emphasizes the economic independence of the Greek household in the Homeric period and examines the Homeric poems for evidence concerning trading practices and metalworking. Includes a summary of the various types of metals mentioned by Homer. Illustrated.

_____. "Women and the Family, Education and Recreation." In *Life in the Homeric Age*. New York: Macmillan, 1908.
Describes eight types of women, distinguished according to age and social status, in the Homeric poems. Considers characters of Helen, Andromache, Hecuba, Penelope, Arete, Nausicaa, Clytemnestra, and Eurycleia. Discusses the occupations and social and property rights of Homeric women, customs concerning marriage and divorce, and children and their education.

Stubbings, Frank H. "Arms and Armour." In *A Companion to Homer*, edited by Alan J. B. Wace and Frank H. Stubbings. New York: Macmillan, 1963.

Comparison of Homeric descriptions with archaeological evidence from the Mycenaean period shows that the epic tradition has preserved some references to military equipment which predates the Trojan War. Individual parts of armor are discussed separately. Contains illustrations of Mycenaean armor in several plates and figures. There are some untranslated Greek words.

_____. "Communications and Trade." In *A Companion to Homer*, edited by Alan J. B. Wace and Frank H. Stubbings. New York: Macmillan, 1963.
A close examination of the Homeric chariot is followed by some discussion of Homeric references to sea travel and trade. There are some untranslated Greek words. Includes three figures.

_____. "Crafts and Industries." In *A Companion to Homer*, edited by Alan J. B. Wace and Frank H. Stubbings. New York: Macmillan, 1963.
Homeric references to such crafts as spinning, weaving, shipbuilding, woodworking, and metalworking are examined and are considered generally to fit any age in the Greek world. Illustrations of these crafts are provided in three plates and three figures; there are some untranslated Greek words.

_____. "Food and Agriculture." In *A Companion to Homer*, edited by Alan J. B. Wace and Frank H. Stubbings. New York: Macmillan, 1963.
An examination of Homeric references to food production and consumption concludes that the poems create an accurate picture of these practices in early Greece. Mycenaean lamps are depicted in figures, and there are two photographs with agricultural scenes. Contains some untranslated Greek words.

Thomas, C. G. "Homer's Kings a Product of Dark Age Greece." In *Homer's History: Mycenaean or Dark Age?*, edited by C. G. Thomas. New York: Holt, Rinehart and Winston, 1970.
In this excerpt from a scholarly article entitled "The Roots of Homeric Kingship," the author finds no sign in the Homeric poems of the centralized and complex socioeconomic system documented for the Mycenaean world by the Linear B tablets. The model for Homeric kings is not to be found in Dorian leaders but in the semi-independent and localized rulers of the Greek Dark Age.

Wace, Alan J. B. "Houses and Palaces." In *A Companion to Homer*, edited by Alan J. B. Wace and Frank H. Stubbings. New York: Macmillan, 1963.
Evidence from archaeology and from the Homeric poems is combined to discuss the major features of a Greek residence, including the *megaron*. There are some untranslated Greek words. Contains several figures.

Wace, H. P., and Alan J. B. Wace. "Dress." In *A Companion to Homer*, edited by Alan J. B. Wace and Frank H. Stubbings. New York: Macmillan, 1963.

By comparing references to dress in the Homeric poems with evidence from Mycenaean frescoes, the authors conclude that Homeric and Mycenaean fashions are not the same and that Homeric dress is unrepresented in Greek art. There are some untranslated Greek words. Includes four plates and three figures illustrating clothing from the period.

Homer's Gods, Myth, Religion, Morality, and Concept of Fate

Adkins, A. W. H. "Homer: Free Will and Compulsion." In *Merit and Responsibility: A Study in Greek Values*. Oxford, England: Clarendon Press, 1960.
Considers the question of compulsion of human beings by the gods, by fate, and by other human beings in the Homeric poems. Occasional interference in human affairs by the Homeric gods and a belief in fate do not diminish Homeric emphasis upon individual responsibility.

_____. "Homer: Mistake and Moral Error." In *Merit and Responsibility: A Study in Greek Values*. Oxford, England: Clarendon Press, 1960.
Examines the Homeric terms used to condemn human mistakes and moral errors and to praise good actions, including the competitive standard of *arete*, or "excellence," and the conflicting claims of an *agathos*, or "good man," and his society.

_____. "'Justice': Homer to the Fifth Century." In *Merit and Responsibility: A Study in Greek Values*. Oxford, England: Clarendon Press, 1960.
Traces the changing concept of justice in the Greek world from Homer through the works of Hesiod and later Greek poets such as Solon and Theognis. In the Homeric poems, pursuit of *arete*, or "excellence," is more important than a concept of justice. Only Greek poets after Homer develop the idea of moral responsibility.

Austin, Norman. Introduction to *Archery at the Dark of the Moon: Poetic Problems in Homer's "Odyssey."* Berkeley: University of California Press, 1975.
Begins with a summary of the long-standing debate concerning interpretation of the Homeric poems as either unsophisticated and primitive or as more complex analyses of the human experience. Opts for the more complex view and outlines in the rest of the essay the way in which this approach is followed in the rest of the book.

_____. "Unity in Multiplicity: Homeric Modes of Thought." *Arion*, n.s. 1/2 (1973/1974): 219-274. Reprinted in *Archery at the Dark of the Moon: Poetic Problems in Homer's "Odyssey."* Berkeley: University of California Press, 1975.
In this study, the author shows that Homeric thought is based upon a symbolism

which requires interpretation. Homeric concepts of the mind, geography, time, and omens are discussed.

Bespaloff, Rachel. "The Comedy of the Gods." In *On the "Iliad,"* translated by Mary McCarthy. New York: Pantheon Books, 1947.
In this essay, the author examines the role of the gods in the *Iliad*. Homer's comic, often irreverent, portrayal of the Greek gods is contrasted with his emphasis on positive relationships between individual gods and humans. Zeus' distance from the force of the *Iliad* is also discussed.

Camps, W. A. "The Supernatural." In *An Introduction to Homer*. New York: Oxford University Press, 1980.
A brief discussion of the role of the Homeric gods in human affairs.

Clay, Jenny Strauss. "Double Theodicy of the *Odyssey.*" In *The Wrath of Athena: Gods and Men in the "Odyssey."* Princeton, N.J.: Princeton University Press, 1983.
The search for reasons why Athena ceases to be angry at Odysseus in the *Odyssey* and begins to help him leads to a study of general statements in the *Odyssey* about the involvement of the gods in human affairs. Two contrasting views about the gods are expressed in the poem: that the gods are the source of divine justice and that the gods distribute good and evil indiscriminately to humans. Suggests that the Homeric gods and mortals share a mutual need for one another and that Athena helps Odysseus not for his own sake but for the sake of the injustices performed by the suitors on Ithaca.

_____. "Gods and Men." In *The Wrath of Athena: Gods and Men in the "Odyssey."* Princeton, N.J.: Princeton University Press, 1983.
Examines the nature of the gods in the Homeric poems, including aspects of their immortality, their superhuman knowledge, their connection with fate, and their ability to transform themselves and the natural world. Considers the differences between the mortals and the Homeric gods, features of interaction between them, including divine epiphanies, and the causes of divine favor and hostility. Suggests that the gods function in human affairs the way spectators act at the funeral games in *Iliad* 22.

Dodds, E. R. "Agamemnon's Apology." In *The Greeks and the Irrational*. Berkeley: University of California Press, 1951. With endnotes and some untranslated Greek. Abridged in *Homer*, edited by Harold Bloom. New York: Chelsea House, 1986. Also reprinted, with original endnotes deleted and Greek transliterated, in *Homer's "The Iliad,"* edited by Harold Bloom. New York: Chelsea House, 1987.
This initial chapter of an influential study of Greek attitudes toward the irrational

examines the role of *ate*, or divine folly in human action, and especially in Agamemnon's behavior toward Achilles in the *Iliad*. The motivations for human behavior in Homer are ascribed to a sense of shame rather than of guilt, to public esteem rather than to conscience.

Edwards, Mark W. "Gods, Fate, and Mortality." In *Homer: Poet of the "Iliad."* Baltimore: The Johns Hopkins University Press, 1987.
In this introduction to the role of the gods in the Homeric epics, Edwards lists the ways in which the gods illustrate the religion of the characters and the ways in which the gods are used by Homer as a compositional tool. The relationship between mortals and immortals is also discussed.

_____. "Honor, Proper Behavior, and Warfare." In *Homer: Poet of the "Iliad."* Baltimore: The Johns Hopkins University Press, 1987.
A brief consideration of such Homeric values as competitiveness and honor. The Homeric code of conduct is discussed in terms of duty to oneself and the community, especially in the context of warfare.

_____. "Personification and Psychology." In *Homer: Poet of the "Iliad."* Baltimore: The Johns Hopkins University Press, 1987.
A short study on the relationship between Homeric psychology and personifications of such abstract concepts as sleep and folly.

Fairbanks, Arthur. "The Gods in Homer." In *The Mythology of Greece and Rome.* New York: D. Appleton, 1907.
A systematic survey of the role of the gods in the Homeric epics. In addition to sections on the individual gods, there are studies of the Homeric view of the afterlife, of the link between mythology and epic, and of the gods' anthropomorphism, differences with humans, and relationship with the world and with one another. Includes illustrations, map, genealogical tables, and index.

Finley, M. I. "Morals and Values." In *The World of Odysseus.* Rev. ed. New York: Viking Press, 1965.
Considers the legal rights of nobles and commoners and the Homeric hero's code of morals and values, including honor and friendship. The Homeric concept of love and Homer's attitude toward women are also discussed. The anthropomorphism of the Homeric gods is seen as part of a religious revolution from old nature gods to humanized deities.

Goodson, Clement. "Homer and Ouranos." In *The Odyssey*, by Homer, edited by Albert Cook. New York: W. W. Norton, 1974.
A study in the Homeric concept of *ouranos* ("sky") as an architectural vault, a solid ceiling of the sky, and as a space of the gods.

Graves, Robert. *The Greek Myths*. 2 vols. Baltimore: Penguin Books, 1960.
   While this handbook on Greek mythology provides useful summaries of many
   Homeric myths and places them in the context of other versions of the story,
   Graves's interpretations of the myths are often controversial. Footnotes must be
   read carefully in order to recognize Homeric sources. Note, in particular, Graves'
   discussions of the following: Aphrodite, with a summary of her love affair with
   Ares in *Odyssey* 8; references to Apollo's relationships with the Muses and with
   the singer Thamyris in the *Iliad*; Homer's version of Heracles' fate after death
   in *Odyssey* 11; Athena's role as arbitrator and judge in Homer; Homer's tale in
   Odyssey 5 about Demeter's love affair with Iasion; Helius, the sun god, mentioned in *Odyssey* 12; the story in the *Iliad* about Hephaestus' fall from Mount
   Olympus, his crippling, and his skills as a blacksmith; the Homeric version of
   the origin of the world, mentioned in *Iliad* 14; Homeric references to Hades, the
   god of the underworld, and to the geography of his realm; myths connected with
   the Greek sea god Poseidon in both Homeric epics; and the relationship between
   the Greek deities Zeus and Hera, including references to such passages as the
   seduction of Zeus by Hera in *Iliad* 14.

Guthrie, W. K. C. "Gods and Men in Homer." In *The Greeks and Their Gods*.
   Boston: Beacon Press, 1950. Reprinted in *Essays on the "Odyssey": Selected
   Modern Criticism*, edited by Charles H. Taylor, Jr. Bloomington: Indiana
   University Press, 1969.
   Explains the Homeric view of the gods by way of an analogy with human
   society. The relationship between man and god in Homer is similar to that
   between man and king. The Homeric concept of justice is also discussed.

Havelock, Eric A. "From Homer to Plato: The Contours of the Problem." In *The
   Greek Concept of Justice: From Its Shadow in Homer to Its Substance in Plato*.
   Cambridge, Mass.: Harvard University Press, 1978.
   Emphasizes the didactic function of the Homeric poems in an oral society. The
   poems are considered a form of collective memory containing information about
   a broad range of cultural and ethical concerns of Greeks in the ninth through
   seventh centuries B.C.

_____. "The Justice of the *Iliad*." In *The Greek Concept of Justice: From
   Its Shadow in Homer to Its Substance in Plato*. Cambridge, Mass.: Harvard
   University Press, 1978.
   An examination of the ideas of individual feud, public assembly, and just resolu-
   tion of conflict in the plot of the *Iliad* suggests that in the poem "justice" is
   portrayed not as a set of laws but as an oral process of negotiation.

_____. "The Justice of the *Odyssey*." In *The Greek Concept of Justice: From Its Shadow in Homer to Its Substance in Plato*. Cambridge, Mass.: Harvard University Press, 1978.
Formulaic statements in the *Odyssey* about just and unjust actions and individuals and about the concept of *hybris*, or "excessive pride," are grouped into eight types which suggest a polarity between a just man and a violent man. The moral code of the *Odyssey* affirms compromise over confrontation.

_____. "Legalities in the *Odyssey*." In *The Greek Concept of Justice: From Its Shadow in Homer to Its Substance in Plato*. Cambridge, Mass.: Harvard University Press, 1978.
A study of assembly scenes in the *Odyssey* shows a dominance of personal feud and private vengeance over a public and negotiated form of justice. The means used to resolve conflict in the *Odyssey* reflect an earlier behavioral stage than that in the *Iliad*.

_____. "The Moralities of the *Odyssey*." In *The Greek Concept of Justice: From Its Shadow in Homer to Its Substance in Plato*. Cambridge, Mass.: Harvard University Press, 1978.
Homeric criteria for the reception of strangers, beggars, and prophets form the basis for the moral lesson of the *Odyssey*, a poem about both the proper treatment of foreigners and social obligation toward the poor in the aristocratic Greek world of trade, travel, and exploration in the ninth through seventh centuries B.C. This moral is not the invention of the poet but is part of the cultural heritage of the poems.

Keller, Albert G. "Religious Ideas and Usages." In *Homeric Society: A Sociological Study of the "Iliad" and "Odyssey."* New York: Longmans, Green, 1913.
Offers an overview of Homeric religious beliefs and practices, including the Homeric concept of the soul, the afterlife, the nature of deity, and its affect on human life. Describes the forms and purposes of Homeric temples and such religious rites as propitiatory cults, funeral ceremonies, burnt sacrifices, and libations. Considers Homeric beliefs and practices concerning prophecy, magic, and religious oaths and the ties of Homeric medicine and poetry with religion.

Lloyd-Jones, Hugh. "The *Iliad*." In *The Justice of Zeus*. Berkeley: University of California Press, 1971.
A response to studies of Homeric morality by A. W. H. Adkins and E. R. Dodds. Argues that Zeus is a god of justice modeled on the attributes of a human ruler. An analysis of Homer's story of the quarrel between Achilles and Agamemnon in the *Iliad* shows how Zeus defends the established order and punishes offenders against justice. Sometimes Zeus inflicts upon mortals a form of temporary insanity (*ate*) in order to further his divine plan. The plot of the *Iliad* is the

story of the just plan of Zeus. At the beginning of the next chapter, Lloyd-Jones briefly illustrates a similar morality operating in the *Odyssey*.

Mireaux, Émile. "The Background and Setting." In *Daily Life in the Time of Homer*, translated by Iris Sells. New York: Macmillan, 1960.
Describes the geography of the Homeric world and the role of the Homeric gods and of fate in the lives of humans and in the universe. Emphasizes the blend between the divine and the natural worlds and the forms of contact between mortals and the gods.

_____. "Popular Festivals: Funeral Rites: Public Games." In *Daily Life in the Time of Homer*, translated by Iris Sells. New York: Macmillan, 1960.
Uses evidence from the Homeric poems, including the funerals of Patroclus and Hector in *Iliad* 23 and 24 and the public games in *Iliad* 23 and *Odyssey* 8, to describe the nature and occasion of various religious festivals, funerals, burial practices, and public games.

_____. "The Religious and Intellectual Professions." In *Daily Life in the Time of Homer*, translated by Iris Sells. New York: Macmillan, 1960.
This discussion of the social position and role of such professions as priest, soothsayer, physicians, exorcists, and bards in Homeric society includes description of such practices as burnt sacrifice, temple worship, prophecy, and rituals of propitiation, healing, and purification.

Morford, Mark P. O., and Robert J. Lenardon. "The Twelve Olympians: Zeus, Hera, and Their Children." In *Classical Mythology*. 3d ed. New York: Longman, 1985.
This introduction to the chief gods of Greece includes extensive quotation from the Homeric poems, including Thetis' plea to Zeus in *Iliad* 1 and the love affair between Ares and Aphrodite in *Odyssey* 8.

Mueller, Martin. "The Gods." In *The Iliad*. Boston: Allen & Unwin, 1984.
A discussion of human and divine motivation in the *Iliad* is followed by a description of the Homeric gods and their society. There are sections on divine intervention and natural causality, on divine motivation and human responsibility, on individual gods, on the social organization of the gods, and on their justice.

Murray, Gilbert. "The Olympian Conquest." In *Five Stages of Greek Religion*. 3d ed. Garden City, N.Y.: Doubleday, 1955.
This essay is divided into two sections, one on the origin of the Olympian gods and a second on the religious value of the Olympians. The origins of individual gods are discussed, especially in the context of evidence from the Homeric poems.

Mylonas, George G. E. "Burial Customs." In *A Companion to Homer*, edited by Alan J. B. Wace and Frank H. Stubbings. New York: Macmillan, 1963.
Considers the contrasting practices of Mycenaean inhumation and Homeric cremation and indicates important similarities between the Mycenaean and the Homeric burial customs, such as the raising of a funeral mound and the giving of death gifts. Includes two figures showing the typical architecture of Mycenaean tombs; there are some untranslated Greek words.

Nilsson, Martin P. "The Homeric Anthropomorphism and Rationalism." In *A History of Greek Religion*, translated by F. J. Fielden. 2d ed. New York: W. W. Norton, 1964. Excerpt reprinted in *The Odyssey*, by Homer, edited by Albert Cook. New York: W. W. Norton, 1974.
This portion of a major study of religious beliefs in ancient Greece includes an examination of Homeric portrayal of the afterlife and a discussion of the nature of deity and the role of fate in human life. Suggests that Greek rationalism led to a belief in anthropomorphic deities which are not always identified in Homer with the divine power controlling human life.

_____. "The Roots of Greek Religion Mycenaean." In *Homer's History: Mycenaean or Dark Age?*, edited by C. G. Thomas. New York: Holt, Rinehart and Winston, 1970.
In this excerpt from a scholarly article entitled "Mycenaean and Homeric Religion," Nilsson, an important Swedish classicist of the first half of the twentieth century, finds evidence for Mycenaean religion in the Homeric poems. The nature of Zeus' rule over the gods is thought to correspond to the Mycenaean feudal organization. Homeric fatalism is traced to the warfare of the Mycenaean age. Mycenaean and Homeric burial practices are compared and the origin of the Greek hero cult is sought in a Mycenaean ancestor cult.

Onians, Richard B. *The Origins of European Thought About the Body, the Mind, the Soul, the World, Time, and Fate*. Cambridge, England: Cambridge University Press, 1951.
An examination of the psychological, metaphysical, and religious beliefs of the ancient Greeks and Romans as the foundation of later European and Christian thought. Compares Greco-Roman beliefs concerning consciousness, the immortal soul, and temporality with those of the Babylonians, Egyptians, Hebrews, Celts, and other early peoples. Includes extensive reference to the Homeric poems and discusses Homeric concepts related to thinking and knowing and the distinction between Homeric words such as *phren* ("mind"), *thymos* ("spirit"), and *psyche* ("soul"). Considers Homeric beliefs about the location of the mind in the body, the five senses, breathing and inspiration, death and dying, fate and necessity (*ananke*). Frequent quotation in Latin and Greek, often without translation. In

addition to a general index, there is a select index of passages quoted from the Bible and from Greek and Latin and an index of the foreign words from seventeen languages quoted in the text. Includes two illustrations.

Otto, Walter F. *The Homeric Gods: The Spiritual Significance of Greek Religion*, translated by Moses Hadas. London: Thames and Hudson, 1954. Excerpts reprinted as "A New Religious Outlook Expressed by Homer," in *Homer's History: Mycenaean or Dark Age?*, edited by C. G. Thomas. New York: Holt, Rinehart and Winston, 1970.
The Homeric poems are shown to have a unified religious viewpoint which is essentially Greek and not Mycenaean. Earlier deities were earth gods dealing with life and death while the Olympian gods of Homer are not so much masters over nature as they are part of the human's awesome experience of nature, especially in the form of divine manifestations to mortals. Discusses the historical origins of gods such as Athena, Aphrodite, and Hermes.

Parkes, Henry Bamford. "The Foundation of Greek Civilization." In *Gods and Men: The Origins of Western Culture*. New York: Alfred A. Knopf, 1959.
A brief history of early Greece and of the development of Greek religion. Emphasizes the important role played by the Homeric epics in the establishment of an Olympian theology and morality. Considers the role of gods in human life and questions of justice and heroic nobility in the Homeric epics.

Redfield, James M. "Error." In *Nature and Culture in the "Iliad": The Tragedy of Hector*. Chicago: University of Chicago Press, 1975.
The fallibility of human and heroic action in the *Iliad* is examined in the context of the role of the gods and of fate. The death of Hector is seen to result from the hero's ignorance and error, his misreading of the god's intentions, and especially his misunderstanding of the plan of Zeus in *Iliad* 1.

Rose, H. J. "Religion." In *A Companion to Homer*, edited by Alan J. B. Wace and Frank H. Stubbings. New York: Macmillan, 1963.
The author uses evidence from archaeological finds, including Linear B tablets, to describe two stages of the religion in early Greece, that of Minoan Crete followed by that of Mycenaean Greece. There are three photographs and eleven figures depicting religious scenes, especially on Bronze Age gems.

Rowe, C. J. "The Nature of Homeric Morality." In *Approaches to Homer*, edited by Carl A. Rubino and Cynthia A. Shelmerdine. Austin: University of Texas Press, 1983.
A review of the main questions about Homeric morality, which has been the subject of scholarly debate since 1960. At issue is the Homeric position concerning justice, the gods, and individual freedom and responsibility. Rowe concludes

that Homeric society limits the freedom of an individual by the need to acknowledge the claims of others.

Russo, Joseph, and Bennett Simon. "Homeric Psychology and the Oral Epic Tradition." *Journal of the History of Ideas* 29 (1968): 483-498. Slightly simplified in *Essays on the "Iliad,"* edited by John Wright. Bloomington: Indiana University Press, 1978.
In this essay, the authors summarize studies of the Homeric mind by Bruno Snell, Hermann Fränkel, and E. R. Dodds and argue that Homeric psychology, the Homeric way of thinking, has its roots in the nature of Greek traditional epic poetry.

Schein, Seth L. "The Gods." In *The Mortal Hero: An Introduction to Homer's "Iliad."* Berkeley: University of California Press, 1984.
Examines the presentation of the gods in the *Iliad*. There are sections on the chthonic gods, on the differences between the powerful, carefree gods and powerless, toiling humanity, and on the ultimate value of achievement. There is a short appendix on the Homeric concept of fate.

Segal, Charles. "Transition and Ritual in Odysseus' Return." In *Masterpieces of Western Literature: Contemporary Essays in Interpretation*, edited by Alex Page and Leon Barron. Dubuque, Iowa: W. C. Brown, 1966. Revised in *The Odyssey*, by Homer, edited by Albert Cook. New York: W. W. Norton, 1974.
The theme of Odysseus' return, viewed as a ritual of transition, is analyzed in terms of four themes: sleep, the bath, purification, and the threshold. These themes, symbolizing the mystery of passage between worlds, transform the return of Odysseus into a ritual rebirth.

Seymour, Thomas D. "Hades and His Realm." In *Life in the Homeric Age*. New York: Macmillan, 1908.
Uses passages from the Homeric poems, such as Odysseus' journey to the underworld in *Odyssey* 11 and the burials of Patroclus and Hector in *Iliad* 18 and 24, to describe Homeric beliefs and customs concerning death and the dead. Discusses general features of the Homeric realm of Hades, the nature of the souls of the dead, and rituals commemorating the dead. Includes an explanation of Homeric psychology, the Greek words for the mind, the soul, and the heart, and their functions in human life and thought.

_____. "Olympus and the Gods." In *Life in the Homeric Age*. New York: Macmillan, 1908.
A detailed description of the anthropomorphic life of the Greek gods in the Homeric poems. Considers the gods' involvement in human affairs and their relationship with fate. Lists the functions, attributes, and epithets of the major

Olympian deities and their participation in the action of the *Iliad*. Also lists a few minor deities, such as Dionysus, Iris, and some of the nymphs. Discusses Homeric ethics, including virtues, vengeance, generosity, and hospitality.

_____. "Temples, Worship, and Divination." In *Life in the Homeric Age*. New York: Macmillan, 1908.
Considers the general features of Greek religious ritual and worship and discusses references in the Homeric poems to temples, altars, cult statues, the duties of priests, procedures for burnt sacrifices, libations, oath-taking, forms of prayer, prophecies, omens, and dreams.

Snell, Bruno. "Homer's View of Man." In *The Discovery of the Mind: The Greek Origins of European Thought*, translated by T. G. Rosenmeyer. Cambridge, Mass.: Harvard University Press, 1953. Reprinted in *Homer*, edited by Harold Bloom. New York: Chelsea House, 1986. Also reprinted in *Homer's "The Iliad,"* edited by Harold Bloom. New York: Chelsea House, 1987.
An examination of various Homeric words for "mind" shows that the Homeric epics represent the first time in European thought that the world is considered not irrational but well-ordered and meaningful.

_____. "The Olympian Gods." In *The Discovery of the Mind: The Greek Origins of European Thought*, translated by T. G. Rosenmeyer. Cambridge, Mass.: Harvard University Press, 1953.
This examination of the Greek view of the gods includes a study of the role of the Homeric gods in human action and the relationship between individual gods and mortals. Especially focuses on Athena's intervention in the quarrel between Achilles and Agamemnon in *Iliad* 1.

Sommer, Richard J. "The *Odyssey* and Primitive Religion." In *The "Odyssey" and Primitive Religion*. Oslo: Norwegian Universities Press, 1962. Reprinted in *Critical Essays on Homer*, edited by Kenneth Atchity, Ron Hogart, and Doug Price. Boston: G. K. Hall, 1987.
Parallels between Odysseus and Agamemnon and the hero's relationships with Circe and Calypso lead the author to seek the beginnings of Odysseus' story in the prehistory of Eurasian primitive culture, in a patriarchal rite of passage from death to rebirth.

Stanford, W. B. "The Favourite of Athene." In *The Ulysses Theme: A Study in the Adaptability of a Traditional Hero*. 2d ed. Ann Arbor: University of Michigan Press, 1968.
Examines the role of the goddess Athena in determining the character of Odysseus in the Homeric poems. Suggests that Athena, functioning as a civilizing

force upon the hero, ensures that Odysseus learns to temper his intelligence with self-control, gentleness, and courtesy.

Vivante, Paolo. "Time and Life in Homer." In *The Homeric Imagination: Homer's Poetic Perception of Reality*. Bloomington: Indiana University Press, 1970. Reprinted in *The Odyssey*, by Homer, edited by Albert Cook. New York: W. W. Norton, 1974.
While the passing of time is shown to be an important aspect of Odysseus' identity, especially in his various recognitions in the poem, the Homeric concept of "life" is shown to lack a sense of duration and to stress only a sense of vitality, of being alive.

Voegelin, Eric. "[Order and Disorder]." In *Order and History*. Vol. 2. *The World of the Polis*. Baton Rouge: Louisiana State University Press, 1957. Reprinted in *Critical Essays on Homer*, edited by Kenneth Atchity, Ron Hogart, and Doug Price. Boston: G. K. Hall, 1987.
In this essay, the author pursues parallels between the Homeric poems and the Hebrew Bible. Examples of disorder in the *Iliad*, especially Achilles' wrath and the erotic passion of Paris and Helen, and observations about disorder in the opening scene of the *Odyssey* lead to a discussion of the etiology of disorder in Homer.

Whitman, Cedric H. "Fate, Time, and the Gods." In *Homer and the Heroic Tradition*. Cambridge, Mass.: Harvard University Press, 1958.
An examination of the role of the gods in the Homeric poems. The gods are considered a figurative means to observe the hero in an eternal dimension.

Wilcock, Malcolm M. "Mythology and the Gods." In *A Companion to the "Iliad."* Chicago: University of Chicago Press, 1976.
In this appendix to a commentary on the *Iliad*, the author discusses the epic in the context of the cycles in the Greek mythological tradition and the relationship between gods and men in Greek mythology.

_____. "Some Aspects of the Gods in the *Iliad*." *Bulletin of the Institute of Classical Studies* 17 (1970): 1-10. Slightly simplified in *Essays on the "Iliad,"* edited by John Wright. Bloomington: Indiana University Press, 1978.
In their relationships with mortals in the *Iliad*, the gods are seen to be simultaneously metaphor and religious force, something more than function separated from god and something less than anthropomorphic deities. Includes individual sections on Aphrodite, Ares, and Athena.

Woodhouse, W. J. "The Wrath of the Gods." In *The Composition of Homer's "Odyssey."* Oxford, England: Clarendon Press, 1930.

Examines the role of the gods in the action of the *Odyssey*. While the anger of the gods, namely Athena, Helius, and, especially, Poseidon, dominates the first half of the story, this theme is replaced by Athena's role as protectress of Odysseus in the second half.

The Authorship of the Homeric Poems

Overviews

Bassett, Samuel Eliot. "An Important Homeric Problem and Its Postulates." In *The Poetry of Homer*. Berkeley: University of California Press, 1938.
A unitarian response to the Homeric question. Emphasizes the poetic qualities of the epics and their composition by a single master poet. Dismisses the apparent contradictions in the epics by noting contradictions in the writers of more historically certain figures such as Plato. Uses the Greek word *poietes* ("poet") to suggest the creative powers of an individual "maker" whose goal was to delight listeners with realistic portrayal of an imagined experience. Qualifies the apparent lack of individual spontaneity suggested by Milman Parry's theory of traditional oral composition by affirming some degree of originality in Homer's use of sources.

Dimock, George E., Jr. Review of *The Making of Homeric Verse: The Collected Papers of Milman Parry*, edited by Adam Parry. *Yale Review* 60 (1971): 585-590. Reprinted in *Critical Essays on Homer*, edited by Kenneth Atchity, Ron Hogart, and Doug Price. Boston: G. K. Hall, 1987.
This review summarizes the contributions made by Milman Parry to the study of Homer's orality and outlines the general nature of the debate about the Homeric question in the twentieth century.

Dodds, E. R. "Homer." In *Fifty Years of Classical Scholarship*. Oxford, England: Basil Blackwell, 1954. Reprinted in *The Language and Background of Homer: Some Recent Studies and Controversies*, edited by Geoffrey S. Kirk. Cambridge, England: W. Heffer & Sons, 1964.
Dodds offers an overview of the scholarly debate about the composition of the Homeric poems. There are separate sections on the analysts, who believe that the Homeric poems are part of a long poetic development, and on the unitarians, who stress the contribution of an individual author. In a third section, Dodds discusses the work of Milman Parry on Homer as an oral poet.

Durant, Will. "The Common Culture of Early Greece." In *The Story of Civilization*. Vol. 2, *The Life of Greece*. New York: Simon & Schuster, 1939.

Included in this essay on the unifying elements of early Greek culture is a discussion of Greek oral poetry, the composition of the Homeric poems and their contribution to Greek education, religion, and morality. Comparison of various features of the *Iliad* and the *Odyssey* suggests that the poems had different authors. Includes chronological table, illustrations, glossary, bibliography, endnotes, and indexes.

Edwards, Mark W. "The Bard, Oral Poetry, and Our Present Text." In *Homer: Poet of the "Iliad."* Baltimore: The Johns Hopkins University Press, 1987.
The question of authorship and composition of the Homeric poems is introduced to the general reader with sections on the depiction of the bard in Homer, Homer as a singer, the techniques of oral poetry, and the establishment of the Homeric text.

Kirk, Geoffrey S. "The Making of the *Iliad*: Preliminary Considerations." In *The "Iliad": A Commentary.* Vol. 1, *Books 1-4.* New York: Cambridge University Press, 1985.
In this essay, the first of four introducing a scholarly commentary on *Iliad* 1-4, Kirk collects evidence for Homer's date and background and for the composition of the *Iliad*. External evidence for the date of Homer, especially the ancient biographical tradition and early references to the poems in art and literature, is combined with internal evidence based upon the language and content of the poems themselves. Questions the contribution of literacy or writing in the formation of the *Iliad* and suggests that the poem, showing a long period of oral formation, could not have assumed its monumental structure without the input of a single poet, who probably lived in the eighth century B.C.

Lord, Albert B. *The Singer of Tales.* New York: Atheneum, 1965.
A basic reference for the oral aspects of the Homeric poems. In the first half of his study, Lord uses the songs of twentieth century Yugoslav epic singers to illustrate the technique of a traditional oral singer and, in the second half, applies these observations to the Homeric poems and to medieval epic. The concepts of composition in performance, the formula, and the theme are highlighted. Includes endnotes, charts, and appendices.

Nagler, Michael N. Introduction to *Spontaneity and Tradition: A Study in the Oral Art of Homer.* Berkeley: University of California Press, 1974.
A reexamination of the Homeric question and a response to the theories of Milman Parry concerning traditional oral language. Asserts the principle of spontaneous composition in the context of inherited, traditional frame of thought and language and affirms the unitarian position that a single poet composed the Homeric epics.

Nilsson, Martin P. "How Old Is Greek Mythology?" In *The Mycenaean Origin of Greek Mythology*. Berkeley: University of California Press, 1932.
In this introductory chapter of a book demonstrating that the heroic myths of the Greeks can be traced back to Mycenaean centers, Nilsson, an important scholar of Greek religion, affirms the parallel development of both Greek epic and Greek mythology, the existence of Mycenaean elements in Greek epic, and, especially, borrowings from the Mycenaean cycle of myths in the Greek epic tradition. Includes an overview of the historical period in which the Greek epics originated and a discussion of the Homeric question.

Thomas, C. G. Introduction to *Homer's History: Mycenaean or Dark Age?*, edited by C. G. Thomas. New York: Holt, Rinehart and Winston, 1970.
This essay divides the Homeric question into four areas: the existence of Homer; composition of the *Iliad* and the *Odyssey* by a single author; the nature of oral epic language; and the historical basis of the poems. Issues related to the first three questions are summarized in this essay while the fourth area is the subject of the fourteen articles which this essay introduces. Also explains the significance of these articles for Homeric studies.

Trypanis, C. A. "The Date of the Homeric Epics and Their Form." In *The Homeric Epics*, translated by William Phelps. Warminster, England: Aris & Phillips, 1977.
Discusses several aspects of the Homeric epics, including hexameter verse, formulas, and, especially, the mix in the poems of linguistic and cultural features from several periods of Greek history. Differences between the two poems, together with other evidence for the dating of the poems, suggests that the *Iliad* was composed in the eighth century B.C. and the *Odyssey* several generations later. The principal stages in the transmission of the written epics are also listed.

Webster, T. B. L. "Homer and His Immediate Predecessors." In *From Mycenae to Homer*. 2d ed. New York: W. W. Norton, 1964.
Elements incorporated into the Homeric poems after 900 B.C. are examined in order to establish a probable date for the *Iliad* and the *Odyssey*, to learn something about the poets of the period, and to consider Homer's debts to the compositional technique and context of performance of his predecessors. Affirms the artistic unity of the *Iliad* and the *Odyssey*. There are sections on Homeric military language, geography, similes, typical scenes, and performance.

Homeric Biography

Boynton, H. W. "Homer." In *The World's Leading Poets*. New York: Henry Holt, 1912. Reprint. Freeport, N.Y.: Books for Libraries Press, 1968.

In this biographical collection about such poets as Vergil, John Milton, and Johann Wolfgang von Goethe, the author implies the unity of Homer and the identity of the poet by lamenting the lack of biographical details and hypothesizing about the personality of the poet. A traditional portrait of Homer is included.

Buckley, Theodore A. Introduction to *The Iliad*, by Homer, translated by Alexander Pope. New York: A. L. Burt, 1902.
In this introductory essay for Pope's eighteenth century translation, the author summarizes the ancient life of Homer attributed to Herodotus and discusses various theories of multiple authorship of the poems. He concludes with an affirmation of the unity of authorship.

Butler, Samuel. "Who Was the Writer?" In *The Authoress of the "Odyssey."* 2d ed. London: Jonathan Cape, 1922. Reprint. Chicago: University of Chicago Press, 1967.
Following his argument in the earlier part of the book that the *Odyssey* was written by a woman, Butler here suggests that the author of the poem was a Sicilian woman named Nausicaa.

Epps, Preston H. "About the Author." In *The Odyssey*, by Homer. New York: Macmillan, 1965.
In this short section, the author simplifies the Homeric question by listing the few "facts" which are known about Homer from the internal evidence of the poem and from remarks by later authors.

Hart, Michael H. "Homer." In *The 100: A Ranking of the Most Influential Persons in History*. Secaucus, N.J.: Citadel Press, 1987.
The single author of both the *Iliad* and the *Odyssey* is ranked as the ninety-sixth most influential person in history, based upon the number of people who have read the poems and the influence of the poems on literature. Includes ilustrations, a historical chart, an index, and statistical summaries in appendices.

Scott, John A. "Homer and Traditions in Homer." In *Homer and His Influence*. Boston: Marshall Jones, 1925.
A summary of the ancient biographical tradition about Homer is followed by the assertion that Homer was a conscious artist who was not so much repeating a traditional tale as he was creating a new tradition.

The "Homeric Question"

Bérard, Victor. *Did Homer Live?* Translated by Brian Rhys. New York: E. P. Dutton, 1931.

An elaborate argument that the core of the *Odyssey* was a poem about Odysseus' wanderings called "Tales at the Court of Alkinoos," written by a single literate poet from Miletos in Asia Minor about 850 B.C. Suggests that this poem was based upon a hypothetical written Phoenician epic modeled upon an earlier sailors' manual about Mediterranean exploration. Includes a brief history of the text of Homer and of Homeric scholarship from 1000 B.C. to the twentieth century A.D., with particular attention to the establishment of the texts of the Homeric poems, their division into twenty-four books, and the history of the Homeric question. The extreme unitarian views of Bérard are, in general, not supported by more recent scholars.

Bowra, C. M. Introduction to *Homer*. New York: Charles Scribner's Sons, 1972.
In addition to discussing the application of the comparative method to Homeric studies, Bowra summarizes several approaches to the Homeric question. The unitarian view of single authorship of the poems is contrasted with the analytic theories that the poems are compilations of separate poems from different hands, or that the poems were expanded and altered over several generations, or that a single poet created the poems from existing oral compositions.

Butler, Samuel. "The Date of the Poem. . . ." In *The Authoress of the "Odyssey."* 2d ed. London: Jonathan Cape, 1922. Reprint. Chicago: University of Chicago Press, 1967.
Because of his belief that the *Odyssey* was written by a woman in Trapani, Sicily, Butler uses references in the poem to Sicily to date the composition of the *Odyssey* to between 1150 and 1050 B.C. Passages from the historian Thucydides are used to support this argument.

_____. "Further Evidence in Support of an Early Ionian Settlement at or Close to Trapani." In *The Authoress of the "Odyssey."* 2d ed. London: Jonathan Cape, 1922. Reprint. Chicago: University of Chicago Press, 1967.
As part of his argument that the *Odyssey* was written by a Sicilian woman from Trapani, Butler gathers historical and archaeological evidence for the existence of an Ionian Greek city near Trapani in Sicily c. 1050 B.C. Includes some untranslated Greek.

_____. "The Importance of the Enquiry. . . ." In *The Authoress of the "Odyssey."* 2d ed. London: Jonathan Cape, 1922. Reprint. Chicago: University of Chicago Press, 1967.
In this introductory chapter to a book arguing that the *Odyssey* was written by a woman, Butler describes how he reached this conclusion and anticipates some of the criticisms of his readers. In particular, he counters several general objections to female authorship by considering the general role of women in Greek poetry and by listing several errors in the *Odyssey* which only a woman could have made.

_____. "The *Odyssey* in Its Relation to the Other Poems of the Trojan Cycle, and Its Development in the Hands of the Authoress." In *The Authoress of the "Odyssey."* 2d ed. London: Jonathan Cape, 1922. Reprint. Chicago: University of Chicago Press, 1967.
References in the *Odyssey* to other poems in the epic cycle are followed by an explanation of Butler's theory that the *Odyssey* was composed in two stages; the first told the story of Odysseus' visit to Phaeacia and the second, only awkwardly attached to the first, the story of Penelope and the suitors.

_____. "That the *Iliad* Which the Writer of the *Odyssey* Knew Was the Same as What We Now Have." In *The Authoress of the "Odyssey."* 2d ed. London: Jonathan Cape, 1922. Reprint. Chicago: University of Chicago Press, 1967.
In order to support his argument that the *Odyssey* was written after the *Iliad*, Butler collects in this chapter passages from the *Iliad* which are echoed in the *Odyssey*; there are some untranslated Greek passages.

Carpenter, Rhys. "Fact, Fable, and Fiction: The Final Verdict." In *Folktale, Fiction, and Saga in the Homeric Epics*. Berkeley: University of California Press, 1946.
Suggests that both heroic epics are fictional products of individual authors. The *Odyssey* is a combination of heroic legend connected with Troy, a folktale about the Bearson, and a quasi-historical incident about a man who disappeared, while the *Iliad* is based upon heroic legend about a distant actual event.

_____. "Literature Without Letters." In *Folktale, Fiction, and Saga in the Homeric Epics*. Berkeley: University of California Press, 1946.
An examination of the Homeric poems as oral literature in which the author discusses aspects of the Homeric question, including the dates of composition and transcription, and suggests a relationship between heroic epics and folktales.

Clay, Jenny Strauss. "Demodocus and Homer." In *The Wrath of Athena: Gods and Men in the "Odyssey."* Princeton, N.J.: Princeton University Press, 1983.
Considers the implications of Demodocus' song about the quarrel between Achilles and Odysseus in *Odyssey* 8 in regard to the Homeric question and the relationship between the two Homeric poems. Argues that the poet of the *Odyssey* knew the *Iliad*, avoided repeating in the *Odyssey* incidents told in the earlier poem, and consciously created in the *Odyssey* thematic correspondences and responses to the *Iliad*.

Davison, J. A. "The Homeric Question." In *A Companion to Homer*, edited by J. B. Wace and Frank H. Stubbings. New York: Macmillan, 1963. Abridged in *The Odyssey*, by Homer, edited by Albert Cook. New York: W. W. Norton, 1974.

A detailed survey of Homeric scholarship in ancient times is followed by a history of the modern debate concerning the composition, authorship, and date of the Homeric poems. Summarizes Homeric scholarship since 1910 under six categories: the artistic unity of the poems; the problem of inconsistencies; the belief that the Homeric poems are the products of a long literary evolution; the sources for the Homeric poems; the theory that the poems are composites of earlier songs; and the question of individual authorship. A figure depicts a scene from the *Odyssey* in early Greek art.

Grene, David. Introduction to *The Authoress of the "Odyssey,"* by Samuel Butler. 2d ed. Reprint. Chicago: University of Chicago Press, 1967.
The reprinting of the 1922 edition of Butler's book occasioned this essay, which provides some historical perspective for Butler's theory and a sympathetic evaluation of Butler's interpretation of the *Odyssey*. Grene explains where Butler anticipated later scholarly discussion on the question of authorship, where his theory remains weak, and where Butler's interpretation is still valuable.

Hainsworth, J. B. "The Criticism of an Oral Homer." *Journal of Hellenic Studies* 90 (1970): 90-98. Slightly simplified in *Essays on the "Iliad,"* edited by John Wright. Bloomington: Indiana University Press, 1978.
The author reacts to the theory of a traditional, oral origin for the Homeric poems with an emphasis on the poet's sense of structural clarity, balance, and proportion and argues that the overall form of the poems is more literary than the typical oral poem.

Jebb, R. C. "The Homeric Question." In *Homer: An Introduction to the "Iliad" and the "Odyssey."* 5th ed. Boston: Ginn, 1894. Reprint. Port Washington, N.Y.: Kennikat Press, 1969.
This essay offers an objective survey of the history of the Homeric question through the end of the nineteenth century. There are good discussions of the theories of such scholars as Robert Wood, F. A. Wolf, and Karl Lachmann as well as an analysis of the evidence. Includes some Greek words in parentheses and notes.

Kirk, Geoffrey S. "Plurality and Unity in Homer." In *The Songs of Homer*. Cambridge, England: Cambridge University Press, 1962.
Considers structural evidence for single and multiple authorship of the epics. Topics discussed include linguistic and archaeological evidence for a cultural amalgam in the epics, as well as the subjects, styles, and structural anomalies of the Homeric poems. The section ends with an argument for the overriding unity of the epics.

Lord, Albert B. "Homer." In *The Singer of Tales*. New York: Atheneum, 1965. Also in *Homer: A Collection of Critical Essays*, edited by George Steiner and Robert Fagles. Englewood Cliffs, N.J.: Prentice-Hall, 1962.
In this chapter, Lord argues that Homer was an oral poet by showing that the oral features of the Yugoslav epic singer can also be found in the Homeric epic.

Lorimer, H. L. "Conclusions." In *Homer and the Monuments*. London: Macmillan, 1950.
This chapter is actually an essay on the composition of the Homeric poems, with a section on each poem. Summarizes the findings of earlier chapters of the book concerning traces of Bronze Age culture in the Homeric poems, suggests the Mycenaean origin of the Greek hexameter, and discusses the so-called aeolisms of Homer. Analyzes both the *Iliad* and the *Odyssey* for signs of multiple authorship and concludes that each poem was probably composed by a single author, the *Iliad* between 750 and 700 B.C. and the *Odyssey* a little later between c. 730 and c. 680 B.C. There are some untranslated Greek words.

Mireaux, Émile. Introduction to *Daily Life in the Time of Homer*, translated by Iris Sells. New York: Macmillan, 1960.
Summarizes the divergent opinions of several Classical scholars concerning the Homeric question in order to establish an approximate time frame for the "Age of Homer." Notes that most scholars, whether analysts such as Victor Bérard or unitarians such as Fernand Robert, date the time of Homer about 700 B.C. Offers a brief historical and political overview of Greece at that date and lists the sources available for a reconstruction of daily life in the time of Homer.

Mueller, Martin. "The Composition of the *Iliad*." In *The Iliad*. Boston: Allen & Unwin, 1984.
A study of repetitions in the *Iliad* reveals a frequency of doublets which do not fit the characteristics of traditional formulaic language. This "contextual surplus" is considered the sign of composition by an individual poet. Suggests that the *Iliad* was composed in several stages by a single literate poet working in the oral tradition. Evidence for such compositional layers is found in the *Iliad*.

Murray, A. T. Introduction to *The Iliad*, by Homer, translated by A. T. Murray. 2 vols. Cambridge, Mass.: Harvard University Press, 1924.
In this essay preceding his translation of the *Iliad*, Murray lists eight principles upon which he bases his belief in the unity of authorship of the Homeric poems.

Nilsson, Martin P. "Views and Methods in the Homeric Question." In *Homer and Mycenae*. London: Methuen, 1933. Reprint. New York: Cooper Square, 1968.
Provides a history of the Homeric question and discusses the arguments of major analytic and unitarian scholars, including Andrew Lang, Gilbert Murray, and

J. A. Scott. Emphasizes one point of agreement, that some sort of earlier poetry served as a source for Homer, and considers the contributions of Mycenaean archaeology and of research on the origin of Greek mythology to the debate concerning the composition of the Homeric poems.

Page, Denys L. "The Beginning of the *Odyssey*." In *The Homeric "Odyssey."* Oxford, England: Clarendon Press, 1955. Reprint. Westport, Conn.: Greenwood Press, 1976.
Considers several problems and inconsistencies connected with the story of Telemachus in *Odyssey* 1-4 and concludes that this theme was woven into the story of Odysseus by a skilled poetic hand.

_____. "The End of the *Odyssey*." In *The Homeric "Odyssey."* Oxford, England: Clarendon Press, 1955. Reprint. Westport, Conn.: Greenwood Press, 1976.
Studies the late language of the scene between Odysseus and his father and inconsistencies in the scenes about the dead suitors and about Odysseus' recognition by Penelope and concludes that all of book 24 was a later addition to the finished poem. There are some untranslated Greek words.

_____. "The Method, Time, and Place of the Composition of the *Odyssey*." In *The Homeric "Odyssey."* Oxford, England: Clarendon Press, 1955. Reprint. Westport, Conn.: Greenwood Press, 1976.
Word studies are used to show that the Homeric poems were composed orally about 700 B.C. in regions of Greece which were isolated from one another. Includes some untranslated Greek words.

_____. "The Middle of the *Odyssey*," In *The Homeric "Odyssey."* Oxford, England: Clarendon Press, 1955. Reprint. Westport, Conn.: Greenwood Press, 1976.
Considers several inconsistencies connected with the role of the prophet Theoclymenus in book 15, the transformation of Odysseus in book 13, and the removal of the armor in book 16. Suggests that themes were added to the *Odyssey* by the editors of the first text of the poem.

_____. "Multiple Authorship in the *Iliad*." In *History and the Homeric "Iliad."* Berkeley: University of California Press, 1959.
In this appendix, signs of multiple authorship of the *Iliad* are sought in two scenes, the building of the Greek defensive wall in book 7 and the embassy to Achilles in book 9, for which there is a particularly detailed discussion of important linguistic and stylistic problems, such as the failure to include Phoenix in the ambassadors' departure scene and the inappropriateness of Phoenix' speech to Achilles.

Parry, Adam. "Have We Homer's *Iliad?*" *Yale Classical Studies* 20 (1966): 175-216. Slightly abridged and simplified in *Essays on the "Iliad,"* edited by John Wright. Bloomington: Indiana University Press, 1978.
In this essay, the author rejects the view of Albert Lord that an oral poet's powers are destroyed if he learns to read and write and the view of G. S. Kirk that orally composed Homeric poems were handed on by the tradition of oral song without fundamental change for a period of time. Parry hypothesizes an *Iliad* somehow put into writing at the time of its composition toward the end of the eighth century B.C.

Perry, Walter Copland. "Homer." In *The Women of Homer*. London: William Heinemann, 1898.
In this introductory chapter to a study of the position and character of the women in Homer, the author considers the authorship of the Homeric poems, recognizes the oral nature of the poems, and describes Homer as a poet more than a historian or a geographer. Includes some untranslated foreign language quotations.

Rouse, W. H. D. "The Critics." In *Homer*. New York: Thomas Nelson and Sons, 1939.
A short discussion of the evidence used and the contradictory conclusions reached by scholars in the debate about authorship of the Homeric poems. Special attention to features of language and to the Homeric digamma, an archaic alphabetic sign.

Scott, John A. "Homeric Poetry and Its Preservation." In *Homer and His Influence*. Boston: Marshall Jones, 1925.
In this essay, the author presents a strong unitarian position, namely that the poems were written by a single poet whose work was never subject to revision.

Seymour, Thomas D. Introduction to *Life in the Homeric Age*. New York: Macmillan, 1908.
Discusses various aspects of the Homeric question and the historical basis of the Homeric poems. Argues that composition of the poems began within a century after the fall of Troy in c. 1200 B.C., that the poems went through several layers of composition, and that a single poet, wandering in Asia Minor c. 900 B.C., finalized these poems. Suggests that, within certain limitations, the poems provide reliable evidence concerning the life of the Greeks in the 9th century B.C. Emphasizes the impersonal, idealized, and cosmopolitan character of the poems and their author.

Silk, M. S. "Homer's World and the Making of the *Iliad*." In *Homer: The "Iliad."* London: Cambridge University Press, 1987.
A significant portion of this chapter is devoted to the way the *Iliad* was composed. Considers evidence concerning the dating of the poem and the ancient

tradition about the man Homer and concludes that the present *Iliad* is not identical with the poem composed in the eighth century B.C. Oral performance and composition are also discussed.

Steiner, George. "Introduction: Homer and the Scholars." In *The Atlantic Monthly* 208 (1961): 77-84. Reprinted in *Homer: A Collection of Critical Essays*, edited by George Steiner and Robert Fagles. Englewood Cliffs, N.J.: Prentice-Hall, 1962.
Considers the historical background to the Trojan War, the composition of the Homeric poems, and, above all, the question of unity. Despite differences between the two poems, Steiner favors authorship of both poems by a single individual.

Trypanis, C. A. "The Poet Homer and the Homeric Question." In *The Homeric Epics*, translated by William Phelps. Warminster, England: Aris & Phillips, 1977.
After a brief discussion of the ancient biographical tradition about Homer, the author summarizes the history and main points of the Homeric question and concludes with an affirmation of the oral nature of the Homeric poems.

Whitman, Cedric H. "Athens, 1200-700 B.C." In *Homer and the Heroic Tradition*. Cambridge, Mass.: Harvard University Press, 1958.
Offers evidence that Athens rather than Ionia was the cultural environment in which the Homeric poems arose.

_____. "Homer and Geometric Art." In *Homer and the Heroic Tradition*. Cambridge, Mass.: Harvard University Press, 1958.
The strict artistic economy shared by Geometric Greek art and the Homeric poems is closely examined. Since much of this art was centered on Athens, the author argues that this city also provided a cultural environment for the creation of the Homeric poems.

_____. "The Meaning of Unity." In *Homer and the Heroic Tradition*. Cambridge, Mass.: Harvard University Press, 1958.
A summary of the scholarly history of the Homeric question leads to an affirmation of the intrinsic unity of the Homeric poems. The well-known inconsistencies in Homer are not as important as the overall cohesiveness of the epics.

_____. "Some Anomalies in the *Iliad* and the Problem of Oral Transmission." In *The Heroic Paradox*, edited by Charles Segal. Ithaca, N.Y.: Cornell University Press, 1982.
Discussion of several problem passages of the *Iliad* which have sometimes been used to argue for multiple authorship of the Homeric poems leads to an outline of the author's theory of individual authorship.

Homeric Poetry

Oral Composition

Austin, Norman. "The Homeric Formula." In *Archery at the Dark of the Moon: Poetic Problems in Homer's "Odyssey."* Berkeley: University of California Press, 1975.
In this chapter, the author shows how the Homeric formula is more than a metrical filler and functions as a fundamental thematic element upon which the poem is based. Epithets for Odysseus, Penelope, and Telemachus are examined. Greek is not translated.

Bassett, Samuel Eliot. "The Poet and His Audience." In *The Poetry of Homer*. Berkeley: University of California Press, 1938.
Suggests ways in which the Homeric narrative is affected by the limitations of oral performance. Homer uses economy of character and repetition in order to ensure comprehension by listeners. Illustrates such repetition especially in Homer's use of ring composition (*abba*) in questions and answers, in the carrying out of commands, and in speeches. Also shows how Homer sometimes involves listeners by making them infer background and motivations for actions, by the use of epic irony, and by overlooking slight inconsistencies in plot and character.

_____. "The Poet as Singer." In *The Poetry of Homer*. Berkeley: University of California Press, 1938.
This appreciation of the poetic nature of Homeric verse is, in part, a reaction to more formalistic studies of Homeric verse. Illustrates the great variety inherent in the dactylic hexameter and the relationship between whole verses and thought units. Emphasizes the naturalness, clarity, fluidity, and variety of Homeric language and discusses the poetic qualities of ornamental epithets and Homeric similes. There is some untranslated Greek.

Beye, Charles Rowan. "Oral Poetry." In *The "Iliad," the "Odyssey," and the Epic Tradition*. Garden City, N.Y.: Doubleday, 1966.
Reconstructs the oral technique which led to the creation of the Homeric poems, with particular focus on formulaic language and digression. Argues that the two poems were composed by separate poets and compares the poems to other sagas in the Greek tradition and to the *Epic of Gilgamesh*.

Bowra, C. M. "Devices of Composition." In *Homer*. New York: Charles Scribner's Sons, 1972.
Techniques used by oral poets differ from literate ones. These include taking the

audience into the poet's confidence, the use of lively invention to maintain the reality and solidity of the narrative, the marking of main features in advance by forecast or prophecy, and the answering of the last question first. Homer avoids the use of negative and mythic similes in favor of similes from the natural world. The construction of a long poem from short episodes or lays, such as the duel between two warriors, is examined in the Homeric and other oral poems.

_____. "Metre." In *A Companion to Homer*, edited by Alan J. B. Wace and Frank H. Stubbings. New York: Macmillan, 1963.
This short introduction to Homer's use of the dactylic hexameter is written for readers of Greek, and Greek quotations are not translated. Nevertheless, the general reader will gain some appreciation for the metrical precision of Homeric epic.

_____. "Obstacles and Difficulties." In *Homer*. New York: Charles Scribner's Sons, 1972.
Considers some of the barriers created by oral composition for the modern reader of the Homeric poems. These obstacles include apparent contradictions in the narrative, the effect of formulas, and the presence in the poems of customs and objects from different time periods.

_____. "Oral Composition." In *Homer*. New York: Charles Scribner's Sons, 1972.
Examines oral features of the Homeric epics, especially the use of formulas and epithets, in the light of the studies of Milman Parry. Includes references to poetic composition in the Homeric poems and to the relevance of the comparative study of other oral heroic poetry, especially that of Yugoslavia.

Camps, W. A. "The Poetic Medium." In *An Introduction to Homer*. New York: Oxford University Press, 1980.
Discusses such aspects of Homeric poetry as verse-form; diction; word length and sound; simplicity and lucidity; epithets; recurrent lines and phrases; and such resources for poetic emphasis as metaphors and similes.

Edwards, Mark W. "Characteristics of Homeric Poetry." In *Homer: Poet of the "Iliad."* Baltimore: The Johns Hopkins University Press, 1987.
This study includes an analysis of such poetic features as narrative, language, meter, word order, type scenes, descriptions, similes, and wordplay. There are also sections on the gods as religious and literary figures, Homeric psychology, warfare, and archaisms.

Finley, M. I. "Bards and Heroes." In *The World of Odysseus*. Rev. ed. New York: Viking Press, 1965.

The role of the bard in the portrayal of a heroic age of the distant past is described in this chapter of a book on the Homeric world. Despite their differences, both Homeric epics are seen to reflect features of heroic or oral epics. The bard's sense of divine inspiration is contrasted with archaeological evidence for the historicity of the Homeric tale in order to show the relationship between the Homeric poems and historical events.

Gaunt, D. M. Introduction to *Surge and Thunder: Critical Readings in Homer's "Odyssey."* New York: Oxford University Press, 1971.
Discusses general characteristics of Homeric oral language and their effects on Homer's poetic style. Considers the possibilities of original composition in the poems in the context of fixed aspects, such as plot, character, theme, and language.

Hainsworth, J. B. "The Epic Dialect." In *A Commentary on Homer's "Odyssey."* Vol. 1. *Introduction and Books I-VIII*, edited by Alfred Heubeck, Stephanie West, and J. B. Hainsworth. Oxford, England: Clarendon Press, 1988.
One of three essays introducing a scholarly commentary on the *Odyssey*. Argues that Homeric language is actually an artistic language, a special dialect used by Greek bards. Describes some of the special features of this dialect and its historical evolution. Considers how changes in the circumstances of performance, and possibly the influence of writing, contributed to this evolution and resulted in more stabilized songs. Includes some untranslated Greek.

Havelock, Eric A. "Epic as Record Versus Epic as Narrative." In *Preface to Plato*. Cambridge, Mass.: Harvard University Press, 1963. Reprinted in *Homer*, edited by Harold Bloom. New York: Chelsea House, 1986.
Suggests that the primary goal of a traditional Greek epic is seen to be not artistic creation but the recording of the typical, of the norms and laws of society, and that memorization rather than improvisation is more important in Homeric oral technique.

_____. "The Homeric State of Mind." In *Preface to Plato*. Cambridge, Mass.: Harvard University Press, 1963. Reprinted in *Homer's "The Iliad,"* edited by Harold Bloom. New York: Chelsea House, 1987.
Considers basic consequences of an oral Homer. Literate and nonliterate cultures speak and think in very different ways.

_____. "Some Elements of the Homeric Fantasy." In *The Greek Concept of Justice: From Its Shadow in Homer to Its Substance in Plato*. Cambridge, Mass.: Harvard University Press, 1978. Reprinted in *Homer's "The Iliad,"* edited by Harold Bloom. New York: Chelsea House, 1987.
One result of the oral composition of the Homeric poems is a blending of

Mycenaean fantasy and Greek reality. There are sections on adversary relationships, kings and queens, exaggeration of dimension, and Homer's use of such words as "king," "hero," "scepter," and *megaron*.

Holoka, James P. "Homeric Originality: A Survey." *Classical World* 66 (1973): 257-293.
An invaluable bibliographical resource for individuals interested in Homeric orality and, especially, the work of Milman Parry and Albert Lord. There are special sections on each of these scholars as well as studies of Homeric epithets, formulas, themes, comparative epic, and structure. Selected entries include detailed annotations which provide summary of the work and comment upon its scholarly significance. There are some references to non-English works.

Kirk, Geoffrey S. "The Development and Transmission of the Great Poems." In *The Songs of Homer*. Cambridge, England: Cambridge University Press, 1962.
In this part of a work on the composition of the Homeric epics, the author outlines the social and historical circumstances surrounding the composition of the Homeric poems. Topics discussed include the Homeric audience, the context of performance, the date of the poems, and the relationship between the *Iliad* and the *Odyssey*. Stages of development of the poems are also considered.

_____. "The Growth of the Oral Epic in Greece." In *The Songs of Homer*. Cambridge, England: Cambridge University Press, 1962.
Suggests the way that the Homeric epics may have evolved from a poetic tradition dating back to the Mycenaean period. Presents the evidence for oral epics in the Mycenaean period, the possibilities for such poetry in Greece in the Dark Age, and Dark Age and Aeolic elements in the Homeric poems.

_____. "Heroic Age and Heroic Poetry." In *The Odyssey*, by Homer, edited by Albert Cook. New York: W. W. Norton, 1974.
This chapter is a brief collation of selections from Kirk's *The Songs of Homer*. There are sections on the heroic age and heroic poetry, the languages and formulas in Homer, and oral tradition and the advent of writing.

_____. "Homer and Modern Oral Poetry: Some Confusions." In *The Language and Background of Homer: Some Recent Studies and Controversies*, edited by Geoffrey S. Kirk. Cambridge, England: W. Heffer & Sons, 1964.
In this essay, Kirk questions Albert Lord's application of observations about modern Yugoslav poetry to the poetry of Homer and argues that the Homeric poems could have been handed down orally from singer to singer with only small changes for several generations.

_____. "The Oral Poet and His Methods." In *The Songs of Homer*. Cambridge, England: Cambridge University Press, 1962.
In this part of a work on the composition of the Homeric epics, the author discusses various aspects of oral composition, including formulaic language in Homer, oral tradition, the advent of writing, the oral poet's use of established themes, and a comparative study of the oral epic in Yugoslavia.

_____. "The Songs and Their Qualities." In *The Songs of Homer*. Cambridge, England: Cambridge University Press, 1962.
Considers the effect of oral composition upon the style, themes, and structure of the individual Homeric poems and discusses some special qualities of the Homeric poems in regard to man, fate, and action.

_____. "The Structural Elements of Homeric Verse." In *The "Iliad": A Commentary*. Vol. 1, *Books 1-4*. New York: Cambridge University Press, 1985.
In this essay, the second of four introducing a scholarly commentary on *Iliad* 1-4, Kirk provides a general overview of the structural components of Homeric verse. He begins by examining ways that Homeric verse can be divided into metrical word groups known as cola and then illustrates the flexibility with which Homeric formulas, particularly noun-epithet combinations, can be placed in these cola. Shows how Homeric verse is built up by means of a process called "progressive enjambment," in which a grammatically complete idea is expanded by the addition of descriptive or contrasting phrases.

Lewis, C. S. "The Technique of Primary Epic." In *A Preface to "Paradise Lost."* New York: Oxford University Press, 1942.
Lewis, a Milton scholar and popular twentieth century author of inspirational books for children and adults, includes in his appreciative study of John Milton's *Paradise Lost* this brief discussion of Homeric diction, especially the use of stock words and phrases. Contains some comparison of Homeric language with that of *Beowulf*. Calls such oral epics "primary" in contrast with more literary "secondary" epics such as *Paradise Lost* which develop from the oral epic tradition.

Lord, Albert B. "The Formula." In *The Singer of Tales*. New York: Atheneum, 1965.
Shows how the repetitious language of oral performance by Yugoslav epic singers is a basic feature of oral composition like the Homeric poems. The formula is a repetitious mnemonic device which enables the performer simultaneously to preserve the tradition and to compose in performance.

_____. "The *Iliad*." In *The Singer of Tales*. New York: Atheneum, 1965.
Discusses the structure of the *Iliad* from the point of view of oral composition.
Themes and structural patterns in the epic are placed in the context of a larger
oral tradition.

_____. "The *Odyssey*." In *The Singer of Tales*. New York: Atheneum,
1965.
Considers the structure of the *Odyssey* in terms of oral composition. Major
themes in the epic are viewed as part of a broader oral tradition. Comparisons
are also made to themes in traditional Yugoslav epics.

_____. "Singers: Performance and Training." In *The Singer of Tales*. New
York: Atheneum, 1965.
In this chapter of his study of oral composition, Lord uses the Yugoslav epic
singer to show how an oral performer is trained and composes in performance.

_____. "Songs and the Song." In *The Singer of Tales*. New York: Athe-
neum, 1965.
Considers the relationship between an individual performer of a song and the oral
tradition and uses Yugoslav oral epics to show how the singer uses formulas and
themes to create songs which can only be understood in the context of other
versions of the same song which are part of the same tradition.

_____. "The Theme." In *The Singer of Tales*. New York: Atheneum, 1965.
Defines a basic feature of the language of oral poets such as Homer and illustrates how a Yugoslav epic singer builds a song by stringing together a series
of themes which can be expanded or contracted in length to suit the context.

Martin, Richard. *The Language of Heroes: Speech and Performance in the "Iliad."*
Ithaca, N.Y.: Cornell University Press, 1989.
Moves from the theories of Milman Parry about an oral Homer to an examination
of Homeric language in the context of public performance. Studies the direct
speech of gods and heroes in the *Iliad*, especially commands, verbal contests,
and feats of memory. Parallels these Homeric speech modes with those used in
traditional cultures in Africa and in Asia. Suggests that the language of Achilles
differs from that of other speakers in the *Iliad* and that the special, expansive
features of Achilles' language are characteristics of Homer's own composition
in performance. Language studies include some untranslated Greek. Bibliography
and indexes.

Nagler, Michael N. "The Motif." In *Spontaneity and Tradition: A Study in the Oral
Art of Homer*. Berkeley: University of California Press, 1974.

Examines the recurring dictional and functional elements associated with the motif of "going" in the Homeric poems and suggests that the basic feature of such motifs is not the formulaic language of Milman Parry's themes but the patterning of ideas and linguistic associations which can make any Homeric narrative episode a type scene. Illustrates the deep semantic fusion of such motifs by comparing scenes of military departure in the *Iliad* with Odysseus' orders to his servants in *Odyssey* 16. Includes some untranslated Greek.

_____. "The Motif Sequence." In *Spontaneity and Tradition: A Study in the Oral Art of Homer*. Berkeley: University of California Press, 1974.
Moves from a study of one recurring sequence of common motifs in the Homeric poems, namely "waking," "preparing," and "convening," to a consideration of the ways that the motif of convening is woven into the structure of both the *Iliad* and, especially, the *Odyssey*. Includes some untranslated Greek.

_____. "The Traditional Phrase (I): Theory of Production." In *Spontaneity and Tradition: A Study in the Oral Art of Homer*. Berkeley: University of California Press, 1974.
An attempt to redefine the traditional Homeric phrases such as noun-epithet groupings not as the fixed oral formulae suggested by Milman Parry but as linguistic transformations generated from a complexity of associations. Includes some untranslated Greek.

_____. "The Traditional Phrase (II): Meaning and Significance." In *Spontaneity and Tradition: A Study in the Oral Art of Homer*. Berkeley: University of California Press, 1974.
Argues that the same traditional oral phrase used by Homer in a variety of poetic contexts can have different essential ideas or meanings generated by the deeper semantic associations of the phrases. Illustrates the varied connotations of the Greek word for "veil" used prominently in Andromache's fainting scene in *Iliad* 22. Includes some untranslated Greek.

Nagy, Gregory. "Introduction: A Word on Assumptions, Methods, Results." In *The Best of the Achaeans: Concepts of the Hero in Archaic Greek Poetry*. Baltimore: The Johns Hopkins University Press, 1979.
Emphasizes the Panhellenic nature of the Homeric epics and the importance of the traditional oral theme in the creation of the poems. Considers the texts of the *Iliad* and the *Odyssey* to be the result of an evolution, an accumulation of a long series of compositions in performance.

Nilsson, Martin P. "Homeric Language and Style." In *Homer and Mycenae*. London: Methuen, 1933. Reprint. New York: Cooper Square, 1968.

Examines features of Homeric language, especially the question of aeolisms and fixed epithets, and concludes that some Homeric words were preserved from the Mycenaean age as a result of oral epic technique, a conclusion later supported by the decipherment of Linear B.

Parry, Milman. "The Traditional Epithet in Homer." In *Homer*, edited by Harold Bloom. New York: Chelsea House, 1986.
An abbreviated and simplified version of Parry's 1928 doctoral dissertation, this examination of such noun-epithet combinations in Homeric verse as "divine Odysseus" concludes that a particular epithet is generally used not according to sense and context but according to the grammatical case.

_____. "The Traditional Metaphor in Homer." In *Homer*, edited by Harold Bloom. New York: Chelsea House, 1986.
An abridged form of a scholarly article published in 1933. Working especially with the metaphors in *Iliad* 1, Parry demonstrates that the Homeric metaphor is regularly part of a fixed noun-epithet combination and is used more for the making of verses than for metaphoric value.

_____. "The Traditional Poetic Language of Oral Poetry." In *Homer*, edited by Harold Bloom. New York: Chelsea House, 1986.
An abridged and simplified version of Parry's second landmark essay entitled "Studies in the Epic Technique of Oral Verse-Making" and first published in 1932. Considers development and change in the language of oral poetry and the role of individual singers within the tradition. Although the process is highly conservative, the archaic language of oral poetry can change over time.

Stewart, Douglas J. "The Artist in the *Odyssey*." In *The Disguised Guest: Rank, Role, and Identity in the "Odyssey."* Lewisburg, Pa.: Bucknell University Press, 1976.
A consideration of artistic features of the *Odyssey* with special reference to the status and role of the poet and the poetic art in the epic, especially in the identification of Odysseus with a poet in book 9. Signs of individual innovation and of the author's intrusion into the poem are discussed in the context of the Homeric question.

Whitman, Cedric H. "Association by Theme in the *Iliad*." In *The Heroic Paradox*, edited by Charles Segal. Ithaca, N.Y.: Cornell University Press, 1982.
Shows how an oral Homer uses thematic associations such as the simile of a star and modulations of traditional themes to create the plot of the epic. Includes comparisons between the *Iliad* and South Slavic oral epics.

Writing and the Transmission of the Homeric Texts

Davison, J. A. "The Transmission of the Text." In *A Companion to Homer*, edited by Alan J. B. Wace and Frank H. Stubbings. New York: Macmillan, 1963.
Summarizes the textual history of the Homeric poems from the first-known Greek text, made in Athens by the Pisistratids in the sixth century B.C., until the introduction of printing in the fifteenth century A.D. Pages from a Homeric papyrus, a manuscript, and the first printed edition of Homer are illustrated in plates. Foreign words are not translated.

Havelock, Eric A. "The Alphabetization of Homer." In *Communication Arts in the Ancient World*, edited by Eric A. Havelock and Jackson P. Hershbell. New York: Hastings House, 1978. Reprinted in *The Literate Revolution in Greece and Its Cultural Consequences*, by Eric A. Havelock. Princeton, N.J.: Princeton University Press, 1982.
A comparison of passages from the *Epic of Gilgamesh* and the *Iliad* suggests the advantages of the Greek alphabet over earlier writing systems. Considers a date for the alphabetization of Homer, the principle of acoustical echoing, the types of recitations upon which the Homeric poems are based, the journey and the dream as metaphors for the process of oral recitation, and the effect of visual organization upon the acoustical form of the poems.

Jeffery, Lilian H. "Writing." In *A Companion to Homer*, edited by Alan J. B. Wace and Frank H. Stubbings. New York: Macmillan, 1963.
A brief history of writing in the ancient world, including a discussion of Linear B writing in the Mycenaean period, the introduction of the alphabet to Greece, and the relationship between writing and the Homeric poems. Values of Linear B signs and ideograms are explained. Accompanied by two plates, figures, and charts of Linear B and alphabet symbols. Some untranslated Greek words.

Kirk, Geoffrey S. "Aristarchus and the Scholia." In *The "Iliad": A Commentary*. Vol. 1, *Books 1-4*. New York: Cambridge University Press, 1985.
One of four essays introducing a scholarly commentary on *Iliad* 1-4, this historical summary traces the transmission of the text of the *Iliad* from its shadowy beginning, probably as an official text made in the sixth century B.C. for rhapsodic competitions at the Athenian Panathenaia, to the major contributions of Aristarchus of Samothrace and other Hellenistic scholars. Evaluates the quality of the various Homeric scholia, or marginal comments by ancient scholars, and considers the evidence Aristarchus and his fellow scholars may have used in forming their opinions about the Homeric text. Includes some untranslated Greek.

Lord, Albert B. "Homer's Originality: Oral Dictated Texts." *Transactions and Proceedings of the American Philological Association* 84 (1953): 124-134.

Reprinted in *The Language and Background of Homer: Some Recent Studies and Controversies*, edited by Geoffrey S. Kirk. Cambridge, England: W. Heffer & Sons, 1964.
In this essay, Lord argues that literacy is incompatible with the creation of oral poetry but that the composers of the Homeric poems may have dictated to literate assistants.

_____. "Writing and Oral Tradition." In *The Singer of Tales*. New York: Atheneum, 1965.
In this chapter of his study of Yugoslav oral epics, Lord contrasts the technique of the oral singer with the skills of the literate bard and argues that the concept of a fixed text is alien to an oral singer and that literacy is incompatible with the traditional oral epic.

Murray, Gilbert. "From Known to Unknown." In *The Rise of the Greek Epic*. 3d ed. Oxford, England: Clarendon Press, 1924.
Considers the history of the written text of Homer. Works from the existing versions, based on Alexandrian scholarship, back toward evidence for earlier written versions. Includes a list of quotations from Homer in Classical Greek texts. Argues that, while an "official" written version of the epics may have been made in Athens by the Pisistratids in the sixth century B.C., Homer's text was still essentially verbal and subject to change as late as the fourth and third centuries B.C. Emphasizes the influence of epic recitations at the Panathenaic festivals upon the text of Homer.

West, Stephanie. "The Transmission of the Text." In *A Commentary on Homer's "Odyssey."* Vol. 1, *Introduction and Books I-VIII*, edited by Alfred Heubeck, Stephanie West, and J. B. Hainsworth. Oxford, England: Clarendon Press, 1988.
One of three essays introducing a scholarly commentary on the *Odyssey*. Argues that the first written version of the *Odyssey* was a manuscript recorded by the author or a scribe in the late eighth century B.C. Considers the problem of alteration and interpolation connected with early rhapsodic performances and discusses the attempt to standardize the texts by Hipparchus, the sixth century Pisistratid ruler of Athens, and outlines the contributions made by ancient scholars such as Antimachus of Colophon, Zenodotus of Colophon, Aristarchus of Samothrace, and Aristophanes of Byzantium. There are some untranslated Greek passages.

Whitman, Cedric H. "Festivals, Pisistratus, and Writing." In *Homer and the Heroic Tradition*. Cambridge, Mass.: Harvard University Press, 1958.
Discounts the theory that the sixth century B.C. Athenian tyrant Pisistratus was responsible for the recording of the Homeric poems and argues that newly

established religious festivals occasioned both Homer's composition of his poems from traditional Greek heroic poetry and the commitment of these poems to writing in the late eighth century.

Homer's Sources

Bradford, Ernle. "The Cave of Polyphemus." In *Ulysses Found*. New York: Harcourt, Brace & World, 1963.
In this attempt to find the geographic reality behind Odysseus' encounter with the Cyclops in *Odyssey* 9, Bradford considers the origin of this story to have been a sea tale based upon an actual encounter with a large and savage inhabitant on the island of Sicily.

Butler, Samuel. "Further Details Regarding the Voyages of Ulysses. . . ." In *The Authoress of the "Odyssey."* 2d ed. London: Jonathan Cape, 1922. Reprint. Chicago: University of Chicago Press, 1967.
The second of two chapters in which the author argues that the description of Odysseus' adventures in *Odyssey* 9-12 reflects not a voyage around the Mediterranean Sea but a trip around the island of Sicily, the home of the reputed female author of the poem. In this chapter, the author suggests Sicilian locations for the adventures with the Cyclops, Circe, the Sirens, Scylla, and Charybdis.

_____. "The Ionian and the Aegean Islands. . . ." In *The Authoress of the "Odyssey."* 2d ed. London: Jonathan Cape, 1922. Reprint. Chicago: University of Chicago Press, 1967.
The first of two chapters in which the author argues that the description of Odysseus' adventures in *Odyssey* 9-12 reflects not a voyage around the Mediterranean Sea but a trip around the island of Sicily, the home of the reputed female author of the poem. In this chapter, the author suggests Sicilian locations for the adventures with Calypso, Aeolus, and the Laestrygonians.

Carpenter, Rhys. "The Cult of the Sleeping Bear." In *Folktale, Fiction, and Saga in the Homeric Epics*. Berkeley: University of California Press, 1946.
Suggests that the origin of the story of Odysseus, the hero who returns from the dead, lies in an Asian myth and cult of a sacred hibernating bear.

_____. "The Folk Tale of the Bear's Son." In *Folktale, Fiction, and Saga in the Homeric Epics*. Berkeley: University of California Press, 1946.
This chapter is a point-by-point comparison of the plot of the *Odyssey* with the folktale of the Bear's son.

_____. "Folktale and Fiction in the *Iliad*." In *Folktale, Fiction and Saga in the Homeric Epics*. Berkeley: University of California Press, 1946.
Contrasts the folktale elements in the story of Achilles with the elements of Attic tragedy in the structure of the *Iliad* and concludes that the *Iliad* is a fictional rather than a traditional story.

Germain, Gabriel. "The Sirens and the Temptation of Knowledge." In *Genèse de l'Odyssée*. Paris: Presses Universitaires de France, 1954. Translated by George Steiner in *Homer: A Collection of Critical Essays*, edited by George Steiner and Robert Fagles. Englewood Cliffs, N.J.: Prentice-Hall, 1962.
Finds the source of Odysseus' adventure with the Sirens in *Odyssey* 12 in ancient Sumerian tales about the temptation of a hero, such as episodes in the *Epic of Gilgamesh* and the story of the "tree of knowledge of good and evil" in *Genesis* 1. The etymology of the word "siren" is also discussed.

Leaf, Walter. Introduction to *A Companion to the "Iliad" for English Readers*. New York: Macmillan, 1892.
In this essay, Leaf focuses on the composition and structure of the *Iliad* and suggests that the epic was formed from three strata of stories: the "Menis," or "Wrath of Achilles"; "Aristeia," or stories about the prowess of other individual heroes; and great individual poems, such as the embassy to Achilles.

Murray, Gilbert. "The *Iliad* as a Traditional Book." In *The Rise of the Greek Epic*. 3d ed. Oxford, England: Clarendon Press, 1924.
Considers the problem of Homer's sources and argues on the basis of expurgations, or changes, in the *Iliad* that the poem is based upon traditional sources. Shows how references to torture and human sacrifice in the earlier tradition may have consciously been removed from the *Iliad* and how changes in customs, such as those connected with burial, temples, and dowries, may have been unconsciously incorporated into the *Iliad*. Suggests that the Homeric *Iliad* is a traditional lay which has developed into a work of fiction.

Nagy, Gregory. "Demodokos, Odyssey, Iliad." In *The Best of the Achaeans: Concepts of the Hero in Archaic Greek Poetry*. Baltimore: The Johns Hopkins University Press, 1979.
Suggests that Demodocus' song in *Odyssey* 8, about a quarrel between Achilles and Odysseus, is part of an earlier epic tradition in which the two heroes vied for status as "the best of the Achaeans." Shows how Homer adapts this tradition in the *Iliad* into the theme that Achilles is "best of the Achaeans."

Nilsson, Martin P. "Mythology in Homer." In *Homer and Mycenae*. London: Methuen, 1933. Reprint. New York: Cooper Square, 1968.
An analysis of the myths of the Homeric poems in order to determine their

probable origin in the myths of the Mycenaean period. Some characters, such as Priam, Aeneas, and Paris, are very old elements in the myth while others, such as Patroclus, are creations of the poet. Argues that the interrelationships between the Homeric gods, and especially the role of Zeus as chief god, are based upon Mycenaean state organization. Suggests that the material in Homeric similes is more recent and tends to replace the mythological elements, which were becoming outdated.

Page, Denys L. "Aeolus; the Cattle of the Sun; and the Sirens." In *Folktales in Homer's "Odyssey."* Cambridge, Mass.: Harvard University Press, 1973.
The folktale origins of three adventures in *Odyssey* 10 and 12 are sought. The story of Aeolus' bag of winds is traced to sea tales of professional wind sellers. The sacredness of the cattle of the sun god is compared to beliefs in ancient Egypt and in India. Odysseus' adventure with the cattle is compared to a story told by Saxo Grammaticus. The Sirens are considered to be based on folktales of dangerous demons masquerading as beautiful maidens.

——————. "Circe." In *Folktales in Homer's "Odyssey."* Cambridge, Mass.: Harvard University Press, 1973.
The origin of the tale about Odysseus' adventure with Circe in *Odyssey* 10 is seen to be a combination of two tales, one in which a beautiful sorceress is on the lookout for a lover and another in which a hero uses a charm to neutralize the magical powers of a sorceress. Similar tales were told in ancient India, Ceylon, and the *Arabian Nights*.

——————. "The Homeric Description of Greece." In *History and the Homeric "Iliad."* Berkeley: University of California Press, 1959.
Shows how certain features of the catalogues in *Iliad* 2 differ in detail from the rest of the *Iliad* and suggests that these catalogues, as essentially Mycenaean compositions, preserve records of actual events which were later incorporated into the *Iliad*.

——————. "The Laestrygonians." In *Folktales in Homer's "Odyssey."* Cambridge, Mass.: Harvard University Press, 1973.
Uses linguistic evidence to show that the story of Odysseus' encounter with the Laestrygonians in *Odyssey* 10 is based upon a very old traveler's tale about a voyage to high northern latitudes. The author of the epic probably borrowed this tale from the legend about Jason and the Argonauts. Includes some untranslated Greek words.

——————. "The Lotus-Eaters." In *Folktales in Homer's "Odyssey."* Cambridge, Mass.: Harvard University Press, 1973.

Odysseus' adventures with the Lotus-Eaters in *Odyssey* 9 is described and compared to stories from various parts of the world in which the living are caught in the realm of the dead by eating food.

_____. "Odysseus and Polyphemus." In *The Homeric "Odyssey."* Oxford, England: Clarendon Press, 1955. Reprint. Westport, Conn.: Greenwood Press, 1976.
Shows how various inconsistencies in the story of Polyphemus in *Odyssey* 9 could have resulted from the blending of several folktales by a single oral poet. A story about a hero at the mercy of a giant shepherd in a cave is joined with a tale in which a devil or demon, outwitted by a human calling himself "Nobody," calls other demons to the rescue. Includes some untranslated Greek words.

_____. "Odysseus and the Underworld." In *The Homeric "Odyssey."* Oxford, England: Clarendon Press, 1955. Reprint. Westport, Conn.: Greenwood Press, 1976.
Suggests that the author of the *Odyssey* used an independent poem about Odysseus' visit to the underworld as a source for *Odyssey* 11. The original roles of Elpenor and Teiresias were modified and a speech by Circe and an intermezzo were added. Includes some untranslated Greek words.

Webster, T. B. L. "Mycenaean Poetry." In *From Mycenae to Homer.* 2d ed. New York: W. W. Norton, 1964. Reprinted in abridged form as "The Material Basis of the Epics Largely Mycenaean," in *Homer's History: Mycenaean or Dark Age?*, edited by C. G. Thomas. New York: Holt, Rinehart and Winston, 1970. The Linear B documents are shown to contain traces of the Homeric poems, including terminology, grammar, poetic formulas, artifacts, and military weapons and tactics. From this evidence, the author draws some conclusions about the general characteristics and content of poetry in the Mycenaean period.

Wilcock, Malcolm M. "The '*Aithiopis*' Theory.'" In *A Companion to the Iliad.* Chicago: University of Chicago Press, 1976.
This appendix to a commentary on the *Iliad* considers the analytical theory that Homer is indebted to other parts of the epic cycle, especially the *Aethiopis*, a lost epic about the Trojan War. Includes a list of parallels between the *Iliad* and the *Aethiopis*.

Woodhouse, W. J. "The Components of the *Odyssey*." In *The Composition of Homer's "Odyssey."* Oxford, England: Clarendon Press, 1930.
Argues that the *Odyssey* was composed from nine sources: a saga of Odysseus concerning the hero's return from Troy and vengeance against his enemies at home; a collection of deep-sea yarns such as the stories of the Sirens and Polyphemus; five folktales (the woman's wit, the test of a husband returned, the grass

widow, the story of the stolen prince, and the suitor contest); the quest of Telemachus; and other original material added by the poet, including the story of Calypso.

_____. "The Deep-Sea Yarns." In *The Composition of Homer's "Odyssey."* Oxford, England: Clarendon Press, 1930.
Shows sea stories to have been a significant source for the plot of the *Odyssey*. Describes the general features of tall tales about sea monsters, magic, and unknown lands and discusses their place in the structure of the *Odyssey*.

_____. "The Exhibition Shot." In *The Composition of Homer's "Odyssey."* Oxford, England: Clarendon Press, 1930.
A close examination of the contest of the double axes in *Odyssey* 21 reveals several indications that the contest originally took place on Phaeacia as part of a suitor contest for Nausicaa's hand.

_____. "Kalypso the Concealer." In *The Composition of Homer's "Odyssey."* Oxford, England: Clarendon Press, 1930.
Suggests that the story of Odysseus' stay with Calypso is derived neither from folktale nor from traditional stories about Odysseus but is invented by the poet in order to fill the temporal gap left between the two years consumed by Odysseus' other adventures and the ten years he was said to have taken between his departure from Troy and his arrival in Ithaca.

_____. "Kirke and Kalypso." In *The Composition of Homer's "Odyssey."* Oxford, England: Clarendon Press, 1930.
Contrasts Homer's elaborate description of the encounter between Odysseus and Circe in *Odyssey* 10 with the passing references to that between Odysseus and Calypso in the *Odyssey* and concludes that the story of Circe is borrowed from folktale sources while that of Calypso is the creation of the poet.

_____. "The Man Far-Travelled." In *The Composition of Homer's "Odyssey."* Oxford, England: Clarendon Press, 1930.
Considers the so-called lying tales of Odysseus on Ithaca and suggests that the account of his adventures which the disguised Odysseus tells first to Eumaeus in *Odyssey* 14 and then to Penelope and the suitor Antinous in *Odyssey* 17 was actually the original version of his travels and that the travels described in *Odyssey* 9-12 are later folktale additions.

_____. "Material Completely Reshaped by Homer." In *Homer's History: Mycenaean or Dark Age?*, edited by C. G. Thomas. New York: Holt, Rinehart and Winston, 1970.
In this excerpt from *The Composition of Homer's "Odyssey,"* Woodhouse shows

how a highly original poem is created from various traditional materials, including Greek deep-sea tales, a saga of Odysseus, and the story of Telemachus' quest. Emphasis on Homer's constructive genius and poetic inspiration over his debt to traditional oral language.

_____. "Nausikaa's Romance." In *The Composition of Homer's "Odyssey."* Oxford, England: Clarendon Press, 1930.
Shows how Odysseus' encounter with Nausicaa and his stay with the Phaeacians in *Odyssey* 6-9 are based upon a folktale about a mysterious stranger competing successfully in a marriage contest for the hand of a princess.

_____. "Penelopeia and Her Web." In *The Composition of Homer's "Odyssey."* Oxford, England: Clarendon Press, 1930.
Examines references to Penelope's deceptive weaving in the *Odyssey* and shows how this story is based upon a folktale of a desperate heroine bargaining for time with trickery. Homer uses only the first part of this folktale in order to emphasize Penelope's trickiness but leaves out the dramatic climax in which the heroine is rescued just as she is discovered in her deception. In the *Odyssey*, the completion of the weaving is generally not seen as a bargain requiring Penelope to choose a new husband.

_____. "The Removal of the Arms." In *The Composition of Homer's "Odyssey."* Oxford, England: Clarendon Press, 1930.
Ponders an inconsistency between two passages concerning the removal of weapons from the hall of Odysseus' house. Although Odysseus instructs his son to remove all but two sets of armor from the hall in *Odyssey* 16, there is no mention of this armor when the arms are actually removed in *Odyssey* 19. Considers other instances in the *Odyssey* where changes of plan occur but finds no evidence for such a change in regard to the armor. This inconsistency appears to be the result of the blending of several sources in the poem.

_____. "The Return of Odysseus." In *The Composition of Homer's "Odyssey."* Oxford, England: Clarendon Press, 1930.
Suggests that Athena's advice to Odysseus in *Odyssey* 13 to disguise himself as a beggar and to return home secretly actually reflects an earlier version of the story, in which the hero consulted both the oracle of Zeus at Dodona and the ghost of Teiresias in the underworld before returning home. Shows that Odysseus' repeated references to the crimes of the suitors in *Odyssey* 22 and elsewhere do not reflect actual events in the poem but are survivals from an earlier saga of Odysseus, in which the suitors were depicted more harshly.

_____. "The Saga of Odysseus." In *The Composition of Homer's "Odyssey."* Oxford, England: Clarendon Press, 1930.

Attempts to reconstruct from evidence in the *Odyssey* the plot of one of the epic's theoretical sources, the so-called "Saga of Odysseus" in which the hero returns home in secret, is recognized by his wife and Eumaeus the swineherd, and with their help deals with the suitors. Suggests that Telemachus did not serve as a helper to his father in the original saga and that his role in the *Odyssey* is an innovation of Homer.

_____. "The Sign of the Bed." In *The Composition of Homer's "Odyssey."* Oxford, England: Clarendon Press, 1930.
Examines the process by which Odysseus is recognized by Penelope in *Odyssey* 23 and suggests that this clue of the bridal bed served as the third token of recognition between husband and wife in the original folktale source for the story.

_____. "The Sign of the Bow." In *The Composition of Homer's "Odyssey."* Oxford, England: Clarendon Press, 1930.
Suggests that the description of Odysseus' stringing the bow in *Odyssey* 21 is based upon a poetic treatment of a folktale about a wife's recognition of her long-lost husband by means of three tests, including his ability to string a bow.

_____. "The Sign of the Scar." In *The Composition of Homer's "Odyssey."* Oxford, England: Clarendon Press, 1930.
The story of the recognition of Odysseus' scar by Eurycleia in *Odyssey* 19 is shown to be derived from a folktale about the return of a long-lost husband who must prove his identity to his wife by means of a series of recognition signs. Homer modifies the story by postponing Penelope's recognition of Odysseus until *Odyssey* 23.

_____. "The Strong-Wing'd Music of Homer." In *The Composition of Homer's "Odyssey."* Oxford, England: Clarendon Press, 1930.
Suggests that the *Odyssey* emerged from a tradition of sea yarns, folktales, and a saga about the return of Odysseus from the Trojan War when a single poet decided to retard the return of Odysseus until his son was old enough to take part in the action. The *Odyssey* was created when the story of Telemachus was merged with these diverse traditional stories.

_____. "The Subject-Matter of the *Odyssey*." In *The Composition of Homer's "Odyssey."* Oxford, England: Clarendon Press, 1930.
A significant difference between the two Homeric epics lies in their sources. While the *Iliad* is composed from semihistorical legends about the Trojan War, the *Odyssey* is shown to be a combination of both historical legend and folktales or tales of fancy, of the realistic story of the return of Odysseus and the more imaginative tales of his adventures on the way home.

——————. "Telemachos in the Dark." In *The Composition of Homer's "Odyssey."* Oxford, England: Clarendon Press, 1930.

Shows how the folktale of the returned husband who plots vengeance with his wife is revised by Homer in the contest of the bow in *Odyssey* 20. Suggests that neither Penelope nor Telemachus considered the contest a plot of vengeance and that even Odysseus did not fully work out his plans until he had the bow in his hands.

——————. "The Twofold Contest." In *The Composition of Homer's "Odyssey."* Oxford, England: Clarendon Press, 1930.

Examines the marriage contest which Penelope proposes to the suitors in *Odyssey* 21 and shows how Homer combines two different types of traditional suitor contest in this story: a test of strength in the stringing of the bow and a test of skill in the shooting of the arrow through the double axes. Argues that the poet blends these tales for dramatic purposes, in order to place the suitors helpless before an Odysseus in possession of a bow and a quiver full of arrows.

——————. "What the Ghost Said." In *The Composition of Homer's "Odyssey."* Oxford, England: Clarendon Press, 1930.

Compares the reaction of the disguised Odysseus in *Odyssey* 19 to Penelope's plan for a bow contest with the statement of the slain suitor Amphimedon in *Odyssey* 24 that Odysseus and Penelope plotted to kill the suitors. Suggests that both passages are survivals of an earlier version of a plotting between husband and wife after the husband is recognized by his wife.

The *Homeric Hymns*, the Epic Cycle, and Background to the Homeric Epics

Distler, Paul F. "The Greek Heritage." In *Vergil and Vergiliana.* Chicago: Loyola University Press, 1966.

This chapter of an introductory study of Vergil includes useful summaries of the plots of the *Iliad* and the *Odyssey* as well as of the events leading up to and following both epics.

Fairbanks, Arthur. "The Legend of Troy." In *The Mythology of Greece and Rome.* New York: D. Appleton, 1907.

Discusses the ancestors of both Greek and Trojan warriors at Troy and summarizes the plots of various epics connected with the war, including the pre-*Iliad Cypria*, the *Iliad*, the post-*Iliad Aethiopis*, the *Little Iliad*, the *Homecomings* (*Nostoi*), and the *Odyssey*. Includes lists of ancient sources for the myths, illustrations, a map, genealogical tables, and an index.

Huxley, G. L. *Greek Epic Poetry from Eumelos to Panyassis.* Cambridge, Mass.: Harvard University Press, 1969.

A survey of lost Greek epic poetry from the eighth through the fifth centuries B.C. Literary and archaeological evidence is used to reconstruct the subject matter of these poems, including the Homeric *Margites*, epics related to events prior to and following plot of the *Iliad*, and stories about the returns of the heroes from Troy. Not all Greek quotations are translated.

Kirk, Geoffrey S. "The Epic Tradition After Homer and Hesiod." In *The Cambridge History of Classical Literature.* Vol. 1, *Greek Literature*, edited by P. E. Easterling and B. M. W. Knox. New York: Cambridge University Press, 1985.

In addition to other poems in the epic tradition besides the *Iliad* and the *Odyssey*, this essay discusses other works falsely attributed to Homer in antiquity, including the mock epic *Margites* and the *Homeric Hymns*.

Romilly, Jacqueline de. "The Epic Cycle and the *Homeric Hymns.*" In *A Short History of Greek Literature*, translated by Lillian Doherty. Chicago: University of Chicago Press, 1984.

In this appendix to a general essay on Homer, the author notes the relationship between the Homeric poems and lost poems in the epic cycle. Together with the extant *Homeric Hymns* and epic parodies like the *Margites*, these poems are considered extensions or continuations of the Homeric epics.

Rose, H. J. "Troy." *A Handbook of Greek Mythology.* New York: E. P. Dutton, 1959.

This chapter is a summary of those myths grouped together as the Trojan cycle. Beginning with the birth of Helen, Rose describes the Judgment of Paris and the Trojan War and ends with the homecoming of the Greeks, including Achilles. The plots of both the *Iliad* and the *Odyssey* are outlined in this summary.

Stanford, W. B. "Developments in the Epic Cycle." In *The Ulysses Theme: A Study in the Adaptability of a Traditional Hero.* 2d ed. Ann Arbor: University of Michigan Press, 1968.

Examines various references to Odysseus in the epic cycle, especially the hero's reluctance to join the Troy campaign, his relationships with Palamedes and Philoctetes, and stories of his fatal inland pilgrimage at the command of Teiresias. Suggests that the variegated tradition about Odysseus resulted from the lack of a definitive version by Homer.

On Translating Homer

Arnold, Matthew. *On Translating Homer.* 2d ed. London: John Murray, 1905. Reprint. New York: AMS Press, 1971.

The well-known Victorian poet offers some general advice to a translator of Homer and suggests that a good translation capture four characteristics of Homeric style: rapidity, directness of expression, directness of thought, and nobility. Applies these criteria to several translations, including those of Alexander Pope and George Chapman, and argues for translation of the Homeric poems into English hexameters. This reprint includes notes, an index, and an introduction by W. H. D. Rouse.

Butcher, S. H., and Andrew Lang. Preface to *The Odyssey*, by Homer, translated by S. H. Butcher and Andrew Lang. 3d ed. New York: Macmillan, 1895.
Most of this short essay deals with the question of translation. The authors of a prose translation of the *Odyssey* provide an overview of English translations of the epic from the seventeenth through the nineteenth centuries, discuss the advantages and disadvantages of various types of translation, and explain their reasons for translating the epic into biblical English.

Butler, Samuel. "Preface to the First Edition." In *The "Iliad" of Homer Rendered into English Prose*. London: Longmans, Green, 1898. 2d ed. New York: E. P. Dutton, 1925.
In this introduction to his prose translation of the *Iliad*, the author of *The Way of All Flesh* describes some of the principles upon which his translation is based. Butler argues for a great degree of freedom of expression on the part of the translator, including the ability to suppress the frequency of epithets. Draws comparison with the translation of Andrew Lang, Walter Leaf, and Ernest Myers.

Cook, Albert. "Preface on the Translation." In *The Odyssey*, by Homer, translated and edited by Albert Cook. New York: W. W. Norton, 1974.
In this short essay, a translator of the *Odyssey* offers some comments which apply to translation of both Homeric poems. A few Greek words are discussed by way of illustration.

Fitzgerald, Robert. Foreword to *A Guide to the "Iliad,"* by James C. Hogan. Garden City, N.Y.: Anchor Books, 1979.
A translator of Homer discusses how he approximates in English significant aspects of the Greek language and of Homer's style.

_____. "Some Details of Scene and Action." In a postscript to *The Odyssey*, by Homer, translated by Robert Fitzgerald. Garden City, N.Y.: Doubleday, 1961.
In this section, the first half of a postscript to his translation of the *Odyssey*, Fitzgerald discusses his trip to Ithaca, reflects on the process of translating Homer, and considers some difficult passages to translate.

Knight, Douglas. "Tradition and Translation." In *Pope and the Heroic Tradition: A Critical Study of His "Iliad."* New Haven, Conn.: Yale University Press, 1951. This discussion of theories of translating Homer centers on Alexander Pope's eighteenth century translation. Pope's theory is based upon a general appreciation of Homer's poetic power and a permanent ideal of epic in regard to the use of fable, characterization, moral sentiments, descriptions, and versification. Pope did not aim to reproduce Homer in English but to capture the spirit of Homer in the language and poetic tradition of his day.

Lord, George de Forest. "Dynamic Allegory in Chapman's *Odyssey*." In *Homeric Renaissance: The "Odyssey" of George Chapman*. New Haven, Conn.: Yale University Press, 1956.
An analysis of several important passages from Chapman's translation shows how allegorical interpretation affected the translation. Odysseus' adventures are presented by Chapman as struggles against the passions. Chapman's version is considered more dramatic and more faithful to Homer than other allegorical interpretations. Passages discussed include Odysseus on Phaeacia in book 6, the Cyclops episode in book 9, and Odysseus' encounter with Circe in book 10. There are some untranslated foreign words.

_____. "Style." In *Homeric Renaissance: The "Odyssey" of George Chapman*. New Haven, Conn.: Yale University Press, 1956.
A detailed comparison of Homer's style with that of George Chapman's translation shows that Chapman's translation is uneven in vigor and clarity, markedly distinctive, and a difficult challenge to readers. Chapman did not feel dependent upon his original but used a range of English styles from the vernacular to the Latinate. Includes some untranslated foreign words.

_____. "Style as Interpretation: Chapman's *Odyssey* and Pope's." In *Homeric Renaissance: The "Odyssey" of George Chapman*. New Haven, Conn.: Yale University Press, 1956.
Compares George Chapman's translation with that of Alexander Pope. Both in style and in meaning, Chapman's translation reveals more freedom and spontaneity than Pope's version. While Chapman emphasizes the specific and immediate, Pope focuses on the general and the universal. There are some untranslated foreign words.

_____. "Translation and Interpretation." In *Homeric Renaissance: The "Odyssey" of George Chapman*. New Haven, Conn.: Yale University Press, 1956.
Suggests that two virtues of George Chapman's 1616 translation are his faithfulness to Homer's conception of Odysseus' career as a moral evolution and a poetic style flexible enough to capture the variety of the original. Includes some untranslated foreign words.

Mason, H. A. "A Conception of the Heroic." In *To Homer Through Pope: An Introduction to Homer's "Iliad" and Pope's Translation*. New York: Harper & Row, 1972.
Comparison of the views of heroism in Alexander Pope's and E. V. Rieu's translations of Homer and Ezra Pound's *Cantos* shows that translation is inevitably affected by the translator's beliefs and perceptions. Both Pope and Rieu translate Homer according to their own conceptions of the heroic.

_____. "Epilogue I. Some Versions of the *Iliad*." In *To Homer Through Pope: An Introduction to Homer's "Iliad" and Pope's Translation*. New York: Harper & Row, 1972.
The problems of translation are considered by comparing six translations of the *Iliad*. While neither prose nor verse translations generally appear to capture the full flavor of Homer's original, the translation of Richmond Lattimore is preferred by the author.

_____. "Epilogue II. Incredible Speech: The *Odyssey* of Homer." In *To Homer Through Pope: An Introduction to Homer's "Iliad" and Pope's Translation*. New York: Harper & Row, 1972.
Praises the translation of Alexander Pope for capturing the humanity of Homer. Pope's translation is preferred to several twentieth century translations of the *Odyssey*, including those of Robert Fitzgerald and Richmond Lattimore.

_____. "Homer's Similes (I): Inanimate Nature." In *To Homer Through Pope: An Introduction to Homer's "Iliad" and Pope's Translation*. New York: Harper & Row, 1972.
This study illustrates how a translation can be affected by the views of the translator. In Alexander Pope's translation of the *Iliad*, Homer's unstructured view of nature is replaced by Pope's orderly worldview. Pope reworked Homer's similes into a *crescendo-decrescendo* form in which physical nature is presented in unity with human nature.

_____. "Homer's Similes (II): Animal Nature." In *To Homer Through Pope: An Introduction to Homer's "Iliad" and Pope's Translation*. New York: Harper & Row, 1972.
In his translation of the *Iliad*, Alexander Pope reworks Homeric similes about animals in order to preserve the decorum of his heroes by avoiding association with lower, animal qualities. Pope's translation of Homer thus helps the reader to understand the original by confronting the reader with a translator's interpretation of Homer's words.

_____. "Pope's and Dryden's Translations of Book I." In *To Homer Through Pope: An Introduction to Homer's "Iliad" and Pope's Translation*. New York: Harper & Row, 1972.

A comparison of Alexander Pope's and John Dryden's translations of *Iliad* 1. Pope instills into the poem a British concept of noble decorum which makes it difficult for his translation always to capture the varied flavor of the Homeric epic. Dryden's translation creates the right balance of dignity and humor, especially in the scene with the gods.

Nicoll, Allardyce. Introduction to *Chapman's "Homer."* Vol. 1, *The Iliad*, edited by Allardyce Nicoll. 2d ed. Princeton, N.J.: Princeton University Press, 1967. The author introduces his edition of George Chapman's seventeenth century translation of Homer's *Iliad* with a history of Chapman's work and some comment upon its importance.

_____. Introduction to *Chapman's "Homer."* Vol. 2, *The "Odyssey" and the Lesser Homerica*, edited by Allardyce Nicoll. 2d ed. Princeton, N.J.: Princeton University Press, 1967.
Includes historical background to George Chapman's seventeenth century translation of Homer's *Odyssey* and some comparison of Chapman's *Odyssey* with his *Iliad*.

Palmer, George Herbert. "A Retrospect." In *The Odyssey*, by Homer. 2d ed. Boston: Houghton Mifflin, 1921.
The second edition of the author's translation of the *Odyssey* provides an opportunity for some reflections upon his general principles of translation and explains some of the features of his own late nineteenth century translation.

Rouse, W. H. D. Introduction to *On Translating Homer*, by Matthew Arnold. 2d ed. London: John Murray, 1905. Reprint. New York: AMS Press, 1971.
The author criticizes Arnold's assertion of the unity of Homer but approves of his general estimation of the Homeric genius and of his advice concerning translation. Considers some of the problems in translating Homer and reviews the poetic qualities of several translations of Homer.

_____. "Translations of Homer." In *Homer*. New York: Thomas Nelson and Sons, 1939.
A close comparison of several translations of the Homeric poems, with extensive quotation. Moves from the seventeenth century verse translation by George Chapman and its influence on John Keats to a comparison of Chapman's translation with the eighteenth century version by Alexander Pope. Discusses features of various prose translations, including those of Samuel Butler and T. E. Shaw ("Lawrence of Arabia"). Rouse advocates the use of simple, direct English in order to capture the tone of the Homeric original.

Scott, John A. "Translations of Homer." In *Homer and His Influence*. Boston: Marshall Jones, 1925.

Discusses the virtues of several translations of Homer, including those by George Chapman, Alexander Pope, and William Cowper. Generally considers prose translations more authentic reproductions of the original Greek.

Shaw, T. E. "Translator's Note." In *The "Odyssey" of Homer*, translated by T. E. Shaw. Oxford, England: Oxford University Press, 1932. Reprinted in *Homer: A Collection of Critical Essays*, edited by George Steiner and Robert Fagles. Englewood Cliffs, N.J.: Prentice-Hall, 1962. Excerpted in *The Poets on the Classics: An Anthology of English Poets' Writing on the Classical Poets and Dramatists from Chaucer to the Present*, edited by Stuart Gillespie. New York: Routledge, 1988.
This translator of the *Odyssey*, better known as T. E. Lawrence, or "Lawrence of Arabia," describes his method of rendering the epic in English and gives his impression of Homer's personality. Shaw laments the limitations of Homer's poetry, including often sketchy characterization, and his own inability to capture in English the flavor of the Homeric poems.

Shewring, Walter. "Epilogue on Translation." In *The Odyssey*, by Homer, translated by Walter Shewring. New York: Oxford University Press, 1980.
A detailed consideration of the problem of translation in general and of translating Homer in particular. Lists some special features of Classical Greek which are difficult to translate into English in their proper social context. Surveys the history of English translations of the *Odyssey* in both verse and prose. Reflects on the difficulty of capturing the poetic flavor of the *Odyssey* in English verse or in everyday prose. Makes some observations on the author's own prose translation of the *Odyssey* and his principles of translation. Gives particular attention to the problems of translating recurring epithets and other forms of repetition in the *Odyssey*. Ends with a historical overview of Homeric criticism and of ways that the poem has been interpreted over the centuries.

Comparative Literary Studies of the *Iliad* and the *Odyssey*

Andersson, Theodore M. "Latent Space in the Homeric Epics." In *Early Epic Scenery*. Ithaca, N.Y.: Cornell University Press, 1976.
Part of a book studying the use of detailed landscapes by the Roman poet Vergil and his medieval imitators, this chapter notes the general absence of natural features in Homeric descriptions and even the poet's indifference to visual aspects of the scene. Compares scenic design in the *Iliad* and the *Odyssey* and suggests that Homer prefers to describe the motivations of his characters from within while Vergil creates an emotional bond between characters and their environments.

Bassett, Samuel Eliot. "The Epic Illusion." In *The Poetry of Homer*. Berkeley: University of California Press, 1938.
Uses scenes from the *Iliad* and the *Odyssey* in order to examine Homer's treatment of time and place and to show how Homer creates the illusion of reality by developing an impression of historicity, vitality, continuity, and movement in the poems.

_____. "The Epic Illusion (Continued)—Personality—the Dramatic in Homer." In *The Poetry of Homer*. Berkeley: University of California Press, 1938.
Shows how direct speech creates the poetic illusion of personality in the Homeric epics. Notes that the *Iliad* and the *Odyssey* use a high proportion of monologues and dialogues, considers the relationship between these speeches and the movement of the narrative, and shows the dramatic qualities of various episodes from the epics, including the speeches in the embassy scene of *Iliad* 9 and the recognition of Odysseus by Eurycleia in *Odyssey* 19.

_____. "The Poet as Realist and as Idealist." In *The Poetry of Homer*. Berkeley: University of California Press, 1938.
Affirms the natural realism of the Homeric poems and shows how the plot of the *Iliad* and the *Odyssey* can be made into the outlines of several hypothetical Greek tragedies, including a "Wrath of Achilles" and a "Hector." Discusses some differences between Greek epic and Greek tragedy, including the significance of the gods in the action and the role of the tragic chorus. Suggests that Homeric epic presents a more realistic portrait of life than the abstract picture painted in Greek tragedy.

Bowra, C. M. "Composition." In *A Companion to Homer*, edited by Alan J. B. Wace and Frank H. Stubbings. New York: Macmillan, 1963.
Considers some effects of oral composition upon the Homeric poems. Discusses several points of similarity between the two poems, including character portrayal and use of similes. Greek quotations are not translated.

_____. "The Poetry of Action." In *Homer*. New York: Charles Scribner's Sons, 1972.
Shows how both Homeric poems, as poems of action, possess objectivity and detail of description. Homer's geographic descriptions of Troy and Ithaca suggest some knowledge of the local terrain. Homer's powerful depiction of human emotions is often achieved by means of directness and concentration on a single mood. The purpose of Homeric poetry is to delight, not to instruct.

_____. "Style." In *A Companion to Homer*, edited by Alan J. B. Wace and Frank H. Stubbings. New York: Macmillan, 1963.

A brief discussion of the origin of Homeric language in the Mycenaean age followed by a survey of various types of Homeric formulas. Greek quotations are not translated.

Butler, Samuel. "The Humour of Homer." In *The Humour of Homer and Other Essays*, edited by R. A. Streatfeild. New York: Mitchell Kennerley, 1914. Reprint. Freeport, N.Y.: Books for Libraries Press, 1967.
In this essay, Butler, the author of *The Way of All Flesh* and a translator of Homer, suggests that there is a broad element of humor in both Homeric poems, especially in scenes depicting the gods. Includes extensive paraphrase of individual episodes from the epics, including several scenes between Zeus and Hera in the *Iliad* and the encounter between Odysseus and Nausicaa in the *Odyssey*. Includes portrait of the author in frontispiece.

Camps, W. A. "Conclusion." In *An Introduction to Homer*. New York: Oxford University Press, 1980.
Summarizes several poetic features shared by the *Iliad* and the *Odyssey*. Two passages, one from each of the Homeric poems, are compared.

_____. "How the Stories Are Told." In *An Introduction to Homer*. New York: Oxford University Press, 1980.
Illustrates the extent to which dramatic form is incorporated into the narrative structure of the two Homeric poems.

_____. "Illustrative Examples in Translation." In *An Introduction to Homer*. New York: Oxford University Press, 1980.
Selections from the two Homeric poems are used to show Homer's use of dialogue and character portrayal. There is no explanatory analysis of the passages.

_____. "Imperfections of Detail and Their Causes." In *An Introduction to Homer*. New York: Oxford University Press, 1980.
Various inconsistencies and incongruities in the plots of the two Homeric poems are discussed and attributed to the oral origin of the poems.

_____. "Omissions from the Outlines." In *An Introduction to Homer*. New York: Oxford University Press, 1980.
Discusses aspects of the Homeric poems which are not illustrated by mere plot summaries, such as the diversity and interest of secondary episodes and the role of the gods in the plot.

_____. "Similarities and Differences Between *Iliad* and *Odyssey*." In *An Introduction to Homer*. New York: Oxford University Press, 1980.

Actually a list of differences between the two poems, especially in regard to structure, setting, subject matter, and attitude toward war.

_____. "Supposed or Real Schemes of Construction in the *Iliad* and *Odyssey*." In *An Introduction to Homer*. New York: Oxford University Press, 1980.
In this appendix to a poetic study of the poems, the author suggests ways in which the twenty-four books of each poem can be divided into groups.

_____. "The Topography of the *Iliad* and *Odyssey*." In *An Introduction to Homer*. New York: Oxford University Press, 1980.
In this appendix to a poetic study of the two Homeric poems, the author compares the way landscape and locality is described in the *Iliad* and the *Odyssey*.

_____. "Unity of Design." In *An Introduction to Homer*. New York: Oxford University Press, 1980.
A brief discussion of the comprehensiveness and compactness of the plots of the two Homeric poems.

Duckworth, George E. *Foreshadowing and Suspense in the Epics of Homer, Apollonius, and Vergil*. New York: Haskell, 1970.
Shows that the same devices are used to forecast future action in four ancient epics, including both the *Iliad* and the *Odyssey*, but that the various poets use these devices in different ways. The epics are discussed as a group rather than individually. A regular and consistent use of foreshadowing is noted in the Homeric epics, where the device is employed, especially in the first two-thirds of each epic, to develop the reader's foreknowledge of and interest in future events. There is an index of passages discussed.

Griffin, Jasper. "Conclusion." In *Homer*. New York: Hill & Wang, 1980.
A short summary of the chief thematic differences between the two Homeric epics. While the *Iliad* focuses on an ideal, supreme hero, the *Odyssey* deals with reality and with a hero of deceit and endurance.

Jebb, R. C. "General Literary Characteristics of the Poems." In *Homer: An Introduction to the "Iliad" and the "Odyssey."* 5th ed. Boston: Ginn, 1894. Reprint. Port Washington, N.Y.: Kennikat Press, 1969.
Summarizes the plots of both Homeric epics and discusses their epic features, including character development and the use of the simile. Aristotle's definition of an epic poem and differences between the Homeric poems and literary epics are also considered. Greek references are in parentheses or notes. Discusses more technical aspects of Homeric language in appendices.

Johnson, W. R. "Lessing, Auerbach, Gombrich: The Norm of Reality and the Spectrum of Decorum." In *Darkness Visible: A Study of Vergil's "Aeneid."* Berkeley: University of California Press, 1976.
Applies the critically influential observations of Longinus, Gotthold Lessing, and Erich Auerbach about the realistic and simple narrative style of the Homeric poems to Vergil's *Aeneid*. The stag episode in *Odyssey* 10 and Homer's description of Helen's love for Paris in *Iliad* 3 are compared with parallel passages in the *Aeneid*. Using E. H. Gombrich's theory of realism in art, Johnson argues that Homer maintains an equilibrium between abstract conceptualization and undifferentiated perception which Vergil sacrifices for a more subjective style.

Knight, Douglas. "The Style of a Heroic Poem." In *Pope and the Heroic Tradition: A Critical Study of His "Iliad."* New Haven, Conn.: Yale University Press, 1951.
A brief discussion of the chief qualities of Homeric style is followed by a study of the style used by Alexander Pope in his translation of the *Iliad*. Pope's style is based upon the nature of heroic writing and the possibilities of English poetry. Particular attention to Pope's choice of vocabulary and method of versification.

Lewis, C. S. "The Subject of Primary Epic." In *A Preface to "Paradise Lost."* New York: Oxford University Press, 1942.
Examines the plots of several "primary" epics, including the two Homeric epics and *Beowulf*, and argues that the greatness of subject associated with epic is a characteristic not of primary epics but of secondary epics such as Vergil's *Aeneid* or John Milton's *Paradise Lost*.

Lukács, George. "To Narrate or Describe?" Excerpted from *Probleme des Realismus*, translated by Hanna Loewy. Berlin: Aufbau-Verlag, 1955. Reprinted in *Homer: A Collection of Critical Essays*, edited by George Steiner and Robert Fagles. Englewood Cliffs, N.J.: Prentice-Hall, 1962.
In this short excerpt, the author praises the precise forms of description found in the epics of Homer, Sir Walter Scott, Honoré de Balzac, and Leo Tolstoy. Includes a passage from Gotthold Lessing's *Laocoön* on the scepters of Agamemnon and Achilles.

Lynn-George, Michael. "Between Two Worlds." In *Epos: Word, Narrative, and the "Iliad."* Atlantic Highlands, N.J.: Humanities Press International, 1988.
Suggests that the straightforward narrative style seen by Erich Auerbach in the scar episode of *Odyssey* 19 is actually a more complicated structure based on two worlds of past and present, of speech and silence. This narrative structure is illustrated through a study of *Iliad* 1 and *Iliad* 3.

Nagy, Gregory. "Praise, Blame, and the Hero." In *The Best of the Achaeans: Concepts of the Hero in Archaic Greek Poetry*. Baltimore: The Johns Hopkins University Press, 1979.

An examination of the themes of strife, praise, and blame in archaic Greek poetry, especially Pindar, Archilochus, and the Homeric epics. Affirms the relationship between praise and blame poetry in the Indo-European poetic tradition and shows the common linguistic and thematic links between Greek epic and Greek poetry of praise and blame.

Perry, Walter Copland. "The Magic of Homer." In *The Women of Homer*. London: William Heinemann, 1898.

A general appreciation of Homer's poetic skill. Attributes Homer's influence to several factors, including his language, humanity, objectivity, and power of personification, the naïveté of his characters, and the varied subject matter of his epics. Includes some untranslated foreign language quotations.

Powys, John Cowper. Preface to *Homer and the Aether*. London: MacDonald, 1959. Reprinted in *Homer: A Collection of Critical Essays*, edited by George Steiner and Robert Fagles. Englewood Cliffs, N.J.: Prentice-Hall, 1962.

Praises Homer for his natural and realistic descriptions, for his musical hexameter, and for his emphasis upon the family.

Pucci, Pietro. *Odysseus Polutropos: Intertextual Readings in the "Odyssey" and the "Iliad."* Ithaca: Cornell University Press, 1987.

A challenging approach to the Homeric epics, based upon the theories of late twentieth century literary criticism, especially those of Jacques Derrida and Oswald Ducrot. Analyzes literary references and allusions to the *Iliad* in the *Odyssey*, including the themes of disguise and recognition, and suggests that the two poems present contrasting views of the hero and of poetry. Suggests that the two epics engage in a dialogue about truth, being, ethics, language, and other aspects of archaic Greek thought. Includes footnotes, a bibliography, and an index.

Redfield, James. Foreword to *The Best of the Achaeans: Concepts of the Hero in Archaic Greek Poetry*, by Gregory Nagy. Baltimore: The Johns Hopkins University Press, 1979.

Presents Nagy's book as a study in the ambiguous nature of the epic hero, about the tension between death and immortality, between heroic force and friendship, in the Homeric poems. Emphasizes Nagy's view of an epic worldview and of the *Iliad* as the mirror of a cultural institution in which there is an important link between ritual and the hero.

Rouse, W. H. D. "Homer as a Poet." In *Homer*. New York: Thomas Nelson and Sons, 1939.
An appreciation of natural poetry and language of Homer, similar to that of Geoffrey Chaucer and William Shakespeare. Using a simple grammar, vocabulary, and imagery, unlike the more artificial style of John Milton, Homer creates a variety of realistic characters. Detailed examination of Homer's treatment of the gods and his portrayal of such human characters as Odysseus, Penelope, Eurycleia, Eumaeus, Achilles, and Agamemnon.

_____. "Homer's Words." In *The Odyssey*, by Homer. New York: New American Library, 1937.
In this essay, which follows a prose translation of the epic, the translator discusses various features of Homer's language, including its natural simplicity, the language of the gods, and oral features such as formulas and epithets. The frequent Greek passages are all translated.

Scott, John A. "The *Odyssey*." In *Homer and His Influence*. Boston: Marshall Jones, 1925.
Despite the title, this essay is a comparison of the two Homeric poems. A list of memorable quotations from the *Odyssey* is included.

_____. "The Reach of His Genius." In *Homer and His Influence*. Boston: Marshall Jones, 1925.
A brief discussion of Homer's similes, religious elements, use of mythology, and ability to create a variety of character types.

Trypanis, C. A. "Epic Narrative Technique." In *The Homeric Epics*, translated by William Phelps. Warminster, England: Aris & Phillips, 1977.
Considers types of epic narrative, speeches, descriptions, similes, metaphors, the Homeric concept of time, and the poet's consideration for the audience.

_____. "The Poetic Achievement of the Homeric Epics." In *The Homeric Epics*, translated by William Phelps. Warminster, England: Aris & Phillips, 1977.
Attributes the poetic success of the poems to three factors: Homer's simple dramatic manner; the nobility and majesty given to the narrative by the hexameter verse form and the formal epic language; and the nobility and depth of Homer's sentiments.

Vivante, Paolo. "Homer and the Reader." In *Homer*. New Haven, Conn.: Yale University Press, 1985.
This essay is an introduction to Homer's use of imagery and description. The Homeric image of reality is seen as concrete and simple.

_____. "Nature." In *Homer*. New Haven, Conn.: Yale University Press, 1985.
In this discussion of Homer's descriptions of nature, the author does not view these similes as mere ornaments of oral composition but emphasizes the poet's own perception of reality. Nature is represented by Homer as a concrete, immediate experience.

_____. "Rose-Fingered Dawn and the Idea of Time." *Ramus* 2 (1979): 125-136. Reprinted in *Critical Essays on Homer* edited by Kenneth Atchity, Ron Hogart, and Doug Price. Boston: G. K. Hall, 1987.
An examination of occurrences of one of the most famous Homeric formulas. Homer's references to dawn are seen to reflect a concrete conception of time in which events take place not during an indefinite period but during a clear series of days.

_____. "The Story." In *Homer*. New Haven, Conn.: Yale University Press, 1985.
This introduction to Homer's narrative technique begins with brief summaries of the plots of the two Homeric epics and discusses such topics as the simplicity of plot, the large scale of the epics, their unity of action, Homer's sense of time, and his method of composition.

Whitman, Cedric H. "Image, Symbol, and Formula." In *Homer and the Homeric Tradition*. Cambridge, England: Harvard University Press, 1958. Reprinted in *Critical Essays on Homer*, edited by Kenneth Atchity, Ron Hogart, and Doug Price. Boston: G. K. Hall, 1987.
In this study of figurative language in the Homeric poems, the formulas and descriptions of Homer are seen to be part of an elaborate symbolic depiction of the hero and the structure of his world. Such passages as the wild description of Odysseus' landing in Phaeacia in *Odyssey* 6 and references to Patroclus as "equal to the gods" in the *Iliad* are shown to create links between formulas and the action of the epics.

Woodhouse, W. J. "The Exordium." In *The Composition of Homer's "Odyssey."* Oxford, England: Clarendon Press, 1930.
A comparison of the invocations at the beginning of the two Homeric poems shows how the *Iliad*'s invocation effectively summarizes the plot while that of the *Odyssey* does not. Concludes that the invocation to the *Odyssey* was not designed to introduce the poem in its present form.

_____. "The Structure and Method of the *Odyssey*." In *The Composition of Homer's "Odyssey."* Oxford, England: Clarendon Press, 1930.

Compares the compositional structures of the two Homeric epics. Shows how novelty of invention is achieved in the *Odyssey* by the use of complicated flash-back techniques while events in the *Iliad* are recounted in a simpler chronological order.

Comparative Character Studies of the *Iliad* and the *Odyssey*

Atchity, Kenneth John. "Helen and Her Galaxy: 1." In *Homer's "Iliad": The Shield of Memory*. Carbondale: Southern Illinois University Press, 1978.
Helen's image in both Homeric poems is an ambiguous blend of disorder and order on both divine and human levels. Artifacts such as Aphrodite's robe and Paris' bed link Helen with other characters and clarify her role in the epic. Helen is seen to be a human form of the divine Aphrodite; both females represent, simultaneously, fertility and barrenness, love and war.

Bloom, Harold. Introduction to *Homer's "Odyssey,"* edited by Harold Bloom. Edgemont, Pa.: Chelsea House, 1988.
In this short essay introducing a collection of interpretative studies of the *Odyssey*, the editor considers the basic differences between the *Iliad* and the *Odyssey* to be reflected in the personalities of their two heroes. Achilles is an isolated, single-minded hero while Odysseus is a realistic man of the world. Passing comparisons to the hero of James Joyce's *Ulysses*, to Dante Alighieri's Ulysses, and to other literary figures.

Camps, W. A. "Characterization." In *An Introduction to Homer*. New York: Oxford University Press, 1980.
A brief survey of the Homeric technique of character portrayal. In addition to the main characters, Achilles and Odysseus, the author discusses several secondary characters.

Clay, Jenny Strauss. "Odysseus." In *The Wrath of Athena: Gods and Men in the "Odyssey."* Princeton, N.J.: Princeton University Press, 1983. Reprinted in abridged form as "Odysseus: Name and Helmet," in *Homer's "Odyssey,"* edited by Harold Bloom. Edgemont, Pa.: Chelsea House, 1988.
Examines the multiplicity of Odysseus' character in Homeric epic from several perspectives. Links the naming of Odysseus in *Odyssey* 19 with the description of his boar-tooth helmet in *Iliad* 10 in order to explain Odysseus' heritage of deception from his maternal grandfather Autolycus and his thematic ties with Meriones, a previous owner of the helmet. Shows how Odysseus earns the status of best of the Greeks through competitive relationships with other heroes, especially with Achilles in the song of Demodocus in *Odyssey* 8 and with Heracles through his identification with a great bow. Suggests that Odysseus reveals

his ability to act with intelligence and self-restraint against the subhuman Cyclops, who, like the Phaeacians, lives near the gods.

Finley, John H., Jr. "Characterization and Theme." In *Homer's "Odyssey."* Cambridge, Mass.: Harvard University Press, 1978.
Homer's portrayal of Odysseus is used to illustrate how characterization in the *Odyssey* is determined by plot and theme, how character conforms to the story rather than vice versa. The theme of the poem is seen to be the sobering retrospection of the old, experienced hero. Frequent comparisons with scenes from the *Iliad*.

_____. "The Heroic Mind." Excerpted from *Four Stages of Greek Thought*. Stanford, Calif.: Stanford University Press, 1966. Reprinted in *The Odyssey*, by Homer, edited by Albert Cook. New York: W. W. Norton, 1974.
The traditional oral language of Homer is seen to reflect an unfaltering confidence in an outer reality. Achilles and Odysseus, the main characters of both epics, sum up the whole Trojan tradition.

Frame, Douglas. "Achilles." In *The Myth of Return in Early Greek Epic*. New Haven, Conn.: Yale University Press, 1978.
The character of Achilles in the Homeric poems is seen to present the antithesis of the linguistic link between the Greek noun *nóos* ("mind") and the verb *néomai* ("to return home") associated with Odysseus. Unlike the hero of the *Odyssey* Achilles has neither mind nor homecoming.

_____. "Nestor." In *The Myth of Return in Early Greek Epic*. New Haven: Yale University Press, 1978.
Linguistic features of Homeric references to Nestor reveal a connection between the Greek noun *nóos* ("mind") and the verb *néomai* ("to return home") which suggests that the Homeric Nestor is a purely mythological figure and is not based upon a historical king of Pylus.

Michalopoulos, Andre. "Two Heroes Compared; the Women of Homer." In *Homer*. Boston: Twayne, 1966.
This chapter is a short comparison of the two major heroes of the Homeric epics. Despite their many differences, both Achilles and Odysseus are seen to share a belief in the inevitability of fate. This essay ends with some comments upon the status of women in Homer.

Perry, Walter Copland. "Andromache." In *The Women of Homer*. London: William Heinemann, 1898.
Considers not only the role of Andromache, the wife of Hector, in the *Iliad* but also that of Helen, Menelaus' wife, who appears in both Homeric epics.

_____. "Aphrodite." In *The Women of Homer*. London: William Heinemann, 1898.
Examines the personalities and roles of Aphrodite, the Greek goddess of love, and of Artemis, the Greek goddess of the hunt, in the Homeric epics. Includes some untranslated foreign language quotations.

_____. "Athene." In *The Women of Homer*. London: William Heinemann, 1898.
A brief examination of the personality and the role of the Greek goddess of war and wisdom in the Homeric epics.

_____. "The Demi-Goddesses or Nymphs—Calypso, Kirke (Circe), Thetis." In *The Women of Homer*. London: William Heinemann, 1898.
Considers the important and beneficent roles which these three minor goddesses play in the lives of Odysseus and Achilles, the heroes of the two Homeric epics. Has some untranslated foreign language quotations.

_____. "Hekabe." In *The Women of Homer*. London: William Heinemann, 1898.
Actually considers not only the role of Hecuba, the mother of Hector, in the *Iliad* but also that of Nausicaa, the daughter of Alcinous, in the *Odyssey*. Compares the Homeric Nausicaa to the later versions of Sophocles and of Johann Wolfgang von Goethe.

_____. "Helen—continued." In *The Women of Homer*. London: William Heinemann, 1898.
A discussion of various views of Helen outside the Homeric tradition leads to an examination of the personality and role of Penelope, the wife of Odysseus.

Stanford, W. B. "The Grandson of Autolycus." In *The Ulysses Theme: A Study in the Adaptability of a Traditional Hero*. 2d ed. Ann Arbor: University of Michigan Press, 1968.
Considers the evidence for a pre-Homeric Odysseus, especially in early folklore, and discusses the significance of the hero's relationship with his wily maternal grandfather, Autolycus, from whom Odysseus inherits a reputation for lying and deceiving. While the Odysseus of the *Odyssey* is a cunning hero, the *Iliad* often depicts a more restrained and prudent hero who constantly strives to avoid a reputation for cleverness. Suggests that Homer portrayed the hero as a noble liar but recognized the potential danger of Odysseus' resourceful character.

_____. "The Untypical Hero." In *The Ulysses Theme: A Study in the Adaptability of a Traditional Hero*. 2d ed. Ann Arbor: University of Michigan Press, 1968. Reprinted in *Homer: A Collection of Critical Essays*, edited by

George Steiner and Robert Fagles. Englewood Cliffs, N.J.: Prentice-Hall, 1962. Also reprinted in *Twentieth Century Interpretations of the "Odyssey,"* edited by Howard W. Clarke. Englewood Cliffs, N.J.: Prentice-Hall, 1983.
An examination of the personality of Odysseus in both Homeric poems reveals significant deviations from the heroic norm. Odysseus stands out in such areas as his physical appearance, his frequent reference to food, his interest in archery, his rhetorical technique, his lack of prudence, and his intellectual curiosity.

Vivante, Paolo. "Characters." In *Homer*. New Haven, Conn.: Yale University Press, 1985.
The concreteness of Homer's characterizations is illustrated by studies of Ajax, Hector, Achilles, Diomedes, Agamemnon, and Helen in the *Iliad* and of Odysseus and Penelope in the *Odyssey*.

Whitman, Cedric H. "The Heroic Paradox." In *The Heroic Paradox*, edited by Charles Segal. Ithaca, N.Y.: Cornell University Press, 1982.
Examines the concept of the hero in the Homeric epics and in Greek drama. Achilles is said to portray to its full tragic effect the heroic paradox of mortal aspiration to divine qualities while Odysseus represents a new, more human hero who rejects the divine and asserts the moral and social values of humanity.

_____. "The *Odyssey* and Change." In *Homer and the Homeric Tradition*. Cambridge, Mass.: Harvard University Press, 1958. Slightly abridged in *Twentieth Century Interpretations of the "Odyssey,"* edited by Howard W. Clarke. Englewood Cliffs, N.J.: Prentice-Hall, 1983.
Suggests that the circular, geometric structure of the *Iliad* is an older epic pattern than the linear, progressive structure found in the *Odyssey*. Illustrates several geometric patterns, especially scenic antithesis and framing patterns, in certain parts of the *Odyssey*, that is, the adventures of Odysseus in books 9-12 and the Phaeacian episode of book 8. This structural change, associated with the transition from Geometric to Proto-Attic art, suggests to Whitman that the *Odyssey* was composed later than the *Iliad*.

The *Iliad*

Greek Text and Commentaries

Clark, Frank Lowry. *A Study of the "Iliad" in Translation*. Chicago: University of Chicago Press, 1927.

This abridged verse translation of the epic includes introductions and summaries of each book and commentary on significant passages. Includes an introduction, bibliography, and index.

Edwards, Mark W. *Homer: Poet of the "Iliad."* Baltimore: The Johns Hopkins University Press, 1987.
The second half of this book consists of a commentary on the ten books of the *Iliad* which the author considers most important. Each of these books is discussed according to its structural and thematic sections. Plot summaries for all twenty-four books are included, and suggestions for further reading are added after each book. Contains an introduction, afterword, bibliography, and index.

Hogan, James C. *A Guide to the "Iliad."* Garden City, N.Y.: Anchor Books, 1979.
This commentary, meant to accompany Robert Fitzgerald's translation of the *Iliad*, is arranged according to the Homeric book divisions and retains Fitzgerald's book titles. A plot summary of each book is followed by some general comments about the book and by a line-by-line commentary with explanation of obscure names and allusions. Contains a foreword by Robert Fitzgerald, a preface, an introduction, a bibliography, a map, and indexes.

Homer. *The Iliad.* 2 vols. Cambridge, Mass.: Harvard University Press, 1924.
This edition of the Greek text in the Loeb Classical Library is accompanied, on facing pages, by an English translation by A. T. Murray plus an introduction, bibliography, and index of Greek words.

Kirk, Geoffrey S. *The "Iliad": A Commentary.* Vol. 1, *Books 1-4.* New York: Cambridge University Press, 1985.
This first of a four-part scholarly commentary on the *Iliad* goes from the beginning of the poem to the encounter between Paris and Menelaus and the other battle scenes in *Iliad* 4. The line-by-line entries include explanations about individual Greek words, background, structure, and themes. Although this commentary is written especially for the Homeric scholar and untranslated Greek is used extensively, there are many features useful to the general reader. These include periodic plot summaries, the extensive introductions and summaries for the catalogues of Greeks and Trojans in book 2, and the series of four introductory essays on the Homeric question and the composition of the *Iliad*, the structure of Homeric verse, the contributions of Alexandrian scholars to the text of the poem, and background to *Iliad* 1-4. Contains three maps and an index.

Leaf, Walter. *A Companion to the "Iliad" for English Readers.* New York: Macmillan, 1892.
This commentary was designed to accompany the translation by Andrew Lang, Walter Leaf, and Ernest Myers. Marginal numbers refer to pages and lines in

this translation. The commentary on each book begins with a general overview and a discussion of various aspects of the book. Provides background and explanation of various words and phrases found in the translation. A large portion of the discussion is devoted to the Homeric question and to Leaf's analytic theories. Includes an introduction, index, and diagram of Achilles' shield.

Owen, E. T. *The Story of the "Iliad."* Ann Arbor: University of Michigan Press, 1966.
This book is a running commentary on the poem, with separate chapters on each book except *Iliad* 23 and 24, which are discussed together. It is a poetic analysis with particular attention to how the story is told, to the artistic purpose of particular scenes, and to the unity of the epic. Includes some untranslated Greek words, an introduction, and footnotes.

Wilcock, Malcolm M. *A Companion to the "Iliad."* Chicago: University of Chicago Press, 1976.
This commentary, based upon the translation by Richmond Lattimore, is arranged according to the Homeric book divisions. A short plot summary of each book is followed by line-by-line commentary on names and phrases. Also includes a preface, three maps, two charts, four appendices, a bibliography, and an index. One appendix provides a brief history of the text and ancient commentaries on the epic and information on the scholia and modern editions.

Translations

Butler, Samuel. *The "Iliad" of Homer Rendered into English Prose.* London: Longmans, Green, 1898. 2d ed. New York: E. P. Dutton, 1925.
This free prose translation of the *Iliad* by the author of *The Way of All Flesh* and *The Authoress of the "Odyssey"* is introduced by a brief plot summary. There are Greek line references on every page, a portrait of the translator, and a preface on his principles of translation. Latinized spellings of Greek names are used.

Clark, Frank Lowry. *A Study of the "Iliad" in Translation.* Chicago: University of Chicago Press, 1927.
The author accompanies his own abridged verse translation of the epic with connecting narrative, commentary, introductions to the various books, and modern literary parallels. Includes an introduction, bibliography, and index.

Homer. *The Anger of Achilles.* Translated by Robert Graves, illustrated by Ronald Searle. Garden City, N.Y.: Doubleday, 1959.

In his translation of Homer's *Iliad*, Graves, a well-known British poet and translator, replaces Homer's hexameters with a combination of prose for narrative passages and lyric for such occasions as prayers, divine messages, and dirges. Some footnotes are incorporated into the text. Headings are provided for each book. Includes an introduction by the translator plus fourteen illustrations.

_____. *The Iliad*. Translated by George Chapman. Vol. 1 in *Chapman's Homer*, edited by Allardyce Nicoll. 2d ed. Princeton, N.J.: Princeton University Press, 1967.
This translation, immortalized in a poem by John Keats, first appeared in various forms between 1598 and 1614. Chapman's Elizabethan translation uses a rare meter called a fourteener, retains the original spelling of the period, and includes a dedication, comments to the reader, and commentaries at the end of eleven books. Some foreign phrases are not translated. This edition includes texts of three separate translations by Chapman, an introduction, an illustration, textual notes, editor's commentary, and a glossary.

_____. *The Iliad*. Translated by Robert Fitzgerald. Garden City, N.Y.: Anchor Books, 1974.
This verse translation of the epic by a well-known translator of the *Odyssey* uses Greek spellings of names and indicates Greek line references at the top of every page. A short, descriptive title is added to each book. A translator's note is appended.

_____. *The Iliad*. Translated by Andrew Lang, Walter Leaf, and Ernest Myers. 2d ed. New York: Macmillan, 1923.
Each translator is responsible for a prose translation of several consecutive books of the epic. Each book begins with a plot summary. Book and line references to the original Greek text appear at the top of every page. Uses Greek spelling of names and includes notes.

_____. *The Iliad*. Translated by Richmond Lattimore. Chicago: University of Chicago Press, 1951.
In this verse translation, Lattimore aims to capture the speed, rhythm, and meaning of the Greek original. Line references to the original Greek appear in five-line increments. Uses Greek spelling of names. Includes a glossary of names, foreword, and introduction by the translator.

_____. *The Iliad*. Translated by A. T. Murray. 2 vols. Cambridge, Mass.: Harvard University Press, 1924.
The chief advantage of this prose translation, written in the formal language of England in the Victorian age, is the facing Greek text, which allows for ready

comparison of original and translation. Uses Latinized spelling of Greek names. Includes an introduction, bibliography, and index of Greek words.

_____. *The Iliad*. Translated by Alexander Pope. New York: A. L. Burt, 1902.
Originally published in 1720, this translation in rhymed couplets by an important eighteenth century English poet has had great influence on later readers. Even in the twentieth century it has been considered one of the best translations of the epic. The translator provides each book with thematic titles as well as a detailed plot summary. A concluding note summarizes events following the *Iliad* and the Trojan war. Latinized spelling of Greek names. Includes an introduction, a preface and footnotes.

_____. *Iliad*. Translated by E. V. Rieu. Baltimore: Penguin Books, 1950.
This prose translation adds a short descriptive title at the beginning of each book. Greek line references at the top of every page. Generally uses Greek spellings of names. Includes an introduction and a glossary that is divided into three lists: Greeks, Trojans, and gods.

_____. *Iliad*. Translated by W. H. D. Rouse. New York: New American Library, 1938.
This straightforward prose translation adds an elaborate descriptive title at the beginning of each book. Uses Greek spellings of names. Includes a preface and a pronunciation guide for Greek names in the index.

_____. *Iliad*. Translated by William Benjamin Smith and Walter Miller. New York: Macmillan, 1944.
This line-for-line English translation uses dactylic hexameter, the meter of the Homeric original. Each book is introduced by two verses from "Another Argument," which George Chapman attached to his translation of the *Iliad* of 1598-1614. Greek line references are included at the top of every page. Illustrated with twenty-six drawings by John Flaxman (1755-1826). Also contains an introduction, a note on the illustrations, and an index.

Background and Plot Summaries

Apollodorus. "The Trojan War (Epitome 3-5)." In *Gods and Heroes of the Greeks: The "Library" of Apollodorus*, translated by Michael Simpson. Amherst: University of Massachusetts Press, 1976.
This epitome, or summary, of Greek myths related to the Trojan war probably dates to the first century A.D. Begins with events connected with the calling of Greek forces at Aulis and the arrival of the Greeks at Troy, includes a paraphrase

of the plot of the *Iliad* and references to events following the end of the *Iliad*. Describes the story of the Trojan horse, the fall of the city, and the fate of the survivors. The book includes notes, a bibliography, and an index.

Camps, W. A. "The Story of the *Iliad* in Outline." In *An Introduction to Homer*. New York: Oxford University Press, 1980.
This chapter is a brief prose summary of the central plot of the epic.

Clark, Frank Lowry. "Analysis of the *Iliad*." In *A Study of the "Iliad" in Translation*. Chicago: University of Chicago Press, 1927.
This last chapter of an abridged verse translation of the epic is a detailed outline of the *Iliad*. Thematic division of each book with references to the original Greek line numbers.

Gayley, Charles Mills. "Houses Concerned in the Trojan War." In *The Classic Myths in English Literature and in Art*. 2d ed. New York: John Wiley & Sons, 1911.
Provides background to the families of several important characters in the *Iliad*: Achilles, Agamemnon, Menelaus, and Helen. Includes extensive quotation from Catullus 64, a poem about the marriage of Achilles' parents, Peleus and Thetis. Commentary section contains a genealogical chart and lists of works of art and literature based upon these myths. Includes a map and an illustration.

_____. "The Trojan War." In *The Classic Myths in English Literature and in Art*. 2d ed. New York: John Wiley & Sons, 1911.
Summarizes the causes of the Trojan War, events connected with the departure of the Greeks for Troy, and the plot of the *Iliad*. Includes brief quotations from a variety of English translations of the *Iliad*. Commentary section contains a genealogical chart and lists of works of art and literature based upon these myths. Illustrated with reproductions of ancient Greek art.

Graves, Robert. *The Greek Myths*. 2 vols. Baltimore: Penguin Books, 1960.
Provides general background to myths connected with Troy and the Trojan War. The following are included: the foundation of Troy; the story of Hesione and the first sack of Troy by Heracles, mentioned in *Iliad* 5; the Judgment of Paris, the abduction of Helen by Paris, and other events leading to the Trojan War; the Greek gatherings at Aulis, with descriptions of the most important Greek warriors who fought at Troy; Odysseus' youth and marriage, the recruitment of Odysseus and Achilles for the war, and the sacrifice of Iphigenia; a summary of events from the arrival of the Greek forces at Troy through the beginning of the *Iliad*; the quarrel between Agamemnon and Achilles and a summary of the plot of the *Iliad*. Includes discussion about the identity of Homer and his source for the

Iliad. Homer's story of the ransom and funeral of Hector is supplemented by other versions.

Guerber, Hélène Adeline. "The Trojan War." In *Myths of Greece and Rome*. New York: American Book Company, 1895.
Describes the events leading up to the Trojan War, including the Judgment of Paris, the abduction of Helen, and the early life of Achilles, and summarizes the plot of the *Iliad* and subsequent events leading to the fall of Troy. Includes quotations from the *Iliad* and other literature, both ancient and modern, and also black and white reproductions of artwork representing these events. Uses both Latin and Greek names. Includes a map, genealogical table, glossary, and index.

Hamilton, Edith. "The Trojan War." In *Mythology*. New York: New American Library, 1942.
This essay complements a summary of the plot of the *Iliad* with background to the war from other ancient sources. The Judgment of Paris leads to the abduction of Helen and to war between the Greeks and Trojans. Includes illustrations, genealogical tables, and an index.

Morford, Mark P. O., and Robert J. Lenardon. "The Trojan Saga." In *Classical Mythology*. 3d ed. New York: Longman, 1985.
This section of a standard mythological handbook summarizes the events surrounding the Trojan War. There are sections on the children of Leda, Troy's early history, preparations for the war, the arrival of the Greeks at Troy, the war, the Trojan and Greek leaders, and the fall of Troy. Includes maps, genealogical charts, illustrations, and a select bibliography.

Rouse, W. H. D. "The Arms of Achilles." In *Gods, Heroes, and Men of Ancient Greece*. New York: New American Library, 1957.
A paraphrase of the main plot of the *Iliad*. Achilles' anger, the death of his friend Patroclus, and the manufacture of new arms for the hero are highlighted.

_____. "The *Iliad*." In *Homer*. New York: Thomas Nelson and Sons, 1939.
This paraphrase of the *Iliad* is preceded by background about the marriage of Peleus and Thetis, the Judgment of Paris, the abduction of Helen, and the outbreak of the Trojan War.

Schwab, Gustav. "Tales of Troy." In *Gods and Heroes: Myths and Epics of Ancient Greece*, translated by Olga Marx and Ernst Morwitz. New York: Pantheon Books, 1946.
A summary of the Trojan cycle of Greek myths, beginning with the building of Troy and ending with the destruction of the city. A detailed paraphrase of the plot of the *Iliad* is included.

Literary Studies

Atchity, Kenneth John. *Homer's "Iliad": The Shield of Memory*. Carbondale: Southern Illinois University Press, 1978.
This interpretative study of the *Iliad* uses artifacts, such as the shield of Achilles and the scepter of Agamemnon, in order to examine the action, characters, and symbolism of the poem. Looks in particular at the symbolic role of artifacts as gift exchanges, such as those between Ajax and Hector in *Iliad* 7 and between Glaucus and Diomedes in *Iliad* 6. Artifacts of warfare, such as Pandarus' bow, are used by Homer to underscore the *Iliad*'s theme of cosmic and human disorder. The theme of the *Iliad* is considered to be the tension between order and disorder on both cosmic and human planes. An appendix includes a chart illustrating the social hierarchy of the Iliadic world, in which action on the most communal level is considered the most noble and memorable. The hierarchy in the *Iliad* is briefly compared with earlier and later Greek social systems. Includes an introduction, appendices, an annotated bibliography, and indexes.

Austin, Norman. "The Function of Digressions in the *Iliad*." *Greek, Roman, and Byzantine Studies* 7 (1966): 295-312. Notes. Slightly simplified in *Essays on the "Iliad,"* edited by John Wright. Bloomington: Indiana University Press, 1978. Reprinted in *Homer*, edited by Harold Bloom. New York: Chelsea House, 1986. Various hortatory, apologetic, and paradigmatic digressions in the *Iliad*, especially those of Nestor, are seen to be forms of dramatic amplification. These digressions do not so much introduce new information or create suspense as much as they focus attention on a particular moment in time.

Bassett, Samuel Eliot. "The Breaking of the Epic Illusion: The Subjective Element— Description." In *The Poetry of Homer*. Berkeley: University of California Press, 1938.
Illustrates how Homer's third-person narrative is not entirely objective, that the subjectivity of the poet intrudes through various indirect ways, especially through descriptions. Detailed examination of the descriptions of Achilles' shield in *Iliad* 18 and of Achilles' pursuit of Hector in *Iliad* 22 in order to emphasize their subjective features and their poetic effects.

_____. "Homer the Poetic Demiurge." In *The Poetry of Homer*. Berkeley: University of California Press, 1938.
Discusses various types of Aristotelian unity and completeness in the Homeric poems, including the unity of individual episodes, the unity of each poem, and the unity of the two poems together. Then illustrates this unity in the *Iliad* by showing how the characters of Achilles, Hector, and Zeus pull the *Iliad* together. Also considers the function of the catalogues in *Iliad* 2, of the hero Diomedes, and of the gods.

Bespaloff, Rachel. "Poets and Prophets." In *On the "Iliad,"* translated by Mary McCarthy. New York: Pantheon Books, 1947.

In this essay on the violence of the *Iliad*, the author reflects on a comparison of biblical and Homeric ways of thinking. Ethics and metaphysics are seen to be linked in both the *Iliad* and the Bible, which both reject magic and philosophy in favor of an emphasis upon fate.

Beye, Charles Rowan. "The *Iliad*." In *The "Iliad," the "Odyssey," and the Epic Tradition*. Garden City, N.Y.: Doubleday, 1966.

A detailed plot summary and discussion of the structure and meaning of the epic, with particular attention to Homer's depiction of the Trojans. Achilles' angry isolation at the beginning of the epic is interpreted as a rejection of the heroic world and is seen to lead, at the end of the epic, to his final, heroic acceptance of humanity in the ransom scene with Priam at the end of the epic.

Bowra, C. M. "The *Iliad*: Its Shape and Character." In *Homer*. New York: Charles Scribner's Sons, 1972.

An analysis of the plot of the *Iliad* shows how the poem is a complex heroic story which blends the theme of the wrath of Achilles with the theme of the fate of Troy. Considers the role of the gods and the portrayal of heroes in the poem.

Cook, Albert. "The Signal Fires." In *The Classic Line: A Study in Epic Poetry*. Bloomington: Indiana University Press, 1966. Index.

Suggests that the use of contrast, both of characters and of events, is the principal poetic and unifying feature in an epic dominated simultaneously by single-minded violence and by complexity of motive. Examines various aspects of Homer's poetic style, including characterization, diction, sound, epithets, and similes. Considers the role of the gods in the epic and shows how the complex structure of the poem is reflected in Achilles' own contradictory character, in the contrast between his wrath and his nobility and between his violent slaughter of Hector and his subsequent pity for Hector's father, Priam.

Greene, Thomas. "The *Iliad*." In *The Descent from Heaven: A Study in Epic Continuity*. New Haven, Conn.: Yale University Press, 1963.

In this chapter of a book on the European epic tradition, Greene discusses Homer's treatment of the theme of divine descent in the *Iliad*. Various instances of this theme are used to consider such topics as fate, free will, grief, honor, and the relationship between gods and men in Homer.

Griffin, Jasper. "The *Iliad*." In *Homer*. New York: Hill & Wang, 1980.

Focuses on the *Iliad* as a heroic epic. Considers how the plot is organized around the theme of Achilles' anger and how the gods are involved in the action. Shows how Homer uses contrasting scenes to develop his main points, namely the clash of heroes and the tension between life and death. Homeric impartiality of description and the themes of noble acceptance of destiny and of the glorification of war are suggested as the main contributions of the *Iliad* to Western thought.

Havelock, Eric A. "The Homeric Encyclopedia." In *Preface to Plato*. Cambridge, Mass.: Harvard University Press, 1963.
Shows how the Homeric poems operate as a tribal encyclopedia containing the laws and customs upon which society is based. The didactic nature of the *Iliad* is illustrated through an analysis of Apollo's plague and the quarrel between Agamemnon and Achilles in book 1.

Hurwitt, Jeffrey M. "Formula and Foreground: Homer and the Dipylon Style." In *The Art and Culture of Early Greece: 1100–480 B.C.* Ithaca, N.Y.: Cornell University Press, 1985. Reprinted in *Homer's "The Iliad,"* edited by Harold Bloom. New York: Chelsea House, 1987.
Compares the artistic form of the Dipylon vase with the structure of the *Iliad*. An eighth century Greek sense of ordered sensibility has given both works their massive size, tight control of formulas, and strong sense of pattern, proportion, and symmetry.

Lang, Mabel L. "Reverberation and Mythology in the *Iliad*." In *Approaches to Homer*, edited by Carl A. Rubino and Cynthia A. Shelmerdine. Austin: University of Texas Press, 1983.
Considers the interaction between the *Iliad* and the poetic tradition of myths in which the epic was composed. An examination of references in the *Iliad* to various myths, especially those about the gods, suggests that for a long period of time the *Iliad* and the poetic tradition borrowed and reworked each other's themes.

Littleton, C. Scott. "Some Possible Indo-European Themes in the *Iliad*." In *Myth and Law Among the Indo-Europeans*, edited by Jaan Puhvel. Berkeley: University of California Press, 1970. Reprinted in *Critical Essays on Homer*, edited by Kenneth Atchity, Ron Hogart, and Doug Price. Boston: G. K. Hall, 1987.
Demonstrates how Georges Dumézil's theories of the tripartite ideology of Indo-European mythology can be applied to the principal characters and events in the *Iliad*.

Lynn-George, Michael. *Epos: Word, Narrative, and the "Iliad."* Atlantic Highlands, N.J.: Humanities Press International, 1988.
This study of the *Iliad* and its narrative structure moves from Erich Auerbach's study of Homeric narrative and from Milman Parry's theory of oral language to

the linguistic theories of Jacques Derrida and Mikhail Bakhtin in pursuit of a reading of the *Iliad* as a complex and multifaceted text. The structure of the *Iliad*, traced throughout the twenty-four books, is seen to be a complex narrative of recurring loss and return, of death and recompense. The narrative functions in a temporal ambiguity between present and past, between now and never, between death and epic immortality. Includes endnotes, a bibliography, and indexes.

MacCary, W. Thomas. "Theme: Theoretical Statement." In *Childlike Achilles: Ontogeny and Phylogeny in the "Iliad."* New York: Columbia University Press, 1982.
The first part of a psychoanalytical study of the *Iliad* as an expression of an "Achilles complex," a preoccupation with the ego and its struggle with the "other" expressed not only in the person of Achilles but also in the development of every male child. Suggests that the timeless appeal of Achilles is based upon this Freudian aspect of the hero and locates this interpretation of the poem in the context of other modern criticism, including the epistemology of Bruno Snell, the structuralism of James Redfield, the humanism of Cedric Whitman, and the orality of Milman Parry.

_____. "Variations: Textual Analysis." In *Childlike Achilles: Ontogeny and Phylogeny in the "Iliad."* New York: Columbia University Press, 1982.
The second part of a psychoanalytical study of the *Iliad*. Shows how the main theme of the poem, centering on the friendship between Achilles and Patroclus, can be expressed in terms of an "Achilles complex," a Freudian preoccupation of a male with himself and his relationship with other males. Uses passages from the *Iliad* to illustrate aspects of this complex in the poems, especially in such themes as the value of women, the role of the gods, narcissism, homosexuality, and the phenomenology of war.

Marshall, David. "Similes and Delay." In *Homer*, edited by Harold Bloom. New York: Chelsea House, 1986.
Considers how similes in the *Iliad* delay the epic narrative just as Achilles tries to postpone his destiny and the poet tries to stall the end of the narrative.

Mason, H. A. "Basic Structures of the First Book of the *Iliad*." In *To Homer Through Pope: An Introduction to Homer's "Iliad" and Pope's Translation.* New York: Harper & Row, 1972.
The structure of the book is a complex unity centered on the theme of wrath and based upon two elements of composition: deliberate parallelism between gods and men and a supple multiplicity of approach. Not all Greek phrases are translated.

_____. "Hector and Andromache." In *To Homer Through Pope: An Introduction to Homer's "Iliad" and Pope's Translation*. New York: Harper & Row, 1972.
The greatness of the *Iliad* is based on its complex concept of heroism. The pattern for this essential structure of the entire *Iliad* is concentrated in varied moods of *Iliad* 6. John Dryden's and Alexander Pope's translations of the farewell scene between Hector and Andromache in *Iliad* 6 are compared.

Mayerson, Philip. "The Trojan War." In *Classical Mythology in Literature, Art, and Music*. Lexington, Mass.: Xerox College Publishing, 1971.
This summary of the ancient Greek myths connected with the Trojan War includes a paraphrase of the plot of the *Iliad* together with references to later literary and artistic treatments of these themes.

Michalopoulos, Andre. "The *Iliad*." In *Homer*. Boston: Twayne, 1966.
Following a summary of the plot of the epic, the author discusses Homeric realism, similes, and descriptions and then considers Homer's use of anthropomorphic gods in order to develop the inner emotions of the heroic characters.

_____. "The Triple Tragedy of the *Iliad*." In *Homer*. Boston: Twayne, 1966.
The epic is presented not only as the tragedy of Achilles, whose wrath leads to the death of his best friend, Patroclus, but also as the tragedy of the House of Troy, seen especially through the eyes of Hector, Andromache, and Priam. The third tragedy of the epic is that of man in conflict with fate.

Mueller, Martin. *The Iliad*. Boston: Allen & Unwin, 1984.
Assumes that this Homeric poem can be interpreted according to the same techniques used for other major literary works. Offers background to the poem, surveys various narrative and thematic aspects, and suggests a general interpretation of the poem. There are chapters on the plot and structure of the poem, battle scenes, similes, the role of the gods, the way the *Iliad* was composed, and the later life of the poem. Includes a bibliography and index.

_____. "The Simile." In *The Iliad*. Boston: Allen & Unwin, 1984. Abridged in *Homer*, edited by Harold Bloom. New York: Chelsea House, 1986. Examines the narrative function and content of similes in the *Iliad*. Study of lion similes and contrast similes shows the relationship between the simile and its narrative context. Includes a brief comparison of Homeric similes with those of Vergil, Dante Alighieri, and John Milton.

Murray, Gilbert. "The *Iliad* as a Great Poem." In *The Rise of the Greek Epic*. 3d ed. Oxford, England: Clarendon Press, 1924.

In this general appreciation of the *Iliad*, a great British classical scholar of the early twentieth century considers some common criticisms of the *Iliad*, including its second-rate subject, its lack of finish, and its fixed descriptions and similes, and suggests that these apparent flaws in the poem are a result of viewing the *Iliad* according to the standards of modern literature instead of those of traditional poetry. Compares the *Iliad* with the Old Testament and discusses the special intensity of imagination which makes such traditional books so appealing.

Nagler, Michael N. "The 'Eternal Return' in the Plot Structure of *The Iliad*." In *Spontaneity and Tradition: A Study in the Oral Art of Homer*. Berkeley: University of California Press, 1974.
Shows how the structure of the *Iliad* can be understood in terms of a triple sequence of the archetypal pattern of withdrawal, devastation, and return. The first sequence is broken in *Iliad* 9 by the abortive embassy scene and the second in *Iliad* 19 by Achilles' fury following the death of Patroclus. The theme of Achilles' return operates within a critical association of disorder with the loss of military responsibilities and an inability to convene assemblies. Includes some untranslated Greek.

Nagy, Gregory. "Beyond Epic." In *The Best of the Achaeans: Concepts of the Hero in Archaic Greek Poetry*. Baltimore: The Johns Hopkins University Press, 1979.
Uses the themes of scapegoat and purification in archaic Greek poetry in order to show the links between the image of hero as warrior and the hero as poet. Links the traditional lives of the poets Aesop and Archilochus with the portrayal of Achilles as a hero in the *Iliad*. Presents the religious aspects of Achilles' heroic nature in the context of Indo-European culture, including parallels in Indo-Iranian religion and epic.

_____. "Poetic Visions of Immortality." In *The Best of the Achaeans: Concepts of the Hero in Archaic Greek Poetry*. Baltimore: The Johns Hopkins University Press, 1979. Reprinted as "Poetic Visions of Immortality for the Hero," in *Homer*, edited by Harold Bloom. New York: Chelsea House, 1986. Also reprinted in *Homer's "The Iliad,"* edited by Harold Bloom. New York: Chelsea House, 1987.
An examination of the diction used in reference to the life span of a hero in the poetry of Homer, Simonides, Pindar, and the Homeric hymn to Demeter. Homeric references to Achilles are compared to the image of Phaëthon in Hesiod. The vocabulary used in this poetry shows that the immortality of the hero is based upon religious cult, a cultural institution connected with the natural process of death. Greek words are deleted in reprints.

Page, Denys L. "Some Mycenaean Relics in the *Iliad*." In *History and the Homeric "Iliad."* Berkeley: University of California Press, 1959.

Outlines several features of oral composition and of Homeric formulas in the *Iliad* and suggests that many formulaic phrases in Homer are probably Mycenaean survivals. Includes close study of specific formulas and comparison with the actual objects they describe, such as Mycenaean armor.

Pope, Alexander. "Preface." In *The Iliad*, by Homer. New York: A. L. Burt, 1902. Excerpted in *The Poets on the Classics: An Anthology of English Poets' Writing on the Classical Poets and Dramatists from Chaucer to the Present*, edited by Stuart Gillespie. New York: Routledge, 1988.
In this introduction to his translation, originally published in 1720, Pope illustrates Homer's superior poetic ability through his amazing invention and simplicity in regard to narrative, character portrayal, description, and language.

Post, L. A. "The Tragic Pattern of the *Iliad*." In *From Homer to Menander: Forces in Greek Poetic Fiction*. Berkeley: University of California Press, 1951.
While the *Odyssey* is considered an Aristotelian comedy of manners, the *Iliad* is interpreted as a study in the tragedy of human existence. Evaluates the moral character of Paris and Helen, examines Homer's portrayal of the gods and their relationship with humans, and outlines the double tragedies of Achilles and Hector.

Redfield, James M. "Landscape and Simile." In *Homer*, edited by Harold Bloom. New York: Chelsea House, 1986.
In this excerpt from *Nature and Culture in the "Iliad": The Tragedy of Hector*, Redfield notes how Homeric similes are dominated by references to *agrou ep' eschatien*, "the land beyond the limit of agriculture," a world of nature which becomes in the epic an image of the battlefield separating the Homeric hero from his community.

_____. Nature and Culture in *The "Iliad": The Tragedy of Hector*. Chicago: University of Chicago Press, 1975.
In this book, Redfield works from the structuralism of Claude Lévi-Strauss and from an interpretation of Aristotle's *Poetics* in order to study the *Iliad* as a unified work of art and Homeric society as a unified cultural system. Two chapters on such Aristotelian concepts as poetic imitation, catharsis, and the nature of tragedy lead to chapters on the hero, error, and purification in the *Iliad*. Achilles and Hector, as warriors, are seen to experience a basic social tension between nature and culture, individual and community, purity and impurity, and reality and art. Includes endnotes, a bibliography, and indexes.

Schein, Seth L. "The Poetic Tradition." In *The Mortal Hero: An Introduction to Homer's "Iliad."* Berkeley: University of California Press, 1984.

An introduction to the structure, traditional form, and mythology of the *Iliad*. The first section describes the meter, formulaic diction, and oral composition of the epic. The second examines the traditional tales upon which the Homeric poem is based. The last section analyzes the structural symmetry of the epic. There is also an appendix on the relationship between the *Iliad* and the *Odyssey*.

_____. "War, Death, and Heroism." In *The Mortal Hero: An Introduction to Homer's "Iliad."* Berkeley: University of California Press, 1984.
Examines the portrayal of death in the *Iliad* and suggests that the poem is not so much a study of death as of mortality, that the beauty and value of human existence is based upon the quest for heroism in the face of mortality.

Scott, John A. "The *Iliad*." In *Homer and His Influence*. Boston: Marshall Jones, 1925.
This essay contains a collection of memorable quotations from the *Iliad*. Running comments by the author show how the poet expresses striking ideas in a few words.

Silk, M. S. "The Poem." In *Homer: The "Iliad."* London: Cambridge University Press, 1987.
Includes a plot summary and comments upon various poetic aspects of the poem. Compares several translations of the epic, considers the style, characterization, and portrayal of gods and heroes in the *Iliad* and concludes that the poem is a balance of such opposites as stylization and immediacy.

Van Doren, Mark. *The Noble Voice*. New York: Henry Holt, 1946.
Ten long poems in the Western poetic tradition are the focus of this book by an important twentieth century American poet and novelist. Besides Homer, the works of Lucretius, Vergil, John Milton, Dante Alighieri, Edmund Spenser, William Shakespeare, George Gordon, Lord Byron, and William Wordsworth are discussed. Van Doren focuses upon the poetic energy of the *Iliad* and, especially, upon the vivacity of its characters.

Weil, Simone. "The *Iliad*: Or, The Poem of Force." From *The "Iliad": Or, The Poem of Force*, translated by Mary McCarthy. Wallingford, Pa.: Pendle Hill, 1945. In *Homer*, edited by Harold Bloom. New York: Chelsea House, 1986. Also reprinted in *Critical Essays on Homer*, edited by Kenneth Atchity, Ron Hogart, and Doug Price. Boston: G. K. Hall, 1987.
In this poetic essay, which argues that the true hero of the epic poem is force, Weil also considers the effects of this force upon individuals.

Whitman, Cedric H. "Fire and Other Elements." In *Homer and the Heroic Tradition*. Cambridge, Mass.: Harvard University Press, 1958. Reprinted in *Homer:*

A Collection of Critical Essays, edited by George Steiner and Robert Fagles. Englewood Cliffs, N.J.: Prentice-Hall, 1962. Also reprinted in *Homer*, edited by Harold Bloom. New York: Chelsea House, 1986.
The author studies the use of fire in the *Iliad* as a symbol for such themes as death, sacrifice, energy, and stress. Other elements, such as the sea, the winds, and the clouds, are also discussed. Includes structural charts.

_____. "Geometric Structure of the *Iliad*." In *Homer and the Homeric Tradition*. Cambridge, Mass.: Harvard University Press, 1958.
The artistic symmetry of Geometric vase design is here seen to be the structural basis of the *Iliad*. The use of circularity and framing by balanced similarity in the epic is illustrated by means of several charts.

Wilcock, Malcolm M. "Methods of Fighting in the *Iliad*." In *A Companion to the "Iliad."* Chicago: University of Chicago Press, 1976.
This appendix to a commentary on the *Iliad* considers such topics as Homeric armor, types of battle, and descriptions of wounds.

Wright, John. *Essays on the "Iliad."* Bloomington: Indiana University Press, 1978.
Eight scholarly essays about various aspects of the *Iliad* are reprinted here for the general reader. Greek quotations have been replaced by English translations, and Greek words have been transliterated. Includes a brief introduction by the editor, a selected bibliography, and endnotes.

Character Studies

Atchity, Kenneth John. "The Central Weaving." In *Homer's "Iliad": The Shield of Memory*. Carbondale: Southern Illinois University Press, 1978.
The image of Helen's loom and her description of the Greek warriors in *Iliad* 3 associate her with the epic singer and illustrate her triple role in the epic as a knower of names, the recorder of human events, and an agent of poetic inspiration.

_____. "Helen and Her Galaxy: 2." In *Homer's "Iliad": The Shield of Memory*. Carbondale: Southern Illinois University Press, 1978.
The roles of Priam, Hector, and Andromache are compared with that of Helen in the *Iliad*. In the ransom scene of *Iliad* 24, Priam is seen to reestablish order by an emphasis on family. Hector's helmet, Andromache's loom and headdress, and Hector's funeral bier link the hero and his family with Helen in the symbolism of order and disorder.

_____. "Hephaistos and the Galaxy of Achilles: 1." In *Homer's "Iliad": The Shield of Memory*. Carbondale: Southern Illinois University Press, 1978.
Through his association with marriage and fire, Hephaestus is seen in the *Iliad* to represent on the divine level the cosmic order for which Achilles stands on the human level. Athena's role in the *Iliad* and her aegis link this goddess also with the cosmic order.

_____. "Hephaistos and the Galaxy of Achilles: 2." In *Homer's "Iliad": The Shield of Memory*. Carbondale: Southern Illinois University Press, 1978.
Through his cup described in *Iliad* 11 and his role throughout the poem as an arbitrator, Nestor is linked with the goal of cosmic order, which the *Iliad* seeks. The shields of Diomedes and Ajax are also discussed as images of order and unity in the Greek army.

_____. "Horses in the *Iliad*." In *Homer's "Iliad": The Shield of Memory*. Carbondale: Southern Illinois University Press, 1978.
This appendix to a study of the theme of order and disorder in the *Iliad* considers Homer's treatment of horses and their importance in connection with major characters, especially Achilles. While Homer's knowledge of horses as animals of war is not always accurate, the poet successfully uses the animals to further the theme of social and cosmic harmony.

_____. "The Identity of Achilles." In *Homer's "Iliad": The Shield of Memory*. Carbondale: Southern Illinois University Press, 1978.
Traces the step-by-step development of Achilles' attitudes throughout the *Iliad*. The hero gradually moves from animosity toward Agamemnon to hatred for Hector and Troy and, finally, to union with Agamemnon, Priam, and humanity at large. By the end of the epic, the angry hero of *Iliad* 1 becomes a fully humanized character linked thematically in several ways with the god Hephaestus and with the epic poet as a creator of social and cosmic order.

_____. "The Queen of the Gods and the King of Men." In *Homer's "Iliad": The Shield of Memory*. Carbondale: Southern Illinois University Press, 1978.
Through her seduction of Zeus in *Iliad* 14, Hera is shown to be a symbol of disorder on the divine plane while Agamemnon's association with his armor and scepter show the king to be a symbol of disorder on the human plane.

Bespaloff, Rachel. "Hector." In *On the "Iliad,"* translated by Mary McCarthy. New York: Pantheon Books, 1947. Reprinted in *Critical Essays on Homer*, edited by Kenneth Atchity, Ron Hogart, and Doug Price. Boston: G. K. Hall, 1987.
Contrasts Hector, the resistance hero, with Achilles, the revenge hero. The duel between these two heroes, rather than the anger of Achilles, is seen to be the central theme of the epic.

_____. "Helen." In *On the "Iliad,"* translated by Mary McCarthy. New York: Pantheon Books, 1947. Reprinted in *Homer: A Collection of Critical Essays*, edited by George Steiner and Robert Fagles. Englewood Cliffs, N.J.: Prentice-Hall, 1962.

Helen's critical attitude toward her Trojan consort, Paris, is contrasted with her affection for her brother-in-law, Hector, and she is seen to be a victim of beauty. Beauty is another form of the destructive force upon which this poem is seen to be based.

_____. "Thetis and Achilles." In *On the "Iliad,"* translated by Mary McCarthy. New York: Pantheon Books, 1947.

In this short essay, the author analyzes the relationship between the hero and his mother. The affection shared by Achilles and Thetis is seen to be an affirmation of the power of love to subdue even the hero of force.

Gransden, K. W. "Prologue: Homer's *Iliad*." In *Virgil's "Iliad": An Essay on Epic Narrative*. Cambridge, England: Cambridge University Press, 1984.

An interesting comparison of Achilles to the portrayal of Napoleon in Leo Tolstoy's novel *War and Peace*. Both characters are said to display simultaneously the contradictory qualities of complete free will and absolute predestination.

King, Katherine Callen. "The Archetype. Homer's Achilles." In *Achilles: Paradigms of the War Hero from Homer to the Middle Ages*. Berkeley: University of California Press, 1987.

The varied Homeric portraits of Achilles as the most complex, the best in speed and beauty, and the most brutal and bloody of the Greek warriors at Troy are traced in the plot of the *Iliad*. Also a study of Achilles' *timê* ("honor") and *kleos* ("glory") in the *Iliad* and the *Odyssey*.

Michalopoulos, Andre. "Achilles' Shield, Character, Reflections." In *Homer*. Boston: Twayne, 1966.

Except for a brief discussion of Achilles' shield, this essay mainly contains comments about the role of various characters in the epic, including Agamemnon, Odysseus, Diomedes, Paris, Glaucus, Hecuba, and Helen.

Mueller, Martin. "Knowledge and Delusion in the *Iliad*." *Mosaic* 3 (1970): 86-103. Revised in *Essays on the "Iliad,"* edited by John Wright. Bloomington: Indiana University Press, 1978.

In separate sections, the author considers the different levels of heroic knowledge illustrated by several characters, including Sarpedon protected by heroic maxims, Hector awakened at the moment of death from cruel disillusionment, and Achilles affected by the death of Patroclus. The role of the god Apollo as a bringer of death in the *Iliad* is then discussed.

Nagy, Gregory. "Hero of Epic, Hero of Cult." In *The Best of the Achaeans: Concepts of the Hero in Archaic Greek Poetry*. Baltimore: The Johns Hopkins University Press, 1979.
Considers the significance of Achilles' name and the deaths of Pyrrhus and of Hector as part of an examination of the nature of the epic hero and of Achilles' character in particular. Presents Achilles' heroic status as a tension between the mortal and the immortal in the context of the fourth generation of humankind described in Hesiod's *Works and Days*.

Parry, Adam. "The Language of Achilles." In *The Language and Background of Homer: Some Recent Studies and Controversies*, edited by Geoffrey S. Kirk. Cambridge, England: W. Heffer & Sons, 1964. Also reprinted in *Homer*, edited by Harold Bloom. New York: Chelsea House, 1986.
An examination of the language used by Achilles reveals a barrier between seeming and being, between the mind of the hero and his formalized language. The hero is shown to be someone who has rejected the common language as unreal and who expresses this disillusionment by misusing this language.

Perry, Walter Copland. "Some Homeric Women." In *The Women of Homer*. London: William Heinemann, 1898.
This chapter is actually a study of the personality of the goddess Hera and her role in the *Iliad*. Includes some untranslated foreign language quotations. There is an appendix of ancient citations in the original languages.

Redfield, James M. "Achilles." In *Homer*, edited by Harold Bloom. New York: Chelsea House, 1986.
In this excerpt from *Nature and Culture in the "Iliad": The Tragedy of Hector*, Redfield focuses on the progression of Achilles' *cholos*, or rage, from the quarrel with Agamemnon in *Iliad* 1 to the embassy scene in book 9 and the sending of Patroclus into battle in book 16.

_____. "The Hero." *In Nature and Culture in the "Iliad": The Tragedy of Hector*. Chicago: University of Chicago Press, 1975.
The Homeric hero as a man on the margin between culture and nature is illustrated by the tragedy of Achilles. While Achilles' role as a warrior has placed him entirely outside culture, his antagonist, Hector, remains within the community. Homeric society is illustrated by the relationship between father and son, the concepts of retribution (*nemesis*) and disgrace (*aidos*), and the social position of women in the *Iliad*.

_____. "Introduction: Achilles and Hector." In *Nature and Culture in the "Iliad": The Tragedy of Hector*. Chicago: University of Chicago Press, 1975.
Summarizes several critical interpretations of the character of Achilles and argues that the *Iliad* does not center on Achilles' moral development. Unlike modern literature, which emphasizes the inner experience of the individual, the *Iliad* focuses on social phenomena, on the individual in society, on the contrast between the heroic Achilles and the human Hector.

Schein, Seth L. "Achilles: One." In *The Mortal Hero: An Introduction to Homer's "Iliad."* Berkeley: University of California Press, 1984.
Considers Homer's portrayal of the character of Achilles through the death of Patroclus in book 18. Achilles is a generous but isolated figure caught between his love for his companions and his resentment toward Agamemnon.

_____. "Achilles: Two." In *The Mortal Hero: An Introduction to Homer's "Iliad."* Berkeley: University of California Press, 1984.
Shows how the death of Patroclus in book 18 transfers Achilles' anger from Agamemnon to the Trojans and alienates him from his natural generosity, humanity, and heroism. Only by the restoration of Hector's body to Priam does Achilles regain his true, compassionate self and his heroism.

_____. "Hector and Troy." In *The Mortal Hero: An Introduction to Homer's "Iliad."* Berkeley: University of California Press, 1984.
Suggests that in the *Iliad* Troy represents domestic and social civilization and that Hector, the hero of Troy, is simultaneously the defender and the destroyer of his beloved city. Compares the character of Hector with that of Achilles and suggests that by following Hector's death with the ransom of his body, Homer affirms at the end of the *Iliad* that love, compassion, and loyalty are stronger than even death.

Whitman, Cedric H. "Achilles: Evolution of a Hero." In *Homer and the Heroic Tradition*. Cambridge, Mass.: Harvard University Press, 1958.
Examines the heroic growth of Achilles, revealed especially through his relationships with Agamemnon, Patroclus, Hector, and Priam. In the *Iliad*, the hero progresses from sanguine youthfulness to horrible violence to final detachment.

_____. "Homeric Character and the Tradition." In *Homer and the Heroic Tradition*. Cambridge, Mass.: Harvard University Press, 1958. Reprinted in *Homer's "The Iliad,"* edited by Harold Bloom. New York: Chelsea House, 1987.
A consideration of the way in which Homer molds his characters from the traditional material of pre-Homeric poetry. The consistent unity of such Homeric characters as Achilles, Diomedes, and Odysseus is shown to be the creation of Homer.

Studies of Individual Books, Episodes, and Passages

Atchity, Kenneth. "Andromache's Headdress." In *Critical Essays on Homer*, edited by Kenneth Atchity, Ron Hogart, and Doug Price. Boston: G. K. Hall, 1987.
This excerpt from "Helen and Her Galaxy: 2," in *Homer's "Iliad": The Shield of Memory*, is a study of Homer's description in *Iliad* 22 of Andromache's reaction to news of her husband's death. The author shows how the loom and the headdress of Andromache are used as symbols of the conjugal disorder caused by war.

_____. "The Great Shield." In *Homer's "Iliad": The Shield of Memory*. Carbondale: Southern Illinois University Press, 1978.
A close examination of the imagery on the shield of Achilles in *Iliad* 18 reveals an emphasis upon the communal dimension of human life in its fullest sense. As an artifact in process of creation, the shield serves a central function in the poem as a image of process and change and as a didactic symbol of cosmic order.

_____. "The Shield of Memory." In *Homer's "Iliad": The Shield of Memory*. Carbondale: Southern Illinois University Press, 1978.
Examines various narrative passages, such as Phoenix's story of Meleager in *Iliad* 9 and Nestor's recollection of the Epeian war in *Iliad* 11, as examples of the creative and mnemonic art of poetry. Together with catalogues and invocations in the *Iliad*, these passages show how Homer uses the imagery of memory as a means of thematic continuity centered on the social order represented on the shield of Achilles.

Bespaloff, Rachel. "Priam and Achilles Break Bread." In *On the "Iliad,"* translated by Mary McCarthy. New York: Pantheon Books, 1947. Reprinted in *Homer*, edited by Harold Bloom. New York: Chelsea House, 1986.
The ransom scene between Achilles and Priam in *Iliad* 24 is seen to be a significant pause from the suffering and violence of the epic. The interaction and motivations of the two characters are analyzed.

Graves, Robert. *The Greek Myths*. 2 vols. Baltimore: Penguin Books, 1960.
Contains background to several myths mentioned in the *Iliad*. These include the story of the hero Bellerophon in *Iliad* 6; Homer's version of the hero's birth in *Iliad* 19; the story of Heracles' capture of Pylos, described in *Iliad* 11; references to Heracles' children and to Ganymede, the Trojan youth abducted by Zeus; the adventure of Jason and the Argonauts on the island of Lemnos mentioned in *Iliad* 7; other myths about Meleager, whose story is told in *Iliad* 9; and information about the grief of Niobe, mentioned in *Iliad* 24.

Havelock, Eric A. "The Method and Manner of Homeric Storage." In *The Greek Concept of Justice: From Its Shadow in Homer to Its Substance in Plato*. Cambridge, Mass.: Harvard University Press, 1978.
An examination of a speech by Sarpedon in *Iliad* 12 is used to show how Homer incorporates into this passage the social code of Homeric society. Comparison of this passage with other parts of the *Iliad* suggests that the sentiments expressed here are not personal ideas of Sarpedon or of the poet but formulaic concepts of society at large.

Henle, Jane. "The Mourning Achilles." In *Greek Myths: A Vase Painter's Notebook*. Bloomington: Indiana University Press, 1973.
Considers several scenes from the *Iliad* on ancient Greek pottery, including the arming of Achilles and the ransom of Hector. The plot of the epic is summarized. Includes three illustrations.

Kirk, Geoffrey S. "The First Four Books of the *Iliad* in Context." In *The "Iliad": A Commentary*. Vol. 1, *Books 1-4*. New York: Cambridge University Press, 1985.
This last of four essays introducing a scholarly commentary on *Iliad* 1-4 includes comments on various ways in which books of the *Iliad* can be divided into subgroups. Emphasizes the structural unity of the epic. Offers a detailed summary of the plot of *Iliad* 1-4 and alerts the reader to some of the textual and interpretative problems contained in these books.

_____. "Introduction to the Achaean Catalogue." In *The "Iliad": A Commentary*. Vol. 1, *Books 1-4*. New York: Cambridge University Press, 1985.
This essay, which interrupts a scholarly commentary on *Iliad* 2, includes an overview of the passage, brief bibliographic comments, an explanation of typical features in the catalogue entries, and some comments on the special historical, geographic, and structural problems which the "catalogue of ships" raises. This introduction is complemented by some conclusions following the actual commentary to the catalogue. In this conclusion, Kirk questions the theory that the catalogue is largely a Mycenaean composition and suggests rather a more gradual development of the catalogue.

Lynn-George, Michael. "The Epic Theatre: The Language of Achilles." In *Epos: Word, Narrative, and the "Iliad."* Atlantic Highlands, N.J.: Humanities Press International, 1988.
Milman Parry's theory of the simplicity and rapidity of Homer's oral language is here countered by a more complex reading of a Homeric text, a study of Achilles' subtle and unstable language in the embassy scene of *Iliad* 9. Achilles' language sends him on a complex journey of words between stability and displacement, between song and silence, between life and death.

_____. "The Homeless Journey." In *Epos: Word, Narrative, and the "Iliad."* Atlantic Highlands, N.J.: Humanities Press International, 1988.
A reading of *Iliad* 24 as the climax of a narrative which modulates between time and timelessness. The *sema*, the tomb of Hector, is also a sign of the multiple meanings of the text.

Mueller, Martin. "Fighting in the *Iliad*." In *The Iliad*. Boston: Allen & Unwin, 1984.
A survey of battle narratives and their function in the *Iliad*. Such scenes include individual encounters, necrologies, gloating speeches, catalogues, *aristeias*, and chains of retribution.

_____. "The Plot of the *Iliad*." In *The Iliad*. Boston: Allen & Unwin, 1984.
This study of the plot and structure of the poem includes studies of Achilles and his anger in book 1, the embassy scene of book 9, the Patrocleia in books 16-18, the portrayal of Hector during Achilles' absence and after Patroclus' death, and the ransom scene in book 24. The overall structure of the *Iliad* is seen to be ring composition, in which the events of book 24 reverse the events of book 1. The poem ends with an affirmation of a common human bond which transcends divisions between individuals like Priam and Achilles.

Nagler, Michael N. "[AUTAR ACHILLES]." In *Spontaneity and Tradition: A Study in the Oral Art of Homer*. Berkeley: University of California Press, 1974.
The title, based upon line 3 of *Iliad* 24, can be translated as "But Achilles." An interpretation of *Iliad* 24 as a final resolution of the pattern of withdrawal, destruction, and return upon which the *Iliad* is based. Shows how mutual consolation for both Achilles and Priam takes place in the context of traditional motifs, such as annunciation, attendance, and the sharing of food. Includes some untranslated Greek.

Nagy, Gregory. "On the Death of Sarpedon." In *Approaches to Homer*, edited by Carl A. Rubino and Cynthia A. Shelmerdine. Austin: University of Texas Press, 1983.
Evidence from archaeology, comparative linguistics, and the study of "oral poetry" is used to shed new light on the death and funeral of Sarpedon in *Iliad* 16. The immortalization of the hero in cult is replaced in the epic by a process of immortalization via epic poetry itself.

_____. "The Worst of the Achaeans." In *Homer*, edited by Harold Bloom. New York: Chelsea House, 1986.
In this excerpt from *The Best of the Achaeans*, Nagy presents the Thersites episode of *Iliad* 2 as the strongest example of blame poetry in Greek epic. The vocabulary associated with Thersites associates him with blame.

Owen, E. T. "The Farewell of Hector and Andromache." In *The Story of the "Iliad."* 2d ed. Toronto: Clarke, Irwin, 1964. Slightly simplified in *Essays on the "Iliad,"* edited by John Wright. Bloomington: Indiana University Press, 1978. The description of the great deeds of Diomedes, and especially his encounter with Glaucus, are seen to be interlocked with the Hector-Andromache scene later in *Iliad* 6 in an anticipation of Troy's approaching fall. The scene with his wife humanizes the doomed warrior.

Redfield, James M. "The Hero." In *Homer,* edited by Harold Bloom. New York: Chelsea House, 1986.
In this excerpt from *Nature and Culture in the "Iliad": The Tragedy of Hector,* Redfield analyzes Sarpedon's speech to Glaucus in *Iliad* 12 as an illustration of the Homeric hero as a man on the margin between culture and nature.

_____. "Nature and Culture in the *Iliad*: Purification." In *Homer's "The Iliad,"* edited by Harold Bloom. New York: Chelsea House, 1987.
This abbreviated version of the final chapter of *Nature and Culture in the "Iliad": The Tragedy of Hector* centers on the ransoming of Hector in *Iliad* 24 and includes sections on the Homeric concepts of human consciousness and death and on art as the negation of culture.

_____. "Purification." *Nature and Culture in the "Iliad": The Tragedy of Hector.* Chicago: University of Chicago Press, 1975.
This final chapter of a literary interpretation of the *Iliad* examines the themes of funeral and willful defilement of the dead in the *Iliad* as part of a larger tension in the poem between culture and nature. The ransom of Hector's body in *Iliad* 24 is the ultimate act of purification for the hero Achilles, defiled by the savage slaying of Hector.

_____. "The Wrath of Achilles as Tragic Error." In *Nature and Culture in the "Iliad": The Tragedy of Hector.* Chicago: University of Chicago Press, 1975. Slightly simplified in *Essays on the "Iliad,"* edited by John Wright. Bloomington: Indiana University Press, 1978.
In this concluding section of a chapter on the Aristotelian concept of tragedy in the *Iliad*, Redfield sees the wrath of Achilles to be the result not of individual action but of collective error and social imbalance. Both Agamemnon and Achilles are shown to be problematic figures who inevitably clash in *Iliad* 1.

Rouse, W. H. D. "Ares in Battle." In *Gods, Heroes, and Men of Ancient Greece.* New York: New American Library, 1957.
This chapter is a paraphrase of the scene in *Iliad* 5, in which Ares, the Greek god of war, is wounded in battle. A short interpretation of the scene is included.

Zarker, John W. "King Eëtion and Thebe as Symbols in the *Iliad.*" *Classical Journal* 61 (1965): 110-114. Reprinted in *Critical Essays on Homer*, edited by Kenneth Atchity, Ron Hogart, and Doug Price. Boston: G. K. Hall, 1987.
Traces Homer's references to Andromache's father and her homeland in the *Iliad* and suggests that these references, which illustrate the character change Achilles undergoes as a result of his wrath, also emphasize the interlocking fate of all the Trojans and their allies.

The *Odyssey*

Greek Text and Commentaries

Heubeck, Alfred, Stephanie West, and J. B. Hainsworth, eds. *A Commentary on Homer's "Odyssey."* Vol. 1. *Introduction and Books I-VIII.* Oxford, England: Clarendon Press, 1988.
The first volume of a three part commentary of the *Odyssey* written for scholars. The general reader, for whom there exists no appropriate commentary on the *Odyssey*, may benefit from three introductory essays on the Homeric question, epic language, and the transmission of the text, as well as from the introductions which precede the commentary on each book of the epic. Includes indexes.

Homer. *The Odyssey.* 2 vols. Cambridge, Mass.: Harvard University Press, 1919.
This edition of the Greek text is accompanied, on facing pages, by an English translation by A. T. Murray, plus a bibliography and an index of Greek names.

Translations

Butler, Samuel. *The "Odyssey" Rendered into English Prose.* London: Jonathan Cape, 1922. Reprint. New York: E. P. Dutton, 1925.
A translation of the epic into the plain prose of the Victorian era by the author of *The Way of All Flesh.* Intended to accompany Butler's *The Authoress of the "Odyssey."* Includes maps, illustrations, and footnotes indicating where the epic shows signs of composition by a Sicilian woman. A preface summarizes Butler's arguments concerning female authorship and his principles of translation. Each book is introduced by a brief summary, and there are line references to the Greek text on every page. Uses Latin forms of Greek names. There is an appendix, reprinted from *The Authoress of the "Odyssey,"* describing the house of Odysseus.

Gaunt, D. M. *Surge and Thunder: Critical Readings in Homer's "Odyssey."* New York: Oxford University Press, 1971.

Contains prose translations of selected passages from the *Odyssey*, including descriptions of Calypso's island in *Odyssey* 5, of Alcinous' palace in *Odyssey* 7, of the Cyclops' island in *Odyssey* 9, of Circe's island in *Odyssey* 10, and of four scattered descriptions of Ithaca. The following passages are also translated: Telemachus' departure from Ithaca in *Odyssey* 2; Odysseus' shipwrecks in *Odyssey* 5 and 12; his struggle to land and his quest for shelter on Phaeacia in *Odyssey* 5; Nausicaa's discovery of Odysseus in *Odyssey* 6; the blinding of the Cyclops in *Odyssey* 9; his disastrous encounters with the Laestrygonians in *Odyssey* 10 and with Scylla and Charybdis in *Odyssey* 12; Odysseus' voyage from Phaeacia to Ithaca in *Odyssey* 13; the story of Eumaeus in *Odyssey* 15; Odysseus' recognitions by his faithful watchdog Argus in *Odyssey* 17 and by his nurse Eurycleia in *Odyssey* 19; the description of Penelope in *Odyssey* 18; Odysseus' stringing of the bow in *Odyssey* 21; and the slaying of the suitors in *Odyssey* 22.

Homer. *The Odyssey*. Translated by S. H. Butcher and Andrew Lang. 3d ed. New York: Macmillan, 1895.

This prose translation uses biblical English in order to capture the flavor of the Homeric language. Each book is introduced by a brief summary, and there are line references to the Greek text at the top of every page. Endnotes contain philological and archaeological information about the poem. An introduction summarizes the action of the epic day by day. Also includes a preface and illustrations.

_____. *The Odyssey*. Translated by George Chapman. In *Chapman's Homer*. Vol. 2, *The "Odyssey" and the Lesser Homerica*, edited by Allardyce Nicoll. 2d ed. Princeton, N.J.: Princeton University Press, 1967.

This translation, first published together with a translation of the *Iliad* in 1614 and immortalized in a poem by John Keats, uses rhymed decasyllabic couplets and retains the original spelling of the period. Includes a dedication and Chapman's translations of several ancient Greek epigrams about Homer. Some foreign phrases not translated. This edition includes Chapman's marginal comments, an introduction, an illustration, textual notes, editor's commentary, and a glossary.

_____. *The Odyssey*. Translated and edited by Albert Cook. New York: W. W. Norton, 1974.

This verse translation of the poem follows the original Greek carefully. There are line references to the Greek text at the top of every page and in five-line increments at the side of the text. Each line of the English translation usually corresponds to a given line of Greek. There are copious aids for the reader, including a preface on the translation, a glossary, a map, a selected bibliography, and a collection of critical essays on the poem.

_____. *The Odyssey*. Translated by William Cooper. London: J. M. Dent & Sons, 1910.
A translation into English blank verse in the style of the Victorian period. Plot summaries are included at the beginning of every book.

_____. *The Odyssey*. Translated by Preston H. Epps. New York: Macmillan, 1965.
This prose translation of the epic is intended for the high school and general reader. Each book is introduced by a brief summary and by a very useful glossary of names. There is also a more comprehensive glossary at the back of the book. Line references to the Greek text are provided at the top of every page. Includes an introduction, map, notes, and study questions.

_____. *The Odyssey*. Translated by Robert Fitzgerald. Garden City, N.Y.: Doubleday, 1961.
An internationally acclaimed verse translation of the epic by an accomplished poet and translator. Fitzgerald's goal is faithfulness to a poetic rather than a literal reading of the poem in English. Line references to the Greek text appear at the top of every page. Titles for each book are provided by the translator. There is a postscript by the translator about various aspects of translation and Homeric studies.

_____. *The Odyssey*. Translated by Robert Fitzgerald. In *Literature of the Western World*. Vol. 1, *The Ancient World Through the Renaissance*, edited by Brian Wilkie and James Hurt. New York: Macmillan, 1984.
This edition of Fitzgerald's translation includes line references and explanatory footnotes. The editors have added an introduction and bibliography.

_____. *The Odyssey*. Translated by Richmond Lattimore. New York: Harper & Row, 1967.
This verse translation follows the formulaic structure of the original Greek as closely as possible. Line references to the Greek text are given in five-line increments. Plot summaries are provided at the top of every page. Glossary and introduction by the translator.

_____. *The Odyssey*. Translated by A. T. Murray. Cambridge, Mass.: Harvard University Press, 1919.
This prose translation of the epic is less accessible to the general reader because of its Victorian language, but the facing Greek text allows for immediate compar-

ison of the original and translation. Includes a bibliography and index of Greek names.

_____. *The Odyssey*. Translated by George Herbert Palmer. 2d ed. Boston: Houghton Mifflin, 1921.
Originally published between 1884 and 1891, this prose translation aims at direct and faithful translation of the Greek original in order to capture Homer's simplicity and realism. Topical titles are added to each book, and there are line references to the Greek text at the top of every page. Also includes an introduction, a retrospect, study questions, a pronouncing vocabulary of proper names, a map, and a frontispiece.

_____. *The Odyssey*. Translated by Ennis Rees. Indianapolis: Bobbs-Merrill, 1977.
In this verse translation, topical titles are provided for each book by the translator. Includes an introduction, selected bibliography, and index but no aids such as a glossary or line references to the Greek text.

_____. *The Odyssey*. Translated by E. V. Rieu. New York: Penguin Books, 1946.
A prose translation with line references to the Greek text at the top of every page. Topical titles are provided for each book by the translator. Introduction and a glossary of Greek gods.

_____. *The Odyssey*. Translated by W. H. D. Rouse. New York: New American Library, 1937.
A prose translation with topical titles added for each book by the translator. An essay on Homer's words is appended. Includes a preface and pronouncing index.

_____. *The Odyssey*. Translated by T. E. Shaw. New York: Oxford University Press, 1932.
This straightforward prose translation is actually the work of T. E. Lawrence, better known as "Lawrence of Arabia." Brief translator's note.

_____. *The Odyssey*. Translated by Walter Shewring. New York: Oxford University Press, 1980.
A translation of the *Odyssey* into twentieth century English prose with some reduction in the frequency of repeated adjectives. Each book is given a descriptive title, and there are line references to the Greek original at the top of every right-hand page and some explanatory footnotes. An unusual feature is the quotation occasionally in the footnotes of earlier translations of the *Odyssey*, including those of Alexander Pope and George Chapman. Introductory essay by

G. S. Kirk and epilogue on translation by Shewring. Also includes maps, a glossary, and an index.

Background and Plot Summaries

Apollodorus. "The Return and Death of Odysseus (Epitome 7)." In *Gods and Heroes of the Greeks: The "Library" of Apollodorus*, translated by Michael Simpson. Amherst: University of Massachusetts Press, 1976.
This epitome, or summary, of Greek myths related to the story of Odysseus begins with the hero's travels following his departure from Troy (*Odyssey* 9-12), his visit with the Phaeacians (*Odyssey* 5-8), and his return to Ithaca (*Odyssey* 13-24). Includes a list of Penelope's suitors and references to alternate versions about Odysseus' return and to stories about Odysseus' death. Includes notes, a bibliography, and an index.

Butcher, S. H., and Andrew Lang. Introduction to *The Odyssey*, by Homer, translated by S. H. Butcher and Andrew Lang. 3d ed. New York: Macmillan, 1895.
This brief essay, devoted to the composition and plot of the *Odyssey*, summarizes Odysseus' ten years of adventure from Troy to Ithaca and analyzes on a day-by-day basis the action of the *Odyssey*, beginning with Zeus' decision to send Odysseus home and ending with Laertes' recognition of his son forty-two days later.

Butler, Samuel. "The Story of the *Odyssey*." In *The Authoress of the "Odyssey."* 2d ed. London: Jonathan Cape, 1922. Reprint. Chicago: University of Chicago Press, 1967.
A detailed paraphrase of the poem accompanying the author's argument that the *Odyssey* was written by a Sicilian woman. The summary is preceded by the author's description of Odysseus' house plan, based upon evidence from the poem. This description is accompanied by a drawing.

Camps, W. A. "The Story of the *Odyssey* in Outline." In *An Introduction to Homer*. New York: Oxford University Press, 1980.
This chapter is a brief prose summary of the central plot of the epic.

Gayley, Charles Mills. "The Wanderings of Ulysses." In *The Classic Myths in English Literature and in Art*. 2d ed. New York: John Wiley & Sons, 1911.
Commentary section contains works of art and literature based upon the epic. This summary of the plot of the poem includes quotations from several English translations of the *Odyssey* as well as excerpts from several original imitations, including "The Lotus Eaters" and "Ulysses" by Alfred, Lord Tennyson. Includes a map, indexes, and reproductions of artwork showing scenes from the *Odyssey*.

Graves, Robert. "Odysseus' Homecoming." In *The Greek Myths*. Vol. 2. Baltimore: Penguin Books, 1960.
A summary of *Odyssey* 13-24, beginning with Odysseus' arrival on Ithaca and ending with the hero's reunion with Penelope, is followed by stories about events which take place after the *Odyssey* ends, including Odysseus' inland journey to placate Poseidon.

_____. "Odysseus' Wanderings." In *The Greek Myths*. Vol. 2. Baltimore: Penguin Books, 1960.
This summary of Odysseus' adventures from his departure from Troy to his departure from the island of the Phaeacians is based especially on *Odyssey* 9-13.

Guerber, Hélène Adeline. "Adventures of Ulysses." In *Myths of Greece and Rome*. New York: American Book Company, 1895.
A straightforward summary of the plot of the *Odyssey* told in chronological order, beginning with Odysseus' departure from Troy and ending with the death of the suitors. Uses both Latin and Greek names. Includes references to the story of Odysseus' last journey. Frequent quotation from the *Odyssey* and other literature, both ancient and modern. Includes black-and-white reproductions of artwork representing scenes from the *Odyssey*, as well as a map, genealogical table, glossary, and index.

Hamilton, Edith. "The Adventures of Odysseus." In *Mythology*. New York: New American Library, 1942.
This retelling of the homecoming of Odysseus begins with the decision of the gods to destroy the homeward-bound Greek fleet and leads into a summary of the plot of the *Odyssey*. Includes illustrations, genealogical tables, and an index.

Henle, Jane. "Odyssey." In *Greek Myths: A Vase Painter's Notebook*. Bloomington: Indiana University Press, 1973.
A plot summary of the epic is accompanied by a discussion of scenes from the *Odyssey* depicted on ancient Greek pottery. Includes four illustrations.

Mayerson, Philip. "The Homecomings." In *Classical Mythology in Literature, Art, and Music*. Lexington, Mass.: Xerox College Publishing, 1971.
Focuses on the returns of Agamemnon and Odysseus from the Trojan War. A detailed plot summary of the *Odyssey* is included together with a survey of later literary and artistic adaptations of the epic.

Morford, Mark P. O., and Robert J. Lenardon. "The Returns." In *Classical Mythology*. 3d ed. New York: Longman, 1985.
This section of a standard mythological handbook is essentially a summary of the plot of the *Odyssey*. Extensive passages from the epic are quoted. Includes

maps, genealogical charts, illustrations, select bibliography, footnotes, and indexes.

Rouse, W. H. D. "Odysseus." In *Gods, Heroes, and Men of Ancient Greece*. New York: New American Library, 1957.
This chapter is a paraphrase of several of Odysseus' adventures in books 9-12 of the *Odyssey*, including the hero's encounters with the Cyclops, Circe, and Calypso.

_____. "The *Odyssey*." In *Homer*. New York: Thomas Nelson and Sons, 1939.
This straightforward paraphrase of the plot of the *Odyssey* includes some comments about the use of flashback and the general unity of the poem's structure and a personal experience of the author in Greece. Includes illustrations, maps, and an index.

Schwab, Gustav. "Odysseus." In *Gods and Heroes: Myths and Epics of Ancient Greece*, translated by Olga Marx and Ernst Morwitz. New York: Pantheon Books, 1946.
This chapter is a summary of the plot of the *Odyssey*. The author does not tell the story chronologically by starting with Odysseus' departure from Troy but follows Homer's order by beginning in the last year of the hero's wanderings and flashing back to earlier adventures.

Literary Studies

Adorno, T. W. "Odysseus: Or, Mythos and Enlightenment." In *Dialektik der Aufklärung: Philosophische Fragmente*. Amsterdam: Querido Verlag, 1947. Translated in *The Odyssey*, by Homer, edited by Albert Cook. New York: W. W. Norton, 1974.
In this philosophical study, the myth of Odysseus is seen to be a quest for self in which rational universality, represented by the hero's cunning, is pitted against the inevitability of fate.

Auerbach, Erich. "Odysseus' Scar." In *Mimesis: The Representation of Reality in Western Literature*, translated by Willard R. Trask. Princeton, N.J.: Princeton University Press, 1953. Reprinted in *Homer: A Collection of Critical Essays*, edited by George Steiner and Robert Fagles. Englewood Cliffs, N.J.: Prentice-Hall, 1962. Also reprinted in *Homer*, edited by Harold Bloom. New York: Chelsea House, 1986.
The first chapter of an influential study of literary style and poetic imitation of the real world, this essay contrasts the straightforward, unambiguous style used

by Homer to describe both scenes and characters with the more suggestive, multilayered style of the author of the biblical book of Genesis. Specifically, the story of Eurycleia and the scar in *Odyssey* 18 is compared with the story of the sacrifice of Isaac in Genesis 22.

Bergren, Ann L. T. "Odyssean Temporality: Many (Re)Turns." In *Approaches to Homer*, edited by Carl A. Rubino and Cynthia A. Shelmerdine. Austin: University of Texas Press, 1983.
An examination of the relationship between narrative and time in the *Odyssey* suggests that the structure of the epic is based upon temporal turns and returns from present to past to present and from present to future to present. Such transitions in time are noted in Odysseus' tale to the Phaeacians in *Odyssey* 9-12 and especially in the Cyclops tale of book 9, the encounter with Teiresias in book 11, and the episode about the cattle of the sun god in book 12.

Beye, Charles Rowan. "The *Odyssey*." In *The "Iliad," the "Odyssey," and the Epic Tradition*. Garden City, N.Y.: Doubleday, 1966.
Includes a discussion of the structure, plot, and meaning of the epic. The *Odyssey* is interpreted as a study in human responsibility and in the tension between appearance and reality, between truth and falsehood. Odysseus' many adventures are considered preparation for the hero's ultimate test in Ithaca, where he must maintain disguise and deception in order to become successfully reoriented into the real world.

Bloom, Harold, ed. *Homer's "Odyssey."* Edgemont, Pa.: Chelsea House, 1988.
A collection of seven interpretative essays on the *Odyssey* originally published between 1966 and 1983. Authors such as H. D. F. Kitto, C. M. Bowra, and Norman Austin consider a variety of topics, including similarities between the Homeric epics and Athenian tragedies, comparisons between the two Homeric epics, and studies of the hero in the *Odyssey*. Includes an introduction, chronological chart, bibliography, and index.

Bowra, C. M. "The *Odyssey*: Its Shape and Character." In *Homer*. New York: Charles Scribner's Sons, 1972. Reprinted in *Homer's "Odyssey,"* edited by Harold Bloom. Edgemont, Pa.: Chelsea House, 1988.
The epic is seen to be based upon a collection of folktales in which the hero struggles against his inferiors and with monsters. The plot of the *Odyssey* is summarized and thematic links between the *Odyssey* and the *Iliad* are discussed. The role of the gods in the two epics is compared. The *Odyssey* is considered more realistic than the *Iliad*, especially in character portrayal. Special problems related to Odysseus' visit to the land of the dead in *Odyssey* 11 are treated in an appendix attached to the original essay.

Butler, Samuel. "Conclusion." In *The Authoress of the "Odyssey."* 2d ed. London: Jonathan Cape, 1922. Reprint. Chicago: University of Chicago Press, 1967.
In this final chapter of a book arguing that the *Odyssey* was written by a woman in Greek-speaking Sicily, the author offers a general appreciation of the poem and its author.

_____. "Preface to the First Edition." In *The "Odyssey" Rendered into English Prose*. London: Jonathan Cape, 1922. Reprint. New York: E. P. Dutton, 1925.
Explains that this translation is meant to accompany Butler's *The Authoress of the "Odyssey."* Summarizes his arguments for female authorship of the *Odyssey* and offers some comments upon his principles of translation.

Clarke, Howard W. Introduction to *Twentieth Century Interpretations of the "Odyssey,"* edited by Howard W. Clarke. Englewood Cliffs, N.J.: Prentice-Hall, 1983.
Provides some historical perspective for a collection of twentieth century essays by summarizing allegorical, unitarian, and analytical approaches to the *Odyssey*.

_____, ed. *Twentieth Century Interpretations of the "Odyssey."* Englewood Cliffs, N.J.: Prentice-Hall, 1983.
Contains reprints of seven essays on various aspects of the *Odyssey*, including an anthropological study of the Telemachy, qualities of Odysseus' heroism, characterization, dating, and problems connected with individual scenes. Includes an introduction, footnotes, bibliography, and notes on the editor and contributors.

Clay, Jenny Strauss. *The Wrath of Athena: Gods and Men in the "Odyssey."* Princeton, N.J.: Princeton University Press, 1983.
A consideration of the ties between gods and men in the Homeric poems, and especially the bond between Athena and Odysseus, leads to a general interpretation of the *Odyssey* centering on the theme of Athena's anger toward Odysseus and its transformation in the *Odyssey* into a more positive relationship. There are individual studies of the beginning of the *Odyssey*, of Athena's encounter with Odysseus in *Odyssey* 13, the character of Odysseus and of the gods as developed in both Homeric poems, and some general comments on the Homeric question. Includes a bibliography and index.

Cook, Albert. "The Man of Many Turns." In *The Classic Line: A Study in Epic Poetry*. Bloomington: Indiana University Press, 1966.
Studies the character of Odysseus and shows how his complexity is reflected in the variety of his experiences in the epic. The psyche of the hero, a man of cunning and infinite resources, dominates and unifies the poem. Illustrates how Odysseus' equanimity in the face of time, change, joy, and sorrow is reflected in the language and tone of the *Odyssey*. Contains an index.

_____, ed. *The "Odyssey" of Homer*. New York: W. W. Norton, 1974.
This volume includes the editor's verse translation of the poem; essays providing useful background on Homeric language and society; a section offering samples of reactions to Homer by ancient authors, such as Pindar, Aristotle, and Longinus; and a selection of comments by modern critics of the poem, including Jean Racine, Ezra Pound, and Cedric Whitman. Includes a glossary, map, and selected bibliography.

Epps, Preston H. Introduction to *The Odyssey*, by Homer. New York: Macmillan, 1965.
In this brief essay attached to a prose translation of the epic, the translator summarizes the plot of the *Odyssey*, the general features of Homeric epic, and such questions as realism and the number of days covered by events in the *Odyssey*.

Finley, John H., Jr. *Homer's "Odyssey."* Cambridge, Mass.: Harvard University Press, 1978.
In this study, the author portrays Odysseus as a hero of experience and interprets the *Odyssey* as an affirmation of human, especially family, attachments. Major sections of the epic are discussed in separate chapters. There are also chapters on characterization and the origin of the travel tales. Not all Greek is translated. Includes a preface, footnotes, two appendices, a bibliography, and indexes.

Foley, Helene P. "'Reverse Similes' and Sex Roles in the *Odyssey*." *Arethusa* 11, no. 1-2 (1978): 7-26. Reprinted without footnotes in *Homer's "Odyssey,"* edited by Harold Bloom. Edgemont, Pa.: Chelsea House, 1988.
Examines a group of similes in which family and social relationships are reversed. These similes of inversion, clustered especially around incidents in Phaeacia and Ithaca, emphasize both the disrupted nature of social life at the beginning of the poem and Odysseus' need for interdependent relationships, especially between husband and wife and between father and son, in order to restore domestic peace to his confused world.

Frame, Douglas. *The Myth of Return in Early Greek Epic*. New Haven, Conn.: Yale University Press, 1978.
A linguistic examination of the *Odyssey* and Indo-European roots reveals a Homeric connection between the "wiles" and the "wanderings" of Odysseus. This connection is based upon a link between the Greek noun *nóos* ("mind") and the verb *néomai* ("to return home"). Introduction, footnotes, endnotes, and index.

Fränkel, Hermann. "The New Mood of the *Odyssey* and the End of Epic." In *Early Greek Poetry and Philosophy: A History of Greek Epic, Lyric and Prose to the Middle of the Fifth Century*, translated by Moses Hadas and James Willis. New

York: Harcourt Brace Jovanovich, 1973. Reprinted in *Homer*, edited by Harold Bloom. New York: Chelsea House, 1986.
As a cunning and energetic man who is able to take his destiny into his own hands, Odysseus is a new type of realistic hero. In the *Odyssey*, the traditional epic form, stretched to its formal limits, is approaching the less stylized poetry of Hesiod and Greek lyric.

Gaunt, D. M. *Surge and Thunder: Critical Readings in Homer's "Odyssey."* New York: Oxford University Press, 1971.
Following an essay on the characteristics of oral poetry, the author provides his own prose translation of twenty significant passages in the *Odyssey*. Each translation is accompanied by an introduction providing the plot background to the passage and by an appreciation section designed to explain fine points of language and meaning to those who cannot read the original Greek. For some passages, there are also commentary sections with more detailed information not connected with poetic appreciation. Includes an introduction, bibliography, pronunciation guide, and index.

Grant, Michael. "Odysseus." In *Myths of the Greeks and Romans*. New York: New American Library, 1962.
This essay includes a plot summary of the *Odyssey* and studies of the character of Odysseus in art and literature, of folktale themes in the epic, and of Odysseus' journey to the land of the dead.

Greene, Thomas. "Form and Craft in the *Odyssey*." In *The Descent from Heaven: A Study in Epic Continuity*. New Haven, Conn.: Yale University Press, 1963. Reprinted in *Homer*, edited by Harold Bloom. New York: Chelsea House, 1986.
In this chapter of a book on the European epic tradition, Greene compares use of the theme of divine descent in the *Odyssey* to that in the *Iliad* in order to make some general observations about the differences between the two epics. the *Odyssey*'s greater sense of form and craft makes it more urbane and refined than the *Iliad*.

Griffin, Jasper. "The *Odyssey*." In *Homer*. New York: Hill & Wang, 1980.
Shows how Homer creates a complex plot from the common narrative theme of a hero returning home. The *Odyssey* differs from the *Iliad* especially in its emphasis on deceit, on an explicit moral code, and on vengeful, testing gods, and in its interest in a broader world which includes not only heroes but also singers, traders, women, the weak, and the ordinary. Discusses the portrayal of women and of the afterlife found in the *Odyssey*.

Kitto, H. D. F. "The *Odyssey*." In *Poiesis: Structure and Thought*. Berkeley: University of California Press, 1966. Reprinted as "The *Odyssey*: The Exclusion of Surprise," in *Homer's "Odyssey,"* edited by Harold Bloom. Edgemont, Pa.: Chelsea House, 1988.

Working from Aristotle's emphasis on plot and from Longinus' description of the *Odyssey* as a comedy of manners, Kitto examines the plot of the *Odyssey*, especially of the first four books, and notes how the author has regularly forestalled occurrences of dramatic surprise. Like fifth century Athenian tragedians, the author of the *Odyssey* operates from a preordained moral structure and a didactic aesthetic which deemphasizes the need for a romantic, suspense-filled plot.

Lattimore, Richmond. Introduction to *The "Odyssey" of Homer*. New York: Harper & Row, 1967. Reprinted in *Twentieth Century Interpretations of the Odyssey*, edited by Howard W. Clarke. Englewood Cliffs, N.J.: Prentice-Hall, 1983.

Lattimore begins this introduction to his verse translation of the *Odyssey* with a short summary of the plot. He also discusses such topics as the Telemachy, the wanderings of Odysseus, the hero on Ithaca, the end of the *Odyssey*, and a comparison of the two Homeric epics.

Lord, George de Forest. "The Allegorical Background." In *Homeric Renaissance: The "Odyssey" of George Chapman*. New Haven, Conn.: Yale University Press, 1956.

Provides historical background for Chapman's allegorical translation of the *Odyssey*. Chapman's allegory differs from earlier, idealized versions in its portrayal of an evolving Odysseus. There are some untranslated foreign words.

Michalopoulos, Andre. "The *Odyssey*." In *Homer*. Boston: Twayne, 1966.

In addition to an outline of the plot of the epic, this study includes comments upon the authorship and date of the *Odyssey*, Telemachus' maturation and quest for his father, the gods in the *Odyssey*, and Odysseus' journeys and homecoming.

Murnaghan, Sheila. *Disguise and Recognition in the "Odyssey."* Princeton, N.J.: Princeton University Press, 1987.

Suggests that the various scenes of disguise and recognition, especially in the second half of the *Odyssey*, provide a critical understanding of the characters of Odysseus and Penelope, an interpretation of the entire epic, and an understanding of the values of Homeric society. Includes specific sections on the themes of hospitality and song in the *Odyssey* and on Odysseus' relationships with the suitors, with Penelope, and with other members of his family. Includes footnotes, bibliography, and indexes.

Page, Denys L. *The Homeric "Odyssey."* Oxford, England: Clarendon Press, 1955. Reprint. Westport, Conn.: Greenwood Press, 1976.

This book is a general introduction to problems related to the composition of the poem. After identifying traditional sources for several sections of the *Odyssey*, the author discusses the method, time, and place of composition of the poem. There are some untranslated Greek words. Includes a preface, endnotes, an appendix, and indexes.

Palmer, George Herbert. Introduction to *The Odyssey*, by Homer. 2d ed. Boston: Houghton Mifflin, 1921.
This essay offers a brief discussion of the question of authorship and provides background to the plot and a detailed plot summary. Special features include a useful division of the plot by days, an analysis of characters, some observations on Homer's style, and comments on several books about and translations of the *Odyssey*.

Post, L. A. "The Pattern of Success: Homer's *Odyssey*." In *From Homer to Menander: Forces in Greek Poetic Fiction*. Berkeley: University of California Press, 1951.
Following an introduction to Greek poetic fiction based especially on the *Poetics* of Aristotle, the author examines the *Odyssey* as a moralizing success story, a comedy of manners in which the wicked are punished and the good rewarded. The plot of the epic is summarized, and Penelope is presented as the emotional center of the epic. Includes a preface, endnotes, and an index.

Redfield, James M. "The Economic Man." In *Approaches to Homer*, edited by Carl A. Rubino and Cynthia A. Shelmerdine. Austin: University of Texas Press, 1983.
A reading of the *Odyssey* according to the economic ethics of Greece in the late eighth century B.C. Tensions between an agricultural and a market economy, between self-sufficiency and decadent affluence, are shown to determine the plot of the *Odyssey* as Odysseus struggles to resolve the conflict between savage violence and the temptations of an excessive culture.

Stewart, Douglas J. *The Disguised Guest: Rank, Role, and Identity in the "Odyssey."* Lewisburg, Pa.: Bucknell University Press, 1976.
Interprets the *Odyssey* as a story of loss and discovery of identity, and uses this theme to analyze the epic, especially in scenes of encounter in the *Odyssey*. Includes an introduction, notes, bibliography, index, and appendix on drugs in the *Odyssey*.

Taylor, Charles H., Jr., ed. *Essays on the "Odyssey": Selected Modern Criticism*. Bloomington: Indiana University Press, 1969.
This collection contains seven essays originally published between 1950 and 1969. All but one focus especially on the *Odyssey*; the other examines the relationship between gods and men in both Homeric poems. There are studies

of personal relationships, the theme of Elysium, the name of Odysseus, obstacles to his return, the reunion of Odysseus and Penelope, and the place of the *Odyssey* in Western tradition.

Van Doren, Mark. *The Noble Voice*. New York: Henry Holt, 1946.
In this study of ten long poems in the Western poetic tradition, Van Doren, an important twentieth century American poet and novelist, considers the works of Homer unrivaled with those of Lucretius, Vergil, John Milton, Dante Alighieri, Edmund Spenser, William Shakespeare, George Gordon, Lord Byron, and William Wordsworth. The *Odyssey* is interpreted as a poem which cannot be contained, which is full of space and distance.

Character Studies

Anderson, William S. "Calypso and Elysium." *The Classical Journal* 54 (1958): 2-11. Reprinted in *Essays on the "Odyssey": Selected Modern Criticism*, edited by Charles H. Taylor, Jr. Bloomington: Indiana University Press, 1969.
Menelaus' description of a blissful afterlife in Elysium in book 4 is compared to Odysseus' life on Calypso's island in book 5. The hero's rejection of an immortal existence with Calypso is seen to be the source of his heroism, an affirmation of his own humanity and mortality.

Bradford, Ernle. "Ancestry." In *Ulysses Found*. New York: Harcourt, Brace & World, 1963.
Emphasizes the maternal ancestry of Odysseus. The hero's crafty nature traced to his maternal grandfather, Autolycus, who was a master thief, and to the tradition that Odysseus was really the son of the trickster Sisyphus, not of Laertes. Includes a genealogical chart of Odysseus' family.

_____. "Youth." In *Ulysses Found*. New York: Harcourt, Brace & World, 1963.
A physical description of Odysseus is followed by the tales associated with his youth, marriage to Penelope, attempt to avoid going to Troy, and expedition to find the hiding place of Achilles.

Budgen, Frank. "James Joyce: An Encounter with Homer." In *James Joyce and the Making of "Ulysses."* Bloomington: University of Indiana Press, 1960. Reprinted in *Homer: A Collection of Critical Essays*, edited by George Steiner and Robert Fagles. Englewood Cliffs, N.J.: Prentice-Hall, 1962.
Describes a meeting between the author and James Joyce while *Ulysses* was being written. In this conversation, Joyce compares Odysseus to Hamlet and Faust and argues that only Odysseus is an all-around or complete man.

Butler, Samuel. "Jealousy for the Honour and Dignity of Women. . . ." In *The Authoress of the "Odyssey."* 2d ed. London: Jonathan Cape, 1922. Reprint. Chicago: University of Chicago Press, 1967.
As part of an argument that the *Odyssey* was written by a woman, the author examines the treatment of several female characters in the poem, the themes of money and religion, and the strong opinions expressed about the conduct of women.

_____. "On the Question Whether or No Penelope Is Being Whitewashed." In *The Authoress of the "Odyssey."* 2d ed. London: Jonathan Cape, 1922. Reprint. Chicago: University of Chicago Press, 1967.
Butler argues that the conduct of Penelope with the suitors is actually scandalous and that a female author has covered up some of Penelope's faults.

_____. "The Preponderance of Woman in the *Odyssey.*" In *The Authoress of the "Odyssey."* 2d ed. London: Jonathan Cape, 1922. Reprint. Chicago: University of Chicago Press, 1967.
As part of an argument that the *Odyssey* was written by a woman, Butler argues that the poem shows a woman's concern and illustrates the importance of females in both the larger and smaller roles of the *Odyssey*. There is a brief comparison of the frequency of female roles in the *Odyssey* with that in Vergil's *Aeneid* and the works of other male authors.

Cook, Albert. "The Man of Many Turns." In *The Classic Line*. Bloomington: Indiana University Press, 1966. Reprinted in *The Odyssey*, by Homer, edited by Albert Cook. New York: W. W. Norton, 1974.
Odysseus' epithet *polytropos* ("of many turns") is seen as both a basic character trait of the hero and an organizing principle for the epic. Odysseus displays equanimity in the face of apparently endless transience.

Finley, John H., Jr. "Penelope." In *Homer's "Odyssey."* Cambridge, Mass.: Harvard University Press, 1978.
An analysis of Penelope's role in the *Odyssey* suggests that she is the key to the unity of a poem about Odysseus as father, son, and husband. Like her husband and her son, she, too, takes a journey, an inner one via her long period of waiting. Utilizes frequent comparisons with the *Iliad*.

Griffin, Jasper. "Characterization." In *Homer on Life and Death*. Oxford, England: Oxford University Press, 1980. Abridged in *Twentieth Century Interpretations of the "Odyssey,"* edited by Howard W. Clarke. Englewood Cliffs, N.J.: Prentice-Hall, 1983.
This study of characterization in both Homeric epics includes discussions of the personalities of Calypso, Circe, and Nausicaa in the *Odyssey* and shows how

these characters are different from one another and how the poet provides motivating psychology for each individual.

Murnaghan, Sheila. "Odysseus and the Suitors." In *Disguise and Recognition in the "Odyssey."* Princeton, N.J.: Princeton University Press, 1987.
Contrasts the suitors' inability to recognize Odysseus with the hero's superior knowledge and reveals the limitations in the collective character of Penelope's suitors by examining their relationship with the disguised hero and with the gods. The suitors' failure to recognize the disguised hero, the presence of gods, or the true meaning of omens justifies their impending deaths not only by the will of the gods but also because of their isolation from the network of proper social obligations and benefits on Ithaca.

_____. "Penelope." In *Disguise and Recognition in the "Odyssey."* Princeton, N.J.: Princeton University Press, 1987.
Considers Odysseus' decision to conceal his identity from his wife, Penelope, until after his vengeance against the suitors. Analyzes her motivations in regard to the bow contest, and her reluctance to recognize her husband. Observes both Penelope's loyalty to Odysseus and her uncertainty, as well as her double role as both deceived and deceiver in the epic.

Segal, Charles. "*Kleos* and Its Ironies in the *Odyssey*." *L'Antiquité Classique* 52 (1983): 127-149. Reprinted in *Homer's "Odyssey,"* edited by Harold Bloom. Edgemont, Pa.: Chelsea House, 1988.
The poet of the *Odyssey* is shown to manipulate several concepts of *kleos*, or Homeric glory, in his portrayal of Odysseus. In the person of Odysseus, glory based on craft and deceit vies with glory derived from heroic deeds. In the *Odyssey*, the tradition of glory as the result of great deeds is contrasted with the concept of glory as the creation of a bardic tradition. Thus, Odysseus gains glory for himself both by his song, by singing to the Phaeacians in *Odyssey* 9-12, and by his deeds, by slaying the suitors in *Odyssey* 21.

Stanford, W. B. "Personal Relationships." In *The Ulysses Theme: A Study in the Adaptability of a Traditional Hero*. 2d ed. Ann Arbor: University of Michigan Press, 1968. Reprinted in *Essays on the "Odyssey": Selected Modern Criticism*, edited by Charles H. Taylor, Jr. Bloomington: Indiana University Press, 1969.
Considers Odysseus' relationships with Circe, Calypso, Nausicaa, Penelope, and his parents. Seeks to explain the apparent contradiction between Odysseus' liaisons with Circe and Calypso and his love for Penelope and home. Suggests that the hero's civilized gentleness and intelligence provided him with a closer affinity to women than to the more violent men of the Heroic Age.

Taylor, Charles H., Jr. "The Obstacles to Odysseus' Return." *The Yale Review* 50 (1961): 569-580. Reprinted in *Essays on the "Odyssey": Selected Modern Criticism*, edited by Charles H. Taylor, Jr. Bloomington: Indiana University Press, 1969.
Odysseus' encounters with Polyphemus, Poseidon, Calypso, and Circe illustrate the hero's quest for identity and his struggles to resist repeated temptations to submit to the powers of the unconscious.

Woodhouse, W. J. "The Faithful Retainer." In *The Composition of Homer's "Odyssey."* Oxford, England: Clarendon Press, 1930.
Examines Homer's portrayal of Eumaeus, the swineherd, suggests that the swineherd loses in the *Odyssey* the central role of Odysseus' helper which he had probably played in earlier versions of the poem, but notes evidence of Homer's detailed and sympathetic characterization of his character.

_____. "The Loyal Wife." In *The Composition of Homer's "Odyssey."* Oxford, England: Clarendon Press, 1930.
Considers Homer's characterization of Penelope and suggests that in the *Odyssey* Homer preferred the more neutral character of the faithful wife in folklore to the strong role Penelope may have played in the Saga of Odysseus. Homer does not emphasize either Penelope's natural beauty or her husband's affection and delays praise of her loyalty to Odysseus until the very end of the epic.

_____. "Penelopeia's Collapse." In *The Composition of Homer's "Odyssey."* Oxford, England: Clarendon Press, 1930.
Considers the possible motives for Penelope's decision in *Odyssey* 19 to announce a marriage contest with Odysseus' bow. Argues that in this decision Penelope does not act in character but is used by the poet as a tool in order to advance the plot.

_____. "The Quest of Telemachus." In *The Composition of Homer's "Odyssey."* Oxford, England: Clarendon Press, 1930.
Suggests that the portrayal of Telemachus, especially in the boy's search for his father in *Odyssey* 1-4, owes nothing to earlier poetic tradition and is the original invention of the poet. Notes that Telemachus is the only figure in the *Odyssey*, and the earliest in Greek literature, to demonstrate growth of character, from a helpless youth to the image of his father.

Studies of Individual Books, Episodes, and Passages

Amory, Anne. "The Reunion of Odysseus and Penelope." In *Essays on the "Odyssey,"* edited by Charles H. Taylor, Jr. Bloomington: University of Indiana Press,

1963. Reprinted in *The Odyssey*, by Homer, edited by Albert Cook. New York: W. W. Norton, 1974.

Examines Penelope's growing awareness in the last part of the *Odyssey* that her husband has returned and analyzes Penelope's motives for deciding in book 21 to hold an archery event to decide her suitor contest. Athena's role in these events is also discussed.

Austin, Norman. "Archery at the Dark of the Moon." In *Archery at the Dark of the Moon: Poetic Problems in Homer's "Odyssey."* Berkeley: University of California Press, 1975. Reprinted in *Critical Essays on Homer*, edited by Kenneth Atchity, Ron Hogart, and Doug Price. Boston: G. K. Hall, 1987.

Austin links Odysseus' homecoming with meteorological events such as the seasons and the cycle of the moon. Odysseus' return, coinciding with the end of the sailing season, occurs at the last possible moment and affirms the struggle of mortals against the inevitability of death and the natural order.

_____. "From Cities to Mind." In *Archery at the Dark of the Moon: Poetic Problems in Homer's "Odyssey."* Berkeley: University of California Press, 1975. Reprinted in abridged form as "The Power of the Word," in *Homer's "Odyssey,"* edited by Harold Bloom. Edgemont, Pa.: Chelsea House, 1988.

The human mind's quest for harmony is examined in the court scenes of the *Odyssey*, at Sparta in book 4, on Phaeacia in books 6-8, and on Ithaca in the last part of the *Odyssey*. The scenes between Odysseus and Penelope show how harmony grows between the reunited couple and how Odysseus is expected to re-create order out of chaos.

_____. "Intimations of Order." In *Archery at the Dark of the Moon: Poetic Problems in Homer's "Odyssey."* Berkeley: University of California Press, 1975.

An interpretation of the symbolism of Odysseus' journey with a concentration on the episodes prior to the hero's arrival in Ithaca. Structural contrasts between the natural and the artificial, between order and disorder, are seen as basic themes. Includes a bibliographical coda on the use of structuralist theory to interpret the *Odyssey*.

_____. "Odysseus and the Cyclops: Who Is Who." In *Approaches to Homer*, edited by Carl A. Rubino and Cynthia A. Shelmerdine. Austin: University of Texas Press, 1983.

On the surface, the Cyclops episode in *Odyssey* 9 is told by a mighty hero recounting his great deeds; on another level, the tale is that of a child telling a Freudian nightmare about an ogre. Analysis of Odysseus' negative description of the Cyclops' island and its social organization suggests the hero's jealousy and the basic parent-child rivalry of the story.

Blanchot, Maurice. "The Song of the Sirens: Encountering the Imaginary." In *The Gaze of Orpheus and Other Literary Essays*, translated by Lydia Davis. Barrytown, N.Y.: Station Hill, 1981. Abridged in *Homer*, edited by Harold Bloom. New York: Chelsea House, 1986.
This reflection upon the Sirens' song considers the relationship between reality and fiction, between the actual event and Odysseus' narration of this event in book 12 of the *Odyssey*. Odysseus becomes a Homer, a narrator of a tale, just like Herman Melville's Ahab after his encounter with Moby Dick.

Bradford, Ernle. *Ulysses Found*. New York: Harcourt, Brace & World, 1963.
This detailed attempt by a modern sailor to trace the route of Odysseus in the Mediterranean offers summaries of the hero's adventures described in *Odyssey* 9-10, including Odysseus' departure from Troy, the pirate raid on the Cicones, the Land of the Lotus-Eaters, his encounter with the Cyclops Polyphemus, and his visits to Aeolus, the wind god, to the Laestrygonians, and to Circe.

Butler, Samuel. "Further Considerations Regarding the Character of Penelope. . . ." In *The Authoress of the "Odyssey."* 2d ed. London: Jonathan Cape, 1922. Reprint. Chicago: University of Chicago Press, 1967.
A female author's description of events in *Odyssey* 1-4, especially Telemachus' journey to search for his father, is thought to contain veiled rebuke of Penelope and of her alleged misconduct with the suitors.

_____. "Further Indications That the Writer Is a Woman. . . ." In *The Authoress of the "Odyssey."* 2d ed. London: Jonathan Cape, 1922. Reprint. Chicago: University of Chicago Press, 1967.
Brief comments on a series of passages from the poem which are thought to suggest that the author of the *Odyssey* was a woman.

Butterworth, E. A. S. "[The Tales Odysseus Told Alkinoos, and the Akkadian Seal]." In *The Tree at the Navel of the Earth*. Berlin: De Gruyter, 1970. Reprinted in *Critical Essays on Homer*, edited by Kenneth Atchity, Ron Hogart, and Doug Price. Boston: G. K. Hall, 1987.
An interpretation of Odysseus' encounter with the Cyclops in which the one-eyed Polyphemus represents the Eastern quest for enlightenment through union with nature while Odysseus' self-naming affirms a Western preference for individuality.

Clark, Raymond J. "The Homeric Nekyia." In *Catabasis: Vergil and the Wisdom Tradition*. Amsterdam: B. R. Grüner, 1979.
In this chapter of a study of various treatments of the descent into the underworld in ancient literatures, the author examines features of Odysseus's descent in *Odyssey* 11. Argues that necromantic elements, such as the prophecy of Teiresias

and of the warning of Agamemnon's ghost, are merged by Homer with an actual *catabasis*, or descent to the underworld.

Clay, Jenny Strauss. "The Beginning of the *Odyssey*." In *The Wrath of Athena: Gods and Men in the "Odyssey."* Princeton, N.J.: Princeton University Press, 1983.
Discusses the invocation at the beginning of *Odyssey* 1, where the poet portrays himself as intermediary between gods and men, summarizes the multiplicity of Odysseus' character, and reveals a sympathetic desire to exonerate Odysseus from any blame for the death of his men. The poet's bias for Odysseus affects the very structure of the epic, which does not begin with Athena's anger toward Odysseus at his departure from Troy but with Athena's intervention on his behalf.

_____. "The Encounter of Odysseus and Athena." In *The Wrath of Athena: Gods and Men in the "Odyssey."* Princeton, N.J.: Princeton University Press, 1983.
A close examination of the meeting between Odysseus and Athena on Ithaca in *Odyssey* 13. Considers this encounter a test of will between mortal and immortal, a deceptive game of knowledge versus ignorance, of reality versus appearance, and suggests that the real reason for Athena's wrath is that Odysseus is too clever, even more clever than the gods.

Combellack, Frederick M. "Wise Penelope and the Contest of the Bow." Abridged from "Three Odyssean Problems." *California Studies in Classical Antiquities* 6 (1974): 17-46. Reprinted in *Twentieth Century Interpretations of the "Odyssey,"* edited by Howard W. Clarke. Englewood Cliffs, N.J.: Prentice-Hall, 1983.
Considers problems connected with Penelope's decision in *Odyssey* 19 to hold an archery contest in order to choose a new husband. The motivations for and timing of Penelope's decision appear inconsistent with her character.

Dimock, G. E., Jr. "The Name of Odysseus." *The Hudson Review* 9 (1956): 52-70. Reprinted in *Essays on the "Odyssey": Selected Modern Criticism*, edited by Charles H. Taylor, Jr. Bloomington: Indiana University Press, 1969. Also reprinted in *The Odyssey*, by Homer, edited by Albert Cook. New York: W. W. Norton, 1974. Also reprinted in *Homer: A Collection of Critical Essays*, edited by George Steiner and Robert Fagles. Englewood Cliffs, N.J.: Prentice-Hall, 1962.
Associates Odysseus' name with a Greek word meaning "to cause pain" and shows how, throughout the epic, Odysseus affirms his identity by causing pain both to others and to himself. Special attention is given to the Cyclops episode in book 9 and to the recognition scenes in the last part of the epic.

Dolin, Edwin. "Odysseus in Phaeacia." In *The Odyssey*, by Homer, edited by Albert Cook. New York: W. W. Norton, 1974.
Suggests that Odysseus' experiences on the island of Phaeacia (books 6-8, 13) are a combination of two traditions, an earlier version in which a picaresque hero decides to maintain a false identity and the Homeric version in which Odysseus heroically chooses truth over deception and reveals his real identity.

Doria, Charles. "[Aphrodite and Ares]." In *The Odyssey*, by Homer, edited by Albert Cook. New York: W. W. Norton, 1974.
In this short piece, the author suggests that the story of Aphrodite and Ares in *Odyssey* 8 is an amorous burlesque of the epic, that the story of Aphrodite's clever husband parallels that of Odysseus.

Eckert, Charles W. "Initiatory Motifs in the Story of Telemachus." *The Classical Journal* 59 (1963): 49-57. Reprinted in *Twentieth Century Interpretations of the "Odyssey,"* edited by Howard W. Clarke. Englewood Cliffs, N.J.: Prentice-Hall, 1983.
Illustrates how the story of Telemachus, not only in the Telemachy (*Odyssey* 1-4) but also in the last half of the *Odyssey*, can be interpreted according to the pattern of a traditional initiation ritual. In Homer's story, ritualized instruction is transformed into an individualized quest for self-knowledge.

Finley, John H., Jr. "The Beggar." In *Homer's "Odyssey."* Cambridge, Mass.: Harvard University Press, 1978.
Examines several of Odysseus' personal encounters in *Odyssey* 13-19, especially those with Athena, Eumaeus, Telemachus, and Penelope. Uses frequent comparisons with the *Iliad*.

_____. "Odysseus' Tale." In *Homer's "Odyssey."* Cambridge, Mass.: Harvard University Press, 1978.
A detailed discussion of the adventures which Odysseus' narrates in *Odyssey* 9-12. These adventures are considered a testimony to the returning hero's store of experience. Includes comparisons between Odysseus' trip to the underworld and trips by other heroes such as those of Gilgamesh, Vergil's Aeneas, and Dante Alighieri. Also uses frequent comparisons with the *Iliad*.

_____. "Ogygia and Scheria." In *Homer's "Odyssey."* Cambridge, Mass.: Harvard University Press, 1978.
Analyzes Odysseus' growth in self-understanding and his progression from a lone man back to a famous hero during his adventures with Circe and with the Phaeacians in *Odyssey* 5-12. There are frequent comparisons with the *Iliad*.

_____. "The Origins of the Tales of Travel." In *Homer's "Odyssey."*
Cambridge, Mass.: Harvard University Press, 1978.
Examines the stories of Odysseus' adventures in *Odyssey* 5-12. Argues that the
various folktale origins hypothesized for these stories are not as important as their
thematic purpose within the poem, namely to illustrate Odysseus as a man of
experience.

_____. "Reunion." In *Homer's "Odyssey."* Cambridge, Mass.: Harvard
University Press, 1978.
Examines several aspects of *Odyssey* 20-24, including the violent slaying of the
suitors and Odysseus' reunions with Penelope and Laertes. Argues strongly for
the authenticity of the last book, including the Second Nekyia.

_____. "The Reunion at the Farm." In *Homer's "Odyssey."* Cambridge,
Mass.: Harvard University Press, 1978.
In this second of two appendices, the author refutes several scholarly objections
to the authenticity of the scene between Odysseus and Laertes in *Odyssey* 24 and
asserts that the scene is genuine. Uses some untranslated Greek phrases.

_____. "The Second Nekyia." In *Homer's "Odyssey."* Cambridge, Mass.:
Harvard University Press, 1978.
In this first of two appendices, the author summarizes scholarly objections to the
authenticity of the suitors' descent into the underworld in *Odyssey* 24 but affirms
that this passage was part of the original epic.

_____. "Telemachus." In *Homer's "Odyssey."* Cambridge, Mass.: Harvard
University Press, 1978.
Suggests that the first four books of the *Odyssey* present not so much a maturation of Telemachus as a revelation of his character and beauty and of the path
of success which the gods have prepared for both Telemachus and his father,
Odysseus. Their future success contrasts with melancholy brooding about the past
by Menelaus and Helen. There are frequent comparisons with the *Iliad*.

Frame, Douglas. "The Return of Odysseus." In *The Myth of Return in Early Greek
Epic*. New Haven, Conn.: Yale University Press, 1978.
Examines linguistic features connected with Homer's description of Odysseus'
return to Ithaca and several of his adventures, including those with Circe and
Cyclops in order to illustrate a connection between Odysseus' "wiles" and his
"wanderings." Odysseus' "return to light and life," based upon a link between
the Greek noun *nóos* ("mind") and the verb *néomai* ("to return home"), is
considered an important strand in the oral tradition upon which the *Odyssey* is
based.

Gaunt, D. M. *Surge and Thunder: Critical Readings in Homer's "Odyssey."* New York: Oxford University Press, 1971.
Translations and commentaries are accompanied by appreciative and interpretative comments on twenty short pieces from the *Odyssey*, including several descriptive passages and such events as Odysseus' arrival on Phaeacia in *Odyssey* 5-6; his encounters with the Cyclops, the Laestrygonians, and Scylla and Charybdis in *Odyssey* 1-12; his recognitions by his faithful watchdog Argus in *Odyssey* 17 and by his nurse Eurycleia in *Odyssey* 19; his stringing of the bow in *Odyssey* 21; and the slaying of the suitors in *Odyssey* 22.

Germain, Gabriel. "Polyphemus and African Initiation Rites." In *Genèse de "L'Odyssée."* Paris: Presses Universitaires de France, 1954. Translated by Clement Goodson in *The Odyssey*, by Homer, edited by Albert Cook. New York: W. W. Norton, 1974.
Associates Odysseus' encounter with Polyphemus in the cave with stories of one-eyed ogres in a variety of cultures, especially in the context of Berber initiation rites.

Graves, Robert. *The Greek Myths*. Vol. 2. Baltimore: Penguin Books, 1960.
This handbook includes discussions of various myths mentioned in the *Odyssey*. References to the epic are often found only in the notes, but the following subjects should be noted: the story of Agamemnon's murder by his wife, Clytemnestra, the avenging of his death by his son, Orestes, and Orestes' trial; parallels between the adventures of Odysseus in *Odyssey* 12 and Jason's voyage on the *Argo*, especially encounters with the Sirens and Scylla and Charybdis; the mythic background for Odysseus' encounter in *Odyssey* 11 with the dead Ajax and with individuals connected with the war known as the Seven Against Thebes; information about the seer Melampus mentioned in *Odyssey* 11; the Homeric version of the fate of Oedipus in *Iliad* 11 compared to other versions of the story; a summary of the story of the creation of the world by union of Earth (Gaea) and Sky (Uranus) with reference to the origin of the Cyclopes and to Odysseus' adventure on their island in *Odyssey* 9; a description of the fates of various Greek warriors returning from the Trojan War, including Menelaus' encounter with Proteus, described in *Odyssey* 4; information about Tantalus, mentioned in *Odyssey* 11; and references to Heracles' capture of Cerberus, noted in *Odyssey* 11.

Greene, Thomas. "Form and Craft in the *Odyssey*." In *The Descent from Heaven: A Study in Epic Continuity*. New Haven, Conn.: Yale University Press, 1963.
In this chapter of a book on the European epic tradition, Greene looks at two episodes of divine descent in the *Odyssey*: Athena's visit to Telemachus in *Odyssey* 1 and Hermes' to Odysseus in *Odyssey* 6.

Harrison, Jane E. *Myths of "The Odyssey" in Art and Literature*. London: Rivingtons, 1883.
In individual chapters, Harrison examines Odysseus' adventures in *Odyssey* 9-12 and traces their influence in the art of ancient Greece and Rome. Paraphrases of the Homeric versions of the stories of the Cyclops, the Laestrygonians, Circe, Odysseus' descent into the underworld, the Sirens, and Scylla and Charybdis are accompanied by descriptions and line drawings of similar scenes on Greek pottery, Roman wall paintings, and other artistic media.

Kafka, Franz. "The Silence of the Sirens." In *Parables*, by Franz Kafka, translated by Willa and Edwin Muir. New York: Schocken Books, 1947. Reprinted in *Homer: A Collection of Critical Essays*, edited by George Steiner and Robert Fagles. Englewood Cliffs, N.J.: Prentice-Hall, 1962.
A reflection upon Odysseus' adventure with the Sirens in *Odyssey* 12. Suggests that the Sirens' most powerful weapon was not really their song but their silence.

Knight, W. F. Jackson. *Cumaean Gates: A Reference of the Sixth "Aeneid" to the Initiation Pattern*. Oxford, England: Basil Blackwell, 1936. Reprinted in *Vergil: Epic and Anthropology*. New York: Barnes & Noble Books, 1967.
This study of comparative anthropology includes a chapter devoted to Odysseus' journey to the land of the dead in *Odyssey* 11. Links between Calypso and the Vergilian Sibyl are discussed.

Mariani, Alice. "The Renaming of Odysseus." In *Critical Essays on Homer*, edited by Kenneth Atchity, Ron Hogart, and Doug Price. Boston: G. K. Hall, 1987.
In this excerpt from her doctoral dissertation, the author reflects on the significance of Odysseus' name, with special attention to the hero's scar and the story of the boar hunt in *Odyssey* 19. Odysseus is seen to be a hero who both gives and endures pain.

Morford, Mark P. O., and Robert J. Lenardon. "Poseidon, Sea Deities, Group Divinities, and Monsters." In *Classical Mythology*. 3d ed. New York: Longman, 1985.
This chapter includes a summary of Menelaus' encounter with the sea god Proteus in *Odyssey* 4. An extensive quotation from the *Odyssey* is included.

_____. "Views of the Afterlife: The Realm of Hades." In *Classical Mythology*. 3d ed. New York: Longman, 1985.
This section includes a summary of Odysseus' journey to the land of the dead in *Odyssey* 11 and comparisons to other such journeys, such as those in the Myth of Er in Plato's *Republic* 10 and in Vergil's *Aeneid* 6. Extensive quotations from all sources are included.

Murnaghan, Sheila. "Recognition and Song." In *Disguise and Recognition in the "Odyssey."* Princeton, N.J.: Princeton University Press, 1987.
Examines the relationship between Odysseus and narratives about his adventures. Considers the occasions, purposes, and effects of various songs and tales about Odysseus' adventures, including those of Phemius in *Odyssey* 1 and of Demodocus in *Odyssey* 8, and of Odysseus, first to the Phaeacians in *Odyssey* 9-12 and later to Penelope in *Odyssey* 23. Evaluates the degrees of truth, fame, and pleasure gained for heroes from third-person narratives, such as those of Phemius and Demodocus, and from the first-person narratives of Odysseus.

_____. "Recognition and the Return of Odysseus." In *Disguise and Recognition in the "Odyssey."* Princeton, N.J.: Princeton University Press, 1987.
Observes the recurrent pattern of scenes of recognition of Odysseus, including those with his mother in *Odyssey* 11, his father in *Odyssey* 24, his son in *Odyssey* 16, his servants in *Odyssey* 19 and 21, and his wife in *Odyssey* 23. Shows how the story of Odysseus' return to Ithaca is intertwined with stories about other members of his household and how all these characters share with Odysseus a process of disguise and recognition during the course of the epic. Observes an important correspondence between the theme of recognition and the Greek custom of guest-friendship in Odysseus' relationships with his hosts both on Scheria and on Ithaca.

Page, Denys L. "Appendix." In *The Homeric "Odyssey."* Oxford, England: Clarendon Press, 1955. Reprint. Westport, Conn.: Greenwood Press, 1976.
Examines several problems and inconsistencies related to the story of Telemachus in *Odyssey* 1-4, including the relation of book 2 with books 3 and 4, references to the suitors in books 3 and 4, and the suitors' ambush of Telemachus in books 4 and 16. Includes some untranslated Greek words.

_____. "The Arrow and the Axes." In *Folktales in Homer's "Odyssey."* Cambridge, Mass.: Harvard University Press, 1973.
In this appendix to a study of folktale motifs in the *Odyssey*, the author explains how the axes are placed for the archery contest in the last part of the *Odyssey*. Includes some untranslated Greek words.

_____. *Folktales in Homer's "Odyssey."* Cambridge, Mass.: Harvard University Press, 1973.
Examines several adventures of Odysseus in *Odyssey* 9-12, including the stories of the Lotus-Eaters, Polyphemus the Cyclops, Aeolus' bag of winds, the cattle of the sun god, the Sirens, the Laestrygonians, Circe, and the journey to the land of the dead. Makes frequent comparison to folktales in other cultural traditions in order to suggest the folktale origin of these Homeric stories.

Stewart, Douglas J. "The Disguised Guest." In *The Disguised Guest: Rank, Role, and Identity in the "Odyssey."* Lewisburg, Pa.: Bucknell University Press, 1976. Reprinted in *Homer*, edited by Harold Bloom. New York: Chelsea House, 1986. In this chapter of a book on Odysseus' identity, the author focuses upon the hero's relationship with his home, Ithaca, and his encounters with his son, Telemachus, and his servant, Eumaeus, in books 13-17.

_____. "The Last Suitor." In *The Disguised Guest: Rank, Role, and Identity in the "Odyssey."* Lewisburg, Pa.: Bucknell University Press, 1976. An examination of the hero's relationship with his wife, Penelope, and their confused relationship in the last part of the *Odyssey*. In particular, the author considers the importance of the stringing of the bow and Penelope's recognition of Odysseus.

_____. "Odysseus and the Cyclops: The Heroic Code Reviewed . . . and Rejected." In *The Disguised Guest: Rank, Role, and Identity in the "Odyssey."* Lewisburg, Pa.: Bucknell University Press, 1976. An examination of the hero's loss of identity in book 9 of the epic and its effect upon the hero's other adventures, including events on the island of Phaeacia.

Thornton, Agathe. "The Homecomings of the Achaeans." Reprinted in *Homer's "Odyssey,"* edited by Harold Bloom. Edgemont, Pa.: Chelsea House, 1988. In this excerpt from *People and Themes in Homer's "Odyssey,"* the author examines Homer's treatment of the homecoming theme, especially the story of Agamemnon in the underworld scene of *Odyssey* 11 and 24 and the stories of Nestor and Menelaus in *Odyssey* 3 and 4. These homecomings, told by the heroes themselves, create dramatic intensity and put the return of Odysseus into greater perspective.

Wender, Dorothea. "In Hades' Halls." In *The Last Scenes of the "Odyssey,"* *Mnemosyne*, supplement 52. Leiden: E. J. Brill, 1978. Reprinted in *Twentieth Century Interpretations of the "Odyssey,"* edited by Howard W. Clarke. Englewood Cliffs, N.J.: Prentice-Hall, 1983. Considers problems connected with the role of Hermes as escort, the failure of Odysseus to bury the suitors, and Amphimedon's inaccurate summary of events in the Second Nekyia (*Odyssey* 24). Wender argues that the scene with the dead suitors in the underworld serves several functions, including a final summary of the poem, a panegyric for Penelope, and an evaluation of Odysseus in comparison with Agamemnon and Achilles.

Whitman, Cedric H. "The *Odyssey* and Change." In *Homer and the Homeric Tradition*. Cambridge, Mass.: Harvard University Press, 1958. Slightly abridged

in *Twentieth Century Interpretations of the "Odyssey,"* edited by Howard W. Clarke. Englewood Cliffs, N.J.: Prentice-Hall, 1983.
This comparative study of the poetic structures used in the two Homeric poems includes a discussion of geometric patterns such as scenic antithesis and framing in the adventures of Odysseus in *Odyssey* 9-12 and the Phaeacian episode of *Odyssey* 8.

Woodhouse, W. J. *The Composition of Homer's "Odyssey."* Oxford, England: Clarendon Press, 1930.
Discusses various scenes from the epic and their possible sources, including Odysseus' stay with Calypso in *Odyssey* 1-5; his meeting with Nausicaa and his stay with the Phaeacians in *Odyssey* 6-9; his encounter with Circe in *Odyssey* 10; the so-called lying tales which Odysseus tells on Ithaca in *Odyssey* 14 and 17; the stringing of Odysseus' bow in *Odyssey* 21; and the recognitions of Odysseus by Eurycleia in *Odyssey* 19 and by Penelope in *Odyssey* 23. Woodhouse is especially interested in narrative inconsistencies as indications of Homer's compositional technique; for example, contradictory references to the contest of the bow in *Odyssey* 19-21 and 24 and to the removal of armor from Odysseus' hall in *Odyssey* 16 and 19.

Homer's Influence

Homer in Later Literature

Apollonius Rhodius. *The Argonautica.* Translated by R. C. Seaton. New York: G. P. Putnam's Sons, 1919.
Unlike the Homeric epics with their oral background, this short Greek epic, telling the story of Jason and Medea and Jason's quest for the Golden Fleece, is a literary work written by a Hellenistic scholar in the late third century B.C. Apollonius uses the conventional epic language of Homer and includes features of Homeric epic, such as an invocation, catalogue, and a divine apparatus. This edition includes a bibliography, an index, and a summary of each book. Greek text and English translation appear on facing pages.

Auden, W. H. "The Shield of Achilles." In *Collected Shorter Poems, 1927-1957.* New York: Random House, 1967. Reprinted in *Homer: A Collection of Critical Essays,* edited by George Steiner and Robert Fagles. Englewood Cliffs, N.J.: Prentice-Hall, 1962. Also reprinted in *Critical Essays on Homer,* edited by Kenneth Atchity, Ron Hogart, and Doug Price. Boston: G. K. Hall, 1987.

This poem, based upon Homer's description of the shield of Achilles in *Iliad* 18, illustrates the continuing contribution of the Homeric epics to twentieth century English literature.

Borges, Jorge Luis. "The Maker." In *Dreamtigers*, translated by Mildred Boyer and Harold Morland. Austin: University of Texas Press, 1964. Reprinted in *Critical Essays on Homer*, edited by Kenneth Atchity, Ron Hogart, and Doug Price. Boston: G. K. Hall, 1987.
This excerpt from the blind author's work *Dreamtigers* is an imaginative reflection by Homer on his blindness.

Cavafy, C. P. "Ithaka." In *C. P. Cavafy: Collected Poems*, edited by George Savidis, translated by Edmund Keeley and Phillip Sharrard. Princeton, N.J.: Princeton University Press, 1975. Reprinted in *Homer: A Collection of Critical Essays*, edited by George Steiner and Robert Fagles. Englewood Cliffs, N.J.: Prentice-Hall, 1962. Also reprinted in *Critical Essays on Homer*, edited by Kenneth Atchity, Ron Hogart, and Doug Price. Boston: G. K. Hall, 1987.
In this poem, a twentieth century Greek poet reflects upon Odysseus' journey to Ithaca and transforms the island into a symbol of human goals and aspirations. The journey itself is considered more valuable than the destination. Illustrates the continuity of Homeric themes in modern Greek literature.

Clark, Frank Lowry. *A Study of the "Iliad" in Translation*. Chicago: University of Chicago Press, 1927.
Included within this abridged verse translation of the epic are frequent quotations from modern literary works which imitate or offer parallels to passages from the *Iliad*. Includes an introduction, bibliography, and index.

Cowper, William. "Lines After the Manner of Homer." In *The Complete Poetical Works of William Cowper*, edited by H. S. Milford. New York: Oxford University Press, 1913.
In this poem, an eighteenth century English poet and translator of the *Iliad* and the *Odyssey* imitates Homer's style and language in his humorous description of the opening of a hamper.

_____. "On a Mistake in His Translation of Homer." In *The Complete Poetical Works of William Cowper*, edited by H. S. Milford. New York: Oxford University Press, 1913.
An eighteenth century translator of Homer responds to a reader's complaint that he has mistakenly translated "wethers" for the Homeric word for "ewes." The poet suggests in this poem that his rhyme scheme demanded this free translation.

_____. "To John Johnson, on his presenting me with an antique bust of Homer." In *The Complete Poetical Works of William Cowper*, edited by H. S. Milford. New York: Oxford University Press, 1913. Reprinted in *The Poets on the Classics: An Anthology of English Poets' Writing on the Classical Poets and Dramatists from Chaucer to the Present*, edited by Stuart Gillespie. New York: Routledge, 1988.
In this eighteenth century sonnet, the poet thanks an acquaintance for the gift of a bust of Homer and suggests that reading Homer is less important and valuable than pursuing Christian ideals.

Day Lewis, C. "Nearing Again the Legendary Isle." In *The Magnetic Mountain*, edited by Leonard and Virginia Woolf. London: Hogarth Press, 1933. Reprinted in *Homer: A Collection of Critical Essays*, edited by George Steiner and Robert Fagles. Englewood Cliffs, N.J.: Prentice-Hall, 1962.
In this poem, the author contemplates a voyage to the island of the Sirens by a shipload of starving sailors.

Donne, John. "A Valediction: Forbidding Mourning." In *The Complete Poetry and Selected Prose of John Donne*, edited by John Hayward. New York: Random House, 1941. Reprinted in *Critical Essays on Homer*, edited by Kenneth Atchity, Ron Hogart, and Doug Price. Boston: G. K. Hall, 1987.
An important seventeenth century English poet offers a poetic study of the love which binds Penelope and Odysseus even in separation.

Du Bellay, Joachim. "Happy the man who, like Ulysses, has had a good journey." In *The Penguin Book of French Verse*. Vol. 2, *Sixteenth to Eighteenth Centuries*, edited by Geoffrey Brereton. Baltimore: Penguin Books, 1967.
In this sonnet about homecomings, a member of the sixteenth century French Pléiade movement shows the movement's interest in Classical antiquity by comparing the return of Odysseus to Ithaca with the poet's return to his own modest home.

Fitzgerald, Robert. "Hellas." In *The Rose of Time*, by Robert Fitzgerald. Norfolk, Conn.: New Directions, 1956. Reprinted in *Homer: A Collection of Critical Essays*, edited by George Steiner and Robert Fagles. Englewood Cliffs, N.J.: Prentice-Hall, 1962.
The poet reflects upon Homer's blindness, Helen's beauty, and her long years in Troy.

Gayley, Charles Mills. *Classic Myths in English Literature and in Art*. 2d ed. New York: John Wiley & Sons, 1911.
This mythological handbook not only summarizes the plots of both the *Iliad* and the *Odyssey* but also includes extensive quotation from various poems based upon

these epics, including Alfred, Lord Tennyson's "Ulysses" and John Keats's "On First Looking into Chapman's Homer." A commentary section contains lists of works of art and literature based upon the epic. Includes illustrations and indexes.

Gillespie, Stuart, ed. *The Poets on the Classics: An Anthology of English Poets' Writing on the Classical Poets and Dramatists from Chaucer to the Present.* New York: Routledge, 1988.
In addition to a collection of poems and excerpts of works by English writers who make reference to Greco-Roman literature, this book includes a general historical overview of Classical influences on the English poets as well as brief summaries of the influence of specific ancient authors, including Homer. The section on Homer contains comments by several translators of Homer, including George Chapman, John Dryden, and T. E. Lawrence, as well as several poems about Homer. A brief glossary, explanatory notes, bibliographies, and indexes are included.

Graves, Robert. "The Authoress of the *Odyssey.*" In *Homer: A Collection of Critical Essays*, edited by George Steiner and Robert Fagles. Englewood Cliffs, N.J.: Prentice-Hall, 1962.
In this excerpt from the concluding chapter of Graves's historical novel *Homer's Daughter*, Nausicaa, the author of the *Odyssey*, describes her working relationship with Phemius, the bard, and her approach to the composition of the poem.

_____. *Homer's Daughter.* New York: Doubleday, 1955.
This historical novel, is based upon the theory of Samuel Butler that the *Odyssey* was written by a Sicilian woman named Nausicaa. In this novel, the plot of the *Odyssey* emerges from a first-person account by Nausicaa of the struggle against her own suitors.

_____. "Ulysses." In *Collected Poems.* New York: Doubleday, 1955. Reprinted in *Homer: A Collection of Critical Essays*, edited by George Steiner and Robert Fagles. Englewood Cliffs, N.J.: Prentice-Hall, 1962.
Associates Odysseus' ties with several women, including Penelope and Circe, with his many terrifying adventures. The hero's quest for adventure is identified with his quest for his home in Ithaca.

Joyce, James. *Ulysses.* New York: Vintage Books, 1961.
This notorious novel by the twentieth century Irish author is based upon a subtle parallel between the plot of Homer's *Odyssey* and a day in the lives of three Dubliners: Stephen Dedalus, Leopold Bloom, and his wife, Molly.

Kazantzakis, Nikos. *The Odyssey: A Modern Sequel.* Translated by Kimon Friar, illustrated by Ghika. New York: Simon & Schuster, 1958.

This book-length modern Greek poem transforms the story of Odysseus into a masterly contemplation of philosophical and religious ideas. Combines Homeric themes and structures with Christian beliefs and the later mythic tradition about Odysseus, especially the story told by Dante Alighieri. In Kazantzakis' poem, the slaying of the suitors is followed by Odysseus' alienation from his wife and son and a second, and final, departure from Ithaca. Leads Odysseus through a series of new adventures, including an abduction of Helen, the destruction of Cnossus, rebellion in Egypt, a divine experience, a journey to the South Pole, and his death. The translator provides an introduction, a synopsis of the plot, a note on meter, and endnotes.

Keats, John. "On First Looking into Chapman's Homer." In *The Complete Poetry of John Keats*, edited by George R. Elliott. New York: Macmillan, 1927. Reprinted in *The Poets on the Classics: An Anthology of English Poets' Writing on the Classical Poets and Dramatists from Chaucer to the Present*, edited by Stuart Gillespie. New York: Routledge, 1988.
This sonnet, a reflection upon the poet's reading of the translation of Homer by George Chapman, suggests that the poet did not fully appreciate the power of Homer's works until he read them in Chapman's translation.

_____. "To Homer." In *The Complete Poetry of John Keats*, edited by George R. Elliott. New York: Macmillan, 1927. Reprinted in *The Poets on the Classics: An Anthology of English Poets' Writing on the Classical Poets and Dramatists from Chaucer to the Present*, edited by Stuart Gillespie. New York: Routledge, 1988.
In this sonnet, Keats contemplates upon the tradition that Homer was blind and suggests that this physical disability enabled the poet to perceive a reality beyond the physical.

Lang, Andrew. "Homer." In *The Poetical Works of Andrew Lang*, edited by Mrs. Lang. New York: Longmans, Green, 1923. Reprinted in *The Poets on the Classics: An Anthology of English Poets' Writing on the Classical Poets and Dramatists from Chaucer to the Present*, edited by Stuart Gillespie. New York: Routledge, 1988.
In this sonnet, an important late nineteenth century translator of Homer rejects a popular comparison of Homer with the sea in favor of one with a river, like the Nile, which is fertile with knowledge of the distant past.

_____. "Homeric Unity." In *The Poetical Works of Andrew Lang*, edited by Mrs. Lang. New York: Longmans, Green, 1923. Reprinted in *The Poets on the Classics: An Anthology of English Poets' Writing on the Classical Poets and Dramatists from Chaucer to the Present*, edited by Stuart Gillespie. New York: Routledge, 1988.

Lang, a popular late nineteenth century translator of Homer, addresses the
Homeric question in sonnet form and asserts his conviction that the *Iliad* and the
Odyssey were written by a single poet. Lang contrasts the indestructibility of the
Homeric poems with the destruction of Troy and of Mycenae, the ruins of which
were discovered by Heinrich Schliemann just before this poem was written.

——————————. "The *Odyssey*." In *The Poetical Works of Andrew Lang*, edited by
Mrs. Lang. New York: Longmans, Green, 1923. Reprinted in *Great Poems of
the English Language: An Anthology of Verse in English from Chaucer to the
Moderns*, edited by Wallace A. Briggs. New York: Tudor, 1933.
In this sonnet, a nineteenth century translator of Homer describes the soothing
effect which reading the *Odyssey* has upon him. The adventures of the *Odyssey*
enable the poet for a while to forget the modern world and briefly to experience
the world of Homer.

Lawrence, D. H. "The Argonauts." In *Last Poems*, edited by Richard Aldington
and Giuseppe Orioli. New York: Viking Press, 1933. Reprinted in *Homer: A
Collection of Critical Essays*, edited by George Steiner and Robert Fagles.
Englewood Cliffs, N.J.: Prentice-Hall, 1962.
A poem about Odysseus voyaging on the sea while the sun sets, the moon rises,
and the poet watches.

Lucretius Carus, Titus. *De Rerum Natura*. Translated by W. H. D. Rouse. 2d ed.
Revised by Martin F. Smith. Cambridge, Mass.: Harvard University Press, 1982.
This Latin epic of the first century B.C. is a philosophical poem describing the
teachings of Epicurus. Homeric influence can be seen not only in Lucretius' epic
language and techniques but also in his direct praise of Homer as the best of
poets in book 3. This edition includes an introduction, bibliography, and index.
Latin text and English translation are on facing pages.

Muir, Edwin. "Telemachos Remembers." In *One Foot in Eden*. New York: Grove
Press, 1956. Reprinted in *Homer: A Collection of Critical Essays*, edited by
George Steiner and Robert Fagles. Englewood Cliffs, N.J.: Prentice-Hall, 1962.
Telemachus recollects the twenty years of his father's absence and his mother's
painful loneliness at the loom.

Parotti, Phillip. *The Greek Generals Talk: Memoirs of the Trojan War*. Urbana:
University of Illinois Press, 1986.
A collection of twelve fictional monologues in which Greek generals reminisce
about events connected with the Trojan War fifty years before. Included are the
tales of Diomedes, Thrasymedes, Meriones, Thersites, and other warriors
mentioned, at least briefly, in the Homeric poems. Includes a glossary and three
maps with an accompanying gazetteer.

_____. *The Trojan Generals Talk: Memoirs of the Greek War*. Urbana: University of Illinois Press, 1988.
This fictional piece is a collection of ten dramatic monologues by Trojan generals who, fifty years after the events, describe their experiences during the war with the Greeks and explain how they survived the fall of the city. Parotti imaginatively develops full personalities and narratives for figures like Merops, Polydamas, and Nastes mentioned only in passing by Homer. Includes a glossary and four maps with an accompanying gazetteer.

Snodgrass, W. D. "*Métis . . . oûtis*." In *Heart's Needle*. New York: Alfred A. Knopf, 1959. Reprinted in *Homer: A Collection of Critical Essays*, edited by George Steiner and Robert Fagles. Englewood Cliffs, N.J.: Prentice-Hall, 1962.
A poetic reflection upon Odysseus' adventure with the Cyclops in *Odyssey* 9, and especially upon Odysseus' deceitful name "Noman."

Stevens, Wallace. "The World as Meditation." In *Collected Poems of Wallace Stevens*. New York: Alfred A. Knopf, 1954. Reprinted in *Critical Essays on Homer*, edited by Kenneth Atchity, Ron Hogart, and Doug Price. Boston: G. K. Hall, 1987.
In this poem, a twentieth century American poet reflects upon the thoughts of Penelope as she contemplates the return of Odysseus after his long absence.

Tennyson, Alfred, Lord. "The Lotus Eaters." In *Poetical Works*. New York: Thomas Y. Crowell, 1900.
Based upon Odysseus' adventure in the land of the Lotus-Eaters in *Odyssey* 9, this poem by the nineteenth century British poet laureate describes the charming appearance of this mysterious land, the arrival of some sailors, and the effect of the lotus on these sailors, who lose the yearning to go home to their families.

_____. "Ulysses." In *Poetical Works*. New York: Thomas Y. Crowell, 1900. Reprinted in *The "Odyssey" of Homer*, translated by Preston H. Epps. New York: Macmillan, 1965.
In this poem, Tennyson describes what might have happened to Odysseus after the events of the *Odyssey*, after the hero had returned to Ithaca and reestablished his position at home.

Vergil. *The Aeneid*. Translated by Rolfe Humphries. New York: Charles Scribner's Sons, 1951.
This epic poem by the first century B.C. Roman poet is a conscious imitation of the Homeric poem. The first half of the *Aeneid*, describing Aeneas' journey from Troy to Italy, parallels and overlaps with the plot of the *Odyssey*, while the second half of Vergil's epic, dealing with the Italian war fought by Aeneas and his followers, is modeled upon the plot of the *Iliad*.

Studies of Homer's Influence

Aristotle. *The Poetics*. Translated by S. H. Butcher. In *Aristotle's Theory of Poetry and Fine Art*, by S. H. Butcher. 4th ed. London: St. Martin's Press, 1907. Reprint. New York: Dover Publications, 1951.
This study of poetry, language, and plot by the fourth century B.C. Greek philosopher includes a comparison of tragedy and epic. The last four chapters of Aristotle's book are particularly devoted to Homer and illustrate the important place held by the Homeric poems among ancient Greeks. Aristotle's book has, in turn, influenced many interpretations of Homer, especially since the Renaissance. In addition to the Greek text and a translation of Aristotle's book, this edition includes a list of editions and translations of *Poetics*, an analysis of the book, a twelve-chapter study of Aristotle's aesthetic theory, and indexes.

Bespaloff, Rachel. "Troy and Moscow." In *On the "Iliad,"* translated by Mary McCarthy. New York: Pantheon Books, 1947.
In this short essay, the author compares the treatment of war in the *Iliad* to that in Leo Tolstoy's *War and Peace* in terms of such themes as human suffering, fatality, the gods, and chastity.

Bloch, Ernst. "Odysseus Did Not Die in Ithaca." In *Homer: A Collection of Critical Essays*, edited by George Steiner and Robert Fagles, translated from *Das Prinzip Hoffnung*, by Hanna Loewy and George Steiner. Englewood Cliffs, N.J.: Prentice-Hall, 1962.
This essay is a reflection upon the story of Odysseus' death told by Dante Alighieri in canto 26 of the *Inferno*. Odysseus is considered a kind of knight errant who faces the unknown.

Bradford, Ernle. "The Flowers of the Sea." In *Ulysses Found*. New York: Harcourt, Brace & World, 1963.
This discussion of stories associated with Odysseus after his return to Ithaca in the *Odyssey* focuses upon Dante's version of the hero's last voyage in the *Inferno* and refers to other literary allusions to the hero's story and its meaning.

Broch, Hermann. "The Style of the Mythical Age." In *On the "Iliad,"* by Rachel Bespaloff, translated by Mary McCarthy. New York: Pantheon Books, 1947.
In this introduction to Bespaloff's study of the *Iliad*, the author reflects on the place of myth in Western literature from Homer to Leo Tolstoy. The relationships between myth and truth, myth and religion, and myth and poetry are pursued in the context of modernistic thought, Nazism, and Bespaloff's identification of the Homeric epic with biblical prophecy.

Camps, W. A. "Making an Episode: Fusion of Inherited Materials Exemplified in the Sixth Book." In *An Introduction to Virgil's "Aeneid."* Oxford, England: Oxford University Press, 1969.
Illustrates the way in which the story of Aeneas' journey to the underworld in *Aeneid* 6 is molded from various sources, including *Odyssey* 11. There is a good discussion of the way in which Vergil has modified the Homeric basis of the episode.

_____. "Making the Story: Fusion of the Legend of Aeneas' Coming to Italy with Matter from *Iliad* and *Odyssey*." In *An Introduction to Virgil's "Aeneid."* Oxford, England: Oxford University Press, 1969.
Discusses the way in which Vergil freely transforms his sources for the *Aeneid*, including the Homeric poems, in his retelling of the legend of Aeneas' journey from Troy to Italy. There is a useful summary of scenes in the *Aeneid* which parallel scenes in the Homeric poems.

Clark, Raymond J. *Catabasis: Vergil and the Wisdom Tradition.* Amsterdam: B. R. Grüner, 1979.
Traces the development of the theme of the descent into the underworld from the Near Eastern literature through *Odyssey* 11 and into later treatments in the Greco-Roman world. Aeneas' journey to the underworld in *Aeneid* 6 is seen to be an innovative adaptation of earlier treatments of the theme, especially that of Homer.

Cook, Albert. "Samples of Reactions to Homer in Antiquity." In *The Odyssey*, by Homer, translated and edited by Albert Cook. New York: W. W. Norton, 1974.
This section is a collection of ancient texts which show the influence of Homer in the ancient Greco-Roman world. Authors represented include Pindar, Proclus, Porphyry, Aristotle, Seneca the Younger, and Longinus.

Distler, Paul F. "Vergil and His *Aeneid*." In *Vergil and Vergiliana*. Chicago: Loyola University Press, 1966.
Includes a partial list of parallel passages between the Homeric epics and Vergil's *Aeneid*, a list of references to Aeneas in Homer, and Vergilian uses of Homeric similes.

Fagles, Robert. "Epilogue: Homer and the Writers." In *Homer: A Collection of Critical Essays*, edited by George Steiner and Robert Fagles. Englewood Cliffs, N.J.: Prentice-Hall, 1962.
Explores interpretations of Homer by and his influence on such twentieth century authors as T. E. Shaw (Lawrence of Arabia), Robert Fitzgerald, James Joyce, Robert Graves, and Ezra Pound.

Foerster, Donald M. *Homer in English Criticism: The Historical Approach in the Eighteenth Century*. New Haven, Conn.: Yale University Press, 1947. Reprint. Hamden, Conn.: Archon Books, 1969.
This scholarly book traces the development of the historical approach toward Homeric studies in eighteenth century Britain, with particular attention to the works of Thomas Blackwell and Robert Wood. Includes a preface, conclusion, appendix, and index.

Friar, Kimon. Introduction to *The "Odyssey": A Modern Sequel*, by Nikos Kazant-zakis, translated by Kimon Friar, illustrated by Ghika. New York: Simon & Schuster, 1958.
The English translator of Kazantzakis' poetic version of the later life of Odysseus offers comments upon the author's philosophy, his life, his portrayal of the hero, and the style and structure of the poem. Illustrates how Kazantzakis transforms the Homeric poem into a modern and Christian reflection upon themes such as human freedom, the life journey, and the relationship between God and human.

Glover, T. R. "Literature: 1. Literary Influences." In *Virgil*. 7th ed. New York: Barnes & Noble Books, 1969.
In one section of this discussion of Vergil's literary antecedents, Glover considers Vergil's relation to Homer. Homer's language is seen as an inspiration for Vergil, who differs from Homer in his greater detachment from his subject.

Gransden, K. W. *Virgil's "Iliad": An Essay on Epic Narrative*. Cambridge, England: Cambridge University Press, 1984.
Throughout this book, which is mostly about the last six books of Vergil's *Aeneid*, there are constant references to Homer's *Iliad* and its influence upon Vergil's epic. Homer's portrayal of Achilles, Patroclus, and Hector receives particular attention.

Harrison, Jane E. *Myths of "The Odyssey" in Art and Literature*. London: Riving-tons, 1883.
Examines the influence of the Homeric poems upon the art of ancient Greece and Rome and the way these artistic versions of the myths evolve over time. Focuses upon the adventures of Odysseus in *Odyssey* 9-12, including the stories of the Cyclops, Circe, and the Sirens. Summaries of the Homeric versions are followed by descriptions of similar scenes on Greek pottery, Roman wall paintings, and other artistic media. Many of these descriptions of artwork are accompanied by line drawings.

Highet, Gilbert. *The Classical Tradition*. New York: Oxford University Press, 1949.
Scattered throughout this major study of the influence of Classical literature are references to the importance of the Homeric poems in the Classical tradition.

Topics covered include translations of the poems in the Renaissance and in the nineteenth and twentieth centuries, criticisms of Homer during the so-called "Quarrel of the Ancients and the Moderns" in the seventeenth and eighteenth centuries, nineteenth century study of the epics as oral poems, Matthew Arnold's essay *On Translating Homer*, and Homer's influence on the symbolist writers of the late nineteenth and twentieth centuries. Includes bibliography, endnotes, and index.

_____. "The Symbolist Poets and James Joyce." In *The Classical Tradition*. New York: Oxford University Press, 1949.
In this chapter of a major study of the influence of Classical literature, Highet considers imitations of Odysseus' journey to the land of the dead in *Odyssey* 11 by such symbolist writers as Ezra Pound and James Joyce. In particular, Highet explains some of the allusions to the *Odyssey* in Joyce's *Ulysses*.

Jebb, R. C. "Homer in Antiquity." In *Homer: An Introduction to the Iliad and the Odyssey*. 5th ed. Boston: Ginn, 1894. Reprint. Port Washington, N.Y.: Kennikat Press, 1969.
This essay offers a summary of Homeric influence and criticism in the ancient world. There is a discussion of such topics as Homer's role in Greek education, his influence on Greek religion, and the studies of ancient Homeric scholars, including Zenodotus, Aristophanes, and Didymus. Greek words are in parentheses and notes.

Kenner, Hugh. "Pound and Homer." In *Ezra Pound Among the Poets*, edited by George Bornstein. Chicago: University of Chicago Press, 1985.
Discusses the influence of Homer on the *Cantos* of Ezra Pound. Begins with an overview of Homeric scholarship during Pound's youth at the end of the nineteenth century and describes the poet's earliest encounters with the Homeric poems. Considers Pound's translations and interpretation of Homer not as accurate translation but as a faithful mutation of the Homeric text. Shows how Pound reads Homer through a sixteenth century Latin version of the *Odyssey* translated by Andreas Divus and through the *Divine Comedy* of Dante Alighieri.

King, Katherine Callen. *Achilles: Paradigms of the War Hero from Homer to the Middle Ages*. Berkeley: University of California Press, 1987.
Studies the image of Achilles in the *Iliad* and traces the changing portrait of the hero in later literature, including his stereotypic images as aristocratic warrior, as wrathful and violent warrior, and as romantic lover in the literature of ancient Greece, Rome, and medieval Europe. Includes illustrations, endnotes, a bibliography, and indexes.

Knight, Douglas. *Pope and the Heroic Tradition: A Critical Study of His "Iliad."*
New Haven, Conn.: Yale University Press, 1951.
Alexander Pope's *Iliad* is considered not a mere translation but an original poem
because of Pope's coherent view of Homer, his poetic style, and his attitude
toward heroic poetry. There are studies of Pope's theory of translation, the style
of his translation of the *Iliad*, and an interpretation of the translation as a whole.
Includes an appendix on Pope's knowledge of Greek and another listing similarities between Pope's poem and earlier translations of the poem; also includes an
index.

_____. "Tradition and Meaning." In *Pope and the Heroic Tradition: A
Critical Study of His "Iliad."* New Haven, Conn.: Yale University Press, 1951.
In his translation of Homer's *Iliad*, Alexander Pope is shown to interpret the
poem through the tradition of heroic poetry, which includes not only Homer's
works but also Vergil's *Aeneid* and John Milton's *Paradise Lost*. Because of this
tradition, Pope's *Iliad* has a stronger sense of divine justice and of a cosmic order
than the Homeric original. Homer and his audience lacked the elaborate set of
prior assumptions which can be found in Vergil, Milton, or Pope.

Lawton, William C. *The Successors of Homer*. London: A. D. Innes, 1898. Reprint.
New York: Cooper Square, 1969.
In this book, the author surveys the mass of Greek literature, written between
800 and 400 B.C., which can be considered "Homeric." This group includes the
other poems in the epic cycle, the poems of Hesiod, the *Homeric Hymns*, and
the works of the pre-Socratic philosophers.

Lord, George de Forest. *Homeric Renaissance: The "Odyssey" of George Chapman.*
New Haven, Conn.: Yale University Press, 1956.
A detailed examination of Chapman's 1616 translation and his allegorical interpretation of the *Odyssey*. There are chapters on translation and interpretation,
allegorical background, dynamic allegory, style, and a comparison of Chapman's
translation with that of Alexander Pope. Includes some untranslated foreign
words. Also includes a preface, illustration, endnotes, and bibliography.

_____. "The *Odyssey* and the Western World." *The Sewanee Review* 72
(1954): 406-427. Reprinted in *Essays on the Odyssey: Selected Modern Criticism*,
edited by Charles H. Taylor, Jr. Bloomington: Indiana University Press, 1969.
The place of the *Odyssey* is considered in the context of the epic tradition of the
West and an interpretation of the epic as the rehabilitation of the hero is offered.

Lotspeich, Henry Gibbons. *Classical Mythology in the Poetry of Edmund Spenser*.
New York: Octagon Books, 1965.
This alphabetical listing of Spenser's references to classical mythology includes

many mythological terms derived from the Homeric epics. Each entry includes a list of places where Spenser refers to a mythological word, a summary of the story told by Spenser, and its ancient sources. Includes a table of abbreviations, an index of mythological names, and an index of authors. The index of authors should be used in order to find the mythological terms which Spenser borrowed from Homer. Also includes an introductory essay which discusses Spenser's use of Classical mythology.

Mackail, J. W. "The Structure of the *Aeneid.*" In *Virgil and His Meaning to the World of To-Day.* Boston: Marshall Jones, 1922. Reprint. New York: Cooper Square, 1963.
In this chapter, the author demonstrates how Vergil used the Homeric poems as structural models for the *Aeneid.*

Mason, H. A. "Introductory: Inevitable Ignorance?" In *To Homer Through Pope: An Introduction to Homer's "Iliad" and Pope's Translation.* New York: Harper & Row, 1972.
A justification for introducing Homer through Alexander Pope's translation. The author considers the different virtues of the Classical scholar and the literary critic as authorities on Homer. Discusses Matthew Arnold's essay on Homer and rejects his interpretation of the Homeric hero as a Victorian gentleman.

Morgan, Gareth. "Homer in Byzantium: John Tzetzes." In *Approaches to Homer*, edited by Carl A. Rubino and Cynthia A. Shelmerdine. Austin: University of Texas Press, 1983.
Examines the career of the twelfth century Byzantine scholar John Tzetzes. Quotations from his letters and from his marginal commentaries on Homer show his teaching methods and his scholarly disposition. Passages from his *Allegories of the "Iliad"* are used to illustrate his interpretation of *Iliad* 1 and his allegorical approach to Homer.

Mueller, Martin. "The Life of the *Iliad.*" In *The Iliad.* Boston: Allen & Unwin, 1984.
Considers imitation, transmission, criticism, and translation of the poem in both the ancient and the modern worlds. Surveys the way that the *Iliad* has influenced such works as the *Odyssey*, Greek tragedy, Vergil's *Aeneid*, the medieval romance, the Renaissance epic, the plays of William Shakespeare, and John Milton's *Paradise Lost.* Also considers the way these works have influenced an understanding of the *Iliad.* Discusses the translations of George Chapman and Alexander Pope.

Otis, Brooks. "From Homer to Virgil: The Obsolescence of Epic." In *Virgil: A Study in Civilized Poetry*. Oxford, England: Clarendon Press, 1963.
Follows the transformation of the epic form from the Homeric poems to the *Aeneid* of Vergil. Includes a survey of the epics of Classical and Hellenistic Greece and Republican Rome, including those of Callimachus, Apollonius of Rhodes, and Ennius. There is an appendix on historical epic in the Hellenistic Greek period. Not all quotations are translated.

_____. "The Odyssean *Aeneid* and the Iliadic *Aeneid*." In *Virgil: A Collection of Critical Essays*, edited by Steele Commager. Englewood Cliffs, N.J.: Prentice-Hall, 1966.
Based upon two chapters of *Virgil: A Study in Civilized Poetry*. Suggests that the theme of Aeneas' internal struggle with piety in *Aeneid* 1-6 is derived from the themes of fate and the supernatural in the *Odyssey* and that Aeneas' external struggle with the impious Turnus in *Aeneid* 7-12 is based upon Achilles' struggle with Hector in the *Iliad*.

_____. "The Originality of the *Aeneid*." In *Virgil*, edited by D. R. Dudley. New York: Basic Books, 1969.
Shows how Vergil created from his Homeric models a new type of epic and a new type of hero. Differences between the Vergilian and Homeric epics and between Achilles' heroic code and Aeneas' sense of piety are stressed. Vergil consistently inverts the Homeric epics by transforming them as he recalls them. Latin quotations are not translated but Greek ones are.

Perry, Walter Copland. "The Wonderland of Homer." In *The Women of Homer*. London: William Heinemann, 1898.
Surveys various opinions of Homer and his influence in both the ancient and modern worlds. The author counters the criticisms of Homer's detractors. Includes some untranslated foreign language quotations. There is an appendix of ancient citations in the original languages.

Pöschl, Viktor. "Basic Themes." In *The Art of Vergil: Image and Symbol in the "Aeneid,"* translated by Gerda Seligson. Ann Arbor: University of Michigan Press, 1962. Reprinted in *Virgil: A Collection of Critical Essays*, edited by Steele Commager. Englewood Cliffs, N.J.: Prentice-Hall, 1966.
Considers how the Homeric structure of the *Aeneid* is symbolically introduced by two scenes, the storm scene in the *Aeneid* 1, which parallels the *Odyssey*, and the Allecto scene in *Aeneid* 7, which initializes the "Iliadic" half of the poem.

Pound, Ezra. "Homer or Virgil?" In *ABC of Reading*. New Haven, Conn.: Yale University Press, 1934. Reprinted in *Homer: A Collection of Critical Essays*,

edited by George Steiner and Robert Fagles. Englewood Cliffs, N.J.: Prentice-Hall, 1962.
This short appreciative essay affirms the continuing relevance of Homer and asserts a significant gulf between Homer and Vergil. The twentieth century reader relates more easily to Homer than to Vergil.

Prescott, Henry W. "The National Epic." In *The Development of Virgil's Art.* Chicago: University of Chicago Press, 1927.
Detailed comparisons of Vergil's treatment in the *Aeneid* of themes from Homer's epics. Includes discussions of Polyphemus, descent to the underworld, and the shipwrecked sailor in the *Odyssey* and of the battle at the ships, the compact and the duel, the night sally, and the funeral games from the *Iliad.*

Redfield, James M. "Imitation." In *Nature and Culture in the "Iliad": The Tragedy of Hector.* Chicago: University of Chicago Press, 1975. Reprinted and abridged in *Critical Essays on Homer,* edited by Kenneth Atchity, Ron Hogart, and Doug Price. Boston: G. K. Hall, 1987.
The author considers the relationship between the Homeric epics and Aristotle's *Poetics.* Such topics as "Imitation as a Mode of Learning," "The Probable as the Universal," and "Plot as Knowledge" are discussed in terms of an Aristotelian concern with ethics and action. For Aristotle, the Homeric stories are, at the same time, both fictional and universally true.

Scott, John A. "Homer Among the Ancient Greeks." In *Homer and His Influence.* Boston: Marshall Jones, 1925. Reprinted as "Homer Synonymous with Poet for the Greeks," in *Homer's History: Mycenaean or Dark Age?,* edited by C. G. Thomas. New York: Holt, Rinehart and Winston, 1970.
This essay illustrates the central position of Homer in ancient Greek civilization. References to and quotations about Homer and his poems by ancient authors are included. Early Christian attitudes toward the Homeric poems are also discussed.

_____. "Homer and England." In *Homer and His Influence.* Boston: Marshall Jones, 1925.
George Chapman's sixteenth century English translation of Homer is followed by imitations of Homer in the works of such authors as William Shakespeare, John Milton, Alexander Pope, and the Romantic poets.

_____. "Homer and His Permanent Influence." In *Homer and His Influence.* Boston: Marshall Jones, 1925.
Explains how the Homeric poems begin the Western tradition of epic, elegiac poetry, drama, literary criticism, history, and philosophy.

_____. "Homer and Roman Italy." In *Homer and His Influence.* Boston: Marshall Jones, 1925.

Traces the place of the Homeric poems in Latin literature from the first Latin translations by Livius Andronicus through the writings of Cicero and Vergil to Homer's influence in late antiquity.

_____. "Homer and the Renaissance." In *Homer and His Influence*. Boston: Marshall Jones, 1925.
The reintroduction of the Homeric poems to the West by Giovanni Boccaccio and Francesco Petrarca (Petrarch) leads to Italian copies of Homer, especially that by Torquato Tasso.

_____. "Proteus in English Literature." In *Homer and His Influence*. Boston: Marshall Jones, 1925.
A summary of the story of Proteus told in *Odyssey* 4 is followed by a series of literary references to the story, including those by Edmund Spenser, William Shakespeare, and Ralph Waldo Emerson. The essay ends with some examples of the influence of this story in modern science and culture.

Silk, M. S. "The *Iliad* and World Literature." In *Homer: The "Iliad."* London: Cambridge University Press, 1987.
Traces the afterlife of the *Iliad* from its position as the norm of Greek poetry in the ancient world through more modern imitation by William Shakespeare and Henry Fielding. Special attention is given to the links between the *Iliad*, the *Odyssey*, Vergil's *Aeneid*, and John Milton's *Paradise Lost*.

Stanford, W. B. "Ulysses as a Figure of Controversy." In *The Ulysses Theme: A Study in the Adaptability of a Traditional Hero*. 2d ed. Ann Arbor: University of Michigan Press, 1968.
This part of a comprehensive study of the treatment of Odysseus in literature follows the Homeric Odysseus through later transformation in the Greco-Roman world. Examines, in particular, the changing portrayals of Odysseus by Greek lyric poets, by fifth century Athenian dramatists, by Alexandrian scholars and Roman Stoic philosophers, and by the Latin writers Vergil, Ovid, Seneca, and Statius. Homer's favorable characterization of Odysseus is eventually discredited by three late Classical writers, Philostratus, Dictys, and Dares, who strongly assert the guilty dissimulation of Odysseus.

Thompson, J. A. K. "Homer and His Influence." In *A Companion to Homer*, edited by Alan J. B. Wace and Frank H. Stubbings. New York: Macmillan, 1963.
In this introduction to a work written primarily for readers of Greek, Thompson offers a historical survey of Homer's influence on literature, beginning with Hesiod, emphasizing Dante and the Italian Renaissance, and ending with the English Romantic poets. Not all foreign words are translated. Includes two plates and a short bibliographical note.

Tolstoy, Leo. "Homer and Shakespeare." In *Recollections and Essays*, translated by Aylmer Maude. Oxford, England: Oxford University Press, 1937. Reprinted in *Homer: A Collection of Critical Essays*, edited by George Steiner and Robert Fagles. Englewood Cliffs, N.J.: Prentice-Hall, 1962.
This short essay by the nineteenth century Russian novelist is a comparison of Homer with William Shakespeare. Homer's works are considered artistic, poetic, and original while Shakespeare's are not.

Trypanis, C. A. "The Influence of the Homeric Epics." In *The Homeric Epics*, translated by William Phelps. Warminster, England: Aris & Phillips, 1977.
Particular emphasis on the influence of Homer on ancient Greek literature, including genres such as drama and didactic epic poetry of the Hellenistic and Byzantine periods. Also mentions the influence of Homer on Western writers such as Vergil, Dante Alighieri, Renaissance authors, and John Milton.

Williams, Gordon. "Connexions with Predecessors: *imitatio exemplorum*." In *Technique and Ideas in the "Aeneid."* New Haven, Conn.: Yale University Press, 1983.
Vergil is shown to echo passages from Homer and other predecessors as a source of irony, as a framework for judgment, and as a way to measure distance from a conventional heroic world.

VERGIL

General Studies

Auslander, Joseph, and Frank Ernest Hill. "The Romans: Horace and Virgil." In *The Winged Horse: The Story of the Poets and Their Poetry*. Garden City, N.Y.: Doubleday, 1927.
A chapter in a book introducing poetry and its appreciation to children. Focuses upon the ties between Vergil and his friend and fellow poet, Horace (Quintus Horatius Flaccus). There are separate sections on each poet. Includes a biography of Vergil, an overview of his works, quotations from the *Aeneid*, and illustrations of Vergil's influence upon later literature.

Bieler, Ludwig. "The Augustan Era (43 B.C.-A.D. 14)." In *History of Roman Literature*, translated by John Wilson. New York: St. Martin's Press, 1966.
An overview of Roman life and letters during the reign of the emperor Augustus, with individual treatments of Vergil, Horace, Livy, the Latin Love Elegists, and Ovid. For Vergil, an overview of his early life and works, including the *Vergilian Appendix*, is followed by separate sections on the *Eclogues*, the *Georgics*, and the *Aeneid*, with background, summaries, and literary analysis of each work. Discusses Vergil's debt to Homer, his characterization, and his later influence. Includes eight plates and an index.

Bloom, Harold, ed. *Virgil*. New York: Chelsea House, 1986.
A collection of thirteen essays on Vergil originally published between 1973 and 1984. These studies of the *Eclogues*, the *Georgics*, and the *Aeneid* include material on Vergil's image of the Augustan age, his pastoral style, his use of politics and his influence. Includes introduction, chronology of Vergil's life, list of contributors, bibliography, and index.

Collins, W. Lucas. *Virgil*. Philadelphia: J. B. Lippincott, 1877.
Contains a biography of the poet, introductions to both the *Eclogues* and the *Georgics*, and a prose paraphrase of the plot of the *Aeneid*. In a concluding chapter, Lucas discusses several drawbacks to the popularity of the *Aeneid* in the late nineteenth century.

Commager, Steele, ed. *Virgil: A Collection of Critical Essays*. Englewood Cliffs, N.J.: Prentice-Hall, 1966.
Seven of these twelve essays by important classical scholars are about the *Aeneid*. Includes a chronology of important dates and a selected bibliography. In an introduction, the editor follows an analogy between Aeneas and the beekeeper

Aristaeus in the *Georgics* as he charts the hero's reorientation from pious respect for his Trojan past toward faith in a Roman future.

Cruttwell, Charles Thomas. "Virgil." In *A History of Roman Literature*. New York: Charles Scribner's Sons, 1893.
Despite its date, this study remains a good general introduction to the poet, with sections on Vergil's life, works, love of nature, aptitude for epic poetry, and on the *Aeneid*'s scope, religious features, and relation to preceding poetry. Includes appendices on Roman imitations of Vergil, parallelism in Vergil, and legends about Vergil, as well as a chronological table, index, and list of essay question topics.

Dimsdale, Marcus S. "The Augustan Age: Virgil." In *A History of Latin Literature*. London: W. Heinemann, 1915. Reprint. Freeport, N.Y.: Books for Libraries Press, 1971.
In this survey of the poet's life and works, a short description of the Augustan age is followed by sections on Vergil's youth and poetic environment, on various features of the *Eclogues* and the *Georgics*, and on the genesis, purpose, and form of the *Aeneid*. There are also sections on Vergilian versification and on character descriptions of Aeneas, Dido, Turnus, and others. The poems attributed to the poet in the *Vergilian Appendix* are summarized in an appendix. Also includes an index.

Distler, Paul F. *Vergil and Vergiliana*. Chicago: Loyola University Press, 1966.
This detailed introduction to the poet was written specifically for the beginning high school and college student. There are fourteen chapters devoted to such topics as Vergil's life, works, and influence. An excellent glossary of names used in the *Aeneid* appears in chapter 12. Also includes eight illustrations, a map, and an index.

Donlan, Walter, ed. *The Classical World Bibliography of Vergil*. New York: Garland, 1978.
A collection of four periodic bibliographic surveys appearing in *Classical World* between 1940 and 1973. More important entries include editorial comments and summaries. There is also a brief introduction by the editor in which the history and scope of these bibliographies is presented. Includes references to non-English works. A good source for additional material on Vergil.

Dudley, D. R., ed. *Virgil*. New York: Basic Books, 1969.
Part of a series on Latin literature and its influence, this collection of essays by several authors includes studies of Vergil's originality in the *Eclogues* and the *Aeneid*; explorations of the use of Vergil as a literary model by later Latin authors, by Dante, and by English poets; observations about links between Vergil

and Western artists such as Nicolas Poussin; and comments on Vergil's beliefs concerning the afterlife. Includes twenty plates, notes, and an index.

Duff, J. W. "Virgil." In *A Literary History of Rome from the Origins to the Close of the Golden Age*. 3d ed. New York: Barnes & Noble Books, 1953.
In this chapter of a standard survey of Latin literature, a brief biography of the poet is followed by overviews of the *Eclogues*, the *Georgics*, and the *Aeneid* as well as discussion of such topics as Vergil's attitude to nature, poetic style, influence, and relation to Lucretius, Augustus, and Maecenas. Not all Latin quotations are translated.

Durant, Will. "The Golden Age." In *The Story of Civilization*. Vol. 3, *Caesar and Christ*. New York: Simon & Schuster, 1944.
In addition to sections on Horace, Livy, and the Latin elegiac poets, this overview of the Age of Augustus offers a biography of Vergil, a summary of the plot of the *Aeneid*, and some comments upon Vergil's poetic goals in writing the epic and the poet's later influence. Includes a chronological table, illustrations, a glossary, a bibliography, endnotes, and indexes.

Fitzgerald, Robert. "Postscript." In *The Aeneid*, by Vergil. New York: Vintage Books, 1984.
In this essay attached to his translation of the *Aeneid*, Fitzgerald summarizes Aeneas' role in Homer's *Iliad*; Rome's relationship with Carthage; the *Aeneid* and Roman history; Vergil's biography and poetic style; and the literary goals of the *Aeneid*.

Glover, T. R. *Virgil*. 7th ed. New York: Barnes & Noble Books, 1969.
A standard introduction, first published in 1904 and revised several times. There are sections on Vergil's life; on his literary background; on his relationships with Italy, Rome, and the emperor; and his interpretations of life. Includes a table of dates and an index.

Grant, Michael. "Virgil." In *Greek and Latin Authors: 800 B.C.-A.D. 1000*. New York: H. W. Wilson, 1980.
An outline of Vergil's life and a discussion of the form and content of his works. For the *Aeneid*, there is a plot summary, an interpretation and a discussion of Vergil's sources and influence. Includes a note on Vergil's lost and spurious works, including the *Vergilian Appendix*. Appendices include a list of works of doubtful attribution and a chronological list of authors arranged by century. Also contains a preface, list of authors included, twenty-five illustrations, pronunciation key, and bibliographies.

Griffin, Jasper. *Virgil*. Oxford, England: Oxford University Press, 1986.
A short introduction to the poet and his work with individual chapters on Vergil's life, the *Eclogues*, *Georgics*, the *Aeneid*, and influence. The moral and political goals of Vergil's poetry are explained and a bibliography and index are included.

_____. "Virgil." In *The Oxford History of the Classical World: The Roman World*, edited by John Boardman, Jasper Griggin, and Oswyn Murray. New York: Oxford University Press, 1988.
A short, introductory essay with sections on each of Vergil's major works, the *Eclogues*, the *Georgics*, and the *Aeneid*. Includes background on the composition and goals of the *Aeneid* and a summary of the plot of the epic. A short bibliography appears at the end of the chapter.

Hadas, Moses. "Vergil." In *A History of Latin Literature*. New York: Columbia University Press, 1952.
A general survey with a biography of Vergil and an overview of his works. Brief quotations from a variety of translations of Vergil's works. For the *Aeneid*, there is a plot summary and discussion of Vergil's literary sources. Includes a bibliography and index.

Haecker, Theodor. *Virgil: Father of the West*. New York: Sheed & Ward, 1934. Reprint. New York: Johnson, 1970.
A study of the Vergilian worldview with an emphasis on duty, fate, and human sorrow so similar in form to Christianity that Haecker called it naturally Christian. Topics for individual chapters include Vergil's life, the *Eclogues*, and the *Georgics*, as well as several chapters on the *Aeneid*.

Hamilton, Edith. "Enter the Romantic Roman: Virgil, Livy, Seneca." In *The Roman Way*. New York: W. W. Norton, 1932.
In the first part of this chapter, Vergil is presented as one of the world's greatest romanticists. The poet's influence and life are summarized and the romantic features of the *Aeneid*, especially in the story of Dido, are analyzed.

John, D. A., and A. F. Turberfield. Introduction to *The Voyage of Aeneas*. New York: St. Martin's Press, 1968.
This introductory essay for a translation of the epic includes material on the poet's life and influence, the form and poetic purpose of the *Aeneid*, the role of the gods and Aeneas' sense of duty.

Johnson, W. R. *Darkness Visible: A Study of Vergil's "Aeneid."* Berkeley: University of California Press, 1976.
A scholarly study of the poetic meaning and narrative form of the *Aeneid*. Includes an overview of interpretations of the *Aeneid*, a study of the poem in the

context of the world of Augustan Rome, and reflections on the influence of the epic in the twentieth century. Compares Vergil's subjective narrative form with Homer's more realistic style. Detailed analyses of various passages from the *Aeneid* are made in order to show the poem's complexity and ambiguity. The *Aeneid* is considered a multilayered poem with aesthetic, political, moral, and philosophical points of view.

Knapp, Charles. Introduction to *The "Aeneid" of Vergil*. Rev. ed. Glenview, Ill.: Scott, Foresman, 1951.
While the primary purpose of this book is to make the Latin text of the *Aeneid* accessible to high school students, the detailed introduction contains very useful material on such topics as historical and poetic background; Vergil's biography; the style of the *Aeneid*; and mythology in Vergil. There are also twenty-one carefully described illustrations, a color map of Aeneas' journeys, and a brief bibliography.

Knight, W. F. Jackson. Introduction to *The Aeneid*, by Vergil. Baltimore: Penguin, 1956.
This introduction to the author's prose translation of the epic is a good general essay on the poet and his epic. Vergil's life, sources, compositional style, language, moral purpose, and influence are discussed.

_____. *Roman Vergil*. 2d ed. London: Faber & Faber, 1944.
A comprehensive study of Vergil containing chapters on Vergil's life, debts to earlier poets, principles of poetic construction, use of historical reality, language, style, and influence. Includes an index.

_____. *Vergil: Epic and Anthropology*. Edited by John D. Christie. New York: Barnes & Noble Books, 1967.
This book, combining three separate studies by the author, includes; a literary examination of *Aeneid* 2; a study of initiation rites and *Aeneid* 6; and an identification of Vergil's Troy with the Eastern concept of the sacred city. Cities in the ancient Near East serve as points of reference. There are two plates, several figures, and extensive notes.

McDermott, William C. Introduction to *Works: The "Aeneid," "Eclogues," "Georgics,"* by Vergil, translated by J. W. Mackail. New York: Modern Library, 1950.
In addition to sections on historical background, Vergil's life, the *Eclogues*, the *Georgics*, and Vergil's influence, the author discusses Vergil's goals and sources for the *Aeneid*, his method of composition, the variety and drama of his style, and his use of Roman imperial ideas and historical development in a multipurposed and complex poem.

Mackail, J. W. *Virgil and His Meaning to the World of To-Day.* Boston: Marshall Jones, 1922. Reprint. New York: Cooper Square, 1963.
This small book by an early twentieth century translator of Vergil is an excellent introduction to Vergil and his poetry. There are chapters on Vergil's predecessors, life, work, style, and influence, as well as several chapters specifically on the *Aeneid.*

Mendell, Clarence W. "Vergil." In *Latin Poetry: The New Poets and the Augustans.* New Haven, Conn.: Yale University Press, 1965.
Vergil's poetic career is surveyed. Extensive quotations in translation, especially from the *Vergilian Appendix.* The structure of the *Aeneid,* Vergil's literary models, and his poetic links with the style of the Augustan poets are outlined. There is a short bibliography, a preface, and an index.

Middleton, George, and Thomas R. Mills. "Virgil." In *The Student's Companion to Latin Authors.* New York: Macmillan, 1896.
A useful listing of ancient sources for information on the poet's life and works. Special sections on the Aeneas legend, sources for the *Aeneid,* and the role of the gods, religion, and politics in the epic. Latin quotations are not translated. Includes bibliography, indices, and appendix on ancient authorities for the history of Roman literature.

Myers, F. W. H. "Virgil." In *Essays Classical.* New York: Macmillan, 1883. Reprinted in *Essays Classical and Modern.* New York: Macmillan, 1921.
A general view of the poet's religion, his relation to Christianity, and his attitudes toward Roman virtue and the government of the emperor Augustus. Discussion of the *Aeneid* includes character portrayals of Aeneas and Dido.

Ogilvie, Robert M. "Between Republic and Empire." In *Roman Literature and Society.* Totowa, N.J.: Barnes & Noble Books, 1980.
This chapter of a survey of Latin literature includes studies of Vergil and his literary contemporaries, Propertius, Tibullus, Horace, and Livy. The section on Vergil considers the poet's major works and their sources. Aeneas is viewed as the prototype of Augustus and as a hero in search of a soul. There are two bibliographies and an index.

Otis, Brooks. "Conclusion." In *Virgil: A Study in Civilized Poetry.* Oxford, England: Clarendon Press, 1963.
In this summary chapter, Otis recapitulates Vergil's poetic growth, beginning in the *Eclogues* and the *Georgics* with his transformation of Theocritus' didactic poetry into symbolic, ideological poetry about Rome, and leading in the *Aeneid* to a new type of subjective and symbolic epic, which asserts both humanity and moral realism as a civilizing force. Not all quotations are translated.

——————. *Virgil: A Study in Civilized Poetry*. Oxford, England: Clarendon Press, 1963.

Shows how Vergil developed a new epic form based upon subjectivity, humanity, moral realism, and Augustanism. A survey of ancient epics from Homer to Vergil is followed by a study of Vergil's subjective style. The growth of his literary style is traced from the *Eclogues* and *Georgics* to the *Aeneid*. There are structural charts and nine appendices, five of which are bibliographical. Not all quotations are translated. Footnotes and index included.

Pearl, Joseph. *Companion to Vergil*. New York: College Entrance Book Company, 1932.

While this small book is meant to be an aid to high school students studying Vergil in the original Latin, there are also many features of value to the general reader, including sections on Vergil's life and works, the Trojan War, the story of the *Aeneid*, a glossary of characters, mythological figures and geographical terms. Sections of particular interest to the Latin student include scansion, Vergil's grammar, rules of syntax, translation passages, vocabulary aids, and sample examination questions. Twelve drawings from ancient Greek vases included.

Pharr, Clyde. Introduction to *Vergil's "Aeneid": Books I-VI*. Lexington, Mass.: D. C. Heath, 1930.

This introduction to a standard textbook for high school and college students of Latin includes brief information on the poet's life and later fame and some background on the Trojan War, Aeneas' wanderings, the purpose of the *Aeneid*, and Roman religion. Contains a chronological table of Vergil's life and a brief bibliography.

Prescott, Henry W. *The Development of Virgil's Art*. Chicago: University of Chicago Press, 1927. Reprint. New York: Russell & Russell, 1963.

In addition to three short chapters on Vergil's literary heritage, the *Eclogues*, and the *Georgics*, there is a detailed discussion of Vergil's youth and early manhood with focus on Vergil's early poems, the *Vergilian Appendix*. Most of the book is devoted to a discussion of the *Aeneid* as a national epic, with chapters on such topics as background, epic tradition, and characters. Includes an index.

Putnam, Michael C. J. *Essays on Latin Lyric, Elegy, and Epic*. Princeton, N.J.: Princeton University Press, 1982.

This collection of Putnam's more important essays includes one on *Eclogues* 1, a general essay on Vergil's poetic achievement, and three on the *Aeneid*. Includes specific reference to the *Aeneid* 3, the *Aeneid* 7, and the relationship between piety and force in the *Aeneid*, as well as notes and indexes.

_____. "The Virgilian Achievement." *Arethusa* 5 (1972): 53-70. Reprinted in *Essays on Latin Lyric, Elegy, and Epic*. Princeton, N.J.: Princeton University Press, 1982.
Surveys Vergil's major works, with special attention to the last three books of the *Aeneid*. Vergil's works are seen to reflect an increasingly tougher view of reality based upon the Roman concepts of piety and the ideal state. Latin quotations are not translated.

Quinn, Kenneth. *Virgil's "Aeneid": A Critical Description*. Ann Arbor: University of Michigan Press, 1968.
Begins with a chapter on the heroic impulse in the *Aeneid*. There are individual chapters on the literary and historical circumstances of the epic, an outline of the poetic structure of the *Aeneid*, an analysis of the text book by book, Vergil's use of form, and his poetic style. Includes two indexes.

Rand, Edward R. *The Magical Art of Virgil*. Cambridge, Mass.: Harvard University Press, 1931.
This comprehensive study of the poet is focused upon Vergil's magic genius, which weaves together history, myth, poetic models, and the poet's own fancy. Epic characteristics of the *Eclogues* and the *Georgics* and features of the drama, tragedy and primitive simplicity in the *Aeneid* are noted. Includes a frontispiece and index.

Rose, H. J. "Vergil and Augustan Poetry." In *A Handbook of Latin Literature*. 3d ed. New York: Methuen, 1954.
A brief discussion of the place of rhetoric and poetry in Augustan Rome leads to a biography of Vergil and a description of his work. The *Aeneid* is summarized book by book. Includes lives of three contemporaries of Vergil: Horace, Propertius, and Tibullus.

Sellar, W. Y. *The Roman Poets of the Augustan Age: Virgil*. Oxford, England: Clarendon Press, 1908.
This Victorian study of Vergil remains a good general introduction to the poet and his work. Includes chapters on Vergil's place in Roman literature; the poet's life and personal characteristics; the *Eclogues*; the *Georgics*; and characteristics of the *Aeneid* as an epic.

Sisson, C. H. Introduction to *The Aeneid*, by Vergil. Manchester, England: Carcanet Press, 1986.
In this short essay, attached to the author's poetic translation of the *Aeneid*, Vergil's influence, lasting two thousand years, is put in the context of the difficulty in translating a poet whose *Aeneid* is remote from the tastes of the late twentieth century reader.

Slaughter, Moses Stephen. "Virgil: An Appreciation." In *Roman Portraits*. New Haven, Conn.: Yale University Press, 1925.
A survey of the poet's works in which Vergil's love of nature and of the Italian countryside is seen to lead him to philosophy and an emphasis on duty and moderation.

Wilkie, Brian. Introduction to *The Aeneid*, by Vergil, translated by Rolfe Humphries. Rev. ed. Edited by Brian Wilkie. New York: Macmillan, 1987.
This essay is divided into three parts. The first section contains a brief biography of Vergil and some background on the politics of the period. The second discusses various features of the *Aeneid*, including Vergil's literary debts, his vision of history, and his use of patterns of imagery. In the last section, the editor considers some of the difficulties involved in translating the *Aeneid* and some of the characteristics of Humphries' translation.

Wilkie, Brian, and James Hurt. "Virgil." In *Literature of the Western World*. Vol. 1, *The Ancient World Through the Renaissance*, edited by Brian Wilkie and James Hurt. New York: Macmillan, 1984.
This brief introduction to selections from Humphries' translation of the *Aeneid* includes a brief life of the poet, historical background to the poem, and comments upon Vergil's literary innovations, meter, and influence. Includes a bibliography.

Williams, R. D. *Aeneas and the Roman Hero*. London: Macmillan, 1973.
Illustrates the ideals of Augustan Rome as reflected in the *Aeneid*. Individual chapters on Vergil's life and times, on patriotic passages in the epic, on Aeneas as the new Roman hero, and on the poet's private voice as expressed through Dido, Turnus, and Juno. Chapter 3 includes a synopsis of the plot. A variety of English translations is used. Includes twelve illustrations, a map of Aeneas' journey, and an index.

_____. Introduction to *The "Aeneid" of Virgil*. Bristol, England: Bristol Classical Press, 1985.
This introductory essay for a companion volume to C. Day Lewis' translation of the *Aeneid* includes a brief biography of Vergil, a summary of the *Aeneid*, and discussion of such topics as the sources, patriotic aspects, major themes, and characters of the *Aeneid*.

Williams, R. D., and T. S. Pattie. *Virgil: His Poetry Through the Ages*. London: British Library, 1982.
A good introduction to the poet, his works, and his influence. The first part, written by Williams, is devoted to Vergil's poetry and includes descriptive introductions to both the *Eclogues* and the *Georgics*; a book-by-book summary; an analysis of the *Aeneid*; and discussion of Vergil's poetic appeal in the twen-

tieth century. The second part, by Pattie, considers the history of Vergil's text and his later influence. Includes twenty plates, some in color, depicting manuscript pages and scenes from Vergil's works, and three appendices on Latin manuscripts of Vergil in the British Museum, as well as select bibliography.

Vergil and His Age

The Social and Political World of Vergil

Camps, W. A. "Echoes of History." In *An Introduction to Virgil's "Aeneid."* Oxford, England: Oxford University Press, 1969.
Individual episodes from the *Aeneid* as well as the whole epic are viewed as analogies and evocations of significant events in Roman history, especially during the Punic wars and during the civil wars of Vergil's own day. Further examples are discussed in an appendix.

Conway, Robert Seymour. *Harvard Lectures on the Vergilian Age.* Cambridge, Mass.: Harvard University Press, 1928. Reprint. New York: Biblo and Tannen, 1967.
A collection of nine essays on various aspects of the Vergilian Age (55-17 B.C.) in which the author attempts to identify the feelings of the time about a variety of topics, including political confiscations, Vergil's farm, the Punic wars, Vergil's philosophy, and the structure of the *Aeneid*. Not all Latin quotations are translated. Several lectures are accompanied by illustrations. Includes an index of proper names, an index of topics discussed, and a list of passages cited from Vergil.

Distler, Paul F. "Political Background." In *Vergil and Vergiliana.* Chicago: Loyola University Press, 1966.
This chapter of a detailed introduction to Vergil summarizes Rome's territorial expansion and political struggles in the first century B.C., two aspects of Roman history which particularly influenced the poet's life and work.

Glover, T. R. "The Age and the Man." In *Virgil.* 7th ed. New York: Barnes & Noble Books, 1969.
Vergil's life is discussed in the context of the literary and political environment in Rome in the first century B.C. Political land confiscations and Vergil's position at the court of Augustus are highlighted.

_____. "The Land and the Nation: 1. Italy." In *Virgil.* 7th ed. New York: Barnes & Noble Books, 1969.

The influence of the Italian countryside and of the Italian people upon Vergil and the *Aeneid* is discussed. Italy is seen as a strong unifying and patriotic theme in the epic.

_____. "The Land and the Nation: 2. Rome." In *Virgil*. 7th ed. New York: Barnes & Noble Books, 1969.
Vergil's feelings toward the city of Rome, its history, and its character are seen to be central to an understanding of the *Aeneid*. Continuity of Roman ritual, heroism, and gravity of character are shown to be important to Vergil.

_____. "The Land and the Nation: 3. Augustus." In *Virgil*. 7th ed. New York: Barnes & Noble Books, 1969.
The relationship between the poet and the Roman emperor is examined closely. Vergil's admiration for and personal debt to Augustus is reflected in Vergil's allusions to the emperor in the *Aeneid*.

_____. "Literature: 2. Contemporaries." In *Virgil*. 7th ed. New York: Barnes & Noble Books, 1969.
Vergil's search for literary themes is placed in the context of contemporary attitudes toward Greek mythology, Roman antiquities, history, and panegyric. In the *Aeneid*, Vergil rejects these themes, popular among other Augustan poets such as Propertius and Ovid, in favor of the story of Aeneas.

Highet, Gilbert. "Vergil." In *Poets in a Landscape*. New York: Alfred A. Knopf, 1957.
The poet is discussed in terms of the places where he lived. There are sections on his birthplace near Mantua, his love of farming, his love of Naples, and the location of his tomb. Includes photographs, notes, and an index.

Johnson, W. R. "The Broken World: Virgil and His Augustus." In *Virgil*, edited by Harold Bloom. New York: Chelsea House, 1986.
In the *Georgics*, the usual contrasts of Vergilian poetry between light and darkness, between order and chaos, between calm and anxiety find an unusual equilibrium and harmony based upon the figure of Augustus. Because of political events in the years 39-30 B.C., Augustus and his world are changed, and the harmony of the *Georgics* is replaced in the *Aeneid* by more uncertain and darker symbols.

_____. "The Worlds Virgil Lived In." In *Darkness Visible: A Study of Vergil's "Aeneid."* Berkeley: University of California Press, 1976. Reprinted in *Virgil*, edited by Harold Bloom. New York: Chelsea House, 1986.
Illustrates the disintegration of traditional social, metaphysical, and moral order in the Rome of Vergil's day and the uncertain permanence of the new Augustan

order reflected in the tension in the *Aeneid* between two worlds, between chaos and civil order, evil and good, falsehood and truth, terror and reason, darkness and light.

Knight, W. F. Jackson. "The World Before Vergil, and Vergil's World." In *Roman Vergil*. 2d ed. London: Faber & Faber, 1944.
Provides background on the philosophical, political, religious, and poetic world in which Vergil lived. Includes discussion of the moral debate between Stoicism and Epicureanism, the problem of divine justice, the relation of individuals to society, and the importance of evocation and allusion in the ancient poetic tradition.

Lyne, R. O. A. M. "Augustan Poetry and Society." In *The Oxford History of the Classical World: The Roman World*, edited by John Boardman, Jasper Griggin, and Oswyn Murray. New York: Oxford University Press, 1988.
In this short essay, Vergil's moralism, his didactic tone, his love of the country-side, and his relationship with his patron Maecenas are considered in the context of literary features of the Augustan age. A discussion of the role of poets and their patrons is followed by individual sections on Vergil, Horace, Propertius, Tibullus, and Ovid. Short bibliography at the end of the chapter. Includes illustrations, color plates, maps, table of events, and an index.

Mackail, J. W. "The Italo-Roman Ideal." In *Virgil and His Meaning to the World of To-Day*. Boston: Marshall Jones, 1922. Reprint. New York: Cooper Square, 1963.
The Augustan vision of Rome as ruler of a peaceful world is traced through the works of Vergil.

_____. "Virgil's Predecessors." In *Virgil and His Meaning to the World of To-Day*. Boston: Marshall Jones, 1922.
Vergil's central position in the history of Latin literature is illustrated by a brief history of Latin poetry from its origins to the time of Vergil.

_____. "Virgil's World." In *Virgil and His Meaning to the World of To-Day*. Boston: Marshall Jones, 1922.
Vergil is presented as the central figure of the Augustan age of Rome. The importance of this period in the history of Rome and of mankind is illustrated by a brief history of the Roman Republic.

Miles, Gary B., and Archibald W. Allen. "Vergil and the Augustan Experience." In *Vergil at 2000: Commemorative Essays on the Poet and His Influence*, edited by John D. Bernard. New York: AMS Press, 1986.

In this essay, the authors study Vergil's poetry, including the *Eclogues*, the *Georgics*, and the *Aeneid*, as a statement not of the Augustan moral order, but of the disorder inherent in Roman *imperium*.

Prescott, Henry W. "The Social and Political Background." In *The Development of Virgil's Art*. Chicago: University of Chicago Press, 1927. Reprint. New York: Russell & Russell, 1963.
Augustan concern for religious and moral reform is reflected in the works of Vergil and his contemporaries. Considers the tradition of literary patronage and national poetry in which Vergil worked. Contains an index.

Quinn, Kenneth. "Genesis." In *Virgil's "Aeneid": A Critical Description*. Ann Arbor: University of Michigan Press, 1968.
Considers some of the literary and historical circumstances in which the *Aeneid* was written. Summarizes what Vergil's audience expected Vergil to write and then demonstrates how the poet fulfilled these expectations by a synthesis of five elements: contemporary relevance, history, myth, rivalry with Homer, and symbolism.

Sellar, W. Y. "The *Aeneid* as an Epic Poem of Human Life." In *The Roman Poets of the Augustan Age: Virgil*. Oxford, England: Clarendon Press, 1908.
Shows how the character of the poem is influenced by various attitudes of the poet and his age. Topics discussed include Roman interest in Homeric life and a romantic Italy, belief in supernatural powers, and Roman attitudes toward government.

_____. "The *Aeneid* as the Epic of the Roman Empire." In *The Roman Poets of the Augustan Age: Virgil*. Oxford, England: Clarendon Press, 1908.
Illustrates how several Roman political attitudes, including imperial pride, national continuity, and antagonism to other races, are expressed in the *Aeneid*. The influence of Roman religious ideas and of the emperor Augustus upon the epic are also discussed.

_____. "General Introduction." In *The Roman Poets of the Augustan Age: Virgil*. Oxford, England: Clarendon Press, 1908.
Sellar's standard nineteenth century study of Vergil begins with this introductory section placing Vergil's life and work in historical context. Topics covered include the influence of patronage and literary and material conditions on literature of the period.

Showerman, Grant. "The Virgil Country." In *Monuments and Men of Ancient Rome*. New York: D. Appleton-Century, 1935.

Vergil's appreciation of nature is considered in the context of the actual Italian countryside described in his poetry. Mentioned in particular are Mantua and the region around Naples.

Williams, R. D. "Virgil's Life and Times." In *Aeneas and the Roman Hero*. London: Macmillan, 1973.
The composition of the *Aeneid* is placed in the context of contemporary political events. The long period of civil war which had followed the assassination of Julius Caesar and the peace brought by Augustus' decisive defeat of Mark Anthony at Actium in 31 B.C. is seen to be reflected in Vergil's friendship for Augustus and his support for the emperor's political agenda.

Vergil's Gods, Myths, Religion, Morality, and Concept of Fate

Bailey, Cyril. "The Dead and the Underworld." In *Religion in Virgil*. Oxford, England: Clarendon Press, 1935.
Vergilian references, especially in *Aeneid* 6, to the importance of burial, the spirits of the dead, the gods of the underworld, and the destiny of souls is shown to consist of an inconsistent blending of Greek and Roman religious concepts, including Platonic ideas, Stoic doctrine, and traditional mythology. Similarly, Vergil's references to funerals and tomb ceremonies, such as those for Misenus in *Aeneid* 6 and for Anchises in *Aeneid* 5, combine Roman and Greek customs concerning the cult of the dead.

_____. "Fate and the Gods." In *Religion in Virgil*. Oxford, England: Clarendon Press, 1935.
A study of the Vergilian concept of fate, particularly in the *Aeneid*, and of the relationship between fate and the Vergilian gods, especially Jupiter, Juno, and Venus. Vergil's concept of fate combines the Greek idea of the lot of the individual with the Stoic belief in providence. While Venus is considered the personification of Aeneas' positive destiny and Juno represents a contrary force, the will of Jupiter is seen to be identical with fate itself. An appendix on the meaning of *fortuna* in Vergil.

_____. *Religion in Virgil*. Oxford, England: Clarendon Press, 1935.
This text is not a study of Vergil's personal religion but of the eclectic religious ideas and practices in his poems. Attention is given to elements of magic and superstition, animistic beliefs, Vergil's treatment of the Greco-Roman anthropomorphic gods, state-cults, and philosophical concepts, such as fate and the afterlife. Vergil's careful distinction between Roman and Greek elements in the religious heritage of his day is illustrated by the author's separate treatments of

gods with Roman names, gods with both Roman and Greek names, and gods with Greek names.

Block, Elizabeth. *The Effects of Divine Manifestations on the Reader's Perspective in Virgil's "Aeneid."* New York: Arno Press, 1981.
This revision of the author's doctoral dissertation deals with the way that perceptions of the role of the gods and, especially, appearances of the gods, enable the reader to participate more fully in the characters and their responses to the gods. Particular emphasis on the Laocoön passage in book 2. Bibliography of works cited.

Brooks, Robert A. *"Discolor Aura*: Reflections on the Golden Bough." In *Virgil: A Collection of Critical Essays*, edited by Steele Commager. Englewood Cliffs, N.J.: Prentice-Hall, 1966.
From an article in the *American Journal of Philology* (74, 1953). Follows the golden bough in *Aeneid* 6 as a symbol of power and an image of the tension between life and death, between the hero and the world.

Camps, W. A. "The Higher Powers: Fate and the Gods." In *An Introduction to Virgil's "Aeneid."* Oxford, England: Oxford University Press, 1969.
The role of the gods in the *Aeneid* is discussed from several points of view: the Roman concept of fate; the traditional Roman belief that the favor of the gods assures the success of individuals and of states; and the Epicurean view of the gods as expressions of an arbitrary fortune.

_____. "Making an Episode: Fusion of Inherited Materials Exemplified in the Sixth Book." In *An Introduction to Virgil's "Aeneid."* Oxford, England: Oxford University Press, 1969.
While the focus of this chapter is on Vergil's sources for Aeneas' journey to the underworld in *Aeneid* 6, there is also some interest in the poet's depiction of the underworld, the religious concept of the reincarnation of souls, and the concept of a limbo for the prematurely dead. *Aeneid* 6 is considered a poem rather than a religious document.

Conway, Robert Seymour. "The Golden Bough." In *Harvard Lectures on the Vergilian Age*. Cambridge, Mass.: Harvard University Press, 1928. Reprint. New York: Biblo and Tannen, 1967.
Links the golden bough mentioned in *Aeneid* 6 with the messianic vision in the 4th *Eclogue* through the natural affection of mother and child.

Glover, T. R. "Interpretation of Life: 4. Olympus." In *Virgil*. 7th ed. New York: Barnes & Noble Books, 1969.

Ancient beliefs in the gods are traced from Homer through later Greek and Roman writers. Platonic and Stoic attitudes are especially emphasized in Vergil's treatment of the gods in the *Aeneid*.

_____. "Interpretation of Life: 5. Results." In *Virgil*. 7th ed. New York: Barnes & Noble Books, 1969.
Vergil's treatment of the problems of death and suffering are examined in terms of the answers offered by Lucretius and by Roman Stoicism and by Christianity. Vergil feels the mystery of death and shows his readers the effects of pain and sorrow upon human character.

Greene, William Chase. "Flammantia Moenia Mundi." In *The Achievement of Rome*. Cambridge, Mass.: Harvard University Press, 1933.
This study of Roman religious beliefs includes a discussion of Vergil as both a priest and a prophet in his vision of Augustan Rome as an incarnation of Roman piety. The Latin title, a quotation from Lucretius (1.73), means "the blazing ramparts of the world." Bibliography and index are included.

Knight, W. F. Jackson. *Cumaean Gates: A Reference of the Sixth "Aeneid" to the Initiation Pattern*. Oxford, England: Basil Blackwell, 1936. Reprinted in *Vergil: Epic and Anthropology*, edited by John D. Christie. New York: Barnes & Noble Books, 1967.
A study of comparative anthropology combining a variety of myths about encounters with the dead, in the South Pacific, in Homer's *Odyssey*, and at Eleusis in Greece. Vergil's Troy is associated with the Cretan labyrinth and with Aeneas' journey to the underworld in *Aeneid* 6. Includes one illustration, several drawings, and extensive notes.

_____. "Virgil's Elysium." In *Virgil*, edited by D. R. Dudley. New York: Basic Books, 1969.
Contrasts the description of the labyrinth on the gate of the Sibyl's temple in the *Aeneid* 6 with the rest of the epic in order to suggest that Vergil had two views on the afterlife, a Platonic moralism and Homeric fatalism.

Prescott, Henry W. "The Life After Death in Popular Fancy and Speculative Theory." In *The Development of Virgil's Art*. Chicago: University of Chicago Press, 1927. Reprint. New York: Russell & Russell, 1963.
Summarizes various ancient beliefs about life after death and their influence upon Vergil's description in *Aeneid* 6. Discussion of Homer's *Iliad*, the Eleusinian Mysteries, Orphic beliefs, Plato's *Phaedo*, and Stoic philosophy.

Williams, Gordon. "The Concept of Fate." In *Technique and Ideas in the "Aeneid."* New Haven, Conn.: Yale University Press, 1983.

Considers Vergil's use of fate in the epic not primarily as a religious concept but as a figurative structure ordering the narrative. Fate is analyzed as a figure of anticipation, as a symbol for the historical process, and as a trope for human aspirations.

_____. "The Gods in the *Aeneid*." In *Technique and Ideas in the "Aeneid."* New Haven, Conn.: Yale University Press, 1983.
The gods are examined here as figurative concepts rather than religious realities. The divine machinery of the epic figures as authorial intervention, human motivation, and the reconciliation of freedom and determinism.

_____. "Moral Ambiguities." In *Technique and Ideas in the "Aeneid."* New Haven, Conn.: Yale University Press, 1983.
An examination of several instances of moral ambiguity in the *Aeneid*, including Aeneas' abandonment of Dido, the motives of Nisus and Euryalus, and Aeneas' pitiless slaying of Turnus. In each case, two opposing viewpoints are left unresolved by the poet. Includes bibliography and indexes.

Wiseman, T. P. "Cybele, Virgil, and Augustus." In *Poetry and Politics in the Age of Augustus*, edited by Tony Woodman and David West. New York: Cambridge University Press, 1984.
Part of a collection of eight essays by Classical scholars, this essay examines references to the goddess Cybele in the *Aeneid* and concludes that Vergil's treatment of the goddess and her relationship with Aeneas reflect her religious rehabilitation in the reign of Augustus. Foreign language quotations are not translated.

Biography

Boynton, H. W. "Virgil." In *The World's Leading Poets*. New York: Henry Holt, 1912. Reprint. Freeport, N.Y.: Books for Libraries Press, 1968.
This biographical collection about such poets as Homer, Dante, and Shakespeare, summarizes the evidence about Vergil's childhood, early poetic works, and artistic development. Focuses on the poet's "genius" and the personal and human side of his poetry. A traditional portrait of the poet is included.

Camps, W. A. "Aelius Donatus' *Life* of Virgil." In *An Introduction to Virgil's "Aeneid."* Oxford, England: Oxford University Press, 1969.
This appendix to a general introduction to the *Aeneid* consists of a translation of the most important ancient biography of Vergil, by Aelius Donatus, a grammar-

ian of the fourth century A.D. This biography, not widely available in English, includes some unreliable information but provides useful background on Vergil's composition of the *Aeneid*.

Conway, Robert Seymour. "The Philosophy of Vergil." In *Harvard Lectures on the Vergilian Age*. Cambridge, Mass.: Harvard University Press, 1928. Reprint. New York: Biblo and Tannen, 1967.
Suggests that the center of Vergil's thought is a belief in human love and kindness as the source of all human joy and sorrow from which the tragedies of Dido, Juturna, Silvia, and Turnus in the *Aeneid* all spring.

_____. "An Unnoticed Aspect of Vergil's Personality." In *Harvard Lectures on the Vergilian Age*. Cambridge, Mass.: Harvard University Press, 1928. Reprint. New York: Biblo and Tannen, 1967.
Discusses several examples of Vergil's poetic shyness or reticence, his hesitation between two positions. Passages discussed include the *Aeneid* 5.95, with its cautious, more poetic explanation for a superstition, and *Aeneid* 4, with Aeneas' apparent ambivalence toward Dido.

_____. "Where Was Vergil's Farm?" In *Harvard Lectures on the Vergilian Age*. Cambridge, Mass.: Harvard University Press, 1928. Reprint. New York: Biblo and Tannen, 1967.
Discusses inscriptional evidence and evidence from Vergil's poetry to argue that Vergil's ancestral farm was located in Calvisano, near Mantua, Italy. Includes a map and several photographs of the region. Several long notes include discussions about the loss of Vergil's farm and an ancient life of the poet.

Copley, Frank O. "Vergil—A Biographical Note." In the *Aeneid*, by Vergil. Indianapolis: Bobbs-Merrill, 1965.
A short, two-page biography of the poet based upon the information found in the ancient biographical tradition of Vergil's life.

_____. "Vergil, the *Eclogues* and the *Georgics*." In *Latin Literature from the Beginnings to the Close of the Second Century A.D.* Ann Arbor: University of Michigan Press, 1969.
A brief biography of the poet at the beginning of this chapter makes some comparison between Vergil and his contemporary Horace and includes the question of Vergil's relationship with the emperor Augustus. Includes a bibliography and an index.

Distler, Paul F. "Life of Vergil." In *Vergil and Vergiliana*. Chicago: Loyola University Press, 1966.

The fourth century biography by Aelius Donatus is the basis of this life of the poet. The ancient biographic tradition is accepted in the main by Distler as historically accurate.

Fairclough, H. Rushton. "Life of Virgil." In *Virgil.* Rev. ed. 2 vols. Cambridge, Mass.: Harvard University Press, 1978.
A brief summary of the poet's life. Portrait in frontispiece and bibliography in appendix.

Frank, Tenny. *Vergil: A Biography.* New York: Henry Holt, 1922. Reprint. New York: Russell & Russell, 1965.
Frank avoids the unreliable ancient lives of the poet in order to reconstruct Vergil's biography and personality from the equally unreliable evidence of Vergil's early poetry, called the *Vergilian Appendix.* Philosophical, political, and literary influences upon Vergil are emphasized.

Griffin, Jasper. "Life and Times: The Unity of Virgil's Work." In *Virgil.* Oxford, England: Oxford University Press, 1986.
In addition to a brief biography of the poet, this chapter includes a discussion of the debt of Latin writers to Greek literature, and of the political agenda and sense of patriotism which unifies Vergil's poetry.

Haecker, Theodor. "Ecce Poeta." In *Virgil: Father of the West.* New York: Sheed & Ward, 1934. Reprint. New York: Johnson, 1970.
This biography presents the poet as an adventist Christian, as a pagan who anticipated Christian beliefs and who links together in his person the pagan and the Christian worlds. The title, translated as "Behold the Poet," is a variation on the words of Pontius Pilate about Jesus in the Gospel of John 19:5.

Humphries, Rolfe. "Virgil's Life and Times." In *The "Aeneid" of Virgil.* New York: Charles Scribner's Sons, 1953.
In this appendix to his verse translation of the poem, Humphries summarizes the life of the poet, with attention to Vergil's education and relationship with the emperor Augustus. There is also a cast of characters and an introduction to the poem by the translator.

Knight, W. F. Jackson. "Vergil's Life and Work." In *Roman Vergil.* 2d ed. London: Faber & Faber, 1944.
A thorough discussion of the poet's background, name, education, poetic career, and ties with such contemporaries as Augustus, Horace, and Propertius. Particular attention to the poems included in the *Vergilian Appendix.*

Mackail, J. W. "Life of Virgil." In *Virgil and His Meaning to the World of To-Day*. Boston: Marshall Jones, 1922. Reprint. New York: Cooper Square, 1963.
Contains a straightforward biography of the poet, including a brief discussion of ancient portraits.

Nardi, Bruno. *The Youth of Virgil*, translated by Belle Palmer Rand. Cambridge, Mass.: Harvard University Press, 1930.
A brief account of the poet's early career with special attention to the historical background to the *Eclogues* and to the *Vergilian Appendix*. The first chapter is about the poet's childhood and education, the second includes discussion of political events before the *Eclogues*, and the third refers to events preceding *Eclogue* 4. The last chapter includes a portrait of the poet and information on Vergil's relationship with his patron Maecenas. There is an appendix on Vergil's birthplace and another on land confiscations, as well as a short bibliography.

Prescott, Henry W. "The Atmosphere of Virgil's Youth and Early Manhood." In *The Development of Virgil's Art*. Chicago: University of Chicago Press, 1927. Reprint. New York: Russell & Russell, 1963.
Combines a biography of the poet's early life with a detailed discussion of his early poems, the *Vergilian Appendix*. Excerpts from these poems are translated into English.

Rand, Edward R. "Virgil's Magic and His Literary Goal." In *The Magical Art of Virgil*. Cambridge, Mass.: Harvard University Press, 1931.
An overview of Vergil's early life and career leads to a study of the magical epic mind of the poet. The poems of the *Vergilian Appendix* are presented as crude experiments for the magical masterpieces to follow in the *Eclogues*, the *Georgics*, and the *Aeneid*, in which the poet creates a new epic form.

Sellar, W. Y. "Life and Personal Characteristics of Virgil." In *The Roman Poets of the Augustan Age: Virgil*. Oxford, England: Clarendon Press, 1908.
This chapter in a standard nineteenth century study of Vergil summarizes the poet's life and discusses the main ancient sources for this information. Includes an outline of Vergil's personal characteristics according to traditional sources.

Showerman, Grant. "Virgil Through Two Thousand Years." In *Monuments and Men of Ancient Rome*. New York: D. Appleton-Century, 1935.
This essay on Vergil's influence begins with a biography of the poet in which Vergil's education, philosophy, and friendship with Horace are featured. Four photographs of Vergil's home region in Italy and an index are included.

Wilkinson, L. P. "Early Life of Virgil." In *The "Georgics" of Virgil*. Cambridge, England: Cambridge University Press, 1969.

This biography of the poet has sections on ancient biographical sources and the poet's education, politics, and poetry. Makes frequent reference to the *Eclogues*, some to the *Vergilian Appendix*, and none to the *Aeneid*. Not all foreign language quotes are translated. Includes a bibliography and an index.

Williams, R. D. "Introduction: Virgil's Life and Times." In *Virgil: His Poetry Through the Ages*, by R. D. Williams and T. S. Pattie. London: British Library, 1982.
A brief life of the poet is followed by an overview of Rome's literary debt to Greece, the civil wars of the first century B.C., and political values during the reign of the emperor Augustus.

_____. "Virgil's Life and Times." In *Aeneas and the Roman Hero*. London: Macmillan, 1973.
The poet's biography and his composition of the *Aeneid* are discussed in the context of political events in the late first century B.C. Augustus' policies, viewed as a restoration of Roman peace and grandeur, are said to be reflected in the values of family, duty, and religion found in the *Aeneid*.

Vergilian Poetry

Vergil and His Sources

Apollonius Rhodius. *The Argonautica*. Translated by R. C. Seaton. New York: G. P. Putnam's Sons, 1919.
To a great extent, Vergil models his characterization of Dido and her relationship with Aeneas on Medea and her love for Jason as described in this literary epic written in the late third century B.C. This Hellenistic epic also uses conventional epic language and features, such as an invocation, a catalogue, and a divine apparatus, which Vergil imitates in his epic. This edition includes a bibliography, an index, and a summary of each book. Greek text and translation appear on facing pages.

Camps, W. A. "Making an Episode: Fusion of Inherited Materials Exemplified in the Sixth Book." In *An Introduction to Virgil's "Aeneid."* Oxford, England: Oxford University Press, 1969.
Illustrates the way in which the story of Aeneas' journey to the underworld in *Aeneid* 6 is molded from various sources, including *Odyssey*, the myth of Er in Plato's *Republic*, and the "Dream of Scipio" in Cicero's *Republic*.

_____. "Making the Story: Fusion of the Legend of Aeneas' Coming to Italy with Matter from *Iliad* and *Odyssey*." In *An Introduction to Virgil's "Aeneid."* Oxford, England: Oxford University Press, 1969.
Discusses the way in which Vergil freely transforms his two main sources for the *Aeneid*, the Homeric poems and legends about Aeneas' journey from Troy to Italy.

Clark, Raymond J. *Catabasis: Vergil and the Wisdom Tradition.* Amsterdam: B. R. Grüner, 1979.
Traces the development of the theme of the descent into the underworld from the Near Eastern through the Greco-Roman world. Vergil's treatment of the theme in *Aeneid* 6 is considered both cumulative and innovative. In addition to the *Aeneid*, major works discussed include *Epic of Gilgamesh* and Homer's *Odyssey* 11. Includes bibliography and indexes.

_____. "Vergil's Golden Bough, the Cumaean Sibyl, and the Eleusinian Catabasis of Heracles." In *Catabasis: Vergil and the Wisdom Tradition.* Amsterdam: B. R. Grüner, 1979.
The golden bough in *Aeneid* 6 is seen to derive from the cult of Diana at Nemi. Vergil's Sibyl is shown to be a conflation of the Cimmerian, Cumaean, and possibly Trojan sibyls. A lost poem about Heracles' descent to the underworld at Eleusis is hypothesized as an additional source for Vergil.

Clausen, Wendell. *Virgil's "Aeneid" and the Tradition of Hellenistic Poetry.* Berkeley: University of California Press, 1986.
Traces the influence of such Hellenistic Greek poets as Callimachus and Apollonius of Rhodes upon Vergil's epic. Studies such literary techniques as similes and *ecphrasis* ("picture-poems"). Includes extensive notes, eleven appendices, a list of bibliographic abbreviations, a general index, and an index of passages cited.

Cook, Albert. "The Refined Style." In *The Classic Line: A Study in Epic Poetry.* Bloomington: Indiana University Press, 1966.
Examines the objective, controlled poetic style which Vergil inherited from the poets of Hellenistic Greece and late Republican Rome and which is known as the classical, or refined style. Characteristics of this style include evenness of poetic voice, repetitiveness, and verbal precision. Illustrates this style in a wide variety of ancient and modern poetry, both lyric and epic, especially in the works of Robert Frost, Catullus, Apollonius of Rhodes, and Theocritus. Contains some untranslated verse. Includes an index.

Distler, Paul F. "The Greek Heritage." In *Vergil and Vergiliana.* Chicago: Loyola University Press, 1966.

In this chapter of a detailed introduction to the poet, a survey of Greek authors who influenced Vergil includes Homer, Hesiod, the Greek tragedians, and Apollonius of Rhodes. Particularly useful are summaries of the plots of the *Iliad* and the *Odyssey*.

_____. "The Latin Heritage." In *Vergil and Vergiliana*. Chicago: Loyola University Press, 1966.
This chapter of a detailed introduction to the poet surveys Vergil's debt to earlier writers of Latin literature and the poet's relationship with such contemporary writers as Horace, Propertius, and Livy.

Glover, T. R. "Literature: 1. Literary Influences." In *Virgil*. 7th ed. New York: Barnes & Noble Books, 1969.
Discussion of Roman attitudes toward literary borrowing leads into a consideration of Vergil's debt to Homer, to Greek tragedians, and to Alexandrian and Latin poets, especially Lucretius.

_____. "Literature: 3. The Myths of Aeneas." In *Virgil*. 7th ed. New York: Barnes & Noble Books, 1969.
Surveys various treatments of the story of Aeneas by ancient authors other than Vergil. These authors include Homer and Livy.

Gransden, K. W. "Catalogue." In *Virgil's "Iliad": An Essay on Epic Narrative*. Cambridge, England: Cambridge University Press, 1984.
Demonstrates how the catalogue in *Aeneid* 7 is a total transformation of the catalogue in *Iliad* 2. While the latter is essentially independent from the rest of the Homeric narrative, Vergil's catalogue has close links with the second half of the *Aeneid*.

_____. "The Council of the Gods." In *Virgil's "Iliad": An Essay on Epic Narrative*. Cambridge, England: Cambridge University Press, 1984.
The council of the gods at the beginning of *Aeneid* 10, modeled on the Homeric council in *Iliad* 20, is shown to be used by Vergil to comment upon the role of the gods and free will in human destiny and history.

_____. "The Council of War." In *Virgil's "Iliad": An Essay on Epic Narrative*. Cambridge, England: Cambridge University Press, 1984.
The war council held by the Latins in *Aeneid* 11 is shown to be an assimilation of three Trojan councils in Homer's *Iliad*. In particular, the speech of Drances is contrasted with that of Thersites in *Iliad* 2 and is interpreted as a crucial point of choice between peace and war for Turnus.

Grant, Michael. "Aeneas." In *Roman Myths*. New York: Dorset Press (Marboro Books), 1984.
A chapter in a study which examines the myths of ancient Rome, their relationship with Greek mythology, and their historical truth. Includes a summary of the plot of the *Aeneid*, background to Evander's story of Hercules and Cacus in *Aeneid* 8, Vergil's reconciliation of Greek myths about Aeneas with Roman political goals, the traditional relationship of Aeneas with the Etruscans and with Latium, and Vergil's mythological and historical sources for the story of Dido. Includes illustrations, endnotes, maps, bibliography, and index.

Harrison, E. L. "The *Aeneid* and Carthage." In *Poetry and Politics in the Age of Augustus*, edited by Tony Woodman and David West. New York: Cambridge University Press, 1984.
Part of a collection of eight essays by Classical scholars, this essay considers links between Augustan politics and various references in the *Aeneid* to Carthage and the Punic wars, and examines the role of Juno in the epic. Harrison shows that the goddess never abandons Carthage in the epic and did not revoke her hostility for Rome until the end of the Second Punic War. Foreign language quotations are not translated.

Knight, W. F. Jackson. "Tradition and Poetry." In *Roman Vergil*. 2d ed. London: Faber & Faber, 1944.
Considers the value of literary derivation in writing poetry. Such poetic integration in Vergil includes adaptation of lines and phrases and literary reminiscences from earlier poets such as Homer, Ennius, and Lucretius. Special attention is given to Vergil's reworkings of his sources for the character of Dido and the structure of the *Aeneid*.

Lucretius Carus, Titus. *De Rerum Natura*. Translated by W. H. D. Rouse. 2d ed. Revised by Martin F. Smith. Cambridge, Mass.: Harvard University Press, 1982.
This Latin epic of the first century B.C., a philosophical poem describing the teachings of Epicurus, was written only a generation before Vergil composed the *Aeneid*. Lucretius' influence upon Vergil can be noted not only in Vergil's emphasis upon Lucretius' special deity, Venus, but also in the many echoes of Lucretius in the *Aeneid*. Lucretius' use of epic language and techniques, part of a Roman tradition inherited from the Greeks, prepared the way for the literary form of the *Aeneid*. This edition includes an introduction, bibliography, and index. Latin text and English translation are on facing pages.

Newman, John Kevin. "Virgil." In *The Classical Epic Tradition*. Madison: The University of Wisconsin Press, 1986.
Illustrates Vergil's position in the epic tradition begun in the third century B.C. by the Hellenistic poet Callimachus. Summarizes Vergil's literary heritage with

a survey of Callimachus' influence on Roman poets who lived before Vergil. Includes close examinations of the *Eclogues*, the *Georgics*, and the *Aeneid* as Hellenistic poems. Considers Vergil's debts to earlier Greek poets such as Homer and Apollonius and his use of time, language, similes, symbols, and history in the *Aeneid*. Includes two illustrations, a valuable glossary of critical terms, a select bibliography, and an index.

Otis, Brooks. "From Homer to Virgil: The Obsolescence of Epic." In *Virgil: A Study in Civilized Poetry*. Oxford, England: Clarendon Press, 1963.
Includes a survey of Vergil's Greek, Hellenistic, and Roman predecessors in epic composition, including Homer, Callimachus, Apollonius of Rhodes, and Ennius. Vergil's *Aeneid* is seen to be a new form of subjective epic which was essentially Augustan and not Greek. There is an appendix on historical epic in the Hellenistic Greek period. Not all quotations are translated.

_____. "The Odyssean *Aeneid* and the Iliadic *Aeneid*." In *Virgil: A Collection of Critical Essays*, edited by Steele Commager. Englewood Cliffs, N.J.: Prentice-Hall, 1966.
Based upon two chapters of *Virgil: A Study in Civilized Poetry*. Shows how Vergil transforms the themes of fate and the supernatural in the *Odyssey* into the theme of Aeneas' internal struggle with piety in *Aeneid* 1-6 and Achilles' struggle with Hector in the *Iliad* into Aeneas' external struggle with the impious Turnus in *Aeneid* 7-12.

_____. "The Originality of the *Aeneid*." In *Virgil*, edited by D. R. Dudley. New York: Basic Books, 1969.
Shows the differences between the Vergilian and Homeric epics, between Achilles' heroic code and Aeneas' sense of piety. Vergil's originality consisted of the transformation of the old epic tradition of the Greeks into a new Roman form. Latin quotations are not translated but Greek ones are. Includes endnotes.

Prescott, Henry W. "Epic Tradition." In *The Development of Virgil's Art*. Chicago: University of Chicago Press, 1927. Reprint. New York: Russell & Russell, 1963.
An extensive study of Vergil's debts to Homer and Apollonius Rhodius. Treats individual themes such as the shipwrecked sailor, the descent to the underworld, and the battle at the ship.

_____. "The Legend of Aeneas." In *The Development of Virgil's Art*. Chicago: University of Chicago Press, 1927. Reprint. New York: Russell & Russell, 1963.
An outline of the story of Aeneas in the *Aeneid* is followed by the history of the tradition from Homer through early Roman writers. Vergil's method of composing an epic poem out of varied prose sources is discussed.

_____. "Virgil's Literary Heritage." In *The Development of Virgil's Art.* Chicago: University of Chicago Press, 1927. Reprint. New York: Russell & Russell, 1963.
Describes the features of Greek literature in the Hellenistic period and provides a brief history of Roman literature through Vergil's youth. Considers the influence of literary trends and individuals upon Vergil's works.

Reinhold, Meyer. "Roman Foundation Myths." In *Past and Present: The Continuity of Classical Myths.* Toronto: Hakkert, 1972.
In addition to a plot summary of the *Aeneid,* there is a discussion of the origin of the Aeneas myth and its influence during the Middle Ages. Includes bibliography and indexes.

Scott, John A. "Homer and Roman Italy." In *Homer and His Influence.* Boston: Marshall Jones, 1925.
This short survey of the influence of Homer on Latin literature includes a section on Vergil's debt to Homer. Scott discusses several parallels between the *Aeneid* and the Homeric poems.

Sellar, W. Y. "The Roman Epic Before the Time of Virgil." In *The Roman Poets of the Augustan Age: Virgil.* Oxford, England: Clarendon Press, 1908.
The differences between primitive and literary epic and the debts of Roman epic to Homer are briefly discussed. Most of the chapter is devoted to a survey of Roman epic writers before Vergil, including Naevius and Ennius.

Vergil's Non-Epic Works

Copley, Frank O. "Vergil, the *Eclogues* and the *Georgics.*" In *Latin Literature from the Beginnings to the Close of the Second Century A.D.* Ann Arbor: University of Michigan Press, 1969.
A short but good introduction to Vergil's chief non-epic works. Emphasizes the debt of Vergil's *Eclogues* to the Greek pastoral poet Theocritus and singles out *Eclogue* 4 for discussion. There is also an overview of the *Georgics.*

Distler, Paul F. "Vergil's Works." In *Vergil and Vergiliana.* Chicago: Loyola University Press, 1966.
Contains brief but useful summaries of all the works of Vergil, including the minor works sometimes called the *Vergilian Appendix.* Summaries of the *Eclogues* and the *Georgics* are preceded by background on sources and context for composition. Detailed summary of the *Aeneid.*

Otis, Brooks. "The *Georgics*." In *Virgil: A Study in Civilized Poetry*. Oxford, England: Clarendon Press, 1963.
Vergil's development as a narrative poet is traced in the *Georgics*. The symbolic structure of the poem is analyzed. In *Georgics* 4 the style of the Aristaeus narrative, is considered more Homeric than that of the Orpheus narrative which contains a subjectivity and moralism similar to that in the *Aeneid*. Includes a bibliographical appendix and an appendix on the ending of *Georgics* 4. Also includes structural charts. Not all quotations are translated.

_____. "The Young Virgil." In *Virgil: A Study in Civilized Poetry*. Oxford, England: Clarendon Press, 1963.
In the *Eclogues*, Vergil develops the neoteric style of sympathetic poetry found in Catullus' works into a subjective style of continuous narrative anticipating the *Aeneid*. *Eclogue* 8 is compared with passages from Theocritus' *Idylls*. A symbolic structure is found in the overall arrangement of the *Eclogues*. Includes structural charts. Not all quotations are translated. There is a bibliographical appendix and an appendix on Apollonius of Rhodes and Theocritus.

Prescott, Henry W. "The Poetry of the Field and Farm." In *The Development of Virgil's Art*. Chicago: University of Chicago Press, 1927. Reprint. New York: Russell & Russell, 1963.
An introduction to Vergil's *Eclogues* and *Georgics* with attention to his literary sources, compositional background, and interpretation. Extensive quotation in translation, especially of the *Georgics*.

Snell, Bruno. "Arcadia: The Discovery of a Spiritual Landscape." In *The Discovery of the Mind: The Greek Origins of European Thought*, translated by T. G. Rosenmeyer. Oxford, England: Basil Blackwell, 1953. Reprinted in *Virgil*, edited by Harold Bloom. New York: Chelsea House, 1986.
In the *Eclogues*, Vergil transforms the Greek pastoral poetry of Theocritus into a completely artificial world of tender feeling and refined language which captures the detached spirit of Classical art. This Arcadian emphasis on a world of poetic imagination rather than on the facts of experience is a new perspective which can also be seen in the *Georgics* and the *Aeneid* and is Vergil's special contribution to later literature.

On Translating Vergil

Anderson, William S. "Translation and Vergilian Style." In *The Art of the "Aeneid."* Englewood Cliffs, N.J.: Prentice-Hall, 1969.
Difficulties in translating the *Aeneid* are illustrated by an examination of some of Vergil's stylistic characteristics, including his emphatic use of adjectives,

positioning of key words, imagery, sound, and rhythm patterns. Analyzes the last fourteen lines of the *Aeneid* and examines the use of five adjectives in particular.

Day Lewis, C. Foreword to *The Aeneid*, by Vergil. Garden City, N.Y.: Doubleday, 1953.
In his foreword, the translator, himself a distinguished poet, discusses some of the problems faced by any translator of Vergil and the goal and circumstances of his own translation.

Distler, Paul F. "Some Hints on Translating." In *Vergil and Vergiliana*. Chicago: Loyola University Press, 1966.
The problems of accurate translation of Vergil from Latin into English are illustrated by comparison of several English translations, and by examples of Vergilian lines which cannot be translated literally into English. An excellent resource even for the reader without Latin.

Dryden, John. "The Translator's Introduction." In *Virgil's Aeneid*. Translated by John Dryden. New York: Heritage Press, 1944.
In this introduction to his translation of 1697, Dryden defends his goals in translating Vergil, including the enrichment of the English languages with Latinized words, and discusses some of the difficulties he faced in this task.

Fitzgerald, Robert. Introduction to *The Aeneid*, by Virgil, translated by John Dryden. New York: Macmillan, 1964.
This introduction to Dryden's 1697 translation of the epic provides literary and biographical background, including Dryden's appreciation of Vergil and method of translation. Dryden's work is presented as a rushed, but brilliant, version of Vergil's epic.

Lewis, R. W. B. "On Translating the *Aeneid*: Yif That I Can." *Yearbook of Comparative and General Literature* X (1961): 7-15. Reprinted in *Virgil: A Collection of Critical Essays*, edited by Steele Commager. Englewood Cliffs, N.J.: Prentice-Hall, 1966.
This scholar of English literature considers the problems of translation in general, and of Vergil in particular, with special attention to Gawin Douglas' translation of the *Aeneid* in 1553.

Pattie, T. S. "Virgil in English." In *Virgil: His Poetry Through the Ages*, by R. D. Williams and T. S. Pattie. London: British Library, 1982.
A short survey of English translations of Vergil beginning with Geoffrey Chaucer in the fifteenth century and ending with C. Day Lewis in the twentieth century. Some discussion of the problems of translation.

The *Aeneid*

Latin Text and Commentaries

Bernardus Silvestris. *Commentary on the First Six Books of Vergil's "Aeneid."*
Translated by Earl G. Schreiber and Thomas Maresca. Lincoln: University of
Nebraska, 1979.
Based upon the text of Jones and Jones (1977), this is a translation of a philosophical commentary attributed to Bernardus Silvestris. Includes an index and
an introductory essay, in which the translators discuss the commentary in the
context of such medieval interpretations of the *Aeneid* as those of Macrobius
(fourth-fifth century), Fulgentius (sixth century), and Cristofor Landino (fifteenth
century).

Di Cesare, Mario A. *The Altar and the City: A Reading of Vergil's "Aeneid."* New
York: Columbia University Press, 1974.
A running commentary and interpretation of the poem. Analyzes individual
scenes, characters, and words. There are separate chapters on *Aeneid* 2, 6, 7,
and 10. *Aeneid* 1 and 4 are treated in a chapter on the Carthage episode of the
epic; books 3 and 5 in a chapter Aeneas' wanderings; books 8 and 9 in a chapter
on the war in Italy; and books 11 and 12 in a chapter on Aeneas and Turnus.
Extensive quotation from the *Aeneid*, but not all Latin is translated. Includes
endnotes, bibliography, and indexes.

Distler, Paul F. "The Text Itself." In *Vergil and Vergiliana*. Chicago: Loyola
University Press, 1966.
A good general introduction to the text of the *Aeneid*, its manuscripts, and its
modern publication history. The major manuscripts are discussed individually,
with a photograph of the *Codex Vaticanus*. Includes brief biographies of ancient
commentators, and a brief comparison of English translations. Latin epitomes
of the *Aeneid* are included but not translated. A bibliographical listing of English
editions, commentaries, and translations is included.

Jones, Julian Ward, and Elizabeth Frances Jones, eds. *The Commentary on the First
Six Books of the "Aeneid" of Vergil Commonly Attributed to Bernardus Silvestris*.
Lincoln: University of Nebraska, 1977.
An important twelfth century commentary on *Aeneid* 1-6, probably written at
Chartres in France. Interprets the poem as an allegorical and philosophical study
of the growth of the human soul. The text of the commentary is in Latin, but
there is a valuable introduction in English with information about the commentary, about its manuscript tradition, and about Bernardus Silvestris, the twelfth
century master of the school of Tours in France, who is usually associated with

this commentary. Includes a selected bibliography and two indexes, one of authors cited and a second of all proper names and important terms appearing in the commentary.

Knapp, Charles. *The "Aeneid" of Vergil.* Rev. ed. Glenview, Ill.: Scott, Foresman, 1951.
This textbook for high school Latin students includes the complete Latin text of the first six books of the *Aeneid* plus selections from books 7-12. Includes a detailed introduction, footnotes, vocabulary, color map of Aeneas' voyages, and twenty-one illustrations with descriptions.

Knight, W. F. Jackson. "Poetry and Manuscripts." In *Roman Vergil.* 2d ed. London: Faber & Faber, 1944.
Offers a general history of the Vergilian manuscript tradition. An excellent introduction to the special problems involved in reconstructing the text of Vergil.

Pharr, Clyde. *Vergil's "Aeneid" Books I-VI.* Lexington, Mass.: D. C. Heath, 1930.
An introductory text of the first six books of the *Aeneid* for high school and college Latin students. Ten to fifteen Latin lines per page with copious vocabulary aids and notes below. Contains a brief introduction to the poet and the epic with bibliography. Includes twenty-four illustrations and a grammatical appendix.

Vergil. *Opera.* Rev. ed. 2 vols. Cambridge, Mass.: Harvard University Press, 1978.
The Loeb Classical Library makes the Latin texts more accessible to the English reader by accompanying the Latin with a facing translation. Latin texts of all Vergil's works, including the *Aeneid*, the *Eclogues*, the *Georgics*, and the *Vergilian Appendix*, are here accompanied by H. Rushton Fairclough's translation. Includes notes and summaries of the manuscripts and modern editions.

Williams, R. D. *The Aeneid of Virgil.* Bristol, England: Bristol Classical Press, 1985.
This companion to C. Day Lewis' translation of the *Aeneid* includes a general introduction and a commentary which surveys the subject matter book by book and provides line-by-line discussion of historical background and detailed explanation of important words and phrases. Four appendices provide samples of fuller literary treatment of specific passages. Includes a cover illustration, bibliography, and glossary.

Translations

Bowen, Sir Charles. *Virgil in English Verse.* London: John Murray, 1889.
Adapts the Latin hexameter to English in order to translate the first six books

of the *Aeneid* as well as the *Eclogues*. Brief plot summaries by the translator precede each book.

John, D. A., and A. F Turberfield. *The Voyage of Aeneas*. New York: St. Martin's Press, 1968.
A straightforward prose translation of the first six books of the *Aeneid*, written for advanced high school students. An introductory essay includes a biography of Vergil, a summary of books 7-12, and sections on various aspects of the *Aeneid*. Basic background information is provided in notes. Includes three maps, a bibliography, and an index.

Vergil. *The Aeneid*. Translated by Frank O. Copley. Indianapolis: Bobbs-Merrill, 1965.
This line-by-line verse translation includes several maps, a biographical note, a selected bibliography, and an extensive glossary of proper names. There is also an introductory essay by Brooks Otis on Vergil's use of Homer.

_____. *The Aeneid*. Translated by Patric Dickinson. New York: New American Library, 1961.
This verse translation includes a brief general essay entitled "Vergil and the *Aeneid*" by Dickinson, who is a British poet and translator. There are no Latin line references. There are several helpful appendices: a list of relevant dates in Roman history; a book-by-book outline of the *Aeneid*; and a glossary of names. Also includes a map showing the wanderings of Aeneas.

_____. *The Aeneid*. Translated by Kevin Guinagh. New York: Rinehart, 1953.
This prose translation of the epic includes an introduction by the translator, a map of Aeneas' voyages, a short bibliography, a genealogical table, and a glossary of names. Also useful are thematic subtitles, several in each book, to indicate the subject of each section. Contains drawings of twelve Roman gods and Aeneas.

_____. *The Aeneid*. Translated by James H. Mantinbrand. New York: Frederick Ungar, 1964.
A verse translation which uses Latin line references and aims for accuracy of translation with a minimum of archaic or colloquial language. Book titles are supplied by the translator. A glossary and an introduction by the translator are included.

Virgil. *The Aeneid*. Edited and with an introduction by Wendell Clausen. New York: Simon & Schuster, 1965.

This text is the prose translation of the Vergilian scholar John Conington, edited by John Addington Symonds and published posthumously in 1872. The introduction, entitled "An Interpretation of the *Aeneid*," was originally a scholarly lecture published in *Harvard Studies in Classical Philology* 68 (1964) and adapted for the general reader. To this introduction, Clausen has added a brief biography of Vergil and some comments upon Conington's translation.

_____. *The Aeneid*. Translated by C. Day Lewis. Garden City, N.Y.: Doubleday, 1953.
A verse translation by a poet and professor of poetry at Oxford University in England. Includes Latin line references. In a brief foreword, Day Lewis discusses some of the problems of translating Vergil. No readers' aids, such as a glossary or an index, are included.

_____. *The Aeneid*. Translated by John Dryden. New York: Heritage Press, 1944.
This edition of Dryden's translation of 1697 includes the translator's own introduction and book summaries as well as illustrations at the beginning of each book by Carlotta Petrina.

_____. *The Aeneid*. Translated by John Dryden, edited by Robert Fitzgerald. New York: Macmillan, 1964.
Dryden's verse translation of the *Aeneid*, first published in 1697, has been the most important in English until the twentieth century and is still very readable, despite the use of rhymed couplets and seventeenth century language. Fitzgerald's introduction provides valuable background on the translation and the translator, an eminent English poet in his own right. Includes Latin line references, one plate from the 1698 edition, and notes prepared by the editor.

_____. *The Aeneid*. Translated by Robert Fitzgerald. New York: Vintage Books, 1984.
An outstanding translator of Homer as well as Vergil, Fitzgerald offers a verse translation which not only remains carefully faithful to the Latin original but also is poetically polished. Book titles are supplied by the translator. There are Latin line references and a brief glossary as well as a short postscript in which Fitzgerald treats such topics as Aeneas in Homer's *Iliad*, the *Aeneid* and Roman history, and Vergil's biography.

_____. *The Aeneid*. Translated by Rolfe Humphries. New York: Charles Scribner's Sons, 1953.
This verse translation of the poem is written in loose iambic pentameters. The language has been simplified somewhat, and there is no attempt to provide a

strictly literal translation. There is a brief introduction by the translator as well as a life of the poet and a cast of characters in an appendix.

_____. *The Aeneid*. Translated by Rolfe Humphries. Rev. ed. Edited by Brian Wilkie. New York: Macmillan, 1987.
This edition of Humphries' verse translation retains the original cast of characters in the appendix but has replaced the translator's introduction and appendix on the poet's life and times with a short explanation of Vergilian meter and a list of important quotations from the *Aeneid* in an appendix. Several useful features have been added, including Latin line references, factual and explanatory footnotes, a map of Aeneas' journey, and a bibliography. There is a preface and introduction by the editor.

_____. *The Aeneid*. Translated by Rolfe Humphries. Abridged in *Literature of the Western World*. Vol. 1, *The Ancient World Through the Renaissance*, edited by Brian Wilkie and James Hurt. New York: Macmillan, 1984.
Contains books 1, 3, and 4 and selections from book 6, as well as an introduction, summary of books 7-12, footnotes, and a bibliography.

_____. *The Aeneid*. Translated by W. F. Jackson Knight. Baltimore: Penguin Books, 1956.
This prose translation of the poem includes a brief but good introduction to the poet and his work. Several useful tools are also included: book titles, Latin line references, a glossary, several maps, and a genealogy of Aeneas. Also includes a list of places where this translation differs from the Latin version of the Oxford Classical Text.

_____. *The Aeneid*. Translated by Allen Mandelbaum. Berkeley: University of California, 1971.
This verse translation by a poet and English professor at the City College of New York includes a brief introduction, Latin line references, a bibliographical note, and a valuable glossary and pronunciation guide. The general reader will find this translation an excellent introduction to the *Aeneid*.

_____. *The Aeneid*. Translated by C. H. Sisson. Manchester, England: Carcanet Press, 1986.
Sisson, a poet and critic, has produced several important English translations, including the works of Lucretius, Jean Racine, and Dante. This poetic translation of the *Aeneid* offers a significant twentieth century perspective on the poem. Includes a short introduction by the translator. The absence of an index of names, Latin line references, and a glossary is regrettable.

_____. *Opera*. Translated by H. Rushton Fairclough. Rev. ed. 2 vols. Cambridge, Mass.: Harvard University Press, 1978.
Includes a literal prose translation of the epic. Originally published in 1916, and Victorian English still appears in the revised edition. The most useful aspect of this translation is the facing Latin text, which allows for ready comparison of original and translation. Includes frontispiece, appendix, and index.

_____. *Works*. Translated by J. W. Mackail. New York: Modern Library, 1950.
This prose translation of the *Aeneid*, the *Eclogues*, and the *Georgics* is written in Victorian English by an important Latin scholar of the early twentieth century. Short descriptive book titles have been added for the *Aeneid* and the *Eclogues*. There are Latin line references, an introduction, and a bibliography.

Background and Plot Summaries

Distler, Paul F. "Of Gods and Men and Places." In *Vergil and Vergiliana*. Chicago: Loyola University Press, 1966.
Contains much useful background to the *Aeneid*, including a brief history of events leading up to the plot and glossaries of the major and minor gods, monsters, mortals, places, and religious terms mentioned in the *Aeneid*.

Gayley, Charles Mills. "Adventures of Aeneas." In *The Classic Myths in English Literature and in Art*. 2d ed. New York: John Wiley & Sons, 1911.
Paraphrases the story of Aeneas' wanderings from Troy to Italy as told in *Aeneid* 1-6. Commentary section contains lists of works of art and literature based upon the epic. Includes illustrations and indexes.

_____. "The Fall of Troy." In *The Classic Myths in English Literature and in Art*. 2d ed. New York: John Wiley & Sons, 1911.
Summarizes the story of the fall of Troy, beginning with the end of the *Iliad* by Homer and including the death of Achilles, and the contest for the arms of Achilles. Covers events from *Aeneid* 2, including the story of the wooden horse, Laocoön, and the death of Priam. Commentary section contains lists of works of art and literature based upon these myths. Includes reproductions of artwork depicting related events.

_____. "The War Between Trojans and Latins." In *The Classic Myths in English Literature and in Art*. 2d ed. New York: John Wiley & Sons, 1911.
Paraphrases the story of Aeneas' conflict with the Rutulian warrior Turnus for the hand of the Latin princess Lavinia as told in *Aeneid* 7-12. Commentary section contains lists of works of art and literature based upon the epic.

Graves, Robert. "The Sack of Troy." In *The Greek Myths*. Vol. 2. Baltimore: Penguin Books, 1960.
This summary of events connected with the fall of Troy places Vergil's story in *Aeneid* 2 in the context of the fuller mythological tradition. Alternate traditions about Aeneas' survival after the war are mentioned.

_____. "The Wooden Horse." In *The Greek Myths*. Vol. 2. Baltimore: Penguin Books, 1960.
This summary of the story of the Trojan horse, based on *Aeneid* 2 and a variety of other ancient sources, includes some details not mentioned by Vergil.

Guerber, Hélène Adeline. "Adventures of Aeneas." In *Myths of Greece and Rome*. New York: American Book Company, 1893.
A summary of the plot of the *Aeneid* told in chronological order, beginning with the appearance of Hector's ghost in *Aeneid* 2 to warn Aeneas to flee burning Troy and ending with the death of Turnus in *Aeneid* 12. There is extensive quotation from the *Aeneid* and other literature. Includes two black-and-white reproductions of artwork related to the epic, as well as a map, genealogical table, glossary, and index.

Hamilton, Edith. "The Adventures of Aeneas." In *Mythology*. New York: New American Library, 1942.
This retelling of Aeneas' travels begins with events from *Aeneid* 1, 3, and 4, including the hero's flight from Troy and encounter with Dido; describes the hero's descent into the lower world from *Aeneid* 6; and ends with a summary of Aeneas' war in Italy from the last half of the epic. Includes illustrations, genealogical tables, and an index.

_____. "The Fall of Troy." In *Mythology*. New York: New American Library, 1942.
Aeneid 2 is combined with several other ancient sources to summarize the events surrounding the fall of Troy, including the return of Philoctetes, the story of the Trojan horse, and the escape of Aeneas. Includes illustrations, genealogical tables, and an index.

Mayerson, Philip. "The Trojan War." In *Classical Mythology in Literature, Art, and Music*. Lexington, Mass.: Xerox College Publishing, 1971.
This summary of Greek myths connected with the city of Troy includes Vergil's story of the wooden horse, Laocoön, and Troy's final hours from *Aeneid* 2. Illustrations of the Trojan horse and the deaths of Laocoön and Priam. Includes genealogical charts, a bibliography, and an index.

Morford, Mark P. O., and Robert J. Lenardon. "Roman Mythology." In *Classical Mythology*. 3d ed. New York: Longman, 1985.
Following a discussion of Roman gods based on the *Aeneid* and other sources, there is a summary of traditions surrounding the founding of Rome, including Aeneas' journey from Troy and his settlement in Italy. Includes maps, genealogical charts, illustrations, select bibliography, footnotes, and indexes.

_____. "The Trojan Saga." In *Classical Mythology*. 3d ed. New York: Longman, 1985.
A summary of events surrounding the Trojan War. In addition to material on the children of Leda, preparations for the war, and Greek and Trojan leaders, the section on the fall of Troy focuses especially on events told in *Aeneid* 2. Extensive quotations from ancient sources are included, as well as maps, genealogical charts, illustrations, select bibliography, footnotes, and indexes.

Rose, H. J. "Italian Pseudo-Mythology." In *A Handbook of Greek Mythology*. New York: E. P. Dutton, 1959.
This summary of the legends connected with the founding and early history of Rome includes a discussion of the myth of Aeneas and a summary of the plot of the *Aeneid*. Includes bibliography, endnotes, and indexes.

Literary Studies

Anderson, William S. *The Art of the "Aeneid."* Englewood Cliffs, N.J.: Prentice-Hall, 1969.
In addition to an introductory chapter outlining some general aspects of the epic, the *Aeneid* is analyzed in a series of six chapters devoted to book-by-book analysis. Books are discussed in pairs. The thematic development, narrative technique, and structural patterns of each book are examined. There is also a final chapter on translation and Vergil's style. Includes map, chronology, bibliography, endnotes, and index.

_____. "Vergil Begins His Epic." In *The Art of the "Aeneid."* Englewood Cliffs, N.J.: Prentice-Hall, 1969.
In this introductory chapter, several features of the poet's art are discussed, including the impersonal stance of the epic poet; Vergil's debt to Homer; the contemporary relevance of the theme in Augustan Rome; characteristics of the Vergilian hero; the importance of the poetic pattern of the *Aeneid* over historical reality; and the role of the gods and "piety" in the epic.

Andersson, Theodore M. "Visible Space in Virgil's *Aeneid*." In *Early Epic Scenery*. Ithaca, N.Y.: Cornell University Press, 1976.

A survey of Vergil's use of landscape in the *Aeneid*. Shows how the poet's control of spatial features of the narrative creates an emotional density and a bond between humans and their surroundings. Especially in Aeneas' encounters with Dido and Turnus, Vergil uses background scenery to project a growing recognition of doom.

Beye, Charles Rowan. "The *Aeneid*." In *The "Iliad," the "Odyssey," and the Epic Tradition*. Garden City, N.Y.: Doubleday, 1966.
Follows the transition from the traditional oral epic represented by the Homeric poems through the work of Apollonius of Rhodes to the literary epic of Vergil. Discusses the structure, plot, political background, and meaning of the *Aeneid*, which is interpreted as a nationalized *Odyssey*, as a Roman version of the theme of the wandering hero. Vergil's hero must sacrifice his personal will to the future destiny of Rome.

Bloom, Harold. Introduction to *Virgil*, edited by Harold Bloom. Edgemont, Pa.: Chelsea House, 1986. Reprinted in *Virgil's Aeneid*, edited by Harold Bloom. Edgemont, Pa.: Chelsea House, 1987.
In this essay, Bloom counters impressions of Vergil as an imitative poet with a refreshing discussion of Vergil's originality and influence, with special attention to the characterizations of Dido and Turnus in the *Aeneid*. A chronology of Vergil's life, a selective bibliography, and an index are included.

_____, ed. *Virgil's "Aeneid."* Edgemont, Pa.: Chelsea House, 1987.
This collection of six critical essays published individually between 1962 and 1984 offers a good general overview of how the *Aeneid* has been interpreted in the second half of the twentieth century. An introduction by the editor focuses on Vergil's originality; the essays deal with the character of Aeneas, Vergil's style, and other topics.

Bowra, C. M. "Virgil and the Ideal of Rome." In *From Virgil to Milton*. New York: St. Martin's Press, 1961.
The *Aeneid* is shown to be a new kind of epic, one which concentrates not on individuals but on the destiny of a nation, of Rome. Examines Vergil's debt to Homer, his portrayal of the gods, his religion, and, especially, his characterizations of Turnus, Dido, and Aeneas. In Aeneas, Vergil depicts a new ideal of heroism, emphasizing moral rather than physical strength.

Camps, W. A. *An Introduction to Virgil's "Aeneid."* Oxford, England: Oxford University Press, 1969.
Offers a good general overview for someone reading the *Aeneid* for the first time. An introductory section deals with Vergil's method of composition. Four chapters are devoted to plot and thematic summary of the poem; two chapters to poetic

structure and language; and four to Vergil's literary and historical sources. Contains endnotes, a selective index, a map of Aeneas' voyages, and five appendices, including a valuable translation of Aelius Donatus' *Life of Vergil*.

_____. "Poetic Expression: Language and Sensibility." In *An Introduction to Virgil's Aeneid*. Oxford, England: Oxford University Press, 1969.
Considers various features of Vergil's poetic diction. Vocabulary, syntax, original phrases, rhythm, figures of speech, and assonance in the *Aeneid* mark the epic as a distinctly poetic creation.

_____. "Preliminary." In *An Introduction to Virgil's "Aeneid."* Oxford, England: Oxford University Press, 1969.
Traditional stories about Vergil's method of writing the *Aeneid* are used to explain the structure of the *Aeneid* and Vergil's debt to Homer in terms of the poet's concentration upon individual scenes and emphasis on an overlying design.

_____. "Principles of Structure: Continuity and Symmetry." In *An Introduction to Virgil's "Aeneid."* Oxford, England: Oxford University Press, 1969.
Illustrates the way in which Vergil uses parallelism as a basic structure of the epic. Events in books 1-6 are shown to prepare for and anticipate those in books 7-12. This symmetry is seen to provide a structure for the episodic form of the epic.

_____. "Relevant and Irrelevant Associations: Conclusion." In *An Introduction to Virgil's "Aeneid."* Oxford, England: Oxford University Press, 1969.
A caution against viewing all allusions and poetic associations in the *Aeneid* as intentional and significant to the meaning of the epic.

_____. "The Story and Its Subject: Rome." In *An Introduction to Virgil's "Aeneid."* Oxford, England: Oxford University Press, 1969.
A summary of the plot of the epic and of the role of the gods is followed by an account of the poet's debt to Homer and his transformation of the story of Aeneas into a tribute to Rome.

Clausen, Wendell. "An Interpretation of the *Aeneid*." *Harvard Studies in Classical Philology* 68 (1964): 139-147. Revised in *Virgil: A Collection of Critical Essays*, edited by Steele Commager. Englewood Cliffs, N.J.: Prentice-Hall, 1966. Also appears in abbreviated form as an introduction to John Conington's translation of the *Aeneid*. New York: Simon & Schuster, 1965.
In this lecture, Clausen discusses the poem as both a literary and a Roman epic and focuses especially on the theme of fate. English translations of Latin and Greek quotations are provided in the reprints.

Cook, Albert. "The Ivory Gate." In *The Classic Line: A Study in Epic Poetry*. Bloomington: Indiana University Press, 1966.
Shows how Vergil adapted the refined, controlled poetic style of Hellenistic Greece and Augustan Rome to the epic form. Traces Vergil's earlier use of this style in the *Eclogues* and the *Georgics* and his reasons for choosing a Homeric model. Illustrates the way that Vergil concentrates language and rhythm in the epic and universalizes the character of Aeneas by unifying in the hero images of the private and the public, of emotion and fate, of death and the future greatness of Rome. Includes an index.

Copley, Frank O. "Vergil, the *Aeneid*." In *Latin Literature from the Beginnings to the Close of the Second Century A.D.* Ann Arbor: University of Michigan Press, 1969.
An interpretative essay in which the *Aeneid* is presented as a poem about empire. Events in the epic are summarized and understood in terms of Vergil's emphasis upon duty and fate and his identification of Aeneas with the emperor Augustus. Includes a bibliography and an index.

Cruttwell, Robert W. *Virgil's Mind at Work: An Analysis of the Symbolism of the "Aeneid."* Oxford, England: Basil Blackwell, 1946. Reprint. New York: Cooper Square, 1969. Reprint. Westport, Conn.: Greenwood Press, 1971.
Mental association as the creative principle of poetic symbolism is followed through the *Aeneid* by such unconscious links as those between the goddess Cybele and Aeneas' mother, Venus, between Aeneas' son Julus and the Julian family of Rome, between Aeneas' Troy and Vergil's Rome, and, most important, between the shield of Aeneas and the labyrinth of Theseus. All of this is accomplished in a very tight book, which the author insists must be read consecutively. For this reason, there is no index.

Dickinson, Patric. "Vergil and the *Aeneid*." In *The Aeneid*, by Vergil. New York: New American Library, 1961.
This brief general essay is attached to the author's verse translation. Vergil's biography and poetic goals are placed in historical context. The *Aeneid* is compared to John Milton's *Paradise Lost*. Discussion of Vergil's influence on the English poet Alfred, Lord Tennyson and of the challenge of translating Vergil.

Distler, Paul F. "The Hexameter." In *Vergil and Vergiliana*. Chicago: Loyola University Press, 1966.
A detailed introduction to the Latin hexameter verse, its history, and its use by Vergil and guide to metrical analysis of hexameter and to reading the hexameter aloud. Contains a useful list of metrically unusual lines in first six books of the *Aeneid* and a glossary of metrical terms.

_____. "Ornaments of Style." In *Vergil and Vergiliana*. Chicago: Loyola University Press, 1966.
A study of Vergilian word order and figures of speech such as alliteration, ellipsis, irony, and metaphor. Definition of each figure is followed by untranslated examples from the *Aeneid*.

_____. "Vergil and His the *Aeneid*." In *Vergil and Vergiliana*. Chicago: Loyola University Press, 1966.
A good, general introduction to the epic, its poetic purpose, its sources, and its unfinished form, with frequent quotations from Donatus' ancient life of Vergil. Includes a useful list of *Aeneid* passages and their Homeric parallels and quotations from ancient references to Vergil's deathbed desire to burn the unfinished *Aeneid*.

_____. "Vergilian Grammar." In *Vergil and Vergiliana*. Chicago: Loyola University Press, 1966.
The distinguishing characteristics of Vergilian grammar are summarized for the Latin student approaching Vergil for the first time. Numerous untranslated examples are cited from Vergil.

Drew, D. L. *The Allegory of the "Aeneid."* Oxford, England: Basil Blackwell, 1927. Reprint. New York: Garland, 1978.
This book attempts to prove that the poem creates an allegorical parallel between Aeneas and Augustus, especially in *Aeneid* 5 and 8. There is a brief appendix citing (in Latin without translation) several passages from ancient commentaries in which such allegory is recognized.

Dryden, John. "The Translator's Introduction." In *Virgil's "Aeneid."* New York: Heritage Press, 1944.
Dryden's introduction to his translation of 1697 is a dedication, written in the flamboyant style of his age. Dryden discusses his preference for epic over drama and defends Vergil against seventeenth century detractors. There are sections on Aeneas' piety, on the language of Vergil, and on Dryden's goals as a translator.

Duckworth, George E. *Foreshadowing and Suspense in the Epics of Homer, Apollonius, and Vergil*. New York: Haskell, 1970.
Shows that the same devices are used to forecast future action in four ancient epics, including the *Aeneid*, but that the various poets use these devices in different ways. The epics are discussed as a group rather than individually. In the *Aeneid*, these devices are not only used, as they are in the other epics, to give the reader foreknowledge of future events of which characters are kept in the dark, but also to create uncertainty in the mind of Vergil's reader as to the outcome of future events. There is an index of passages discussed.

_____. *Structural Patterns and Proportions in Vergil's "Aeneid."* Ann Arbor: University of Michigan Press, 1962.
Shows that a mathematical symmetry based upon the golden mean ratio governs each book of the *Aeneid* as well as the *Eclogues* and the *Georgics*. Includes seven appendices, twenty-seven tables, an index, and a bibliography.

Garrison, Daniel H. *The Language of Virgil: An Introduction to the Poetry of the Aeneid.* New York: Peter Lang, 1984.
Primarily a textbook written as a short introduction to the *Aeneid* for college students. The Latin language, as used by Vergil, is concisely but clearly explained in the first half, and Latin passages from the *Aeneid* are explained in the second half. Copiously illustrated with maps and drawings from all areas of Roman life.

Gransden, K. W. *Virgil's "Iliad": An Essay on Epic Narrative.* Cambridge, England: Cambridge University Press, 1984.
Argues the paramount importance of the last six books of the *Aeneid*, which are often not as well known as the first six and which are carefully analyzed here. Gransden suggests that a full understanding of the epic requires a reconsideration of Homer's *Iliad* as well as *Aeneid* 1-6 in the light of books 7-12. Includes a bibliography and index.

Grant, Michael. "The Quest for a New Home." In *Myths of the Greeks and Romans.* New York: New American Library, 1962.
This overview of the *Aeneid* is divided into three sections: a plot summary; a discussion of such topics as a comparison of the *Aeneid* and the Homeric epics, the characterizations of Aeneas, Dido, and Turnus, the growth of the Aeneas legend in Rome, and the influence of the epic on later literature and art; and a section on religion, dreams, and the underworld in Vergil. Includes illustrations, maps, genealogical charts, myth summaries, bibliographical notes, endnotes, and an index.

Greene, Thomas. "Virgil." In *The Descent from Heaven: A Study in Epic Continuity.* New Haven, Conn.: Yale University Press, 1963. Abridged in *Virgil*, edited by Harold Bloom. New York: Chelsea House, 1986.
In this chapter of a book on the European epic tradition, Greene focuses on Mercury's descent from Olympus to speak to Aeneas in the *Aeneid* 4 and discusses such topics as the inaccessibility of Vergil to the twentieth century reader, the poet's transformation of Homeric elements, the character of Aeneas, and Vergil's poetic style.

_____. "Virgil's Style." In *Virgil's "Aeneid,"* edited by Harold Bloom. Edgemont, Pa.: Chelsea House, 1987.

In this excerpt from *The Descent from Heaven*, Greene accounts for Vergil's inaccessibility to readers in the second half of the twentieth century in terms of the poet's stylistic originality: his adaptations of Homer to a uniquely moral and Roman context; his portrayal of Aeneas as a hero only in so far as he surrenders self to duty; and his expansive use of geography and history to create a poetic unity.

Griffin, Jasper. "The *Aeneid* and the Myth of Rome." In *Virgil*. Oxford, England: Oxford University Press, 1986.
In addition to a summary of the plot and some comments on Vergil's poetic language, Griffin interprets the *Aeneid* as an ambiguous statement concerning Roman history and the nature of imperial power in which the molding of the story of Aeneas into an epic on the career of Augustus ensures that a revival of Roman virtue would actually occur under Augustus' rule.

Guinagh, Kevin. Introduction to *The "Aeneid" of Vergil*. New York: Rinehart, 1953.
In this introduction to his prose translation of the epic, Guinagh provides historical and literary background to the epic. There are individual sections on the works of Vergil, Aeneas as a hero, and Vergil in literary tradition.

Harrison, E. L. "The *Aeneid* and Carthage." In *Poetry and Politics in the Age of Augustus*, edited by Tony Woodman and David West. New York: Cambridge University Press, 1984.
Part of a collection of eight essays by Classical scholars. Rejects the theory that contemporary Augustan politics explains the prominence of Carthage in the first part of the *Aeneid* and considers various references in Vergil's epic to Carthage and the Punic wars. The role of the goddess Juno in the epic is also examined. Foreign language quotations are not translated. Includes frontispiece, endnotes, bibliography, and index.

Highet, Gilbert. *The Speeches in Vergil's "Aeneid."* Princeton, N.J.: Princeton University Press, 1972.
Several aspects of speeches in the *Aeneid* are discussed, including the various types of speeches, Vergil's sources for these speeches, and the importance of speeches within the epic. Seven appendices group the speeches in several different ways. Bibliography and indexes are also included.

Hornsby, Roger. *Patterns of Action in the "Aeneid": An Interpretation of Vergil's Epic Similes*. Ames: University of Iowa Press, 1970.
Similes are discussed according to the following groupings: nature; characters; gods and men; and *Aeneid* 12. Vergil's similes are shown to develop characters as well as the organization and theme of the *Aeneid* as a whole. Latin passages are not translated. An index and bibliography are included.

Humphries, Rolfe. Introduction to *The "Aeneid" of Virgil*. New York: Charles Scribner's Sons, 1953.
In this short introduction to his verse translation of the poem, Humphries discusses various aspects of the epic, including its incompleteness, its purposes for Augustan propaganda, the character of Aeneas, and the relationship between Vergil and Homer. The goals of his translation are also mentioned. There are a life of the poet and a cast of characters in an appendix.

Hunt, J. William. *Forms of Glory: Structure and Sense in Virgil's "Aeneid."* Carbondale: Southern Illinois University Press, 1973.
An alternative to extrinsic, partial, and one-sided analyses of the structure of the epic is provided in this study of the interwoven architectural design of Vergil's metaphoric narrative. There are chapters on the general structure of the poem, on imagery, and on character development. Some translations of the Latin are provided only in endnotes. Includes a select bibliography, list of passages cited, and index.

_____. "Labyrinthine Ways." In *Forms of Glory: Structure and Sense in Virgil's "Aeneid."* Carbondale: Southern Illinois University Press, 1973. Reprinted in *Virgil*, edited by Harold Bloom. New York: Chelsea House, 1986.
This final chapter of a study of imagery and structure in the *Aeneid* examines the links among Aeneas, Dido, and Turnus in terms of the tripartite scheme around which the epic is organized. These three characters reveal in the *Aeneid* an ambiguous tension between tragic destruction and violent glory. Some translations of the Latin are provided only in endnotes.

_____. "Pictures at an Exhibition." In *Forms of Glory: Structure and Sense in Virgil's "Aeneid."* Carbondale: Southern Illinois University Press, 1973.
Vergil's pictorial imagery, such as his description in book 1 of the engraved panels on the temple of Juno in Carthage depicting the fall of Troy, provides a basis for summarizing the general structure of the epic. A tripartite rather than a bipartite division of books is preferred. Some translations of the Latin are provided only in endnotes.

_____. "Promise and Performance." In *Forms of Glory: Structure and Sense in Virgil's Aeneid*. Carbondale: Southern Illinois University Press, 1973.
Aeneas' reaction to the visit of Mercury in the *Aeneid* 4 provides an introduction for an analysis of Vergil's use of two thematic images in the epic: betrayal of trust, expressed through reference to gifts, prizes, and trophies; and the caprice of the gods, who are seen as symbols of action in the epic. Some translations of the Latin are provided only in endnotes.

_____. "Shadows and the Sea." In *Forms of Glory: Structure and Sense in Virgil's Aeneid*. Carbondale: Southern Illinois University Press, 1973.
An examination of four important images—land, sea, glory, and shadow—in the epic. The role of Palinurus and Aeneas' reaction to the burning of the ships by the Trojan women in *Aeneid* 5 provide a framework for this discussion. Some translations of the Latin are provided only in endnotes.

Johnson, W. R. "Lessing, Auerbach, Gombrich: The Norm of Reality and the Spectrum of Decorum." In *Darkness Visible: A Study of Vergil's "Aeneid."* Berkeley: University of California Press, 1976.
Beginning with E. H. Gombrich's theory of artistic realism and such classic comparisons of the *Aeneid* and the Homeric poems as those of Longinus, Gotthold E. Lessing, and Erich Auerbach, Johnson argues that Vergil consciously avoids the Homeric form of realistic and simple narrative in favor of a more ambiguous, complex, and subjective style. Compares such passages as the stag episodes in *Odyssey* 10 and in *Aeneid* 1 and passages of erotic compulsion in *Iliad* 3 and *Aeneid* 1.

_____. "*Varia Confusus Imagine Rerum*: Depths and Surfaces." In *Darkness Visible: A Study of Vergil's "Aeneid."* Berkeley: University of California Press, 1976. Reprinted in abridged form as "Depths and Surfaces," in *Virgil's Aeneid*, edited by Harold Bloom. Edgemont, Pa.: Chelsea House, 1987.
An analysis of the ways in which "light," expressed in themes of compassion and moral worth, is overshadowed by the reality of "darkness," of despair and futility in Vergil's epic. Compares Vergil's similes and descriptive passages, including the shield of Aeneas in *Aeneid* 8, with parallel Homeric passages. Includes special studies of Turnus' decision to confront Aeneas and Turnus' death in *Aeneid* 12, the death of Euryalus in *Aeneid* 9, and the death of Dido in *Aeneid* 4. The Latin quotation in the title, translated as "bewildered by the varied image of things," is taken from *Aeneid* 12.665.

Jones, J. W., Jr. "The Allegorical Traditions of the *Aeneid*." In *Vergil at 2000: Commemorative Essays on the Poet and His Influence*, edited by John D. Bernard. New York: AMS Press, 1986.
A survey of the two major allegorizing traditions of the *Aeneid*, the classical interpretation of Servius and the medieval approach represented by the commentary attributed to Bernardus Silvestris. While the author suggests that some of Servius' comments are valuable, those of Bernardus are seen as a misrepresentation of the epic.

Knight, W. F. Jackson. *Accentual Symmetry in Vergil*. Oxford, England: Basil Blackwell, 1950. Reprint. New York: Garland, 1979.

Demonstrates the relationship between sound and thought, between rhythm and emotion, in the *Aeneid* by examining various patterns caused by stress accent in Vergil's verse. While Latin quotations are not translated, the sound qualities are indicated by notations. Includes notes.

_____. "Form and Reality." In *Roman Vergil*. 2d ed. London: Faber & Faber, 1944.
Shows how alternation and reconciliation, two basic structural principles of Vergil's poetry, determine his use of similes, imagery, and tonality. In the *Aeneid*, Vergil reconciles the Alexandrian epyllion, or "little epic," with the characteristics of longer Homeric epic and of Euripidean tragedy.

_____. "Language, Verse, and Style." In *Roman Vergil*. 2d ed. London: Faber & Faber, 1944.
In this central chapter of his book on Vergil, the author suggests that compression into density of meaning is the main principle of Vergilian versification and language. There are detailed studies of Vergil's use of specific Latin words, alliteration, rhymes, and figures of speech.

Lewis, C. S. "Virgil and the Subject of Secondary Epic." In *A Preface to "Paradise Lost."* New York: Oxford University Press, 1942. Reprinted in *Virgil: A Collection of Critical Essays*, edited by Steele Commager. Englewood Cliffs, N.J.: Prentice-Hall, 1966.
In this excerpt from a book on John Milton's *Paradise Lost*, this English poet and novelist discusses the way in which Vergil remodeled the traditional Roman epic form used by Naevius and Ennius into a national epic told through the experiences of a single hero.

Mackail, J. W. "Concentration on the Epic." In *Virgil and His Meaning to the World of To-Day*. Boston: Marshall Jones, 1922. Reprint. New York: Cooper Square, 1963.
Suggests a list of twelve goals which directed Vergil's composition of the *Aeneid* from historical and legendary sources about the origin of Rome. The structure of the epic is seen to harmonize these various goals.

_____. "The Structure of the *Aeneid*." In *Virgil and His Meaning to the World of To-Day*. Boston: Marshall Jones, 1922. Reprint. New York: Cooper Square, 1963.
In this chapter, the author summarizes the plot of the epic and shows how Vergil organized his Homeric sources into a tightly knit structure in which Aeneas' mission gradually emerges.

_____. "Style and Diction." In *Virgil and His Meaning to the World of To-Day*. Boston: Marshall Jones, 1922. Reprint. New York: Cooper Square, 1963. Includes a brief history of the Latin hexameter and illustrates the challenges this meter presented to the poet. Vergil's skill is illustrated in several untranslated quotations from the *Aeneid*.

Mantinbrand, James, H. Introduction to *The Aeneid*, by Vergil. New York: Frederick Ungar, 1964.
In this introduction to his verse translation, Mantinbrand summarizes the poem, discusses Vergil's debts to Homer, and cites Vergil's language, the quality of the narrative, and Vergil's moral tone as ways in which the *Aeneid* is a highly original poem.

Mayerson, Philip. "Aeneas and the Quest for a New Troy." In *Classical Mythology in Literature, Art, and Music*. Lexington, Mass.: Xerox College Publishing, 1971.
A detailed paraphrase of the plot of the *Aeneid* is followed by a short summary of subsequent events including the founding of Rome and a discussion of Vergil's influence on later literature and art. Includes genealogical charts, illustrations, bibliography, and index.

Otis, Brooks. "The Iliadic *Aeneid*." In *Virgil: A Study in Civilized Poetry*. Oxford, England: Clarendon Press, 1963.
In *Aeneid* 7-12, Vergil continues the subjective and ideological goals of *Aeneid* 1-6 by presenting a humane and pious hero who sees war as a terrible and violent necessity. The structure, themes, and symbolism of each book are discussed scene by scene. Not all quotations are translated.

_____. Introduction to the *Aeneid*, by Vergil. Indianapolis, Ind.: Bobbs-Merrill, 1965.
In this introduction to Copley's translation, Otis suggests that the *Aeneid* is a classic because of its timelessness, because Vergil went beyond contemporary politics to create from his Homeric sources an image of heroism which transcends time and culture. Uses examples especially from the *Aeneid* 1-6.

_____. "The Mystery of the *Aeneid*." In *Virgil: A Study in Civilized Poetry*. Oxford, England: Clarendon Press, 1963.
In this introductory essay for a general study of Vergil's poetry, Otis suggests that the mystery of the success of the *Aeneid* is not Vergil's imitation of Homer but his creation of a new type of epic which is both Roman and subjective.

_____. "The Odyssean *Aeneid*." In *Virgil: A Study in Civilized Poetry*. Oxford, England: Clarendon Press, 1963.

Illustrates the ideological emphasis on death and resurrection which the *Aeneid* shares with the *Eclogues* and the *Georgics*. Vergil combines this ideology with subjective narrative to show the growth of his Augustan hero in *Aeneid* 1-6. Each book is carefully analyzed scene by scene according to structure, themes, and symbolism. Not all quotations are translated.

_____. "The Odyssean *Aeneid* and the Iliadic *Aeneid*." In *Virgil: A Collection of Critical Essays*, edited by Steele Commager. Englewood Cliffs, N.J.: Prentice-Hall, 1966.
Based upon two chapters of *Virgil: A Study in Civilized Poetry*. Establishes for the *Georgics*, the *Eclogues*, and the *Aeneid* an ideological similarity and schematic structure based upon optimism and pessimism, death and resurrection, fate and piety. These themes determine Vergil's choice of Homer's *Odyssey* as model for *Aeneid* 1-6, focusing on Aeneas' internal struggle with piety, and of Homer's *Iliad* as model for *Aeneid* 7-12, focusing on Aeneas' struggle with external forces of impiety.

_____. "The Subjective Style." In *Virgil: A Study in Civilized Poetry*. Oxford, England: Clarendon Press, 1963.
Comparison of scenes of athletic contests from *Aeneid* 5 and *Iliad* 23 and of Vergil's story of Dido and Apollonius of Rhodes' story of Medea in order to show how Vergil's style is more subjective, psychological, dramatic, and empathetic than Homer's. Vergil's narrative style, including sentence structure, tense usage, meter, and choice of words and similes enables him to describe events through the eyes of his characters. Not all quotations are translated.

Pöschl, Viktor. *The Art of Vergil: Image and Symbol in the "Aeneid,"* translated by Gerda Seligson. Ann Arbor: University of Michigan Press, 1962.
An investigation of the ways in which poetic symbols illustrate the central themes and characters of the *Aeneid*. The first chapter deals with basic themes, including the tragedies of Roman history and of human life; the second with the main characters, Aeneas, Dido, and Turnus; and the last with artistic principles, especially sequence of mood. Includes endnotes and an index.

_____. "Artistic Principles." In *The Art of Vergil: Image and Symbol in the "Aeneid,"* translated by Gerda Seligson. Ann Arbor: University of Michigan Press, 1962.
An examination of the way in which the poet controls narrative and creates transition by means of sequence of mood. The ordering of images within scenes and the symbolic importance of landscape descriptions are emphasized. A survey of books 1, 7, and 8 demonstrates that Vergil organizes his narrative around a balance of dark and light moods.

_____. "Basic Themes." In *The Art of Vergil: Image and Symbol in the "Aeneid,"* translated by Gerda Seligson. Ann Arbor: University of Michigan Press, 1962. Reprinted in *Virgil: A Collection of Critical Essays*, edited by Steele Commager. Englewood Cliffs, N.J.: Prentice-Hall, 1966.
The storm scene in *Aeneid* 1 and the Allecto scene in *Aeneid* 7 are seen as symbolic anticipations of the whole epic tragedy depicted in the myth of Aeneas, in Roman history, and in human life.

_____. "Introduction: The Problem." In *The Art of Vergil: Image and Symbol in the "Aeneid,"* translated by Gerda Seligson. Ann Arbor: University of Michigan Press, 1962.
Obstacles to interpreting the pervasive imagery of the *Aeneid* include centuries of scholarly misinterpretation. Comparison with Homer is seen as the best way to understand Vergil. Roman attachment to Homer and respect for authority establish the concept of a "classical," or "standard," text and secure Vergil's place in the Western world.

Prescott, Henry W. "The National Epic." In *The Development of Virgil's Art*. Chicago: University of Chicago Press, 1927. Reprint. New York: Russell & Russell, 1963.
Examines various aspects of the *Aeneid*, including background, sources, characters, and Vergil's attitude toward the afterlife. There are special sections on the story of Dido, the fall of Troy, Aeneas' wanderings, his descent into the lower world, and the war in Italy.

Putnam, Michael C. J. *The Poetry of the "Aeneid."* Cambridge, Mass.: Harvard University Press, 1965.
Aeneid 2, 5, 8, and 12 are interpreted individually not only in terms of special imagery and thematic devices which give the books unique qualities but also in terms of unifying features such as repetition of key words and symbols which create a larger design for the epic. There are detailed endnotes.

Quinn, Kenneth. "Did Virgil Fail?" In *Cicero and Virgil: Studies in Honor of Harold Hunt*, edited by John R. C. Montagu. Amsterdam: A. M. Hakkert, 1972. Abridged in *Virgil*, edited by Harold Bloom. New York: Chelsea House, 1986. Comparison of *Aeneid* 1-6 with *Aeneid* 7-12 suggests that Vergil composed *Aeneid* 7-12 first and considered his unfinished epic a failure because he did not live to complete fundamental changes designed to make the conventional heroic epic with which he began into a poem about a more humane hero fighting a fated, inevitable war.

_____. "Form and Technique." In *Virgil's "Aeneid": A Critical Description*. Ann Arbor: University of Michigan Press, 1968.

The first section, on epic form, centers on Vergil's use of Homer and Vergil's exploitation of form for political purposes. A second section on technique considers Vergil's use of the gods, characterization, fate, and divine and psychological motivation. A final section outlines tragic features of the *Aeneid*, including Vergil's use of tragic suspense and irony.

_____. "The Poet as Storyteller." In *Texts and Contexts: The Roman Writers and Their Audience*. London: Routledge & Kegan Paul, 1979.
Compares the narrative styles of the *Aeneid* with that of Ovid's *Metamorphoses* and Lucan's *Pharsalia*. Vergil, considered more tragic, subtle, and poetic than either Ovid or Lucan, challenges his audience with a new type of hero. Includes bibliography and indexes.

_____. "Structure." In *Virgil's "Aeneid": A Critical Description*. Ann Arbor: University of Michigan Press, 1968.
This chapter of a general study of the epic includes a discussion of the structure of the twelve books of the *Aeneid*, the types of episodes, the role of the narrator, types of narrative, and narrative tempo.

_____. "Style." In *Virgil's "Aeneid": A Critical Description*. Ann Arbor: University of Michigan Press, 1968.
Considers features of the poetic style of the *Aeneid*, first in the context of the tradition of Latin poetry from Ennius to Catullus and second from the point of view of Vergilian innovations, such as his use of a semantic gap, latent metaphor, and syntactical ambiguity. There is also a section on the Vergilian sentence, including features such as meter, theme, and imagery.

_____. "The Tempo of Virgilian Epic." In *Latin Explorations*. London: Routledge & Kegan Paul, 1963.
This chapter of a book on Roman poetry in the first century B.C. is a study in the tight and swift-moving tempo of the *Aeneid*. Special attention is paid to the techniques of elliptical narrative, interweaving, allusion, and tense usage. Analyzes the "Death of Priam" scene in *Aeneid* 2. There is an index and a list of passages discussed.

Ridley, M. R. "Literary Epic." In *Studies in Three Literatures*. London: J. M. Dent & Sons, 1962.
Differences between primitive and literary epic are illustrated by means of an examination of the *Aeneid* and John Milton's *Paradise Lost*. Examines the qualities of literary epic and judges Vergilian narrative, description, and character portrayal inferior both to Homer and to Milton. Foreign language quotations are not translated. Includes an index.

Sellar, W. Y. "Form and Subject of the *Aeneid.*" In *The Roman Poets of the Augustan Age: Virgil.* Oxford, England: Clarendon Press, 1908.
Argues that both the literary and political motives of the poem determined its form. Sellar shows how Vergil adapted the legend of Aeneas to these purposes. Several scenes of the epic are analyzed in this context.

_____. "On the Style, etc. of the *Aeneid.*" In *The Roman Poets of the Augustan Age: Virgil.* Oxford, England: Clarendon Press, 1908.
A brief consideration of the characteristics of speeches in the *Aeneid* as well as Vergil's poetic imagery, rhythm, and diction.

Showerman, Grant. "The Meaning of the *Aeneid.*" In *Monuments and Men of Ancient Rome.* New York: D. Appleton-Century, 1935.
A summary of the plot is followed by a discussion of Vergil's characters. The many interpretations of the epic through the ages are noted, and the epic is seen as a diverse celebration of the Italian countryside, the greatness of the Roman character, and the destiny of Rome.

Van Doren, Mark. *The Noble Voice.* New York: Henry Holt, 1946.
In this book, an important twentieth century American poet and novelist studies ten long poems in the Western poetic tradition. Besides Vergil, the author discusses the works of Homer, Lucretius, John Milton, Dante Alighieri, Edmund Spenser, William Shakespeare, William Wordsworth, and George Gordon, Lord Byron. The *Aeneid* is presented as a political poem which does not inspire "higher criticism."

Williams, Gordon. "Connexions with Predecessors: *imitatio exemplorum.*" In *Technique and Ideas in the "Aeneid."* New Haven, Conn.: Yale University Press, 1983.
Passages of the *Aeneid* which echo Homer and Apollonius of Rhodes are shown to serve several points of view: irony; a framework for judgment; and a measure of the distance from a conventional heroic world. The Latin phrase in the title, translated as "imitation of models," refers to Vergil's relationship with his sources.

_____. "Figures of Movement and Linkage." In *Technique and Ideas in the "Aeneid."* New Haven, Conn.: Yale University Press, 1983.
Examines ways in which Vergil creates narrative movement and coherence. Techniques of thematic anticipation, ring composition, and the interlacing of narrative threads are discussed.

_____. "Ideas and the Epic Poet." In *Technique and Ideas in the "Aeneid."*
New Haven, Conn.: Yale University Press, 1983. Reprinted in *Virgil*, edited by
Harold Bloom. New York: Chelsea House, 1986.
In this conclusion to a book on Vergil's epic technique, the author confronts two
equally valid but contradictory interpretations of the *Aeneid*: the first, the epic
as propaganda for Augustan ideology; and the second, the epic as hostile to these
very ideals. Williams suggests that the presence of these two irreconcilable points
of view in the epic is a result of tension between the optimism of the Augustan
age and the poet's more pessimistic view of the human condition.

_____. *The Nature of Roman Poetry*. New York: Oxford University Press,
1970.
An abbreviated and simplified version of *Tradition and Originality in Roman
Poetry*. In particular, there is a discussion of Vergil's description of the landing
of Aeneas in North Africa in *Aeneid* 1 and a comparison to Lucretius' descriptive
techniques. All foreign language quotations are translated. Includes a bibliography
and index.

_____. "The Poet's Voice." In *Technique and Ideas in the "Aeneid."* New
Haven, Conn.: Yale University Press, 1983.
Examines the way Vergil's point of view intrudes into the epic via such conventions as the invocation, similes, apostrophes, epitaphs, and authorial comments.
In a final section, the author suggests that these conventions reflect Vergil's
pessimistic Epicurean view of human life, in which the gods are only a metaphor
for a hostile universe.

_____. "Retrospective Judgement Enforced." In *Technique and Ideas in
the "Aeneid."* New Haven, Conn.: Yale University Press, 1983.
Considers Vergil's use of irony and suspension of judgment, especially in *Aeneid*
4 and 6.

_____. "Signs of Changes of Plan in the *Aeneid*." In *Technique and Ideas
in the "Aeneid."* New Haven, Conn.: Yale University Press, 1983.
In this appendix to a study of Vergil's use of figures of thought, Williams
discusses evidence from the epic that the poet originally planned to begin with
Aeneas' journey (book 3), followed by the funeral games for Anchises (book 5),
and the storm off Carthage (book 1). Books 2, 4, and 6 then followed much in
their present form.

_____. *Technique and Ideas in the "Aeneid."* New Haven, Conn.: Yale
University Press, 1983.
Examines how figures of thought and speech are used in the *Aeneid* not only as
a means of indirect communication but also as a source of coherence for the

entire poem. The first part of the book considers the variety of features used to create narrative unity. The second examines figures which convey a point of view. Includes an appendix discussing signs in the *Aeneid* of Vergil's changes of plan for the epic, a bibliography, and two indexes.

_____. *Tradition and Originality in Roman Poetry*. Oxford, England: Clarendon Press, 1968.
Scattered throughout this study of Latin poetry are references to Vergil, and especially to the *Aeneid*, in order to illustrate that the nature of this poetry is a dynamic blending of imitation and originality. Not all foreign language quotations are translated. Includes indexes.

Williams, R. D. "The *Aeneid*." In *Latin Literature*. Vol. 2, *The Cambridge History of Classical Literature*, edited by E. J. Kenney. Cambridge, England: Cambridge University Press, 1982.
Includes sections on the historical and literary background of the epic, composition and structure, major characters, style, meter, and Vergil's portrayal of destiny and religion in the *Aeneid*. The epic is seen as a poem of conflicting attitudes, of a tension between the poet's public and private voices. There is an appendix of authors and works, a bibliography, and an index.

Character Studies

Bono, Barbara J. "The Dido Episode." In *Virgil's "Aeneid,"* edited by Harold Bloom. Edgemont, Pa.: Chelsea House, 1987.
In this essay, an excerpt from *Literary Transvaluation*, Bono analyzes the Aeneas-Dido episode as an expression not of Aeneas' lack of feeling for Dido but of his dutiful suppression of such feeling. For Bono, Dido's death is a tragedy for both Dido and Aeneas, a tragedy rooted in Aeneas' sacrifice of self.

Camps, W. A. "The Hero: Aeneas." In *An Introduction to Virgil's "Aeneid."* Oxford, England: Oxford University Press, 1969.
In this chapter, Camps follows Aeneas' mission and piety through three stages in the *Aeneid*: the quest, books 1-6; arrival, books 5-7; and victory, books 10-12. The hero's painful relationship with Dido is discussed at the end of the chapter.

_____. "The Secondary Heroes: Dido and Turnus." In *An Introduction to Virgil's "Aeneid."* Oxford, England: Oxford University Press, 1969.
Camps suggests that Vergil's portrayal of Dido as Aeneas' lover is balanced in the *Aeneid* by the role of Turnus as Aeneas' rival. Both characters represent unreasoned opposition to the plans of Providence for the future of Rome.

Glover, T. R. "Interpretation of Life: 1. Dido." In *Virgil*. 7th ed. New York: Barnes & Noble Books, 1969.
Dido's important role in the *Aeneid* as the tragic love of Aeneas is examined carefully. Discussion centers on a character study as well as the literary background for Vergil's portrayal of Dido.

_____. "Interpretation of Life: 2. Aeneas." In *Virgil*. 7th ed. New York: Barnes & Noble Books, 1969.
Aeneas' complex character, based upon the Homeric hero and upon Roman attitudes toward piety, is summed up in William Wordsworth's picture of the "Happy Warrior," the man who follows his duty cheerfully.

Haecker, Theodor. "Odysseus and Aeneas." In *Virgil: Father of the West*. New York: Sheed & Ward, 1934. Reprinted in *Virgil: A Collection of Critical Essays*, edited by Steele Commager. Englewood Cliffs, N.J.: Prentice-Hall, 1966.
Discusses the transformation of Odysseus, the Greek sacker of cities, into Aeneas, the Roman builder of cities, and interprets the *Aeneid* as an expression of an adventist humanity which looks toward the rebuilding of Greek thought in Roman form and anticipates a Christian emphasis on eternal truths.

Hunt, J. William. "The Burden of Vocation." In *Forms of Glory: Structure and Sense in Virgil's "Aeneid."* Carbondale: Southern Illinois University Press, 1973.
Examines the state of mind of Aeneas throughout the epic. The hero is seen to be motivated by an intensity of vision, a vocation which calls him from self-interest to a higher sense of duty. Some translations of the Latin are provided only in endnotes.

_____. "The Realm of Tragic Guilt." In *Forms of Glory: Structure and Sense in Virgil's "Aeneid."* Carbondale: Southern Illinois University Press, 1973.
A close parallel is seen between Dido and Turnus, who both obstruct the heroic goal of Aeneas and whose tragic deaths frame the central Aeneas section of the epic. Considers the question of guilt and the concept of a tragic hero. Some translations of the Latin are provided only in endnotes.

_____. "Shadows and the Sea." In *Forms of Glory: Structure and Sense in Virgil's "Aeneid."* Carbondale: Southern Illinois University Press, 1973.
The character of Palinurus is seen to provide a focus for a cluster of several important images in the *Aeneid*: land, sea, glory, and shadow. Some translations of the Latin are provided only in endnotes.

Johnson, W. R. "The Figure of Laertes: Reflections on the Character of Aeneas." In *Vergil at 2000: Commemorative Essays on the Poet and His Influence*, edited by John D. Bernard. New York: AMS Press, 1986.

Uses the relationship between Laertes and Hamlet in William Shakespeare's play as a metaphor for the way Turnus functions with Aeneas in the *Aeneid*, as a dynamic foil for the introverted hero.

Mackail, J. W. "The Human Element." In *Virgil and His Meaning to the World of To-Day*. Boston: Marshall Jones, 1922. Reprint. New York: Cooper Square, 1963.
A brief look at Vergil's romantic character studies. Piety, a sense of duty to God and man, is seen to be central to the portrayal of the hero Aeneas, while Dido is the image of human tenderness. Latin quotations are not translated.

Parry, Adam. "The Two Voices of Virgil's *The Aeneid*." *Arion* 2 (Winter, 1963): 66-80. Reprinted in *Virgil: A Collection of Critical Essays*, edited by Steele Commager. Englewood Cliffs, N.J.: Prentice-Hall, 1966. Reprinted in abridged form in *Virgil*, edited by Harold Bloom. New York: Chelsea House, 1986. Also reprinted in *Virgil's "Aeneid,"* edited by Harold Bloom. Edgemont, Pa.: Chelsea House, 1987.
Shows how the character of Aeneas in the *Aeneid* is a blend of two voices: the public, epic voice of heroic triumph and the private, elegiac voice of personal regret which dominate the personality of Aeneas. Not all Latin words are translated.

Pöschl, Viktor. "Aeneas." In *Virgil's "Aeneid,"* edited by Harold Bloom. Edgemont, Pa.: Chelsea House, 1987.
An excerpt from the author's *Art of Vergil*. Interprets the character of Aeneas as a unique blend of Homeric heroism, Stoic emphasis on "greatness of soul," and a special Vergilian sense of humanity.

_____. "The Principal Figures." In *The Art of Vergil: Image and Symbol in the "Aeneid,"* translated by Gerda Seligson. Ann Arbor: University of Michigan Press, 1962.
In this central chapter of his study of imagery, the author considers how characterizations of Aeneas, Dido, and Turnus are developed by means of poetic associations and symbols.

Prescott, Henry W. "The Characters of the *Aeneid*." In *The Development of Virgil's Art*. Chicago: University of Chicago Press, 1927. Reprint. New York: Russell & Russell, 1963.
The discussion moves from the ancient emphasis on generalized rather than individual characterizations to Vergil's treatment of Camilla, Pallas, Turnus, and Aeneas.

Putnam, Michael C. J. "Tragic Victory." In *The Poetry of the "Aeneid."* Cambridge, Mass.: Harvard University Press, 1965.
In this poetic analysis of the *Aeneid* 12, the character of Turnus is seen as a personification of violence and mad passion, which identifies him, together with Dido, as a special victim of Aeneas.

Quinn, Kenneth. "The Heroic Impulse." In *Virgil's "Aeneid": A Critical Description*. Ann Arbor: University of Michigan Press, 1968.
In this introductory chapter to a general study of the epic, the author examines the heroic qualities of several characters, including Priam, Aeneas, Dido, and Turnus. An essential feature of the Vergilian hero is seen to be a tragic urge to kill.

_____. "Virgil's Tragic Queen." In *Latin Explorations*. London: Routledge & Kegan Paul, 1963.
This chapter of a book on Roman poetry in the first century B.C. is an essay on the character of Dido, who is shown to be an exceptional woman not only in her intense ability to love but also in her high standards of queenliness. Some Latin quotations are not translated.

Rand, Edward R. "Tragedy from Romance." In *The Magical Art of Virgil*. Cambridge, Mass.: Harvard University Press, 1931.
An examination of Vergil's treatment of the love theme. Vergil transforms his romantic sources for the characters of Aeneas and Dido into tragic and heroic figures. Shows how the romantic figure of Medea in Apollonius of Rhodes' epic becomes the tragic Dido in the *Aeneid*.

Sellar, W. Y. "The Conception and Delineation of Character in the *Aeneid*." In *The Roman Poets of the Augustan Age: Virgil*. Oxford, England: Clarendon Press, 1908.
Suggests the weakness of Vergil's character development. Brief consideration of the characters of Aeneas, Turnus, Mezentius, and Dido.

Stanford, W. B. "Virgil's Ulysses." In *The Ulysses Theme: A Study in the Adaptability of a Traditional Hero*. 2d ed. Ann Arbor: University of Michigan Press, 1968.
Shows how early Roman genealogies connecting the Greek Odysseus with Italy and Rome were rejected in favor of descent from the Trojan Aeneas. Examines Vergil's treatment of Ulysses, especially in *Aeneid* 2 and 3. Despite the poet's reluctance to criticize Homer's hero directly, and his emphasis upon qualities such as compassion and long-suffering, which Vergil's Aeneas shares with the Homeric Odysseus, Aeneas' description of Ulysses in *Aeneid* 2 created an impression of Ulysses the scoundrel which carried over into the medieval romances.

Stewart, Douglas J. "Aeneas the Politician." *The Antioch Review* 32, no. 4 (1973): 649-664. Reprinted in *Virgil*, edited by Harold Bloom. New York: Chelsea House, 1986.
A reading of the *Aeneid* as a poem about political institutions and the education of a political leader. Vergil presents in Aeneas not a simple epic hero but a fallible political leader willing, in the case of Dido, to sacrifice personal ties in favor of a political agenda but unwilling, in the case of Turnus, to abandon personal vengeance in the interest of the state.

Williams, R. D. "Aeneas—the New Hero." In *Aeneas and the Roman Hero.* London: Macmillan, 1973.
In contrast with the Homeric hero, Vergil's hero is seen to be a man of social responsibility. A book-by-book analysis of the plot of the *Aeneid* from the point of view of Aeneas' heroic development supports this view of Aeneas.

_____. "Virgil's Private Voice: Dido, Turnus, Juno." *Aeneas and the Roman Hero*. London: Macmillan, 1973.
All three characters represent obstacles to Aeneas' fulfillment of his divine mission. Vergil's treatment of these three characters contrasts with his public voice of praise for Rome's greatness and illustrates the poet's more private sensibility for the defeated and for human suffering.

Studies of Individual Books, Episodes, and Passages

Anderson, William S. "Ambiguities in Defeat and Victory: Books Nine and Ten." In *The Art of the "Aeneid."* Englewood Cliffs, N.J.: Prentice-Hall, 1969.
These ambiguities deal with the complex qualities needed by a victorious general and with the moral prerequisites for victory and defeat. In *Aeneid* 9, Turnus' violence and fury contrasts with the noble passion of Nisus and Euryalus. In *Aeneid* 10, the pious savagery of Aeneas is balanced by the impious grandeur of Mezentius.

_____. "Carthage and Troy: Books One and Two." In *The Art of the "Aeneid."* Englewood Cliffs, N.J.: Prentice-Hall, 1969.
Summarizes the first two books of the *Aeneid* and examines the symbols and imagery in the scenes describing Aeneas' arrival at Carthage and the fall of Troy. Homeric sources and structural patterns for both books are discussed.

_____. "The Search for Home: Books Three and Four." In *The Art of the "Aeneid."* Englewood Cliffs, N.J.: Prentice-Hall, 1969.
The plots of these books and their thematic interrelationship are examined.

Aeneas' wanderings in book 3 are presented as Aeneas' gradual introduction to his destined home in Italy. The tragedy of Dido in book 4 is understood in terms of Dido's failure to remember her responsibilities to her first husband and Aeneas' failure to remain faithful to his destiny.

——————. "Sicily and Italy: Books Five and Six." In *The Art of the "Aeneid."* Englewood Cliffs, N.J.: Prentice-Hall, 1969.
Includes summaries of the plots of *Aeneid* 5 and 6 and discussion of themes found in the funeral games for Anchises and in Aeneas' journey to the underworld.

——————. "Turnus or Aeneas? Books Eleven and Twelve." In *The Art of the "Aeneid."* Englewood Cliffs, N.J.: Prentice-Hall, 1969. Examines how Vergil develops suspense concerning the outcome of the war between Aeneas and Turnus and shows how the poet complicates his sympathetic treatment of Aeneas by describing the hero as an angry killer instead of a noble victor and by making Aeneas a tragic hero.

——————. "Vergil Begins His Epic." In *The Art of the "Aeneid."* Englewood Cliffs, N.J.: Prentice-Hall, 1969.
In this introductory chapter, the author analyzes the first thirty-three lines of the *Aeneid*. Discussion of this prologue or invocation is divided into several units, each of which reflects an important aspect of the poet's art.

——————. "War, a Monster of Two Faces: Books Seven and Eight." In *The Art of the "Aeneid."* Englewood Cliffs, N.J.: Prentice-Hall, 1969.
Examines the first stages of Aeneas' war in Italy. War is seen as a monster of destruction in book 7 and as a necessary evil in book 8. This depiction of war is climaxed at the end of book 8 in the description of Aeneas' shield, which symbolizes war as an honorable means to peaceful rule, first by Aeneas and later by his Roman descendants.

Basson, W. P. *Pivotal Catalogues in the "Aeneid."* Amsterdam: Hakkert, 1975.
This work focuses on an important feature of the epic, the list, or catalogue. Four Vergilian lists are studied: Jupiter's prophetic genealogical summary of the Julian family in *Aeneid* 1; the parade of famous Romans, which the author calls the Heroscopia, in *Aeneid* 6; the catalogue of Italian heroes in *Aeneid* 7; and the catalogue of Etruscan allies in *Aeneid* 10. Includes a bibliography, index of names, and index of the *Aeneid* passages cited.

Camps, W. A. "Making an Episode: Fusion of Inherited Materials Exemplified in the Sixth Book." In *An Introduction to Virgil's "Aeneid."* Oxford, England: Oxford University Press, 1969.

Discusses the way Vergil fashions the story of Aeneas' journey to the underworld from the *Odyssey* and other sources. Vergil's depiction of the underworld is compared to the poet's view of fate and life after death.

Di Cesare, Mario A. "Aeneas and Turnus." In *The Altar and the City: A Reading of Vergil's "Aeneid."* New York: Columbia University Press, 1974.
An interpretative commentary on *Aeneid* 11 and 12. The Latin conference of war and the Camilla episode of book 11 are seen to enhance Turnus' heroic glory and to lead to the tragedy of his death in book 12, where Turnus' furious valor and human frailty, reenforced by Amata and Juturna, is contrasted with Aeneas' piety and divine destiny. Extensive quotation from the *Aeneid*, but not all Latin is translated.

_____. "Carthage: Search for the City." In *The Altar and the City: A Reading of Vergil's "Aeneid."* New York: Columbia University Press, 1974.
A running commentary on and interpretation of *Aeneid* 1 and 4 with special attention to the invocation (1.1-1.11), the description of the Carthaginian temple (1.467-1.493), and the structure of book 4. Discusses the humanity of Aeneas, his search for a city and home, and the primitive, elemental symbolism of the Dido-Aeneas story. Extensive quotation from the *Aeneid*, but not all Latin is translated.

_____. "Hades: Journey Through the Wood." In *The Altar and the City: A Reading of Vergil's "Aeneid."* New York: Columbia University Press, 1974.
In this interpretative commentary on *Aeneid* 6, the author highlights the importance of Aeneas' conversation with the Sibyl and Anchises' vision of Rome's future greatness. Extensive quotation from the *Aeneid*, but not all Latin is translated.

_____. "Italy." In *The Altar and the City: A Reading of Vergil's "Aeneid."* New York: Columbia University Press, 1974.
This study of *Aeneid* 7 examines the roles of Juno, Latinus, Turnus, Amata, and Camilla and emphasizes important structural and thematic links between books 7 and 1. Extensive quotation from the *Aeneid*, but not all Latin is translated.

_____. "*Pius* Aeneas and the Wages of War." In *The Altar and the City: A Reading of Vergil's "Aeneid."* New York: Columbia University Press, 1974.
An interpretative commentary on *Aeneid* 10 with particular emphasis on the council scene in lines 1-117, the deaths of Pallas, Lausus, and Mezentius, and the rages of Turnus and Aeneas. In book 10, war and weapons are seen to overpower justice and piety. Extensive quotation from the *Aeneid*, but not all Latin is translated.

_____. "Troy: Fall of the City." In *The Altar and the City: A Reading of Vergil's "Aeneid."* New York: Columbia University Press, 1974.
In this commentary on and interpretation of *Aeneid* 2, the author emphasizes the themes of deception connected with the Trojan horse and the Sinon episode, of unavoidable fate in the death of Laocoön, and of vision and prophecy connected with Aeneas' departure from the doomed city. Extensive quotation from the *Aeneid*, but not all Latin is translated.

_____. "The Wanderer." In *The Altar and the City: A Reading of Vergil's "Aeneid."* New York: Columbia University Press, 1974.
The dominance of Anchises as a symbol of Aeneas' piety and the sea-weariness of Aeneas are the focus of this commentary on and interpretation of *Aeneid* 3 and 5. Includes discussion of the Helenus episode in book 3 and the funeral games for Anchises, the burning of the ships, and the death of Palinurus in book 5. Extensive quotation from the *Aeneid*, but not all Latin is translated.

_____. "War in Italy." In *The Altar and the City: A Reading of Vergil's "Aeneid."* New York: Columbia University Press, 1974.
An interpretative commentary on *Aeneid* 8 and 9. Discussion of *Aeneid* 8 centers on the significance of the Evander and shield scenes and the pastoral atmosphere of the first half of the book. Book 9 is considered to be a dramatization of the irrelevant heroic quest for military glory. Extensive quotation from the *Aeneid*, but not all Latin is translated.

Fowler, William Warde. *Aeneas at the Site of Rome.* Oxford, England: Basil Blackwell, 1917. Reprint. New York: Garland, 1978.
The Latin text of *Aeneid* 8, describing Aeneas' visit to the home of Evander, is preceded by a brief introductory note discussing the importance of this book and an English commentary on various lines and phrases. An endnote on Vergil's idea of fate is particularly important.

_____. *The Death of Turnus.* Oxford, England: Basil Blackwell, 1919. Reprint. New York: Garland, 1978.
In addition to the Latin text of *Aeneid* 12, there is an introductory note summarizing the plot of the book and a detailed English commentary which discusses features of the book line by line.

_____. *Virgil's Gathering of the Clans.* Oxford, England: Basil Blackwell, 1916. Reprint. New York: Garland, 1978.
This small book is about the passage in *Aeneid* 8 describing the gathering of the Italian tribes for war against the Trojans. Fowler supplies a commentary to this passage, which he compares to its Homeric source and its imitation in John Milton's *Paradise Lost.* Includes the Latin text and a verse translation.

Gaunt, D. M. "Shipwreck." In *Surge and Thunder: Critical Readings in Homer's "Odyssey."* New York: Oxford University Press, 1971.
Vergil's description of a shipwreck in *Aeneid* 1 is compared with Odysseus' shipwreck in *Odyssey* 12. Vergil's more elaborate rhetorical effects are contrasted with the brevity of Homeric language. Includes Latin text with metrical scansion.

Glover, T. R. "Interpretation of Life: 3. Hades." In *Virgil*. 7th ed. New York: Barnes & Noble Books, 1969.
Vergil's portrayal of the underworld in *Aeneid* 6 is traced from its Homeric beginnings through Greek religious ideas such as Orphism, Pythagoreanism, and Platonism as well as Italian ideas about the afterlife.

Gransden, K. W. "Absence." In *Virgil's "Iliad": An Essay on Epic Narrative*. Cambridge, England: Cambridge University Press, 1984.
Shows how Vergil modifies the Iliadic theme of the burning of the ships in *Aeneid* 9. In Aeneas' absence, narrative attention is directed toward his antagonist, Turnus.

_____. "Camilla's Last Stand." In *Virgil's "Iliad": An Essay on Epic Narrative*. Cambridge, England: Cambridge University Press, 1984.
The glorified deeds and death of the female warrior Camilla in *Aeneid* 11 are seen to be an assimilation of characteristics of several figures in the epic, including Dido and Turnus, and a preparation for the death of Turnus in *Aeneid* 12.

_____. "Diplomatic." In *Virgil's "Iliad": An Essay on Epic Narrative*. Cambridge, England: Cambridge University Press, 1984.
Discusses the significance of several scenes in *Aeneid* 8, including Aeneas' visit to the simple hut of Evander, based upon *Odyssey* 14; the introduction of Pallas as Aeneas' equivalent of the Homeric Patroclus; and the description of Aeneas' shield.

_____. "Dynastic." In *Virgil's "Iliad": An Essay on Epic Narrative*. Cambridge, England: Cambridge University Press, 1984.
Considers the structural purposes of the Trojan embassy to Latinus in *Aeneid* 7 and shows how Vergil employs a dynastic argument to transform the Iliadic plot of wrath into an Odyssean one of homecoming.

_____. "The Funeral of Pallas." In *Virgil's "Iliad": An Essay on Epic Narrative*. Cambridge, England: Cambridge University Press, 1984. Reprinted in *Virgil*, edited by Harold Bloom. New York: Chelsea House Publishers, 1986.
Special attention is given to the contrast between the furor of Aeneas in *Aeneid* 10 and the sympathetic sense of loss he displays at the funeral of Pallas at the beginning of *Aeneid* 11.

_____. "Homecoming." In *Virgil's "Iliad": An Essay on Epic Narrative*. Cambridge, England: Cambridge University Press, 1984.
Focuses on Vergil's presentation of King Latinus and Turnus, of the portents concerning Lavinia's betrothal, and of the appearance of Rumor to Iarbas in *Aeneid* 7. Links with book 4 are discussed.

_____. "Invocation." In *Virgil's "Iliad": An Essay on Epic Narrative*. Cambridge, England: Cambridge University Press, 1984.
Analyzes Vergil's role as prophet, or seer, in the second invocation of the *Aeneid*, in book 7.

_____. "Juno." In *Virgil's "Iliad": An Essay on Epic Narrative*. Cambridge, England: Cambridge University Press, 1984.
The role of Juno in *Aeneid* 7 is seen as the source of discord and bloodshed. Themes discussed include the abrupt transition of Juno's furious monologue from the Trojan embassy to Latinus; correspondences of this speech with divine tirades in *Aeneid* 1, *Odyssey* 5, and *Iliad* 14; the visit of Allecto to Turnus; and comparisons between Turnus' maddened love for battle with Dido's passionate frenzy in *Aeneid*.

_____. "Nisus and Euryalus." In *Virgil's "Iliad": An Essay on Epic Narrative*. Cambridge, England: Cambridge University Press, 1984.
This episode of *Aeneid* 9, based upon the embassy scene and Doloneia of *Iliad* 9 and 10, is shown to have a central importance in the epic because of the poet's sympathetic introduction of the theme of erotic loyalty into the heroic epic.

_____. "The Return of Aeneas." In *Virgil's "Iliad": An Essay on Epic Narrative*. Cambridge, England: Cambridge University Press, 1984.
The focal scenes of *Aeneid* 10 are discussed, including the return of Aeneas; the death of Pallas; the episode of the phantom Aeneas; and the death of Mezentius. Highlighted themes are Aeneas' role as an Achillean avenger and the dialogue between Jupiter and Juno as an illustration of Jupiter's all-seeing power.

_____. "Siege." In *Virgil's "Iliad": An Essay on Epic Narrative*. Cambridge, England: Cambridge University Press, 1984.
Shows how Vergil's description of the assault on the Trojan camp at the end of *Aeneid* 9 develops and extends the fighting narratives of Homer's *Iliad*. Aeneas' role as the absent Achilles is compared to Turnus' re-creation of the role of Hector.

_____. "Transition." In *Virgil's "Iliad": An Essay on Epic Narrative*. Cambridge, England: Cambridge University Press, 1984.

Discusses the beginning of *Aeneid* 7 as a bridge between the Odyssean and the Iliadic halves of the *Aeneid*. Links between *Aeneid* 1 and *Aeneid* 7 are noted.

——————. "War and Peace." In *Virgil's "Iliad": An Essay on Epic Narrative.* Cambridge, England: Cambridge University Press, 1984. Reprinted in *Virgil's Aeneid*, edited by Harold Bloom. Edgemont, Pa.: Chelsea House, 1987.
The death of Turnus in *Aeneid* 12 is seen to be the key to an interpretation of the *Aeneid* as a study in war's brutality and lack of personal choice and an affirmation of peace and freedom.

Knight, W. F. Jackson. *Vergil's Troy: Essays on the Second Book of the "Aeneid."* Oxford, England: Basil Blackwell, 1932. Reprinted in *Vergil: Epic and Anthropology*, edited by John D. Christie. New York: Barnes & Noble Books, 1967.
Contains chapters on the poetry, tragedy, legends, and events of *Aeneid* 2. Latin quotations are not translated. Has one illustration and extensive notes.

Knox, Bernard M. W. "The Serpent and the Flame: The Imagery of the Second Book of the *Aeneid.*" In *Virgil: A Collection of Critical Essays*, edited by Steele Commager. Englewood Cliffs, N.J.: Prentice-Hall, 1966.
Based upon an article published in the *American Journal of Philology* (71, 1950). Knox follows the images of serpent, violence, concealment, and flames in Aeneas' description of the fall of Troy in *Aeneid* 2.

Morford, Mark P. O., and Robert J. Lenardon. "Views of the Afterlife: The Realm of Hades." In *Classical Mythology*. 3d ed. New York: Longman, 1985.
This chapter includes a summary of Aeneas' journey to the underworld in *Aeneid* 6 and comparisons to other such journeys, such as those in the Myth of Er in Plato's *Republic* 10 and in *Odyssey* 11. Extensive quotations from all sources are included, as well as maps, genealogical charts, illustrations, select bibliography, footnotes, and indexes.

Pöschl, Viktor. "Basic Themes." In *The Art of Vergil: Image and Symbol in the "Aeneid,"* translated by Gerda Seligson. Ann Arbor: University of Michigan Press, 1962. Reprinted in *Virgil: A Collection of Critical Essays*, edited by Steele Commager. Englewood Cliffs, N.J.: Prentice-Hall, 1966.
Considers the storm scene in *Aeneid* 1 as symbolic anticipation of the whole poem and as a initial symbol of the Odyssean half of the poem in the same way that the Allecto scene in *Aeneid* 7 initializes the Iliadic half of the poem.

Prescott, Henry W. "The Descent to the Lower World." In *The Development of Virgil's Art*. Chicago: University of Chicago Press, 1927. Reprint. New York: Russell & Russell, 1963.

In this summary and analysis of *Aeneid* 6, Prescott shows how Vergil organizes the first part of the narrative around the Sibyl's three conditions for Aeneas' journey: the golden bough, the burial of Palinurus, and special sacrifices. For the second half of the narrative, the emphasis is upon the topography of Vergil's underworld, the stylistic variety, and Vergil's adaptations of the *Odyssey*.

_____. "The Fall of Troy." In *The Development of Virgil's Art*. Chicago: University of Chicago Press, 1927. Reprint. New York: Russell & Russell, 1963. Discusses Aeneas' narrative about the fall of Troy in *Aeneid* 2. Individual scenes, such as those with Sinon, Laocoön and Panthus, are summarized. Episodes such as the Helen scene, Aeneas' vision of the gods, and events in Aeneas' home are shown to create a thematic unity for the narrative.

_____. "The Story of Dido." In *The Development of Virgil's Art*. Chicago: University of Chicago Press, 1927. Reprint. New York: Russell & Russell, 1963. Includes a summary and analysis of *Aeneid* 1 and 4 with careful attention to the role of the gods and character development.

_____. "The Wanderings of Aeneas." In *The Development of Virgil's Art*. Chicago: University of Chicago Press, 1927. Reprint. New York: Russell & Russell, 1963.
Aeneas' wanderings in *Aeneid* 5 are shown to create an inner unity based upon gradual revelation to Aeneas of his destiny and destination. Particular discussion of the Palinurus and Helen scenes. Some attention to Vergil's debts to Homer's *Odyssey*.

_____. "The War in Latium." In *The Development of Virgil's Art*. Chicago: University of Chicago Press, 1927. Reprint. New York: Russell & Russell, 1963. The last six books of the *Aeneid* are summarized in this short chapter. The author shows how the poet combines his goals of artistic unity and variety with patriotic appeal to organize the material of these books. Vergil's debts to Homer's *Iliad* are also mentioned.

Putnam, Michael C. J. "*Aeneid* 7 and the *Aeneid*." *American Journal of Philology* 91 (1970): 408-430. Reprinted in *Essays on Latin Lyric, Elegy, and Epic*. Princeton, N.J.: Princeton University Press, 1982.
Deals with the theme of metamorphosis in the *Aeneid*. Monstrous apparitions throughout the epic set a pattern for the personification of Allecto in book 7 and for the transformation of peace into war. Latin quotations are not translated.

_____. "Game and Reality." In *The Poetry of the "Aeneid."* Cambridge, Mass.: Harvard University Press, 1965.

The funeral games for Anchises and the death of Palinurus in *Aeneid* 5 are shown to contain themes and images, such as victory through sacrifice, which are echoed in the entire epic. The themes of loss of pilot, narrow escape, and safe arrival in the boat race mirror Aeneas' journey to Italy, for which Palinurus serves as a sacrificial victim.

—————. "History's Dream." In *The Poetry of the "Aeneid."* Cambridge, Mass.: Harvard University Press, 1965.
A study of the poetic structure of *Aeneid* 8 and its central theme of the identification of Aeneas and his descendants with Roman glory. Aeneas' journey up the Tiber River is compared to his journey to the underworld in book 6. The interplay of contrasting episodes seen in Aeneas' visit to the house of Evander and the love scene between Venus and Vulcan in the Cyclopes' cave is reflected in the imagery of Aeneas' shield, which summarizes the themes of birth and generation found in book 8.

—————. "Madness and Flight." In *The Poetry of the "Aeneid."* Cambridge, Mass.: Harvard University Press, 1965.
A study of the poetic design of *Aeneid* 2, with special attention to Sinon, the Trojan horse, and Laocoön's sea serpents as monstrous symbols of violence and madness, by which Aeneas' journey through the burning city can be compared to his later journey into the underworld. Ends with a brief discussion of ties with book 9, especially with the story of Nisus and Euryalus.

—————. "*Pius* Aeneas and the Metamorphosis of Lausus." *Arethusa* 14 (1981): 139-156. Reprinted in *Essays on Latin Lyric, Elegy, and Epic.* Princeton, N.J.: Princeton University Press, 1982. Also reprinted in *Virgil*, edited by Harold Bloom. New York: Chelsea House, 1986.
Considers the relationship between piety and force in the *Aeneid.* The portrayal of Lausus in *Aeneid* 10 as a model of filial devotion toward his father, Mezentius, is reflected in Aeneas' own attitude toward Anchises in *Aeneid* 1-6 and in his treatment of Turnus in *Aeneid* 12.

—————. "The Third Book of the *Aeneid*: From Homer to Rome." *Ramus* 9 (1980): 1-21. Reprinted in *Essays on Latin Lyric, Elegy, and Epic.* Princeton, N.J.: Princeton University Press, 1982.
Vergil's alterations and additions to the legend of Aeneas' voyage effect in Aeneas a vision of reconciliation, a transition from savage hatred to civilizing forgiveness.

—————. "Tragic Victory." In *The Poetry of the "Aeneid."* Cambridge, Mass.: Harvard University Press, 1965.

The themes of love, disease, violence, and fury are traced through the character of Turnus in *Aeneid* 12, which is filled with poetic associations with the rest of the poem and with the *Georgics* 3. The monstrous, winged Terror which helps Aeneas kill Turnus is like the winged sleep which destroys Aeneas' helmsman Palinurus in book 5.

Quinn, Kenneth. "The Tempo of Virgilian Epic." In *Latin Explorations*. London: Routledge & Kegan Paul, 1963.
This chapter of a book on Roman poetry in the first century B.C. contains an analysis of the narrative describing the death of Priam in *Aeneid* 2. A good illustration of the tight and swift-moving tempo of the *Aeneid*.

_____. "The Twelve Books." In *Virgil's "Aeneid": A Critical Description*. Ann Arbor: University of Michigan Press, 1968.
This central chapter of a general study of the *Aeneid* includes, for each book, a short paraphrase of the plot, a tabulated synopsis of the book's structure, and a prose restatement of Vergil's text. More detailed discussion of books 10-12.

Rand, Edward R. "Primitive Simplicity from Imperial Rome." In *The Magical Art of Virgil*. Cambridge, Mass.: Harvard University Press, 1931.
Examines the way in which Vergil focuses in the second half of the *Aeneid* not on the grandeur of Augustan Rome but on the admirable simplicity of the primitive city. Aeneas' visit to the plain home of Evander is a focus of the discussion.

_____. "Virgil and the Drama." In *The Magical Art of Virgil*. Cambridge, Mass.: Harvard University Press, 1931.
Vergil's vision of tragic fate, developed in Aeneas' journey to the underworld in the *Aeneid* 6, is shown to unite two dramatic narratives, the tragic stories of Dido in *Aeneid* 4 and of Turnus in the second half of the *Aeneid*.

Williams, R. D. "Rome's Destiny: The Golden Age." *Aeneas and the Roman Hero*. London: Macmillan, 1973.
Vergil's patriotism and vision of Roman destiny linked with the Augustan restoration is illustrated in analysis of four passages: Jupiter's prophecy in book 1; the pageant of Roman heroes in book 6; the pictures on Aeneas' shield in book 8; and the reconciliation between Juno and Jupiter in book 12. Various English translations are used.

Wills, Gary, ed. *Roman Culture: Weapons and the Man*. New York: George Braziller, 1966.
An anthology of short passages from major Roman authors by a wide variety of translators from the Elizabethan period through the twentieth century. Selections

are grouped thematically. Excerpts from the *Aeneid* include the death of Palinurus (book 5) and Nisus and Euryalus (book 9). Includes a general introduction to Roman civilization by the editor, thirty-three illustrations, and an index.

Vergil's Influence

Vergil in Later Literature

Ariosto, Ludovico. *Orlando Furioso*. Translated by Sir John Harinton, edited by Rudolf Gottfried. Bloomington: Indiana University Press, 1963.
This volume includes selections from the sixteenth century English translation of a contemporary Italian literary epic based upon the romance tradition about Charlemagne and Roland. The hero becomes the *Mad Roland* of the title because of his love for Angelica. The influence of the Classical epic tradition, and especially of Vergil, can be seen in such scenes as Astolfo's descent into the underworld and the description of Merlin's paintings in canto 33, which parallels Vergil's description of Dido's palace and of the Sibyl's temple.

Auden, W. H. "Secondary Epic." In *The Poets on the Classics: An Anthology of English Poets' Writing on the Classical Poets and Dramatists from Chaucer to the Present*, edited by Stuart Gillespie. New York: Routledge, 1988.
This poem by a twentieth century British poet is based upon Vergil's description of the shield of Aeneas in *Aeneid* 8. Reacting to Vergil's use of prophecy in this scene, Auden reflects upon knowledge and time, upon Vergil's celebration of the Roman past as future on Aeneas' shield, and upon Auden's knowledge of the sack of Rome and the fall of the Roman empire, which is future for Vergil but past for Auden.

Baudelaire, Charles. "The Swan." In *66 Translations from Charles Baudelaire's "Les Fleurs du Mal,"* translated by James McGowan. Peoria, Ill.: Spoon River Poetry Press, 1985.
Dedicated by the French symbolist poet to Victor Hugo in exile, this poem, originally titled "Le Cygne," considers the theme of exile by apostrophizing Andromache, widow of Hector, whom Aeneas meets in *Aeneid* 3. The poem uses the image of a swan to combine Baudelaire's personal experiences in Paris with reflections upon the fate of Andromache. The poet includes a quote from *Aeneid* 3. This edition of the poem has an English verse translation on a facing page with the original French poem.

Berlioz, Hector. *The Trojans in Carthage*. Translated by Henry Edward Krehbiel. New York: G. Schirmer, 1910.

The plot of this mid-nineteenth century opera, originally composed in French, is based in large part upon Vergil's story of Dido and Aeneas. This translation includes an essay on the opera.

Broch, Hermann. *The Death of Virgil*. Translated by Jean Starr Untermeyer. New York: Pantheon Books, 1945.
This psychological German novel describes the last eighteen hours of Vergil's life. It begins with the poet's arrival in Brindisi harbor and ends with his death in Augustus' palace the following afternoon. While written in the third person, this book offers an imaginative reflection by Vergil himself upon his life and work, its successes and failures. Focuses especially on the poet's desire to have the unfinished *Aeneid* destroyed.

Camoëns, Luís de. *The Lusiad (Os Lusíadas)*. Translated by Richard Fanshawe. Cambridge, Mass.: Harvard University Press, 1940.
A sixteenth century Portuguese epic poem is translated here by a seventeenth century English diplomat. This historical epic, describing Vasco da Gama's discovery of a sea route around Africa to India, is greatly indebted to Vergil, especially in its use of Greco-Roman deities as divine protectors of the Portuguese explorers.

Cowper, William. "On Receiving Heyne's Virgil from Hayley." In *The Complete Poetical Works of William Cowper*, edited by H. S. Milford. New York: Oxford University Press, 1913.
This short poem, expressing the author's gratitude to his friend and fellow poet William Hayley for a copy of Christian Gottlob Heyne's German translation of Vergil, illustrates the high esteem in which the Roman poet was held by an eighteenth century English poet.

Dante Alighieri. *The Divine Comedy*. Translated by Geoffrey L. Bickersteth. Oxford, England: Basil Blackwell, 1972.
This epic journey through hell, purgatory, and heaven by the late thirteenth century Italian poet is filled with Vergilian influences. In addition to adapting the general epic style of Vergil and basing his plot upon Aeneas' descent into the underworld in *Aeneid* 6, Dante makes the Roman poet himself his guide through hell and purgatory. This edition includes both an English translation and the Italian text on facing pages.

Flaccus, Gaius Valerius. *Argonautica*. Translated by J. H. Mozley. Cambridge, Mass.: Harvard University Press, 1972.
This unfinished Latin epic by an obscure poet of the late first century A.D. uses a Vergilian style to tell the story of Jason and Medea and the quest for the

Golden Fleece. Includes both the Latin text and the English translation on facing pages.

Gayley, Charles Mills. *Classic Myths in English Literature and in Art*. 2d ed. New York: John Wiley & Sons, 1911.
This mythological handbook not only summarizes the plot of the *Aeneid* but also includes an extensive quotation from Alfred, Lord Tennyson's poem "To Virgil" and, in the commentary section, lists of works of art and literature based upon the epic. Includes illustrations and indexes.

Gillespie, Stuart, ed. *The Poets on the Classics: An Anthology of English Poets' Writing on the Classical Poets and Dramatists from Chaucer to the Present*. New York: Routledge, 1988.
Includes a collection of poems and excerpts of works by English writers who make reference to Greco-Roman literature, a general historical overview of Classical influences on the English poets, and brief summaries of the influence of individual ancient authors, including Vergil. The section on Vergil contains comments by such authors as John Dryden, Alexander Pope, and Samuel Johnson, as well as several poems about Vergil. Includes a brief glossary, explanatory notes, bibliographies, and indexes.

Johnson, Lionel. "Propheta Gentium." In *The Poets on the Classics: An Anthology of English Poets' Writing on the Classical Poets and Dramatists from Chaucer to the Present*, edited by Stuart Gillespie. New York: Routledge, 1988.
The English translation of the title of this poem by a Victorian poet is "Prophet of the Races." In this poem, Johnson accepts the medieval image of the Roman poet as a prophet and celebrates Vergil not only as the master of Dante Alighieri but also as a divinely inspired teacher for Johnson, and his readers.

_____. "Sortes Virgilianae." In *The Poets on the Classics: An Anthology of English Poets' Writing on the Classical Poets and Dramatists from Chaucer to the Present*, edited by Stuart Gillespie. New York: Routledge, 1988.
A Victorian English poet celebrates Vergil as both poet and prophet, as the voice of Rome's golden age and as the inspiration for Dante Alighieri. The Latin title of this sonnet means "Vergilian Lots" and refers to medieval attempts at reading the future by random selection of lines from Vergil's works. The medieval custom is imitated by Johnson, who includes in the poem several phrases from the *Aeneid*.

Lucan, Marcus Annaeus. *The Civil War ("Pharsalia")*. Translated by J. D. Duff. Cambridge, Mass.: Harvard University Press, 1977.
This Latin epic poem, written during the reign of Nero (A.D. 54-68) by the nephew of the statesman Lucius Annaeus Seneca, portrays the first century B.C.

political war between Gnaeus Pompey ("the Great") and Julius Caesar as a futile Republican struggle against despotism. While many Vergilian techniques can be seen in this epic, Lucan does not imitate Vergil's use of divine machinery. Includes both the Latin text and English translation on facing pages.

Milton, John. *Paradise Lost*. In *The Poetical Works of John Milton*, edited by H. C. Beeching. 2d ed. Oxford, England: Oxford University Press, 1944.
Milton's English epic poem in twelve books about the temptation of Adam and Eve by Satan is a conscious adaptation of the biblical story of the fall of man to the Classical epic form derived especially from Homer, Vergil, and Dante. Includes reader's guide and index.

Ovid (Publius Ovidius Naso). *The Metamorphoses*. Translated by Frank J. Miller. 3d ed. Revised by G. P. Gould. Cambridge, Mass.: Harvard University Press, 1977.
This poem by a Roman poet of the late first century B.C. represents a conscious effort to rival Vergil with a different kind of epic. Instead of a heroic theme, Ovid writes about changes of form, beginning with a creation story and ending with the apotheosis of Julius Caesar. Ovid uses many epic features, including dactylic hexameter, invocation, and divine apparatus. Latin text and English translation appear on facing pages. Includes a bibliography.

Parotti, Phillip. *The Greek Generals Talk: Memoirs of the Trojan War*. Urbana: University of Illinois Press, 1986. Among these twelve fictional monologues by Greek generals reminiscing fifty years later about events connected with the Trojan War are the tales of Thoas, Machaon, Neoptolemus, and Sinon, who are mentioned by Vergil in *Aeneid* 2. Contains a glossary and three maps with an accompanying gazetteer.

_____. *The Trojan Generals Talk: Memoirs of the Greek War*. Urbana: University of Illinois Press, 1988.
A collection of ten fictional monologues by Trojan generals who survived the fall of their city. Modeled upon Vergil's story of Aeneas' escape from burning Troy and his journey to a new life in Italy. While most of these Trojans are not mentioned in Vergil's poem, the tale of Keas describes the escape of his lord Aeneas from the city. Includes a glossary and four maps with an accompanying gazetteer.

Petrarch (Petrarca, Francesco). *Africa*. Translated and annotated by Thomas G. Bergin and Alice S. Wilson. New Haven, Conn.: Yale University Press, 1977.
This unfinished Latin epic poem, composed by the fourteenth century Italian poet, is based upon the history of the Second Punic War, fought between Rome and Carthage at the end of the third century B.C. The plot, centered on the tragic love

story of Sophonisba and Massinissa, is indebted to a great extent to Vergil's tale of Dido and Aeneas.

Silius Italicus. *Punica*. Translated by J. D. Duff. Cambridge, Mass.: Harvard University Press, 1934.

This Latin epic, composed in old age by a public official of first century A.D. Rome, narrates the story of Rome's struggle with the Carthaginian general Hannibal in the Second Punic War, fought at the end of the third century B.C. While the poet owed much of his plot to the *Histories* of Titus Livy, the style is greatly influenced by Vergil. Includes both the Latin text and English translation on facing pages.

Spenser, Edmund. *The Faerie Queene*. In *The Complete Poetical Works*. Boston: Houghton Mifflin, 1908.

Written as a "courtesy book" for the moral education of gentlemen, this unfinished poem by a central sixteenth century English poet is, in part, a Vergilian epic celebrating the glory of Elizabethan England and the struggle between Protestantism and Catholicism.

Stafford, William. "Publius Virgilius Maro." In *Forms of Glory: Structure and Sense in Virgil's Aeneid*, by J. William Hunt. Carbondale: Southern Illinois University Press, 1973.

In this poem reflecting on the relationship between writing and reality, the poet refers to Vergil's perception of human experience and alludes to *Sunt lacrimae rerum* (1.470), a famous and untranslatable quotation from the *Aeneid* about the sorrows of life.

Statius, Publius Papinius. *Thebaid*. Translated by J. H. Mozley. Cambridge, Mass.: Harvard University Press, 1967.

This Latin epic poem about the story of the mythical war known as "The Seven Against Thebes" was composed by a celebrated poet of the first century A.D. and is written in a Vergilian style. Includes both Latin text and an English translation on facing pages.

Tasso, Torquato. *Jerusalem Liberated*. Translated by Edward Fairfax. New York: Capricorn Books, 1963.

This semihistorical epic composed in Italian by an important sixteenth century Italian poet is based upon the capture of Jerusalem in 1099 by the First Crusade under the leadership of Godfrey of Boulogne. Vergilian influence is notable in the use of an invocation to the Muse, a divine apparatus, and many parallels in plot, such as the message of the angel Gabriel to Godfrey in Tasso's poem and the message of the god Mercury to Aeneas in the *Aeneid*.

Tennyson, Alfred, Lord. "To Virgil." In *Poetical Works*. New York: Thomas Y. Crowell, 1900. Reprinted in *The Poets on the Classics: An Anthology of English Poets' Writing on the Classical Poets and Dramatists from Chaucer to the Present*, edited by Stuart Gillespie. New York: Routledge, 1988.

This poem by the celebrated Victorian poet laureate was subtitled "Written at the request of the Mantuans for the nineteenth centenary of Virgil's death." In ten quatrains, Tennyson sings of Vergil not only as the author of the *Aeneid* but also as the poet of the *Georgics* and the *Eclogues*, and shows his great admiration for the Roman poet.

Studies of Vergil's Influence

Andersson, Theodore M. *Early Epic Scenery*. Ithaca, N.Y.: Cornell University Press, 1976.

Shows how such Vergilian techniques as detailed landscapes, panoramic perspectives, and the use of scenic mood to create emotional density are imitated in three Latin epics of Carolingian Germany and Anglo-Saxon England: *Charlemagne and Pope Leo (Karolus Magnus et Leo Papa)*; *In Honor of Hludowici (In Honorem Hludowici)*, by Ermoldus Nigellus; and *Waltharius*, attributed to Geraldus. While medieval epics written in the vernacular, such as *The Romance of Aeneas (Roman d'Eneas)*, move away from the epic scenery of Vergil, the Anglo-Saxon *Beowulf* is shown to contain many imitations of Vergil's style.

Ayrton, Michael. "The Path to Daedalus." In *Virgil*, edited by D. R. Dudley. New York: Basic Books, 1969.

A twentieth century sculptor and painter analyzes the influence of Vergil on his own work by tracing his use of the myth of Daedalus. Ayrton encounters Vergil through Hector Berlioz' opera *The Trojans*, through the books of W. F. Jackson Knight, and through visits to Cumae.

Bernard, John D., ed. *Vergil at 2000: Commemorative Essays on the Poet and His Influence*. New York: AMS Press, 1986.

This collection of fifteen scholarly essays celebrating the two thousandth year since Vergil's death includes both interpretative studies and essays which focus on Vergil's influence in later periods. Also includes a bibliography, an index, and several illustrations. In his introductory essay, "Vergil: 'Prince of Song,'" the editor gives an overview of the other studies which, he suggests, reflect a revision of the traditional "Augustanism" of the poet and a tension in Vergilian imitators between tradition and innovation.

Bowra, C. M. *From Virgil to Milton*. New York: St. Martin's Press, 1961.
A study of the literary epic and its history. A chapter on characteristics of the literary epic form is followed by individual studies of Vergil's *Aeneid*, Luís de Camões' *The Sons of Lusus (Os Lusíadas)*, Torquato Tasso's *Jerusalem Delivered (Gerusalemme Liberata)*, and John Milton's *Paradise Lost*. Discusses the debts of Camões, Tasso, and Milton to Vergil and compares various aspects of the four epics, including artistic goals and themes. Includes an index.

Clark, John. *A History of Epic Poetry*. Edinburgh, Scotland: Oliver & Boyd, 1900.
A historical survey of the epic form in medieval and modern Europe with individual chapters on Latin epics after Vergil, and on French, German, Italian, and Spanish and Portuguese epics. Includes plot summaries of individual poems and observations about their literary characteristics and their position in the Classical epic tradition of Homer and Vergil.

Comparetti, Domenico. *Virgil in the Middle Ages*. Translated by E. F. Benecke. New York: Macmillan, 1895. 2d. ed. London: Allen & Unwin, 1908. Reprint. Hamden, Conn.: Archon Books, 1966.
This book is divided into two parts. The first deals with Vergil's influence on the medieval literary tradition, especially in such areas as philosophical allegory, biography, and poetic form. The second half surveys the appearance of Vergil as magician and sage in medieval popular legends. Foreign language quotations are not translated.

Cook, Albert. *The Classic Line: A Study in Epic Poetry*. Bloomington: Indiana University Press, 1966.
In this study of the classical epic as a literary genre, Cook shows how Vergil combined the Homeric epic tradition with a refined poetic style in order to create the epic form imitated by Dante Alighieri and John Milton. In separate chapters, Cook examines the characteristics of Vergil's, Dante's and Milton's epics. Index.

Cowling, George H. "Virgil in English Poetry." In *Shelley and Other Essays*. Melbourne, Australia: Melbourne University Press, 1936. Reprint. Freeport, N.Y.: Books for Libraries Press, 1967.
Attached to a biography of the English poet Percy Bysshe Shelley is a short essay which surveys the influence of the *Aeneid* and other Vergilian works on such poets as Geoffrey Chaucer, Christopher Marlowe, William Shakespeare, Ben Johnson, John Milton, and the English Romantic poets.

Curtius, Ernst Robert. "Rudolf Borchardt on Virgil." In *Essays on European Literature*, translated by Michael Kowal. Princeton, N.J.: Princeton University Press, 1973.
A transcript of a BBC broadcast in October, 1951, in which the author describes

his own rediscovery of Vergil and talks about Vergil's place in the European Classical tradition, especially in German Classicism and in the work of Rudolf Borchardt.

_____. "Virgil in European Literature." In *Essays on European Literature*, translated by Michael Kowal. Princeton, N.J.: Princeton University Press, 1973. Reprinted in *Virgil*, edited by Harold Bloom. New York: Chelsea House, 1986. Argues that Vergil's artistic imitation in a historical and poetic tradition makes him great but is difficult to appreciate in the twentieth century. Vergil presents this imitation in a refined pastoral world of simple nature and perfection of style which is impossible to translate into another language. Links between Vergil and Dante Alighieri are mentioned.

Distler, Paul F. "Vergil Through the Centuries." In *Vergil and Vergiliana*. Chicago: Loyola University Press, 1966.
Traces Vergil's influence through the twentieth century by citing many passages imitating or admiring the poet by later Roman authors, by Dante Alighieri, and by many English writers. Discusses Vergil as a magician, as an allegorist, and as a natural Christian.

Eliot, T. S. "Vergil and the Christian World." In *On Poetry and Poets*. New York: Farrar, Straus, 1957.
In this essay, Eliot suggests that Vergil has been so appealing to the Christian mind over the centuries because of his poetic emphasis on words such as *labor*, *pietas* (reverence and duty), and *fatum* (fate).

_____. "What Is a Classic." In *On Poets and Poetry*. New York: Farrar, Straus, 1957.
In this important essay by a major twentieth century poet, Vergil's *Aeneid* is used to define the characteristics of a piece of classic literature as comprehensiveness, universality, and, especially, maturity of language, style, and manners. Some comparative reference is made to other works of literature, such as those of William Shakespeare, John Milton, and Johann Wolfgang von Goethe.

Fichter, Andrew. *Poets Historical: Dynastic Epic in the Renaissance*. New Haven, Conn.: Yale University Press, 1982.
Begins with the *Aeneid* as an early example of dynastic epic, which uses a prophetic narrative poem to describe the rise of a ruling family, race, or nation. Discusses the influence of Vergil on later writers of dynastic works, including Augustine of Hippo, the Italian Renaissance poets Ludovico Ariosto and Torquato Tasso, and the English poet Edmund Spenser. Includes an index.

Fitzgerald, Robert. Introduction to *The Aeneid*, by Virgil, translated by John Dryden. New York: Macmillan, 1964.

This introduction to Dryden's 1697 translation of the epic provides excellent background to the place of Vergil in English letters at the end of the seventeenth century. The challenge of translating Vergil into rhymed couplets and characteristics of Dryden's style are discussed.

Foerster, Donald M. *The Fortunes of Epic Poetry: A Study in English and American Criticism, 1750-1950.* Washington, D.C.: Catholic University of America Press, 1962.
This overview of British and American literary criticism traces the popularity and influence of the Homeric and Vergilian epics from the Neoclassical and Romantic periods into the twentieth century. Contrasts Neoclassical respect for these poems as models of the epic form with Romantic redefinitions of the form. A good source of information about attitudes displayed toward Homer and Vergil by major figures in English letters, including Alexander Pope, Samuel Taylor Coleridge, and John Ruskin. Includes notes and index.

Gossage, A. J. "Virgil and the Flavian Epic." In *Virgil*, edited by D. R. Dudley. New York: Basic Books, 1969.
Reviews imitations of Vergil by the first century A.D. Latin epic poets Silius Italicus, P. Paninius Statius, and C. Valerius Flaccus. More attention to character study and the role of the gods than to vocabulary and general poetic technique. Latin quotations are not translated.

Griffin, Jasper. "Posthumous Career and Influence." In *Virgil*. Oxford, England: Oxford University Press, 1986.
A short survey sketching the poet's influence and importance in Western culture from his immediate popularity among contemporaries to his continued significance in the twentieth century.

Highet, Gilbert. *The Classical Tradition.* New York: Oxford University Press, 1949.
In this major study of the influence of Classical literature, scattered references to the importance of Vergil and his *Aeneid* in the Classical tradition include Vergil's influence on Francesco Petrarca (Petrarch), translations of the *Aeneid* in the Renaissance, and the role of Vergil as a school text and as a model in nineteenth century Britain. Includes bibliography, endnotes, and index.

_____. "Dante and Pagan Antiquity." In *The Classical Tradition.* New York: Oxford University Press, 1949.
A significant portion of this chapter in an important study of the influence of Classical literature is devoted to the role of Vergil in the *Divine Comedy* of Dante Alighieri. Highet lists several reasons why Dante chose Vergil as his guide in the *Inferno*.

_____. "The Renaissance: Epic." In *The Classical Tradition*. New York: Oxford University Press, 1949.
Considers the all-pervading influence of ancient epics, and especially the *Aeneid* of Vergil, upon such epics of the European Renaissance as *The Franciad* of Pierre de Ronsard, *The Sons of Lusus (Os Lusíadas)* of Luís de Camões, *The Madness of Roland (Orlando Furioso)* of Ludovico Ariosto, *The Liberation of Jerusalem (Gerusalemme Liberata)* of Torquato Tasso, and *Paradise Lost* of John Milton.

Hughes, Merritt Y. *Virgil and Spenser*. Berkeley: University of California, 1929. Reprint. Port Washington, N.Y.: Kennikat Press, 1969.
This study of Vergil's pastoral features and their influence on Edmund Spenser looks especially at the *Eclogues* and the *Georgics* but includes some discussion of allusions to the *Aeneid* in *The Faerie Queene*. Foreign language quotations are not translated. Includes a bibliography and index.

Johnson, W. R. "Eliot's Myth and Vergil's Fictions." In *Darkness Visible: A Study of Vergil's "Aeneid."* Berkeley: University of California Press, 1976.
Starting from the writings of Matthew Arnold and T. S. Eliot, Johnson surveys the use of the *Aeneid* in the nineteenth and twentieth centuries as a classic school text and divides twentieth century criticism of the *Aeneid* into two philosophical groups, an optimistic "European" school, which considers the poem an ideal expression of the myth of Europe, and a more pessimistic "Harvard" school, which emphasizes the political disorder and ambiguity in the poem. Suggests that limited approaches to the epic as a myth have obscured its deeper meaning as a poem and argues for a multilayered interpretation of the poem as political, moral, and philosophical allegory.

Knight, W. F. Jackson. "Vergil and After." In *Roman Vergil*. 2d ed. London: Faber & Faber, 1944.
Surveys Vergil's literary influence on contemporaries Ovid and Livy and the growth of his intellectual authority in the works of Quintilian, Servius, and Macrobius. Includes discussion of allegorical interpretations of Vergil, the medieval distortions of the poet as magician, his influence on Dante Alighieri and later poets, and Vergil's reputation as a natural Christian.

Lewis, C. S. *A Preface to "Paradise Lost."* New York: Oxford University press, 1942.
This appreciative study of John Milton's *Paradise Lost* includes several chapters which illustrate Milton's literary debt to Vergil. Contrasts the "primary" epic of Homer with the "secondary" epic of Vergil and shows how Milton inherited his grandeur and elevated style from Vergil. Includes an appendix and index.

Lotspeich, Henry Gibbons. *Classical Mythology in the Poetry of Edmund Spenser.* New York: Octagon Books, 1965.
Spenser's references to Classical mythology are collected here in an alphabetical listing. Many of these mythological terms are derived from Vergil's *Aeneid.* Each entry includes a list of places where Spenser refers to this mythological word, a summary of the story told by Spenser, and its ancient sources. Includes a table of abbreviations, an index of mythological names, and an index of authors. The index of authors can be used in order to find the mythological terms which Spenser borrowed from Vergil. Also includes an introductory essay which discusses Spenser's use of Classical mythology.

Mackail, J. W. "Virgil in the Medieval and Modern World." In *Virgil and His Meaning to the World of To-Day.* Boston: Marshall Jones, 1922. Reprint. New York: Cooper Square, 1963.
Surveys the popularity of the *Aeneid* in Vergil's lifetime and in the medieval and modern world and the poet's influence on Christianity, Dante Alighieri, and the Renaissance.

McKay, A. G. "Virgilian Landscape into Art: Poussin, Claude, and Turner." In *Virgil,* edited by D. R. Dudley. New York: Basic Books, 1969.
Specific paintings are used to compare the way three painters use Vergilian qualities in their landscapes. Nicolas Poussin's heroic classicism is contrasted with Claude Lorraine's idyllic view of the Italian countryside and with John Turner's touch of human reality. Includes endnotes and six plates.

Mandelbaum, Allen. Introduction to *The Aeneid,* by Virgil. Berkeley: University of California, 1971.
This essay, accompanying the author's verse translation of the *Aeneid,* explains that in order to appreciate Vergil the author had to overcome a twentieth century preference for Homer. In this, he was aided by the poetry of Giuseppe Ungaretti, by Dante, and by his own poetic development.

_____. "'Taken from Brindisi': Vergil in an Other's Otherworld." In *Vergil at 2000: Commemorative Essays on the Poet and His Influence,* edited by John D. Bernard. New York: AMS Press, 1986.
In a poetically dense and sophisticated article, the author, a translator of both Vergil and Dante, considers several ways in which the Italian poet appropriates his Roman model and guide. The paper ends with a warning that Vergil is not completely open to assimilation, that he cannot be totally transported into another's "otherworld."

Miola, Robert S. "Vergil in Shakespeare: From Allusion to Imitation." In *Vergil at 2000: Commemorative Essays on the Poet and His Influence,* edited by John

D. Bernard. New York: AMS Press, 1986.
A survey showing the growth of William Shakespeare's use of Vergil, from
learned allusion in early plays such as *Titus Andronicus* to more integrated
references in *Julius Caesar* and *Hamlet* and finally to a complete transformation
of Vergilian models in *Antony and Cleopatra* and *The Tempest*.

Mortimer, Ruth. "Vergil in the Light of the Sixteenth Century: Selected Illustrations." In *Vergil at 2000: Commemorative Essays on the Poet and His Influence*,
edited by John D. Bernard. New York: AMS Press, 1986.
This paper reproduces twelve sixteenth century Renaissance woodcuts connected
with Vergil, four from the edition of Vergil produced in Strasbourg by Johann
Grüninger in 1502; four from Vergilian texts produced in Lyons by Jean de
Tournes in 1552 and 1560; and four woodcuts with portraits of Vergil from
several sources. Illustrations are accompanied by a brief description of the
woodcut and information about the edition.

Nelson, Lowry, Jr. "Baudelaire and Virgil." *Comparative Literature* 13 (1961): 332-
345.
A specific example of Vergil's influence on Western literature. This study of
Baudelaire's allusion in his poem "Le Cygne" ("The Swan") to the Andromache
scene in *Aeneid* 3 is shown to be a remarkable blend of literary allusion and
originality. Latin and French quotations are not translated.

Nethercut, William R. "American Scholarship on Vergil in the Twentieth Century."
In *Vergil at 2000: Commemorative Essays on the Poet and His Influence*, edited
by John D. Bernard. New York: AMS Press, 1986.
The author sees three important stages in Vergilian scholarship in America: an
emphasis on the *Vergilian Appendix*, Vergil's minor and spurious poems, in the
period 1920-1940; a reassessment of the *Aeneid* in the period 1965-1979; and
a renewed appreciation of the *Eclogues* and the *Georgics* since 1979. Includes
a bibliography entitled "American Scholarship on Vergil."

Newman, John Kevin. *The Classical Epic Tradition*. Madison: University of
Wisconsin Press, 1986.
Vergil's *Aeneid* is here viewed as the product of the poetic tradition founded by
the third century B.C. Hellenistic poet Callimachus and as the central epic of
European civilization. Broadly traces the continuity of this poetic tradition in
Western culture, not only in poetry but also in other art forms, including novels
and the modern cinema. There are separate chapters on epic features of post-
Vergilian Latin epic poets such as Ovid and Statius, on the poems of Dante
Alighieri and Francesco Petrarca (Petrarch), on the Italian Renaissance epics of
Ludovico Ariosto and Torquato Tasso, on the epic works of the English poets
Geoffrey Chaucer and John Milton, on the cinema of the Russian directors Sergei

Eisenstein and Vsevolod Pudovkin, and on the epic novels of Leo Tolstoy and Thomas Mann. Includes two illustrations, a valuable glossary of critical terms, a select bibliography, and an index.

Paterno, Joseph V., and Bernard Asbell. "Virgil." In *Paterno: By the Book*. New York: Random House, 1989.
In this chapter of his autobiography, the coach of the Pennsylvania State football team reminisces about his high school years and his study of Vergil. Paterno compares Aeneas' attitude toward "fate" and his philosophy of life with modern sports values. Shows the kind of lingering influence which the study of Vergil has had upon those who, like Paterno, studied the poet in high school Latin classes.

Pattie, T. S. "Virgil Through the Ages." In *Virgil: His Poetry Through the Ages*, by R. D. Williams and T. S. Pattie. London: British Library, 1982.
Summarizes the manuscript tradition of Vergil. Discusses the popular medieval tradition of the poet as Christian and magician as well as literary imitations and English translations of Vergil. Twenty plates, some in color, depict manuscript pages and scenes from Vergil's works. Includes three appendices on Latin manuscripts of Vergil in the British Museum.

Pound, Ezra. "Homer or Virgil?" In *ABC of Reading*. New Haven, Conn.: Yale University Press, 1934. Reprinted in *Homer: A Collection of Critical Essays*, edited by George Steiner and Robert Fagles. Englewood Cliffs, N.J.: Prentice-Hall, 1962.
This short essay asserts a strong preference for Homer over Vergil. There is a strong gulf between the two poets, and Homer is more relevant than Vergil in the twentieth century.

Reinhold, Meyer. "Vergil in the American Colonial Experience from Colonial Times to 1882." In *Vergil at 2000: Commemorative Essays on the Poet and His Influence*, edited by John D. Bernard. New York: AMS Press, 1986.
This paper surveys American attitudes toward the poet. Vergil's traditional place in the academic curriculum is contrasted with the negative attitudes of many early Americans to Vergil, who was more popular in the United States as a pastoral poet than as an epic poet.

Sellar, W. Y. "Virgil's Place in Roman Literature." In *The Roman Poets of the Augustan Age: Virgil*. Oxford, England: Clarendon Press, 1908.
In this chapter of his standard nineteenth century study of Vergil, Sellar considers the reputation of Vergil beginning with his contemporary Romans and ending with the nineteenth century. The poet is presented as a representative writer of his age and country.

Showerman, Grant. "Virgil Through Two Thousand Years." In *Monuments and Men of Ancient Rome*. New York: D. Appleton-Century, 1935.
An overview of Vergil's influence upon later Roman and medieval writers and upon Dante leads to a summary of celebrations in honor of the two thousandth anniversary of Vergil's birth in 1930.

Silk, M. S. "The *Iliad* and World Literature." In *Homer: The "Iliad."* London: Cambridge University Press, 1987.
This discussion of the later influence of Homer's *Iliad* focuses in particular on the ties of the Homeric epics with the *Aeneid* of Vergil and *Paradise Lost* of John Milton.

Spargo, John Webster. *Virgil the Necromancer: Studies in Virgilian Legends*. Cambridge, Mass.: Harvard University Press, 1934.
Traces the development of the popular legends about Vergil as sage, magician, saint, and frustrated lover in the medieval period, in Renaissance romance literature, and among later travellers in Italy. Considers Vergil's association with a mouth of truth and with the death and burial site of Julius Caesar. Includes twenty-nine illustrations from manuscripts and woodcuts, an appendix with a German poem about Vergil the magician, endnotes, and an index.

Stanford, W. B. "Modern Variations on the Classical Themes." In *The Ulysses Theme: A Study in the Adaptability of a Traditional Hero*. 2d ed. Ann Arbor: University of Michigan Press, 1968.
This part of a comprehensive study of the figure of Odysseus deals with the image of the hero in the Renaissance and modern world and illustrates how several modern types evolve from the ancient hero portrayed by both Homer and Vergil. Sometimes Odysseus is a realistic, calculating politician, as he is in William Shakespeare's *Troilus and Cressida* and in Neoclassical French drama, and other times he is the eternal wanderer who appears in Dante Alighieri's *Divine Comedy*. The integrated hero of Homer is not restored until the twentieth century portrayals offered in James Joyce's *Ulysses* and in Nikos Kazantzakis' *Odyssey*.

Tunison, J. S. *Master Vergil: The Author of the "Aeneid" as He Seemed in the Middle Ages*. 2d ed. Cincinnati, Ohio: Robert Clarke, 1890.
The medieval traditions about Vergil are considered to be the result of literary rather than popular sources. There are separate chapters on Vergil and the Devil, Vergil in the literary tradition of late antiquity, Vergil's book of magic, Vergil as a man of science, Vergil as the savior of Rome, Vergil as a lover, Vergil as a prophet, and Vergil in literature of the Renaissance.

Whitfield, J. H. "Virgil into Dante." In *Virgil*, edited by D. R. Dudley. New York: Basic Books, 1969.
Shows that Dante's epic is based upon a tension between the authentic Vergil and the one who guides Dante through the underworld. Dante has recast Vergil in his own image, into a mouthpiece for Dante's, not the authentic Vergil's, thoughts. Latin and Italian quotations are not translated.

Wilkinson, L. P. "The 'Georgics' in After Times." In *The "Georgics" of Virgil*. Cambridge, England: Cambridge University Press, 1969.
This study shows that Vergil's later influence was not based on the *Aeneid* alone. The influence of the *Georgics* is surveyed from antiquity through eighteenth century English vogue for didactic pastoral poetry, into early twentieth century. Includes bibliography and index.

Williams, Gordon. "Statius and Vergil: Defensive Imitation." In *Vergil at 2000: Commemorative Essays on the Poet and His Influence*, edited by John D. Bernard. New York: AMS Press, 1986.
Studies some examples of imitations of the *Aeneid* by the second century Latin poet Statius especially in his epic poem called *Thebiad*. Williams is particularly interested in the way in which Statius deals with the problem of the subtext, of poetic imitation of a great predecessor.

Williams, R. D. "Changing Attitudes to Virgil: A Study in the History of Taste from Dryden to Tennyson." In *Virgil*, edited by D. R. Dudley. New York: Basic Books, 1969.
A survey of British opinions of Vergil from the late seventeenth to the nineteenth century. The idolatry of Neoclassical poets such as John Dryden is followed by rejection by Romantic poets such as Samuel Coleridge and rehabilitation by Victorians such as Matthew Arnold.

Zwicker, Steven N. "Reading Vergil in the 1690s." In *Vergil at 2000: Commemorative Essays on the Poet and His Influence*, edited by John D. Bernard. New York: AMS Press, 1986.
This paper is actually an attempt to reconstruct the way Vergil was read and understood by his famous seventeenth century translator John Dryden and his contemporaries. Dryden's prefaces and postscripts, together with his translation, are used to show how Vergil was reconstructed to fit the specific personal and political circumstances of Dryden and his readers.

THE CLASSICAL EPIC

INDEX

INDEX